PROCEEDINGS

OF THE

HARVARD CELTIC COLLOQUIUM

Volume 38, 2018

Edited by

Celeste Andrews
Heather Newton
Shannon Parker
Elizabeth Gipson

Published by
The Department of Celtic Languages and Literatures
Faculty of Arts and Sciences, Harvard University

ISBN: 978-0-674-24131-2

The cover design is based on the medallion of an
Early Christian belt shrine from Moylough, Co. Sligo.
Drawing by Margo Granfors

Designed and typeset by JKD Publishing
Cambridge, Massachusetts

CONTENTS

iii

PREFACE

The annual Harvard Celtic Colloquium has its origins in a Graduate Student conference established in 1980 by students at Harvard University's Department of Celtic Languages and Literatures. Since that date, the conference has developed into an internationally recognized, event, drawing together scholars and students from around the world to present work on all facets of Celtic Studies. The Colloquium is the oldest graduate-run conference in the field of Celtic Studies, and, true to its origins, it remains entirely run and organized by graduate students.

Papers given at each Colloquium may be submitted for peer review and subsequent publication in the journal *Proceedings of the Harvard Celtic Colloquium*. The journal is distributed through Harvard University Press, including subscriptions and back issues if they are still available. Information on the Colloquium and the *Proceedings* may be obtained through the web site of the Department of Celtic Languages and Literatures of Harvard University. The managing editor for PHCC may be contacted directly at phcc@fas.harvard.edu.

Acknowledgements:

The editors are indebted to Professor Catherine McKenna for her advice and encouragement, and to the Celtic department staff, Ms. Mary Violette and Mr. Steven Duede, for their help with the Colloquium and administrative matters. We also wish to thank the Managing Editor of PHCC and the staff of JDK Publishing for their help with the publication of this volume.

Celeste Andrews
Heather Newton
Shannon Parker
Elizabeth Gipson

Iceberg Tip or Floating Island?
The Harlaw *Brosnachadh* revisited

William Gillies

I am deeply honoured to have been invited to give the fifteenth John V. Kelleher Lecture. I hope that my chosen topic will be found to be germane to the interests of Professor Kelleher, inasmuch as it will lead me into the borderlands between history, literature and myth-making, where he laboured with such perspicacity and to such great effect. I should not neglect to mention that this specific topic is also one on which Harvard Celtic scholars have made significant contributions, for both Charles Dunn and Edgar Slotkin have given us thoughtful and perceptive insights on the Harlaw *Brosnachadh*. [1] I wish to honour their memory as well as that of Professor Kelleher. [2]

First, a word about Scottish Gaelic *brosnachadh*. The verb *brosnaich* (sometimes with initial *p-* in early printed sources) corresponds to Early Gaelic (and Modern Irish) forms with medial *-st-*. [3] The Scottish *-sn-* development is already present in John Carswell's translation of the Book of Common Order (1567). By contrast, *-st-* is retained in the more conservative language of the Gaelic translation of Calvin's Catechism (1631). Scottish bardic verse, like Carswell, shows a few examples of *-sn-*, e.g. *brosnagh* (: *cosnamh*) occurs in a 1636 elegy, and *brosnadh* occurs twice in a 1738 elegy. [4] A seemingly hybrid form *broistni* (for *brostnaidh*)

---

[1] C. W. Dunn, "Highland song and Lowland ballad*"*, *University of Toronto Quarterly*, 18.1 (October 1948), pp. 1–19; E. M. Slotkin, "The formulaic nature of the Harlaw *Brosnachadh*?", *Proceedings of the Third International Conference of Scottish language and literature (Medieval and Renaissance)* (Glasgow/Stirling: Dept. of Scottish Literature, University of Glasgow, 1983), pp. 143–60.

[2] I reiterate here the reference I made on the occasion of the Lecture to the recent death of another good friend of the Department and of Celtic Studies, Professor Anders Ahlqvist. *A chuid fhèin de Phàrrthas dha.*

[3] For these forms see *Dictionary of the Irish Language (DIL),* Dublin (Royal Irish Academy), s.v. *brostaid* and *brostaigid.*

[4] For Carswell, see R. L. Thomson (ed.), *Foirm na nUrrnuidheadh*, Scottish Gaelic Text Society (hereafter SGTS), vol. 11. (Edinburgh: Oliver & Boyd, 1970), l. 247 *do*

occurs in the Fernaig Manuscript of 1688, in a poem which also contains *deisnig* (for *d'éisneadh* = *d'éisteadh*).[5] It means 'incite' or similar, and its verbal noun *brosnachadh* is often used to denote a form of poetic composition which calls for action. A number of instances occur in an evangelical context in which the soldiers of Christ are called on to rally to a spiritual crusade, while others are calls to arms in a variety of political and social contexts. Underlying all these is the idea of a military incitement, as is made clear by the fairly numerous class of poems entitled *Brosnachadh do na Gàidheil* (An incitement to the Gaels) or similar which is associated with the Jacobite Risings of 1715 and 1745. There are also examples of the term *brosnachadh* applied by Gaelic poets to harangues supposedly given by generals before famous battles, e.g. Bruce at Bannockburn or Calgacus at Mons Graupius. In other words, there is a strong association between *brosnachadh* and fighting.[6]

With this in mind, we can render 'The Harlaw *Brosnachadh*' more expansively as 'The Battle-incitement associated with the Battle of Harlaw'. In form it is best described as a sort of poem, and it was composed in Gaelic; we shall have to say more shortly about the specific form of the *Brosnachadh* and about the sort of Gaelic it was composed in. As to the occasion that gave rise to it, it is usually said to have been uttered by the MacMhuirich chief-poet of Donald, Lord of the Isles, before the Battle of Harlaw, in the district known as the Garioch in Aberdeenshire, in 1411. Donald had brought an army deep into the

---

bhrosnaidh, etc.; for Calvin, see R. L. Thomson (ed.), *Adtimchiol an Chreidimh*, SGTS, vol. 7. (Edinburgh:Oliver & Boyd, 1962), 91 b 6 *bhrostughadh*, etc.; for bardic verse, see A. Cameron (ed.), *Reliquiae Celticae*, 2 vols, (Inverness:Northern Counties Newspaper and Printing and Publishing Company/ Northern Chronicle Office, 1892–94), 2, p. 234, l. 3 (1636), and pp. 276, l. 2 and 280, l. 14 (1738).

[5] See C. MacPhàrlain (ed.), *Làmh-sgrìobhainn Mhic Rath* (Dundee: C.S. MacLeoid, 1923), no. VI, verse 4 and verse 10. Cf. also, in *id.*, no. II, *eisnighk* (for *éisneacht* = *éisteacht*) verse 5; *chostnū* (for *chostnamh* = *chosnamh*) verse 7; *brijstnig* (for *bristneadh* = *bris(t)eadh*) verse 17.

[6] Examples may be found in Corpas na Gàidhlig (i.e. https://dasg.ac.uk/corpus/), s.v. *brosn-*, *prosn-*. Note also the musical application of the term in "the *Brosnachadh Catha* or Battle March" of the MacDougalls, in 'Fionn' [i.e. Henry Whyte], *The Martial Music of the Clans* (Glasgow: John MacKay, 1904), p. 138.

mainland in pursuance of his claim to the Earldom of Ross, which was contested by Alexander Stewart, Earl of Mar.[7]

The Harlaw *Brosnachadh* (hereafter HB) is preserved in several eighteenth-century manuscript versions, and it appears in several of the printed Gaelic poetry collections of the eighteenth and nineteenth centuries, including the earliest, i.e. the Eigg Collection, which was published by Ronald MacDonald.[8] Ronald (also known as Raghnall Dubh) was the son of Alexander MacDonald (Alastair mac Mhaighstir Alastair), the most famous of all the eighteenth-century Gaelic poets. The superscription in the Eigg Collection reads:

> *Prosnuchadh-catha   roinaidh   le   Lachun-Moir-*
> *Macmhuireach-Albinnich, do Dhomhnil a Iola, Riodh*
> *Inshagaill, agus Eairla Rois; la Machrich Cathgariach,*
> *Thugidh è June 11.1411.*

> The Battle-incitement which was made by Lachlann Mór,
> Son of Muireadhach Albanach, for Donald of Islay, King
> of the Isles and Earl of Ross on the day of the engagement
> of the Battle of Harlaw; it was fought on June 11, 1411.[9]

To give an indication of the form in which we find HB, its main part consists of a series of unrhymed couplets, each containing seven syllables and ending with a tri-syllabic word, giving a dactylic ($-\cup\cup$) cadence to each line.[10] It has heavy alliteration throughout. It opens with an address to

---

[7] For some recent studies on the Battle of Harlaw, its causes and significance, see note 16 below.

[8] The Eigg Collection, entitled *Comh-chruinneachidh Orannaigh Gaidhealach, le Raonuill Macdomhnuill, Ann 'N Eilean Eigg*, was published in Edinburgh in 1776. HB is on pp. 5–6. For the MS sources see note 14 below. The most recent edition and translation is in W. McLeod and M. Bateman (eds), *Duanaire na Sracaire* (Edinburgh: Birlinn, 2007), pp. 228–33.

[9] Note that *MacMhuireach-Albinnich* (literally 'Son of Muireadhach Albanach') needs to be taken as a patronymic style denoting the head of the family at a given time, since Muireadhach Albanach, founder of the Scottish poetic dynasty, lived some two hundred years before Harlaw.

[10] The poem has been seen by modern editors as containing a continuous series of lines; in fact, the lines in the abecedarian part fall naturally into pairs. Several lines as printed contain more or less than seven syllables, but the irregularity can usually be

the descendants of Conn of the Hundred Battles, one of the mythical ancestors of the Clan Donald: *A Chlanna Cuinn cuimhnichibh cruas an am na h-iorghaile* 'Descendants of Conn, remember hardihood at the time of the conflict'; and it proceeds to list in great detail the ways in which the MacDonalds are to comport themselves in the imminent battle. This opening leads into a highly schematised set of epithets, arranged in such a way that each pair of lines contains adverbs beginning with one letter of the alphabet. In Professor Derick Thomson's 1968 edition of HB the letters A and B are covered as follows:[11]

> *Gu h-àirneach, gu h-arranta,*
> *Gu h-athlamh, gu h-allanta,*
> *Gu beòdha, gu barramhail,*
> *Gu brìoghmhor, gu buan-fheargach,* . . .

> Be watchful (?), daring (?),
> Be dexterous, winning renown
> Be vigorous, pre-eminent,
> Be strong, nursing your wrath, . . .

This arrangement is continued down to the letters T and U, which in the same edition are given as follows:[12]

> *Gu teannta, gu [togarrach]*
> *Gu talcmhor, gu traigh-èasgaidh,*
> *Gu h-urlamh, gu h-ùr-mhaiseach* . . .

> Be compact [in your ranks], elated,
> Be vigorous, nimble-footed,
> Be ready, fresh and comely, . . .

---

eliminated by disregarding an epenthetic vowel (e.g. *cal(a)ma* 'brave') or simple emendation (e.g. *dùr* 'hard' > *dùrdha* 'hard'); the creators of the early texts of HB often added *is* 'and' to provide a seventh syllable where this seemed to be needed.

[11] Derick S. Thomson, "The Harlaw Brosnachadh: An early fifteenth-century literary *curio*", in James Carney and David Greene (eds), *Celtic Studies: Essays in memory of Angus Matheson* (London: Routledge and Kegan Paul, 1968), pp. 147–69, at 151 and 160; hereafter HBT.

[12] Thomson, "Literary *curio*", pp. 152 and 161; note that U has only two epithets in the versions utilised by Thomson.

4

After this HB concludes with a fresh appeal to the descendants of Conn telling them that now is the time for them to win recognition: "you . . . whelps, . . . bears, . . . lions, . . . battle-hounds, . . . firebrands of the progeny of Conn of the Hundred Battles."[13]

It should be noted at the outset that the text of HB has a dynamic quality. The earliest versions we have are more or less contemporary with one another–they are clustered in the 1770s–and they seem *prima facie* to be quite closely related productions, albeit with considerable superficial variation.[14] In the following decades, however, the specific form of the poem seems to have provided an invitation or challenge to subsequent readers to beef up the text by inserting additional epithets. The extravagant version first published in Alexander and Donald Stewart's collection (1804) contains literally hundreds of extra lines.[15]

This brings us to the central question posed by HB: can it really be what it purports to be? In other words, is the variation we see in the extant versions the product of a long period of oral transmission during the centuries before they were written down? This would be a bold assertion, because the lapse of time between 1411 and the 1770s is *prima facie* a very considerable one for a purely oral survival. Should we rather be thinking of a text transmitted orally at first, but then committed to writing? In which case, when did it attain written status, and was there a time when oral and written versions existed side by side? Alternatively, is the visible variation the result of recent editorial activity, e.g. during the period when the controversy over MacPherson's *Ossian*, published in the early 1760s,

---

[13]HBT, ll. 40–49.

[14] They are Glasgow University MS Gen. 1042 (i.e. the McLagan Manuscript Collection), no. 97, f. 3 [hereafter ML97], and no. 222a, f. 13 [hereafter ML222]; the Eigg Collection (on which see note 8 above) [hereafter E]; and the MacDiarmaid MS (in the Department of Gaelic and Celtic, Glasgow University), pp. 60–62, on which see D. S. Thomson, *The MacDiarmaid MS Anthology*. SGTS, vol. 17. (Edinburgh: Scottish Academic Press, 1992), pp. 1–10 [hereafter MacD]. I am grateful to Glasgow University Library and to the University's Department of Gaelic and Celtic for allowing me to quote from these sources.

[15] A. and D. Stewart, *Cochruinneacha Taoghta de Shaothair nam Bard Gaeleach* (Edinburgh: T. Stiuart, 1804), pp. 1–19. The Stewarts gave the *Brosnachadh* pride of place, where other early editors tended to give this honour to Ossian himself or to Ossianica like *Miann a' Bhàird Aosta* "The Aged Bard's Wish".

led to a surge of interest in Gaelic antiquity? Indeed, could HB have been created *de novo* at that time, perhaps to further a spurious claim to antiquity for Gaelic literature?

There are two main reasons why it is important to be as clear as possible about the status of HB. In the first place, the Battle of Harlaw itself was an occasion of great historical significance. It has often been seen as a supreme moment of confrontation between Gaelic and Scots culture, and an important juncture in the emergence of the modern consciousness of Highlands and Lowlands. Its outcome and after-effects have been hotly debated.[16] As a consequence, any composition associated with this battle has a special aura about it; by the same token, however, it has to be treated with caution, inasmuch as it may have been subjected to politically charged interference of one sort or another along the way. In the second place, if its authenticity can be validated, HB offers a rare insight into Scottish Gaelic literature and language at a time when alternative sources are few and far between. For although we have vernacular literature–mostly song-poetry–from the seventeenth, sixteenth and possibly earlier centuries, it is found almost exclusively in eighteenth, nineteenth and twentieth-century sources. Moreover, much of the potentially earlier material is anonymous and hard to date. By contrast, the author, occasion and date of HB are knowable–again, if it can be shown to be authentic.

This dilemma is implicit in my title, which may be glossed as follows. By 'iceberg tip' I mean to suggest the possibility that we have in HB a rare survival, hinting at poetic, linguistic and cultural riches, unplumbed and lying beneath the surface. By 'floating island' I mean to signify one of those patches of aquatic surface weed whose alluring verdancy and apparent substantiality on the surface of a loch could lead unwary cattle or children to step out onto it and sink into the depths.

Resolving the dilemma requires one to have dealt adequately with a third issue. For *brosnachadh* itself, when one tries to engage with it, is a shadowy category of composition. It is obviously harder to establish

---

[16] Recent studies include J. Sadler, *Clan Donald's greatest defeat* (Stroud: Tempus, 2005), and I. A. Olson, *Bludie Harlaw: Realities, myths, ballads* (Edinburgh: John Donald, 2014). The political background is explained helpfully by S. Egan, "The early Stewart Kings, the Lordship of the Isles, and Ireland, c. 1371–c. 1433", *Northern Studies*, 49 (2018), 61–78.

whether HB is or is not a member of a category if that category is itself poorly attested. This difficulty combines with those already mentioned– the uncertain durability of the Gaelic oral tradition and the possibility that politically charged intervention may have distorted the form or substance of the poem, or even engendered it–to produce a definite presentational challenge.

I propose to approach these questions in the following order. First, I shall attempt to identify and date the extra-literary influences. The principal ingredients here are, in my view,

(1) in the late eighteenth and early nineteenth centuries, Scottish patriotic and nationalistic reverberations of the Jacobite Risings and responses to the Ossianic controversy;

(2) in the later nineteenth and early twentieth centuries, Highland and Gaelic self-assertion and identity-promotion; and

(3) in the later twentieth century, scholarly anxieties and public concerns about authenticity and the bogus.

Secondly, I shall look into the historical evidence for poetical incitement to battles, and also for the existence of a literary genre of *brosnachadh catha* 'battle incitement' associated with such historical events. Thirdly, I shall examine, in the light of current understanding, the circumstances in which fifteenth-century Gaelic material could have survived till the late eighteenth century, and the likelihood (or not) of this having happened in the case of HB. Fourthly, I shall summarise the internal evidence which the texts of HB itself allow us to bring to bear on the same question. Fifthly and finally, I shall present some additional evidence to fuel some conclusions of my own, including a hopefully improved way of regarding HB. To anticipate, I shall suggest that we are dealing with more than a floating island, if not quite a *bona fide* iceberg.

It will be expedient to start with some characteristic views on HB, and attitudes towards it. To represent the late eighteenth century, we may cite the Rev. Donald McNicol, who, in his *Remarks on Dr. Samuel Johnson's Journey to the Hebrides*, wrote as follows, in or around 1776:

> There are at present two very old manuscripts in the possession of a gentleman in Argyleshire. . . .
> The same gentleman is likewise possessed of Prosnachadh

7

Catha Chlann Domhnaill,[17] at the battle of Harlaw, in 1411, composed by Lachlan More Macvurich, the bard. This performance is in exact alphabetical order, like the Doctor's famous Dictionary. It contains four epithets upon every letter of the alphabet, beginning with the first letter, and ending with the last. Every epithet upon the same letter begins with that letter; which proves to a demonstration, that some of the bards at least, were not unacquainted with letters in that age.[18]

As his use of the *anno domini* date 1411 indicates, McNicol was *au fait* with standard accounts of Scottish history, and his reference to "four epithets" for each letter of the alphabets shows that he was describing the poem pretty much as we find it in our earliest sources. McNicol's words are loaded. In the 1770s the first flush of the Ossianic controversy had come and gone, but Scottish and Highland indignation had been re-kindled by Doctor Johnson's publication of his account of the trip he and James Boswell made to the Hebrides in 1773. McNicol's *Remarks* took the form of a comprehensive critique of the injustices done by Dr. Johnson to McNicol's countrymen and their language and culture. At this point he is incensed by Johnson's well-known opinion, repeated in *A Journey*, that there could be no venerable literature without letters to preserve it.[19] That is why McNicol stresses the antiquity of the "two very old manuscripts", and makes the point about HB being as alphabetical as the Doctor's own *Dictionary*. Note, however, that there is no note of doubt, and no protective bluster about the authenticity of the *Brosnachadh*; its occasion, author, title and purpose are unquestioned.

To represent the earlier nineteenth century, I have chosen John Mackenzie, the editor of *Sàr Obair nam Bard Gaelach*, who was (amongst

---

[17] A footnote at this point in the *Remarks* reads as follows: "A speech to cheer up the MacDonalds, when beginning the battle."

[18] See *Remarks* (London: printed for T. Cadell, in the Strand, 1779), pp. 263–4. In the following paragraph (p. 264) McNicol writes "Since I began these Remarks, the poem has been published by Mr. Macdonald in his collection [i.e. the Eigg Collection, published in 1776], where it may be seen by the curious."

[19] S. Johnson, *A Journey to the Western Islands of Scotland* (London: W. Strahan & T. Cadell, 1775). See pp. 258–62 for offensive remarks about Gaelic illiteracy.

many other things) one of the fathers of Gaelic literary criticism.[20] In the very extensive introduction to this work he made the following reference to HB:

> Of the works of this famous poet [i.e. Lachlann Mòr Mac Mhuirich], all now extant is an extraordinary one–a war song, composed almost wholly of epithets arranged in alphabetical order, to rouse the Clan Donuil to the highest pitch of enthusiasm before the Battle of Harlaw. . . . This piece has a part for every letter of the Gaelic alphabet till near the end consisting of three hundred and thirty-eight lines. It would occupy to[o] much space to print it in this work. . . . This poem is very valuable [because] it is the best proof that could be given of a language, so copious and abounding in epithets, that the number poured out under each letter is almost incomprehensible. . . . Our poet, therefore, exhausted the almost exhaustless *copia verborum* of the language, for the purpose of infusing the spirit of the greatest heroism and love of conquest into the breasts of the warriors.[21]

Mackenzie's first audience was one of cultured Gaels, expatriate Gaels and Gaelic sympathisers who were acquainted with the idea of 'great literature' and were pleased by references to the grandeur, magnitude, antiquity and sublimity of Gaelic poetry, which deserved admiration and respect rather than the disparagement which critics like Dr. Johnson had accorded it. That is why Mackenzie exults in the size of the version of the *Brosnachadh* which he takes as his source: not one of the early sources, which do not exceed fifty lines in all, but the extended version as found in the Stewarts' Collection.[22] He is quick to include a reference to the copiousness of Gaelic descriptive vocabulary–a big point with defenders of Gaelic since Alastair Mac Mhaighstir Alastair's poem

---

[20] Full title: *Sàr Obair nam Bard Gaelach: or, The Beauties of Gaelic Poetry, and Lives of the Highland Bards* (Glasgow: Polson and Co, 1841).

[21] Ibid. These remarks are on pp. 62–3.

[22] Stewarts' Collection, see note 15.

on the *Seann chànain Albannach* ('the Old Scottish tongue'),[23] if not before–but links this with the somewhat eccentric argument that the verbosity of the *Brosnachadh* exhausts the resources of the language as it increases the ardour of the Gaelic warriors who hear it. For present purposes, however, the point to note is that no question as to the authenticity of the *Brosnachadh* intrudes. If Mackenzie had any doubts about the relative value of the later and earlier versions, he suppressed them.

Of these early writers on Gaelic literature one more may be mentioned here, as a representative of late nineteenth century views. The Rev. Nigel MacNeill mentions HB in the following terms:[24]

> Lachlan Mor MacVurich . . . is the author of one of the most extraordinary poems in Gaelic or in any language. . . This war song or battle incitement (Stewart's Collection) consists of three hundred and thirty-eight lines. . . . Round this subject Lachlan Mòr has gathered some six hundred and fifty adverbial adjectives, arranged alphabetically, and every one of them bearing specially and martially on the great theme of the song. There is nothing in the poem but these adjectives, which certainly in themselves are not very poetical; but rehearsed unhesitatingly from a good memory "in all their astonishing alliterative array by a ready speaker gifted with a strong and sensitive voice, they could not but have offered a rare opportunity for impetuous, vehement, and effective declamation."[25]

Interestingly, MacNeill calls HB a "song" as well as a "poem" and a "declamation". One gets the feeling that he is stretching his imagination and his vocabulary, trying to envision the circumstances that gave rise to this "extraordinary" production, and the reception it might have enjoyed. But he follows his literary predecessors in offering no challenge to the

---

[23] Rev. A. and Rev. A. MacDonald, *The Poems of Alexander MacDonald* (Inverness: Northern Counties Newspaper & Print. & Pub. Co., 1924), pp. 2–9.

[24] N. MacNeill, *The Literature of the Highlanders* (Inverness: J. Noble, 1892), p. 153.

[25] The quotation within this quotation is from Thomas Pattison, *Selections from the Gaelic Bards* (Glasgow: printed by A. Sinclair, 1866), p. 39.

credibility of the *Brosnachadh* as a genuine product of the late Middle Ages.

Moving on to the scholarly era, we find that Charles Dunn used HB as one of three Gaelic and three Scots texts which he compared in a thoughtful exploration of differences in the temper and consistency of the two contiguous literatures. He juxtaposed HB with the well-known Scots ballad "The Battle of Harlaw", which is still sung today, whenever it may have been composed.[26] Although Professor Dunn did not explicitly question the authenticity of our text, he had clearly asked himself some searching questions about it, and in response to these he highlighted certain Early Modern Gaelic analogues or points of contact.[27] The most notable of these was with bardic verse; for example, the animals whose qualities the warriors are urged to emulate in the final section of HB were those used by the Classical poets. Dunn also pointed out that HB has a *dúnadh* or closure echoing its beginning, again in the manner of earlier Gaelic verse. At the same time he linked the 'florid' alliteration of the *Brosnachadh* with the inflated style of prose found in Early Modern texts like the Fenian romance *Cath Fionntrágha* ("The Battle of Ventry"). Specific suggestions like these were long overdue, and we shall see shortly that they were well-founded.

The greatest advance in the study of HB, however, was Derick Thomson's 1968 paper "The Harlaw Brosnachadh: a fifteenth-century literary *curio*?". Thomson had entered the field of 'literary curios' in his research on the relationship between genuine Scottish Gaelic heroic lays and their echoes in James MacPherson's Ossianic poems, and had followed this up by investigating some of the forgers and fabricators who, following in MacPherson's wake, created a little home industry producing what Thomson called "bogus Gaelic literature".[28] He was therefore well placed to ask the question others had shied away from: could this production really date from 1411? He faced the fact which twentieth-

---

[26] The Scots ballad (on which see note 40 below) is discussed by Olson, *Bludie Harlaw*, pp. 74–84.

[27] Dunn, "Highland Song and Lowland Ballad", 6–9.

[28] D. S. Thomson, *The Gaelic sources of MacPherson's 'Ossian'*, Aberdeen University Studies no. 120, (Edinburgh: Oliver & Boyd, 1952); "Bogus Gaelic literature, c.1750–c.1820", *Transactions of the Gaelic Society of Glasgow*, 5 (1958), 172–88. For Thomson's article on HB see note 11 above.

century scholarship had gradually brought into clearer perspective: that such a survival would be highly remarkable, and the real onus on scholars was surely to show how it could have happened, against considerable odds.

In his paper Thomson investigated the affinities between the earliest extant texts of HB, which date from the 1770s. Amongst other things, he drew attention to the statement in one of the MS sources that it was derived from "an old MS. in Galic character" (p. 150). At the same time, he pointed out (p. 166) that the extended version of HB, first seen in the Stewarts' Collection, is heavily indebted to William Shaw's Gaelic Dictionary, published in 1780, for its flood of extra epithets.[29] Those accretions at least, had no claim to antiquity, and this fact alone puts beyond doubt the correctness of Thomson's decision to deal solely with the earliest group of sources. Thomson also showed (p. 151) how the early sources themselves show signs of editorial tinkering, including what he saw as the "plundering" of vowel sections to interpolate a H-section into the alphabetical sequence. But the main thrust of his investigation was to enquire whether the vocabulary of the text was a credible product of the early fifteenth century; his conclusion (p. 163) was that this was a genuine possibility. He further noted (pp. 163–5) a significant overlap in vocabulary between HB and a late fifteenth-century prose-poem addressed to John, the last Lord of the Isles. Finally, he found parallels for the abecedarian format of HB in medieval Latin sources, and for its heavy alliterative technique in poems like that known as *Rosg Guill*, a Fenian poem found in the early sixteenth-century Book of the Dean of Lismore and elsewhere (p. 167).[30] Although this assessment contains a number of points which will require further consideration, it will suffice to say for now that this paper at last exposed HB fully to scholarly examination.

The next contribution to be mentioned, responding directly to Thomson's, is Edgar Slotkin's "The formulaic nature of the Harlaw *Brosnachadh*?". Slotkin approached our text with a very different perspective from that of Thomson's literary-historical enquiry. He

---

[29] Rev. W. Shaw, *A Gaelic Dictionary* (London: printed for author by W. and A. Strahan, 1780).

[30] This is the poem beginning *Ard aigneach Goll* or *Ard aigneadh Guill*, for which see N. Ross, *Heroic Poetry from the Book of the Dean of Lismore*, SGTS, vol. 3. (Edinburgh: Oliver & Boyd, 1939), pp. 60–68, 218–20.

suggested (p. 145) that, although this had been partially concealed by subsequent transmission, HB was originally composed in an old *rosg* metre, comparable in form to passages from Early Irish saga literature describing "a hero, his appearance, clothing, horses, chariot, weapons, and so on." Applying distinctions derived from his work on formulaic and traditional texts in medieval Irish, he categorized the text of HB as highly traditional but only minimally formulaic (in the Parry-Lord sense), and he placed it some way along a spectrum of textual development that saw formulaic compositions gradually give way to literary-antiquarian reprises of the 'surface' features of the truly formulaic. He identified certain features of HB which hinted at relatively recent, literate activity, including the abecedarian format and the repeated use of the adverb-marker 'gu' with every adjective (p. 151). Other features, however, were suggestive of a relatively old and oral background, e.g. hints of a "performative" dimension, highly traditional vocabulary and very short lines (p. 152). This led him to entertain the idea that HB might have started life as an oral rendition, along the lines that the traditional accounts claimed for it. He saw the objection based on its abecedarian format as "not insuperable", if one could postulate, say, a learned poet giving an extra spin to an old oral genre (p. 157). [31] There are several valuable ideas in this reading of HB, to which we shall return in our own conclusions.

The last estimate I wish to cite, representing the scholarship of the twenty-first century, is that of Wilson McLeod and Meg Bateman, whose anthology *Duanaire na Sracaire* includes HB in a section entitled "Incitement". [32] They venture the following cautiously negative statement:

> This poem is cast in the form of an incitement to the Clann Domhnaill warriors before the celebrated Battle of Harlaw . . . [It] may be the earliest surviving metrical text in vernacular Scottish Gaelic . . . Unfortunately, it is now considered somewhat doubtful that the poem is a genuine survival of the early fifteenth century; it may be best

---

[31] See note 1, Slotkin, "The formulaic nature of the Harlaw *Brosnachadh?*", pp. 145, 151–52, 157.

[32] W. McLeod and M. Bateman (eds), *Duanaire na Sracaire*, pp. 219–45 (228–33).

understood as a historical re-imagining composed at some later date, probably with feelings of nostalgia for the glory days of the Lordship of the Isles . . .[33]

A tipping point had been reached, and the authenticity of HB was now regarded with suspicion by some if not all scholars.[34] Of course, many popular writers down to the present day still refer to HB with the same degree of acceptance as the nineteenth-century writers; so far as I am aware, there has been no further critical scrutiny of its status or of its form.

Although that is where the matter rests for HB itself, there have been significant developments in our understanding of other aspects of the Gaelic literary tradition germane to the present enquiry; and it will be expedient to take account of these developments. But I should begin by declaring my own prejudices. I first became interested in HB as a Scholar of the Dublin Institute for Advanced Studies, while working on an Early Modern Gaelic account of the Harrowing of Hell under the guidance of Professor Brian Ó Cuív. There are several descriptions of the horrors of Hell in Gaelic literature, and the subject clearly brought out a desire to indulge in verbal pyrotechnics in authors and scribes. My version of the Harrowing was an abecedarian side-shoot from the main stock, one which I regarded as the height of precious scholasticism.[35] That perception predisposed me to be sceptical about the alphabetical treatment in HB. Was this not excess to requirements on the battlefield? Would its alphabetism not have been lost on fighters who were mostly illiterate?

---

[33] See p. 229 and cf. W. McLeod, *Divided Gaels: Gaelic cultural identities in Scotland and Ireland, c.1200–c.1650* (Oxford: Oxford University Press, 2004), p. 75: "The earliest surviving Mac Mhuirich poem may be the so-called 'Harlaw Brosnachadh' . . . possibly composed by Lachlann Mór . . ." ; id., p. 126: "A *brosnachadh catha* . . . was apparently composed by Lachlann MacMhuirich (though it may be a forgery of sorts, composed much later)".

[34] Ronald Black, commenting on Hector MacLeod's poem *An Taisbean* (see below, p. 17) in his anthology *An Lasair* (Edinburgh: Birlinn, 2001), p. 462, is more charitable towards the traditional view, simply calling HB "an extraordinary medieval poem".

[35] "An Early Modern Irish 'Harrowing of Hell'", *Celtica*, 13 (1980), 32–55. Further examples of such pyrotechnics are cited on pp. 36–7; even Geoffrey Keating departed from the measured exposition of the Three Shafts of Death when he came to describe the horrors of Hell; see O. J. Bergin, ed., *Trí Biorghaoithe an Bháis,* second edition (Dublin: Hodges, Figgis & Co., 1931), pp. 208-11.

Was it not equally implausible to imagine that it was meant to be savoured by a minority of *cognoscenti*? On a different tack, could the alphabetical treatment have been devised as a mnemonic aid to help the reciter? But surely the Gaelic trained poets had other, more sophisticated, methods for developing the memory. And if such Gaelic poets were involved, why use the Latin/English alphabet rather than the native *Beithe-LVS-Nin*? I have to confess that I regarded HB with a considerable degree of suspicion from the outset.

It was also the case that Derick Thomson's writings on MacPherson's treatment of his Gaelic sources, and on "bogus Gaelic literature" in general, strongly influenced my thinking about the *Brosnachadh*; for he was, as I say, the leading investigator of this sort of Gaelic literature at that time. Yet when I studied his treatment of HB I noted that he did not dismiss it out of hand. And I realised that I too would need to treat it with a measure of seriousness that I had at first been minded to deny it. That tension, which has remained with me over the years, was the starting-point for the present paper.

Because of those early misgivings, however, I resolved to take nothing for granted. Rather, I determined that one should try to answer some prior questions before engaging in literary or linguistic analysis of the text of HB. How strong, in point of fact, is the evidence that there really was a battle-incitement at Harlaw in 1411? If there was, how plausibly can we claim to know anything about it? And how far back can we trace the credentials of the text that has come down to us? To start with, we need to get behind the 1770s texts and references with their hints of inter-connectedness and shared agenda.[36]

John MacCodrum, the North Uist bard, has a slightly earlier, apparently independent reference to a *brosnachadh* associated with Harlaw:

---

[36] The question of late eighteenth-century Gaelic literary and scholarly networks has lately been receiving fresh attention; see the proceedings of the conference "The Rev. James McLagan (1728–1805) and his manuscripts", Glasgow, 9 September 2016 (forthcoming, ed. by S. Innes and G. Parsons, Edinburgh, 2020); D. E. Meek, 'The Gaelic Literary Enlightenment: The Making of the Scottish Gaelic New Testament and Associated Books', http://meekwrite.blogspot.com (2018).

HARLAW *BROSNACHADH*

Bha Clann Raghnaill treun aig Àrla
nuair bhrosnaich Lachlann am Bàrd iad.[37]

My use of the qualification 'apparently' here acknowledges the fact that the bard was not only in touch with traditional Gaelic learning through friendship with surviving members of Clann 'ic Mhuirich in South Uist, but was also being cultivated by Lowland-educated scholars and antiquarians around the time when he composed this song.[38] This could possibly explain why MacCodrum used *Àrla*, i.e. 'Harlaw', for the battle which was usually termed *Cath Gairbheach* 'The Battle of Garioch' by the Gaelic poets. It has to be noted that two of the manuscript versions of HB have *La Tharlà*, and that an earlier example of this form is provided by Alastair Mac Mhaighstir Alastair, who has *Harlà* in one of his Jacobite poems.[39] There is a difference, however: in the HB texts the accent is marked on the final syllable, and metre confirms that Alastair put stress and length on the second syllable, whereas the same criterion shows that MacCodrum stressed and lengthened the first syllable. One might hazard a guess that MacCodrum's acquaintance with the toponym 'Harlaw' derived from normal Scots pronunciation, and that the others reflect acquaintance with the Scots ballad "The Battle of Harlaw", in which (at least in twentieth-century versions) the final syllable is musically lengthened.[40] At

---

[37] "The Clanranald were brave at Harlaw when Lachlan the Bard incited them." These lines are from *Tàladh Iain Mhùideartaich*: see W. Matheson, *The Songs of John MacCodrum*, SGTS, vol. 2, (Edinburgh: Oliver & Boyd, 1938), ll. 1757–8. Matheson dated this song to 'c. 1763'.

[38] See my "The Mavis of Clan Donald: Engaging with John MacCodrum", in A. Ahlqvist and P. O'Neill (eds), *Germano-Celtica. A Festschrift for Brian Taylor*, Sydney Series in Celtic Studies, vol. 16 (Sydney: Celtic Studies Foundation, University of Sydney, 2017), pp. 123–51.

[39] This reading is in ML97 and MacD (see note 14 above) the other sources having forms of *Cath Gairbheach*. Alastair's *Harlà* is in Rev. A. and Rev. A. MacDonald, *The Poems of Alexander MacDonald*, p. 138.

[40] See F. J. Child, *The English and Scottish popular ballads*, 5 vols (1882–98), vol. 3, (Boston: Houghton, Mifflin and Co.) pp. 316–20. Verse 1 of Version A of Child 163 reads: "As I cam in by Dunidier,/ an' doun by Netherha,/ there was fifty thousand Hielanmen/ a-marching to Harlaw". The last syllables of 'Netherha' and 'Harlaw' are accented.

16

all events, there is more than a suggestion of clear water between MacCodrum and the HB texts.

Another reference, this time an apparent echo of the *Brosnachadh* itself, can be found in *An Taisbean* "The Revelation", a vision-poem ascribed by John Mackenzie in *Sàr Obair nam Bard Gaelach* to "Eachunn Mac-Leoid, or Hector MacLeod, the South Uist bard".[41] This puzzling poem consists of a sort of political prophecy into which is inserted, near the end, a call to arms. This begins with an appeal to the "tribes of Mìl" (i.e. the Gaels, as descendants of *Mìl Easpáine* 'Mìl of Spain') to rise up and avenge Culloden. At this point the metre changes from quatrains to a continuous sequence of lines similar in form to HB, prescribing how the warriors should make their attack:

> *Tòisichibh gu h-àrdanach,*
> *gu bras-rìoghail, mòralach,*
> *gu mear-leumnach, dearg-chneadhach,*
> *gu luath-làmhach, treun-bhuilleach . . .*

> Set out proudly,
> actively-royally, magnificently
> lively-leaping, bloody-wounding,
> swift-handed, brave-striking . . .

The debt this section owes to HB is obvious: it includes the heavy use of grandiloquent compounds and some specific correspondences in vocabulary, as Thomson and Black have rightly pointed out.[42] The whole poem is explicitly post-Culloden, and it shows a general dependence on the works of Alastair Mac Mhaighstir Alastair, including echoes of *Birlinn Chlann Raghnaill*, which is supposed to have been composed in the early 1750s. Unfortunately, there is nothing more definite to say about the date of composition of *An Taisbean*; it does, however, provide additional evidence for the presence of HB 'in the tradition' some time during the

---

[41] Mackensie, *Sàr Obair*, 161–62. Ronald Black dubs him "the 'mystery man' of eighteenth-century Gaelic verse" (*An Lasair*, p. 461). Even his name seems an unlikely one for a South Uist man; it may be a *nom de guerre*.

[42] HBT, p. 168, note 7; Black, *An Lasair*, pp. 462, 464.

decades after Culloden.[43] We may note the absence of an abecedarian dimension in *An Taisbean*, where 'Eachunn Mac-Leoid' might have been expected to seize on this feature if he had encountered it; but that is mere speculation.

Mention of Mac Mhaighstir Alastair makes this an appropriate point at which to mention that his *Òran nam Fineachan Gàidhealach* (a rallying call to the Highland clans composed shortly before 1745) also has lines that carry a clear echo of HB; we shall have to return to these when discussing the texts of the latter.[44] For now it is enough to say that we can document HB back as far as the 1740s in Scottish Gaelic poetry. But helpful as these testimonies are to confirm that HB was not simply concocted in the 1770s to discomfit Dr. Johnson and his like, it is noteworthy that neither the presence of a MacMhuirich poet at the battle nor the reciting of a *brosnachadh catha* on that occasion are referred to in the Books of Clanranald or in other seventeenth-century MacMhuirich sources in connections with the Battle of Harlaw; nor are they mentioned in the fuller account of the battle in the seventeenth-century MacDonald history ascribed to "the Sleat Shennachie".[45] For a MacMhuirich endorsement of these aspects of the battle we have to wait until 1775, when the Niall who was then head of the family recited his genealogy before witnesses, referring in it to Lachlann Mòr, *do reinn prosnachadh Catha Chath-caireabhach 1411* "who made the Battle-incitement of the

---

[43] The *Birlinn* is supposed by local tradition to have been composed while Alastair was living in Canna, i.e. between c. 1751 and c. 1755 (cf. Black, *An Lasair*, p. 470). *An Taisbean* was first published by John Gillies in *The History of the Feuds and Conflicts among the Clans* (Perth: printed by J. & J. Robertson for John Gillies, 1780), pp. 115–20.

[44] Compare HBT, p. 156. See discussion of Mac Mhaighstir Alastair's lexicon and orthography in relation to HB below, pp. 36-37, 40-41.

[45] In the so-called 'Red Book of Clanranald', i.e. Royal Museum of Scotland MS MCR 39, p. 40, Niall says simply: *Do brisd se cath gaifech cairfech ar diúc murchadh* "He defeated Duke Murdoch in the perilous Battle of Harlaw" (cf. *Reliquiae Celticae*, 2, p. 160). Note that 'Red Book', although a useful tag, is a misnomer for MCR 39: see R. Black, "In search of the Red Book of Clanranald", *The Clan Donald Magazine*, 8 (1979), 43–51. For 'the Sleat Shennachie', see "History of the MacDonalds", in J. R. N. MacPhail (ed.), *Highland Papers, Volume 1* (Edinburgh: Scottish History Society, 1914), pp. 5–72 (29–31).

Battle of Harlaw in 1411".[46] Mention of the date 1411, which is prominent in three of our 1770s sources for HB and in the statement quoted above from Donald MacNicol's *Remarks*, suggests that this testimony belongs together with these contemporary sources.

If we turn to clan histories, writers like the reverend authors of *The Clan Donald* refer admiringly to both poet and poem, as one would expect:[47]

> The courage of the men of the Isles was roused to the most patriotic fervour by the stirring appeal of MacVuirich, the Tyrtaeus of the campaign, to remember the ancient valour of the race of Conn.

This tone is adopted by most clan historians and popular writers. So far as I can see, none adds anything concrete to our knowledge of the Harlaw *brosnachadh* that is not already present in the 1770s sources.[48] The key elements in their shared message can be summarised as follows: (i) the *brosnachadh* was delivered by the chief-poet; (ii) it was associated with the actual battle; (iii) it was addressed to the warriors; (iv) it exhorted them to display certain qualities as fighting men.

To put the propositions in this summary into perspective, mention may be made of one other account of Highland battle incitement from a significantly earlier source. It uses the term *brosnachadh catha* explicitly,

---

[46] Quoted from the McNicol MSS in HBT, p. 148. See also Appendix, No. XVII, "Declaration of Lachlan Mac Vurich", in H. Mackenzie (ed.), *Report of the Committee of the Highland Society of Scotland . . . into the Authenticity of the Poems of Ossian* (Edinburgh: A. Constable, 1805), pp. 275–9, for confirmation of the MacMhuirich genealogy (though without any reference to Harlaw) supplied in 1800 by Niall's son Lachlann; and *id.*, Appendix, No. II (pp. 38–51), for the testimony of Hugh MacDonald, Kilpheder (confirming Mac Mhuirich authorship of the *Brosnachadh* at Harlaw, though he attributes the poem to "Niall Mòr Mac Mhuirich").

[47] Rev. A. and Rev. A. MacDonald, *The Clan Donald*, 3 vols (Inverness: Northern Counties Pub. Co., 1896–1904), vol. 1, pp. 160–61. They print the full text of "this extraordinary poem", from the extravagant version in the Stewarts' Collection, in an appendix (id., pp. 516–24).

[48] Whereas the variation between the primary texts of HB is mostly a matter of minor detail, there are significant differences in the superscriptions, most notably in the name of the poet: Lachlann in two of our texts, Iain in the other two. See Thomson, HBT, pp. 147–9 for discussion.

though it does not mention Harlaw. It occurs in Martin Martin's *Description of the Western Isles of Scotland*, written '*circa* 1695', in a section on 'the Antient and Modern Customs of the Inhabitants':[49]

> Before they engag'd the Enemy in Battle, the Chief Druid harangu'd the Army to excite their Courage. He was plac'd on an Eminence, from whence he address'd himself to all of them standing about him, putting them in mind of what great things were perform'd by the Valour of their Ancestors, rais'd their hopes with the noble Rewards of Honour and Victory, and dispell'd their Fears by all the Topicks that natural Courage could suggest. After this Harangue, the Army gave a general Shout, and then charg'd the Enemy stoutly. This in the antient Language was call'd *Brosnichiy Kah*, i.e. an Incentive to War.

The key elements for us to take from this account are: (i) the "chief Druid" (presumably to be equated with 'chief poet')[50] did the inciting; (ii) the timing was "before [the] battle"; (iii) the poem was "addressed . . . to all of [the men]"; (iv) it was termed *brosnachadh catha* (*sic leg.*); (v) it referred to "great things . . . performed by the valour of their ancestors" and the "noble rewards of honour and victory", and at the same time it "dispelled . . . fears". We should note that this is obviously compatible (or should we say, suspiciously compatible?) with what we have gleaned so far about the Harlaw *Brosnachadh*. We should also note that there is no reference to an abecedarian framework, or to alliteration or adjective packing, or indeed to versification of any sort, though that omission does not of itself prove anything in a generalised account like this.

Martin's wording suggests that *brosnachadh catha* was an established custom. But apart from this account, and inferences which have been drawn from our sources for HB itself, there is (to my knowledge) very little historical evidence for such a formalised institution of battle incitement in the Scottish Highlands. Indeed, there has to be at

---

[49] Cited here from the second ('very much corrected') edition (London: Printed for A. Bell, et al., 1716), pp. 104–5.

[50] Elsewhere in this section Martin equates the Druids with the Orators, and the Orators with the *Is-Dane*, i.e. the *aos dána* 'poets'.

least a suspicion that Martin's own account may be based on traditions of Harlaw. If this were so, it would of course remain valuable as testimony to the existence of those traditions in the late seventeenth century; but it would not widen the evidential base for the putative genre of *brosnachadh catha* in the way that we would like.[51]

In the circumstances, it may be worth stepping back for a moment and viewing our information on *brosnachadh* and the Battle of Harlaw in a wider literary context. Incitement as such is widely diffused through the literature: the call to 'rise up' and take action is present from the archaic *Audacht Morainn*, with its opening *At-ré, tochomla / a mo Neiri Núallgnáith* "Arise, set forth, O my Neire accustomed to proclaiming", through to Eibhlín Dubh Ní Chonaill's cry to her murdered husband to spring to life in *Caoineadh Airt Uí Laoghaire*.[52] This element of incitement to some sort of action, which we see in so much of Gaelic poetry, seems like something inherent in the dramatic framing of a substantial part of it. Incitement to bravery is an important part of this, given the martial constitution of Gaelic society, or that part of it whose literature best survives. Its occurrence in early Gaelic literature has been explored by Proinsias MacCana, who identified a nucleus of texts in which incitement to battle had a special significance as part of the "mystery" of fighting and warriors. He argued that the key examples of battle incitement occur in the Ulster Cycle, where the incitement has two

---

[51] An apparent exception to this silence may be disposed of here. Robert Armstrong's Gaelic Dictionary of 1825 is prefaced by a Gaelic grammar, which includes a discussion of prosody. His "exemplification of Gaelic verse" concludes (pp. lxvi–lxvii) with "one of those famous songs of incitement to battle, called *Brosnachadh catha*. These songs were not all precisely in the same measure; but they were all quick, rapid, and animating, descriptive of hurried movements, activity, and exertion." Unfortunately, this "incitement to battle" is a Gaelic rendering of a passage from James MacPherson's *Fingal, Book IV*, itself loosely modelled on the Fenian poem *Rosg Guill* (note 30). See Mackenzie, *Sàr Obair*, pp. li–lii (who quotes the lines and translates them back into English, while acknowledging their MacPhersonic source), and D. S. Thomson, *The Gaelic Sources of MacPherson's 'Ossian'*, pp. 39–40.

[52] F. Kelly (ed.), *Audacht Morainn* (Dublin: Dublin Institute for Advanced Studies, 1976), pp. 1–2; S. Ó Tuama (ed.), *Caoineadh Airt Uí Laoghaire* (Dublin: An Clóchomhar Tta, 1961), ll. 86, 181.

standard modes: praise for success alternating with castigation for weakness.[53]

MacCana saw this phenomenon as having its roots in Early Gaelic (or Celtic) society and its *floruit* in the early literature, though with definite echoes in the Early Modern period. His acknowledgment of Early Modern echoes was clearly correct; in a recent discussion of the poems which are found in many versions of the Early Modern Gaelic "Death of Cú Chulainn", Lára Ní Mhaoláin has classified at least two of them as "incitements to battle".[54] Similarly, Pádraig Ó Macháin has used the term "panegyric poems of incitement" to characterise the short-line Fenian poem *Goll mear míleata* and a small group of similar specimens from the *Fianaigheacht*.[55]

Conversely, we should recognise that these examples of literary incitement in Early Modern literature have clear fore-runners in the Medieval period.[56] They can perhaps be best seen as reflexes of what was once a double-edged weapon, wielded by inciters who applied 'carrots' and 'sticks' alternately to make the incited ones dance to their tune, though in the later texts we are more likely to meet 'carrots' alone (in what are effectively eulogies), and occasionally 'sticks' alone (effectively satires). This is certainly an interesting way of viewing poems of incitement, i.e. within the ideological framework of praise and satire. Yet there is a problem for the present inquiry: these compositions are about inciting action from an individual rather than an army.

Moreover, when we ask who was empowered to deliver incitement, we encounter another difficulty. In literary sources, the characters we meet who can provide the needful stimulus include scald-crows, fairy women,

---

[53] P. MacCana, "*Laíded, gressacht* 'Formalized incitement'", *Ériu* 43 (1992), 69–92.

[54] "Poetry in *Brislech Mhór Maighe Muirtheimhne agus Deargruathar Chonaill Chearnaigh* considered", in G. Toner and S. Mac Mathúna (eds), *Ulidia 3: Proceedings of the Third International Conference on the Ulster Cycle of Tales* (Berlin, 2013), pp. 299–306.

[55] Forthcoming in the 2016 McLagan Conference proceedings (note 36). I am grateful to Professor Ó Macháin for allowing me to access and refer to the written version of this talk.

[56] According to MacCana, it was the formalised or ritual aspect of *gressacht* and *laíded* that died away after the heyday of the Ulster Cycle ("*Laíded, gressacht*" pp. 83, 89).

goddesses and charioteers (MacCana); warriors' girl-friends (Ní Mhealláin); or Fenian warriors (Ó Macháin). But there is not so much evidence for poets in this role. Moreover, if we turn to descriptions of historical battles, we can find prayers, saints and relics, musical accompaniments (whether vocal or instrumental), war-cries and slogans. But references to poets on battlefields are not so common, at least in the Scottish Gaelic world.[57] There are indeed references to warriors being incited to fight well in historical circumstances; but the exhortation or incitement they receive, before or during battles, is usually given by leaders and generals. For instance, in the Civil War section of the Clanranald Histories, the Marquis of Montrose encourages his army at a critical juncture in the Battle of Auldearn, while Lord Gordon and the leader of the Covenanters shout threats at one another in the presence of the armies before the Battle of Alford.[58] We need to have a care with these supposedly *verbatim* quotations, since historians have been using generals' speeches before battles as a fictive way of representing the hopes and fears of combatants ever since Classical times. Yet the Clanranald examples just cited are pretty circumstantial and are embedded in battle-descriptions which include undoubted reportage by eye-witnesses.[59]

---

[57] MacCana mentions comparative evidence for poets and satirists leading the battle charge, with an Early Irish instance from *Cath Maige Tuired*, in "*Laíded, gressacht*", pp. 71–2. He cites as an Early Modern literary example the incitement of Oisín by Fergus Finnbhél in *Cath Fionntrágha* (pp. 73–4), and compares the encouraging *draoi* 'druid' who accompanies the hero in some Gaelic romances (p. 82).

[58] MCR 39, pp. 152, 157 (cf. *Reliquiae Celticae,* 2, pp. 190, 194). Note that Montrose's words carry a hint of *gressacht* as he urges the other troops to emulate Alastair Mac Colla and his soldiers: *Is mor a[n] náire duinn an d-aonduine ag tabhair[t] ar clú dhinn* "It is a great shame for us that one man is taking our reputation from us".

[59] See my "The Clanranald Histories: Authorship and purpose", in G. Evans, B. Martin and J. Wooding (eds), *Origins and Revivals. Proceedings of the First Australian Conference of Celtic Studies* (Sidney: Centre for Celtic Studies, University of Sidney), pp. 315–40 (330–31); and "After 'the backward look': Trials of a Gaelic historian", in T. van Heijnsbergen and N. Royan (eds), *Literature, Letters and the Canonical in Early Modern Scotland* (East Linton:Tuckwell Press, 2002), pp. 121–37 (126–7). The same appears to be true of the report of Cameron of Lochiel's speech before the Battle of Killiecrankie (1689), cited by MacCana, "*Laíded, gressacht*", pp. 70–71.

If the poets were not conspicuous in front of real-life battle-lines, they nevertheless had their part to play more generally in the context of strife and warfare. Inciting a patron to take action was of course included in the bardic repertoire, and there are examples where the action prescribed is military, as can be seen from the motif-list of the Bardic Poetry Database.[60] The poem in the Book of the Dean of Lismore in which the Earl of Argyll is exhorted to attack the *Goill* is a well-known example; if it is correctly associated with the Scots expedition which culminated in disastrous defeat at Flodden, the Earl took the bard's advice, with fatal consequences.[61] To generalise, one might say that bardic eulogy almost always contains a measure of incitement, implicitly if not overtly, in the sense that it puts forward a code of conduct if not a course of action. Moreover, it carries with it the sanction of satire if the patron should fail to step up to the mark, reminding us of Mac Cana's juxtaposition of *laíded* (praise for 'correct' behaviour) and *gressacht* (castigation for 'wrong' behaviour). From the perspective of the present inquiry, however, bardic incitement seems to take place in the chief's hall; i.e. it is delivered either before or after, but not at the scene of the battle.[62] Additionally, it is addressed to the chief, not the men, though the chief's officers and leaders would doubtless have been present in the hall. To me at least it seems likely that the *ollamh* who sat beside the chief at the feast, listening while the *reacaire* declaimed his eulogy, would surely have either stayed close by his patron's side or headed for a safe vantage point as the hosts prepared to charge, and would not normally have thought it necessary or appropriate to flaunt himself in front of the battle-lines.[63]

---

[60] See https://bardic.celt.dias.ie, s.v. "Poet incites patron to battle", which yielded 28 hits on 9/30/2018; cf. McLeod and Bateman, *Duanaire na Sracaire*, pp. 219–45 ('Incitement'), and M. Pía Coira, *By poetic authority* (Edinburgh, Dunedin Academic Press, 2012), p. 40.

[61] *Duanaire na Sracaire*, pp. 238–45.

[62] Wilson McLeod's reference to "eve of battle" in this context (*Divided Gaels*, p. 125), tacitly acknowledges this point. For eulogies on battle successes *after* the event, see K. Simms, "Images of warfare in bardic poetry", *Celtica*, 21 (1990), pp. 608–19 (610).

[63] Hugh Cheape, in *Bagpipes: a national collection of a national instrument* (Edinburgh: National Museums of Scotland, 2008), p. 42, accepts the idea that a

This pattern of behaviour was not confined to the Gaelic professional poets, but recurs more widely. One can find a parallel in the case of the Carmelite Robert Baston, the Oxford-trained poet and rhetorician whom King Edward II of England brought with him on his expedition to Scotland in 1314 so that he could compose an ode celebrating Edward's expected victory over the Scots. In point of fact, he was captured by the Scots and forced to compose an ode in honour of Robert the Bruce's victory at Bannockburn.[64] But even if Edward had been successful, Baston's poem would have graced the celebrations after the battle. There was never any question of his inciting the English soldiers during the action of the battle. For an example of this mind-set amongst the vernacular Scottish Gaelic poets we may cite Iain Lom, i.e. John MacDonald the Keppoch bard, who is said to have told Alastair Mac Colla Ciotaich, the Royalist Major-General, *Cathaichibh sibhse is innsidh mise* "You (warriors) fight and I'll celebrate", as he made his way to the vantage-point from which he would oversee the destruction of the Campbells at Inverlochy in 1645.[65] From this perspective, the action ascribed to Lachlann Mac Mhuirich, in front of the battle-lines at Harlaw, begins to look less like a standard occurrence.

To sum up the argument so far, some of the elements which we identified as central in descriptions of *brosnachadh catha* certainly appear in literary incitements and historical accounts of battles, but there are also significant discrepancies. By contrast with the widely based and specific evidence we have for poets officiating at inauguration ceremonies, the evidence for their having a formal role on the battle-field is fairly slender.[66] It is not entirely lacking, however. In the course of his

---

brosnachadh could have been delivered on the battle-field, but suggests that it was addressed only to "a few, a select band of the élite of the clan".

[64] Partial text and references in W. Macray, *English Historical Review*, 19 (1904), pp. 507–8; translation and notes in www.royaldunfermline.com/Resources/ robert_ the_ bruce.pdf.

[65] A. Mackenzie, *Òrain Iain Luim*, SGTS, vol. 8, (Edinburgh: Oliver and Boyd, 1964), pp. xxvii (the tradition) and 20 (the poet's testimony).

[66] E.g. Martin, *Description* (see note 49), p. 102, refers to the poet's "Rhetorical Panegyrick" at inaugurations, in which were described "the ancient Pedigree, Valour, and Liberality of the Family, as Incentives to the young Chieftain." See more generally K. Simms, *From Kings to Warlords* (Woodbridge: Boydell Press, 1987),

examination of the Fenian 'panegyric poems of incitement' referred to above, Pádraig Ó Macháin has drawn attention to an intriguing comment by Standish Hayes O'Grady on the copy of *Goll mear míleata* found in British Library Egerton MS 111, which O'Grady called a "Warsong in honour of the Ossianic chief Goll mac Morna". Here is what O'Grady says:[67]

> [This is a] specimen of the rhapsodies called '*rosg*' and supposed to be run off extempore. ... Their style is jerky and disjointed, structure not always homogeneous; but in their day they were used very effectively on occasions of triumph or of mourning; at inaugurations; and just before battle, when they were delivered either by a leader or by the tribal poet (himself often a good man of action) *ag iarraidh na hionnsaighthi* i.e. 'calling for the charge': a technical term.

There is clearly a lot of information to be unpacked, sifted and checked here. As we have just indicated, "inauguration" was, indeed, an institution which involved the professional poets. But the idea of a battle-incitement delivered by someone who could be either a "leader" or a "tribal poet" is less clear-cut. It is true that "leader" accords with some descriptions of real-life battles, as we have seen; but "tribal poet" raises more questions. Was this term meant to denote a chief-poet, or did O'Grady mean to distinguish a "tribal poet" from an *ollamh (flatha)*? If they were the same, we have seen reason to doubt whether this could be correct. If they were different personages, or at least distinct functions, perhaps we have been wrong to concentrate our search on the professional poets–looking, as it were, in the directors' box for a phenomenon that really took place 'in the huddle'. The mention of *rosg* metre and 'extempore' recital may be significant in this context, for it could suggest that O'Grady was referring not to an *ollamh* or *file* but to some other class or grade of poet. In a Scottish Gaelic context we might recall the variety of strophic metre used by Eachann Bacach for his eulogies and elegies for the Maclean chiefs, composed at a time when the Ó Muirgheasáin family

---

pp. 21–40.
[67] S. H. O'Grady, *Catalogue of Irish Manuscripts in the British Museum*, vol. 1 (London: [s.n.] for the Trustees, 1926), p. 346.

provided their official poets.[68] On the Irish side, Katherine Simms has raised the possibility that the type of metre known as *brúilingeacht* was used in poems, mostly now lost, about battles and fighting; her reference to the O'Brien poets chanting menacing lines of *rosg* on the way to battle (as found in *Caithréim Thoirdhealbhaigh*) is also suggestive for the present inquiry.[69] Then again, reference to 'mourning' conjoined with 'extempore' composition invites comparison with *caoineadh*; in that case, battle-incitement could perhaps have belonged at one time alongside the "other musics" described in Breandán Ó Madagáin's *Caointe agus Seancheolta eile* (Indreabhán: Cló Iar-Chonnachta, 2005). Considerations like these might lead us to ask whether the Harlaw *Brosnachadh* could represent a type of composition that usually fell 'below the radar' in terms of learned recognition. We should here recall Edgar Slotkin's comparison of the Harlaw *Brosnachadh* with passages in the old *rosg* metres, and Derick Thomson's comparison of the metrical structure of the Harlaw *Brosnachadh* with short-line metres in the *fianaigheacht*.[70] Most intriguing of all is O'Grady's claim that "calling for the charge" was a "technical term". I confess I have only one example of a poet *ag iarraidh na hionnsaighthe*, and that occurs in O'Grady's own Irish Texts Society edition of *Caithréim Thoirdhealbhaigh*.[71] Disappointingly, the poem which this statement introduces contains an incitement to warriors to join an expedition (*toisc*) rather than to charge into battle. However, the *Caithréim* as a whole contains 69 poems, relating to all aspects of its unremittingly martial narrative; and of these, several could justly be called battle incitements by poets.[72] Although some of O'Grady's assertions have

---

[68] C. Ó Baoill (ed.), *Eachann Bacach and other Maclean poets*, SGTS, vol. 14, (Edinburgh: Scottish Academic Press, 1979). This metre is classed as Type V(b) in my survey "The form of Scottish Gaelic poetry", in C. Sassi (ed.), *The International Companion to Scottish Poetry* (Glasgow: Scottish Literature International, 2015), pp. 94–108 (104).

[69] See Simms, "Images of warfare", pp. 611 (*brúilingeacht*) and 617 (*rosgadha*).

[70] Slotkin, pp. 153–4; HBT, p. 167.

[71] S.H. O'Grady, *Caithréim Thoirdhealbhaigh*, 2 vols, (Irish Text Society vols 26 and 27), (London: Irish Texts Society, 1929), vol. 1, p. 96.

[72] E.g. *Dénaid báig, a chlanna Bloid* (p. 36), a poem in *rannaigheacht* ascribed to *fili síl Bhloid*; *Éirged suas bar sluaghcatha* (p. 125), a heptasyllabic *rosg* poem ascribed to *fili na bfialcath* (rendered in vol. 2, p. 129, as 'the poet of the host'). But most of the

to be taken with a pinch of salt, and the present one may stem from an over-generous estimate of the authentic element in the poems in *Caithréim Thoirdhealbhaigh*, I believe it would be mistaken to dismiss the evidence of this text entirely.[73] At the very least, *Caithréim Thoirdhealbhaigh* tells us that in the eyes of Seán Mac Craith, the fifteenth-century poet who composed it, poets and poetry had a significant role to play in the rough and tumble of Irish warfare in the fourteenth century.

To return to the Scottish evidence, it is worth asking whether there could have been a time when battle incitement (*brosnachadh catha*) co-existed with bardic poems of incitement, rather in the way that the Highland bag-pipe or *pìob mhòr* was later associated with the battle-field while the harp or *clàrsach* was the instrument of the chief's hall. For it is actually 'classical' bagpipe music (*pìobaireachd*) and its traditions that provide the nearest Scottish parallel to O'Grady's scenario, in the form of pipe tunes commemorating famous battles in the history of particular clans. Several of these take us back to battles fought in the fifteenth century or earlier, including one linked with the Battle of Harlaw.[74] But it is believed nowadays that such 'battle' tunes need to be seen as retrospective rather than contemporary with the events they commemorate, and the hey-day of composition of the *pìobaireachd* or *ceòl mòr* "big music" tunes is put in the seventeenth and eighteenth centuries. The piping tradition is also the place where we can find references to pipe tunes associated with particular aspects of warfare, such as the rallying of the clan, the march to battle, or the call to arms and the stimulus to heroism during the actual battle. Henry Whyte's *Martial Music of the Clans*, which synthesized a variety of nineteenth-century traditions

---

battlefield incitements are put in the mouths of the war-leaders, and most of the poems attributed to poets are set before or after the actual engagements.

[73] See further A. Nic Ghiollamhaith, "Dynastic warfare and historical writing", *Cambridge Medieval Celtic Studies*, 2 (Winter 1981), pp. 73–89 (especially pp. 82–3).

[74] The late Roderick Cannon, in a posthumously posted paper entitled "Gaelic names of pibrochs: a classification", claimed that the *pìobaireachd* tune known as "The Battle of Harlaw" is "melodically related" to that named *An Cath Gailbheach*, translated into English as "The Desperate Battle", but sounding suspiciously like a garbling of *Cath Gairbheach*, "The Battle of Garioch", i.e. the older Gaelic poetical name for the Battle of Harlaw: see www.cl.cam.ac.uk/~rja14/musicfiles/preprints/Gaelicnames.pdf.

and speculations, provides such Gaelic and English terms as *Cruinneachadh* "gathering" and *Cath-ghairm* "war-cry" (p. 1), *Spaidsearachd* "march" (pp. 95, 107), *Caismeachd* "warning" (p. 139) and even *Brosnachadh Catha* "Battle March" (p. 138). It is likely enough that some grains of truth are preserved in the piping and clan traditions in which these terms occur; for example, *caismeachd* (defined as 'alarm, warning' in Scottish Gaelic dictionaries) occurs in the earlier language as *caismert* 'signal, battle-cry, battle'.[75] However, there are clearly imprecision and crossed wires, and not a little invention, in the reported terms and meanings; and it is unclear how much, if any, of the information they provide pre-dates the incorporation of piping into the routines of the Highland Regiments of the British Army in the eighteenth and nineteenth century.[76] As regards our difficulty in visualising a *locus* for a poetic *brosnachadh catha*, Roderick Cannon's "Gaelic names of pibrochs" (see note 74) has a valuable comment on the piping term "gathering", as used to denote a call signal on the battle-field. In Cannon's view, a formal ground with variations could not have been effective in a real-life battlefield; one needed a short, instantly recognisable musical phrase or line, one which could be played on the move, in the midst of military manoeuvrings. This dictum would doubtless apply even more strongly to a poet trying to declaim in the heat of preparation for battle.

To revert to the question of different classes or grades of poet, Edgar Slotkin suggested a link between incitement and the early *rosg* metre

---

[75] Whyte, *Martial Music,* see note 6. Cf. *DIL*, s.v. *caismert*. The form *caismeart* is cited separately in Dwelly with the meaning 'heat of battle'. ScG *caismeachd* presumably developed before the ScG sound-change of /xt/ to /xk/ took place. It was perhaps influenced by a folk etymology of *cas* + *imeachd*, thought of as 'foot-marching'; compare the meaning 'Highland march' also provided by Dwelly, and the metrically supported form *caisimeachd* in A. MacLeod (ed.), *The Songs of Duncan Bàn Macintyre*, SGTS, vol. 4, (Edinburgh: Oliver and Boyd, 1952), l. 3539.

[76] Whyte, *Martial Music,* prints (p. 27) a passage reputedly extracted from the "orderly book" of the 72nd Regiment (Seaforth Highlanders), in which no less than twelve prescribed tunes are specified, from "Daybreak" to "When dinner is ready". They include the following field-of-battle terms: "Gathering, or turn on", "The Charge", "While engaged" and "Lament (burying dead)".

known as *anamain*, which was reserved for poets with the rank of *ollam*.[77] But his reason for making this proposal was in order to explain the abecedarian format of the Harlaw *brosnachadh* by associating it with the most exalted grade of the professional poets. If we reject that association, as I do, then we are free to link the putative genre of incitement with other personnel from within the poetic order in the widest sense. Whatever the truth may be with regard to O'Grady's puzzling reference to the "tribal poet", it seems unnecessary to assume that there was a defined poetic genre of battle-incitements to armies delivered by a chief-poet on a battle-field.

This does not mean that pre-battle incitement, verbal or musical or whatever, did not take place before Highland battles; indeed, there is every reason to believe that rituals or formalities of some sort existed, and the Battle of Harlaw was surely a suitable occasion for them to be rehearsed. But if there was a *brosnachadh catha* associated with the Battle of Harlaw, there are still serious questions to be asked about how such a production could have survived from the early fifteenth to the late eighteenth century. For present-day Celtic scholars need to be more cautious than the early writers on HB. We cannot endorse their casual assumption that 'the tradition' could deliver changeless texts over hundreds of years. Saying that is not to endorse the crude negativity of Dr Samuel Johnson on the subject, but to acknowledge that while the oral traditions of some cultures preserve material for much longer than others (usually because of the deliberate efforts of designated custodians, and the continuing intelligibility and importance of the materials in question to later generations), there is a general tendency for newer, more relevant items and genres to replace older, more remote ones, resulting in a notional life-span for a given cultural artefact. In terms of global comparisons, a span of three and a half centuries seems like a long period for a purely oral survival; and in the case of the Gaelic literatures massive cultural dislocation between the seventeenth and nineteenth centuries should have tended to lessen the chances of survival. Yet while this is generally true for Scottish Gaelic, we have a few examples of items that bridge the chasm between the late Medieval and the Modern period. For

---

[77] Slotkin, *"Formulaic Nature"*, pp. 156–7; cf. F. Kelly, *A Guide to Early Irish Law* (Dublin: Dublin Institute for Advanced Studies, 1988), pp. 45–7.

instance, a couple of poems found in the Book of the Dean of Lismore (compiled between 1512 and 1542), are matched by versions which crop up in eighteenth-century sources.[78] Although these examples are exceptional, they at least allow one to make a case for HB; to judge by these examples, such a case would have to include the presence of manuscript transmission somewhere in the background.

If no manuscripts were involved, real longevity is even more questionable. Yet here too we can point to some impressive cases of oral survival in Gaelic–including, of course, some of the Fenian ballads. Where the normal processes of attrition and loss of oral texts are in suspense, however, and in the absence of a manuscript dimension, there seems usually to be some other special factor involved. For example, the Gaelic waulking-song tradition seems to have captured some old Gaelic song-texts and given them an afterlife long after they would have perished in the ordinary way. That is how we have orally preserved women's songs to Alastair Mac Colla after the Battle of Inverlochy (1645) and to Dòmhnall mac Iain 'ic Sheumais after the Battle of Càirinis (1601).[79] Again, the allegedly oldest example of Gaelic song preserved till modern times is *Pìobaireachd Dhomhnaill Duibh* "The pibroch of Black Donald", which is supposed to go back to a battle fought at Inverlochy in 1431.[80] For this tradition to be credible, I believe one should look for some special explanation. Conceivably, the fame of the 1645 Battle of Inverlochy might have lent interest to the song from the earlier battle, thereby extending its life-span. Despite questions about its own authenticity, this song may offer a helpful parallel to HB in terms of longevity. And although *Pìobaireachd Dhomhnaill Duibh* is an isolated example, a number of the Gaelic waulking songs (*òrain luaidh*) can confidently be accepted as involving oral survival from the seventeenth to the twentieth century. Could some

---

[78] See P. Ó Macháin, "Irish and Scottish traditions concerning *Ceathrar do bhí ar uaigh an fhir*", *Éigse*, 30 (1997), pp. 7–17 (16); "Scribal practice and textual survival: the example of Uilliam Mac Mhurchaidh", *Scottish Gaelic Studies*, 22 (2006), pp. 95–122 (98–104).

[79] J. L. Campbell and F. Collinson (eds), *Hebridean Folksongs* (3 vols, Oxford: Clarendon Press, 1969–81), 2, pp. 134–7 and 239–41; 3, pp. 94–9 and 250–5.

[80] See Whyte, *Martial Music*, pp. 6, 106; cf. F. Collinson *The Traditional and National Music of Scotland* (London: Routledge & K. Paul, 1966), p. 50; A. L. Gillies *The Songs of Gaelic Scotland* (Edinburgh: Birlinn, 2005), pp. 124–8.

comparable set of special circumstances have carried HB intact from the fifteenth to the eighteenth century? Although no oral-popular Gaelic texts now survive to commemorate the Battle of Harlaw, Donald of Islay's incursion into the Mearns was still a living memory to the inhabitants of that area when Montrose's army encamped there in 1645, as an anecdote in the Clanranald Histories reveals.[81] Bearing in mind the iconic status of *Cath Gairbheach* in Gaelic tradition, as evidenced by references in the poetry, one could perhaps conclude that an oral survival–say, of an item of traditional lore (*seanchas*) with accompanying verse, preserved in a Clan Donald territory–from 1411 to the 1770s, while improbable, is not impossible.[82]

Setting these general considerations to one side for the moment, I should like to ask now what the actual text of HB can contribute to the question of its origins and background. I accept that the three versions on which Derick Thomson based his edition–ML97, ML222 and E–are prime witnesses to the text of HB, together with MacD, which was not available when Thomson wrote.[83] I would argue as follows. The alphabetical sequence of adjectives in each surviving version is gapped or has its order disturbed in one or more ways, but I presume that there was a moment in the textual history of HB when a whole alphabet was present, with each letter equally represented and in the correct alphabetical order.[84] The gaps in the extant versions occur in different and potentially instructive ways: all four versions lack one half of the U-section; ML222 lacks the whole E-section and the whole O-section; E lacks half of the E-section and half of the O-section; MacD lacks the whole of the H-section; ML97 is complete except for the missing half of the U-section. Taking this evidence in isolation we might conclude that:

---

[81] RMS MS MCR 39, p. 165; see *Reliquiae Celticae*, vol. 2, pp. 196–7.

[82] For *Cath Gairbheach* in Scottish Gaelic poetry see W. McLeod, *Divided Gaels*, p. 126.

[83] See notes 8 and 14 for details of these sources. The MacDiarmaid MS was presented to Glasgow University's Celtic Department in 1968, having till then lain unnoticed in private hands.

[84] See p. 12 above and p. 46 (n. 115) below for the question whether this alphabet included a H-section at that stage.

1.) all four versions derive from an archetypal source which had lost half of its U-section;

2.) because of their gaps, neither ML222 nor MacD nor E could easily be seen as the direct source of the others, but ML97 could be nearer to the archetype than the rest.

In fact, ML97 does seem, in one obvious respect, to occupy a position superior to E's in stemmatic terms. ML97's G-section is followed directly by its I-section, and its H-section is added in a box at the foot of the page, following the L-section. In E, the H-section is incorporated between its L-section and its M-section without comment. This suggests that the compiler of E had access to ML97.

If we examine the readings of the four versions, however, this first impression is quickly seen to be inadequate. For if we exclude obviously mistaken forms, there are still points at which each source has a reading different from and not inferior to what we find in the other three, points at which each pair of sources has a reading different from and not inferior to what we find in the other pair, and points at which all four sources differ.[85] It is true that the list of unique readings in ML222 is considerably longer than those of the other versions; and that ML97 and MacD share a significant-looking number of divergences from ML222 and E; but we lack the means to move from these impressions to constructing a stemma for the surviving descendants of the archetypal version of the *Brosnachadh*. The suspicion has to be that we are dealing with missing versions, contamination between sources, editorial repair-work or a combination of these and similar factors.

At this point it is worth recalling the statement in ML97 quoted earlier, to the effect that its version had been copied from "an old MS in Galic character", which I take to mean in the Gaelic hand or *corr-litir*.

---

[85] Examples: ML222 *toghannta* (others *togarrach* or similar); ML97 *fortail is* (others *fortail* or similar); MacD *brìoghmhor* (others *brioghor* or similar); E *furichair* (others *furachail* or similar); ML222 and ML97 *talcmhor/talcor* (MacD and E *talcorra/talcarra*); ML222 and MacD *làn-ealamh* or similar (ML97 and E *lanathlif*); ML222 and E *deagh-fhulang/deugh-fhuillin* (ML97 and MacD *deugh-fhulinich/deagh-fhulangach*); all different: ML222 *mor-chneathach*, ML97 *mor-chriodhich*, MacD *mor-chritheach*, E *moir-chriadhach*.

Although it is perfectly reasonable to suppose on general grounds that there could have been such a manuscript (or indeed manuscripts) in circulation, clear-cut evidence for the presence of such a source is scarce in ML97 and, for that matter, in the other surviving versions. This could, of course, be because those who created our versions were adept at reading the Gaelic script and did not make many transcriptional errors. On the other hand, I have noticed a couple of sets of variant readings which could embody mistakes triggered by the Gaelic MS contraction $\bar{s}$ for *acht*. For example, in its T-section, ML222 has *traidh-easgidh* and E has *froigheasgi*, both presumably representing *troigh-éasgaidh* 'nimble-footed' (I take the initial *f-* in E as a printer's error for *t-*), but ML97 and MacD have, respectively, *troigheachdich* and *traoigheachtach* (perhaps thought of as involving *éacht* 'deed', though MacD glosses the whole word obscurely as *"ciosach"*).[86] These difficulties may or may not count as a sufficient indication of the presence of a manuscript "in Galic character". One should add, in any case, that the word 'old' applied to this putative source has to be treated with caution, since the writing of manuscripts in the *corr-litir* survived, albeit tenuously, till the eighteenth century in Gaelic Scotland; and I see almost no signs of medieval spelling traits (e.g. absence of lenition marking on *b*, *d*, *g*, *m*, etc., or the use of *e* and *i* for later *ea* and *io*) in our versions of HB.[87]

If pressed to give a view on the circumstances lying behind HB as we find it, I would speculate that a MS source (or perhaps more than one MS source) containing our text was being circulated and copied between several individuals, with omissions and mistakes occurring and being rectified, versions being compared and spellings being modernised in a relatively casual way. Reference was made earlier to the activities of a circle of Gaelic scholars, including collectors of poetry like Rev. James McLagan and Rev. Donald MacNicol, Biblical translators like Rev. James Stuart of Killin, his son Rev. Dr. John Stuart of Luss and Dugald Buchanan, and gentleman-scholars like James Macintyre of Glenoe, who–as we now begin to understand–were looking to create a fuller picture of

---

[86] See also the word *dàsannach* in the D-section, to be discussed below on pages 39-40.

[87] The word *laomsgair*, which had a lenited *m* in the earlier language (see *DIL*, s.v. *láemscar*, defined as a "vaguely laudatory" term; cf. *láem* 'flame', *láemda* 'flaming') is a possible exception; cf. HBT, p. 156.

what Gaelic literature had been and could be like, asking their own questions about its antecedents and properties.[88] I believe we need look no further than the efforts of these late eighteenth-century scholars to explain the textual patterning and linguistic forms we see in the primary texts of HB.

Identifying this phase of literary activity, of course, does nothing to explicate the earlier history of our text. Unfortunately for us, the HB texts not only lack early orthographical traits; they are also devoid of meaty verb-forms on which to found linguistic arguments for or against a fifteenth-century origin. In any case, when considering Early Modern Gaelic texts, we need to keep in mind both the progressive forms sanctioned in the Grammatical Tracts and found in strict-metre poetry from the twelfth century onwards, and the persistent archaistic tendencies of annalistic and similar texts from as late as the seventeenth century. While we can confirm on linguistic and orthographic grounds that the origins of our text lie within the Early Modern period of Gaelic literature, this could signify an origin as late as the eighteenth century.

Can we do anything to illuminate the darkness between 1411 and the 1770s? We can certainly try. Professor Thomson's edition of HB made several references to the poet Alastair Mac Mhaighstir Alastair, including echoes of HB in Alastair's *Òran nam Fineachan Gàidhealach* and a possible link between his wife's family and ML222.[89] Thomson also reminded us that the printed source within our primary group of texts, the Eigg Collection, was made by Alastair's son Raghnall. We may well ask whether there could have been a connection between the text of HB and Alastair himself.

The connection which Professor Thomson noted between HB and Alastair's work could, in my view, have been stated a good deal more strongly. There are actually up to a dozen potentially significant lexical overlaps involving HB and Alastair's *Birlinn Chlann Raghnaill*, a similar number in *Òran nam Fineachan Gàidhealach*, and a good scattering in his other poems, especially the political ones; there are even a dozen or so

---

[88] Cf. note 36 for these literary and cultural circles.

[89] See p. 149 for his wife Jane's family, the MacDonalds of Dalness, and p. 156 for *Òran nam Fineachan Gàidhealach*. Thomson also referred to Alastair's use of words which occur in HB: the "rare" word *frithir* (p. 163) and the "obsolete" word *confadhach* (p. 169 n. 19).

such shared items in Alastair's *Vocabulary*.[90] While some of these terms are part of the stock-in-trade of vernacular praise poetry of the eighteenth century, some are distinctly uncommon. Taken together, they suggest that Alastair would have been pretty comfortable with the lexicon of HB. But if it is hard to be categorical about the significance of coincidences like these in sources like these, we can broaden and strengthen our argument by reference to a different criterion and a different sort of text: a version of the Early Modern Gaelic Fenian romance *Cath Fionntrágha* [hereafter *CF*] written in Gaelic script in Alastair's own hand.[91]

When Charles Dunn compared the style of the *Brosnachadh* with that of the "florid" descriptions in *Cath Fionntrágha*, he did not know of the existence of this copy of *Cath Fionntrágha*. Textually it is readily comparable with other versions of *CF* in Irish MSS. Linguistically speaking, although it contains some spectacular vernacularisms, it is basically standard Early Modern Gaelic. In palaeographic terms, it is written in a competent, workmanlike script and shows a good command of the usual repertoire of MS contractions. Orthographically, however, it reveals a set of distinctive, even idiosyncratic practices. For example, when spelling words containing the sequence /iu/ or /ju/, Alastair tends to write *ui* rather than *iu* or *io*, e.g. *ionnsaigh* becomes *uinsi(th)*. Again, he tends to write epenthetic vowels pronounced in Scottish Gaelic but not usually written, e.g. *oirragheirc* for *oirdheirc*. Again, he often misses out spirants which would have been pronounced in the Classical language but presumably not in his own Gaelic, e.g. *tiolicich* for *tiodhlaiceach*, a

---

[90] Those in the *Birlinn*, for which see A. MacLeod, *Sàr Òrain* (Glasgow: An Comunn Gaidhealach, 1933), include *àibheiseach*, *furachair* and a distinctive use of *socair*. Those in *Òran nam Fineachan*, for which see D. S Thomson, *Alasdair Mac Mhaighstir Alasdair: Selected Poems*, SGTS, new series, vol. 1, (Edinburgh: Scottish Academic Press, 1996), include *athlamh*, *innealta* and *togarrach*. Those in the Jacobite poems, for which see J. L. Campbell, *Highland Songs of the 'Forty-five*, vol. 15, (revised edition, Edinburgh: Scottish Academic Press, 1984), include *tailceanta*, *furachair* and *arranta*. Those in the *Vocabulary*, i.e. A. M'Donald, *A Galick and English Vocabulary* (Edinburgh: [s.n.] printed by R. Fleming, 1741), include *ruai[m]neach*, *frithaire* (cf. *frithir*), *furachair* and a distinctive use of *inntinneach*.

[91] NLS Gaelic MS 72.2.11. It is incomplete; Ronald Black in his introduction to the reproduction of this MS in Irish Script on Screen (https://www.isos.dias.ie/) reckons that roughly the last ten out of a total of about 50 pages are missing .

spelling which also shows his frequent practice of writing final *-ach* as *-ich*. He is also prone to uncertainty over the spelling of the sound /xk/ in his spoken Gaelic, which sometimes represents *-c(-)* and sometimes *-cht(-)* in the Classical language; for example, he writes *do ghlachtidh* for *do g(h)lacadh* 'was caught' (also involving *-idh* for *-adh*, another feature of Alastair's 'system').

Now this set of spelling traits can likewise be seen in the other main instance of Alastair's writing in the *corr-litir*, namely the specimens of his own poems contained in the surviving sections of NLS Gaelic MS 72.2.13.[92] Intriguingly, it can also be glimpsed intermittently in Alastair's *Vocabulary*, whatever that may portend.[93] Most importantly for our purposes, the self-same traits, which John Lorne Campbell (p. 74) called "weird [albeit] with a certain rough consistency", recur conspicuously and in numbers that take us beyond the possibility of coincidence, in the HB texts–especially in ML97 and E.[94] The presence of these spelling traits, involving both Classical Gaelic and vernacular Scottish Gaelic texts

---

[92] See J. L. Campbell, *Scottish Gaelic Studies*, 4 (1934–5), pp. 70–84 and 153–204. Examples include: *pechdich* for *peac(th)ach*, *Huil* for *Shiubhail*, *Gherich* for *Dh'éireadh*, *chuinn* for *chionn*.

[93] Examples include *guimhlain* for *giúlain* (p. 44), *deudhebholtrach* for *deagh-bholtrach* (p. 53), *Uibhair* for *Iubhair* (p. 66), *uinsachadh* for *ionnsachadh* (p. 156). Conceivably, an earlier draft of the *Vocabulary* had more such spellings, and most but not all of them were edited out before publication. Note that the Modern Gaelic love-poem written into NLS Gaelic MS 72.1.39, which Ronald Black suggested might be in Alastair's hand, is less likely to have been written by Alastair, since its 'execrable' spelling lacks the specific features we are associating with him: see 'Mac Mhaighstir Alastair in Rannoch: a reconstruction', *Transactions of the Gaelic Society of Inverness*, 59 (1994–96), pp. 341–419 (377).

[94] Examples from the HB texts include the following: (1) *uinsi(th)*: E *uima-ghonach*; (2) *oirragheirc*: ML97 *oirradheirc*, E *merragha*, MacD and E *olla-ghniomhach*, ML222 *ollabhorb*; (3) *tio[dh]licich*: ML97 and ML222 *nai[mh]demhail*, E *briogh[mh]or*; (4) *-ich* for *-ach*: ML97 *gruamich*, E *-ghniomhich*; (5) /k~xk~xt/ confusion: ML97 *ericol* (= ScG *eireachdail*), E *èicoil* (= ScG *euchdail*); (6) *-idh* for *-adh*: ML97 and E *cosnidh*. Additionally, *CF* consistently has *deudh-* for *deagh-* 'excellent', and this spelling is echoed in ML97 and E *deugh-*. Note that orthographic parallels with *CF* are much less frequent in ML222 (cf. Thomson, 'Harlaw Brosnachadh' pp. 148-9) and MacD.

written by Alastair himself, is important because they put it beyond doubt that he played a significant role in the pre-history of HB.

To ascertain the nature of that involvement we need to consider another set of relationships. These were recognised by Professor Thomson in the form of a set of lexical correspondences between HB and two putatively fifteenth-century texts found in the Red Book of Clanranald: the "Arming of John" and the bardic eulogy *Fìor mo mholadh ar Mhac Colla*.[95] These lexical correspondences are undeniable; but to fully understand their significance we must add that they are also present in the Clanranald History which is the main text in the Red Book.[96] Such a connection with the Red Book should not surprise us. It was stated by Lachlan MacMhuirich, a descendant of the bardic family, in his testimony to the Highland Society's inquiry into the authenticity of Ossian (previously noted), that Alastair (and likewise his son Raghnall) had carried off Gaelic manuscripts after visits to Clann 'ic Mhuirich in South Uist.[97] And John Lorne Campbell suggested back in 1934 that Alastair had very likely seen the Red Book, when discussing the Gaelic use of the English word 'faction' in a poem of Alastair's.[98] The Red Book would

---

[95] The "John" in question was the last Lord of the Isles, according to HBT, pp. 163–4. The texts are in RMS MS MCR 39, pp. 219–28, and are printed in *Reliquiae Celticae*, vol. 2, pp. 259–65.

[96] An edition with translation of this text can be found in *Reliquiae Celticae*, vol. 2, pp. 138–309. Ignoring repeated items, I calculate that about 45 of the 70–plus epithets in the abecedarian section of the primary texts of HB recur in the Red Book texts. Of these, 12 are in both the "Arming of John" and the Clanranald History, 22 (including the noteworthy *séanamhail, toirteamhail, bunanta* and *foirniata*) are in the "Arming" alone, and 11 (including the noteworthy *furachair, talcmhor, traigh-éasgaidh* and *sanntach*, all occurring in the description of the Battle of Auldearn) are in the Clanranald History alone.

[97] See note 46, H. Mackenzie (ed.), *Ossianic Enquiry*, Appendix, pp. 276, 279.

[98] 'Gaelic MS. 63 of the National Library', *Scottish Gaelic Studies*, 4 (1934–5), pp. 70–84 and 153–204 (p. 74). Niall MacMhuirich had used the word in his Clanranald History (MCR 39, p. 71, ll. 14, 18), cf. *Reliquiae Celticae*, vol. 2, p. 170.

presumably have been available in Uist until it was carried away by James MacPherson in 1760.[99]

Professor Thomson thought that HB had been drawn on by the composer of the "Arming" text and the bardic poem, and used this interpretation as an argument in favour of a fifteenth-century date for HB. I would prefer to see these texts as relatively run-of-the-mill specimens of learned literary output, extracted by Niall MacMhuirich from MacMhuirich family records or similar sources elsewhere, and used by him to embellish his accounts of the Battle of Auldearn and the Battle of Alford for the purposes of his Clanranald History.[100] And I would see the unique text that is HB as the derivative rather than the source, a creative response to the Red Book texts, inspired by one of Alastair's visits to South Uist.

There is a piece of specific evidence which tends to support this reading of the facts. The adjective *dàsannach* (with minor spelling variations) occurs in our four primary sources and is hence archetypal to HB as we have it. This word occurs in a handful of Modern Scottish Gaelic texts, but it is not in *DIL* or in Early Modern or Modern Irish sources known to me. It is explained variously: as "bold" in a gloss in ML222, as *dòchasach* ('hopeful, confident') in a footnote in MacD, and as "furious, fierce" in the *Focalair Gearr* which accompanies the Stewarts' Collection. In the Fieldwork Archive of the Digital Archive of Scottish Gaelic we find instances of *dàsannach* explained as "audacious" (Applecross) and as "determined" (Harris). [101] On this evidence, the

---

[99] For historical references see Black, "MacMhaighstir Alastair in Rannoch", p. 394 (n. 121); for an echo in Gaelic tradition see my "Alexander Carmichael and Clann Mhuirich", *Scottish Gaelic Studies*, 20 (2000), 1–66 (pp. 31 and 34).

[100] I gave some reasons to support this view in "The Clanranald Histories–Authorship and Purpose", in G. Evans, B. Martin and J. Wooding (eds), *Origins and Revivals: Proceedings of the First Australian Conference of Celtic Studies* (Sydney, 2000), 315–40 (330, 334). Also note that Christopher Beaton, when making the copy of the Red Book which is extant in the Black Book of Clanranald (i.e. RMS MS MCR 40), edited out most of Niall's florid adjectives.

[101] See https://dasg.ac.uk/fieldwork/, s.v. *dàsannach*. The Harris example does not have an accent in the Field-worker's copy. Note also *dàsanta* 'foolhardy' (Skye) in the same source. The form *dàisneachd* 'ferocity' (applied to winter weather) was

twentieth-century meaning of the word is somewhat indeterminate, but its existence in the literature and language is not in doubt; the earliest dateable example is from the late seventeenth century in a poem by Duncan Macrae, the compiler of the Fernaig MS.[102] It clearly has a certain affinity with *dásachtach* 'furious, raging', as found in Early and Modern Irish sources, and in Early Modern Scottish Gaelic MSS including the Red Book of Clanranald. In the Fenian lay *Duan an Deirg* the equivalence is manifest: *gu dasanach* (MacNicol's version, v. 18) corresponds to *gu dàsachdach* (Kennedy's version, v. 21).[103] As it happens, one of the examples of *dásachtach* in the Clanranald Histories occurs in a florid passage in MacMhuirich's description of the Battle of Auldearn. On p. 151 of the Red Book, line 11 ends with *dáſ* and line 12 begins with *uiđ*, which needs to be corrected to *dá[s]ſuiđ* and expanded as *dhásachtuidh*. Since this word was printed in *Reliquiae Celticae* (vol. 2, p. 190) as *dháchtuidh* with a footnote reading 'thtápuidh ?' this MS reading could clearly cause difficulty.

I suspect that this reading in the Red Book was seen by Alastair and misread as *dhásanuidh*, and suggest that that is why *dàsan(n)ach* (as opposed to *dásachtach*) appears in Alastair's version of *CF* and in his published poem *Iorram Cuain*.[104] This cannot be the source of the example in the Fernaig MS, of course, but later poetical examples could be explained as deriving from Alastair's use of the word. A second starting-point for the word in Scottish Gaelic could be the jingling phrase *dèisinneach dàsan(n)ach* which occurs in a run describing two warriors pitching into one another in the well-known heroic-romantic tale

---

used by Neil Morison (1816-1882), Bàrd Phabaigh: see G. Henderson, *Leabhar nan Gleann* (Edinburgh: Norman MacLeod, 1898), p. 52, verse 4.

[102] See W. Matheson, *The Blind Harper*, SGTS, vol. 12, (Edinburgh, Glasgow: Scottish Gaelic Texts Society, 1970), p. 177 (*gu dàsannach*, translated "furiously").

[103] J. F. Campbell, *Leabhar na Féinne* (London: printed for author, Spottiswoode & Co., 1872), pp. 108b, 122a.

[104] For *CF* see NLS MS 72.2.11, p. 18, l. 10, where it is adjacent to other adjectives recurring in HB, including the noteworthy words *ruaimneach, cnedhach* and *aithasich,* and p. 27, l. 30. Alastair's *Iorram Cuain* was first published in 1776 in the Eigg Collection (pp. 121–5), but Ronald Black ("Mac Mhaighstir Alastair in Rannoch", pp. 406–7) has argued persuasively for an early date of composition, possibly 1738.

Gaisgeach na Sgèithe Deirge.[105] Be that as it may, even if this specific explanation is not robust enough to bear the weight assigned to it, I believe the evidence for Alastair's involvement in the 'pre-history' of HB is more than adequately established by the general considerations outlined above.[106]

This begs the question, how can we best view HB in the light of other available information about Alastair's literary and intellectual development. We have had occasion to mention his *Iorram Cuain* (composed 1738?) and his *Vocabulary* (published 1741); and Ronald Black's reconstruction of his activities in the late 1730s also brings up his poem on the Gaelic language (*Moladh na seann chànain Albannaich*), which may have been stimulated by reading Rev. David Malcolm's *An Essay on the Antiquities of Great Britain and Ireland* (Edinburgh, 1738).[107] Bearing in mind the way he entitled his own collection of poems *Ais-eiridh na Sean-chanoin Albannich*, "The Resurrection of the Old Scottish Tongue", I wonder if Alastair, the linguistic and literary experimenter and explorer of Gaelic manuscripts, could have become interested in HB as part of his project to bring about that "resurrection". Answering this question could be important for our understanding of Alastair's poetic aims and his contribution to Gaelic literature more generally. For present purposes, however, a more pertinent question

---

[105] E.g. W. J. Watson, *Rosg Gàidhlig*, second edition, (Glasgow: An Comunn Gàidhealach, 1929), p. 93; for further examples of *dàsan(n)ach*, see https://dasg.ac.uk/corpus/. This phrase (originally *déistinneach dàsachtach*?) could have inspired Macrae and might be the ultimate source of the colloquial examples. It could likewise have been known to Alastair and might have helped to suggest the misreading of *dàsachtach* in the first place. A third possible starting-point for *dàsannach* is explored by R. Ó Maolalaigh, "Am buadhfhacal meadhan-aoiseach *meranach* agus *meran, meranach, dàsachdach, dàsan(n)ach* na Gàidhlig", *Scottish Studies*, 37 (2014), 183–206 (196–8).

[106] A similar case could be made out for *laomsga(i)r* (cf. note 87) which recurs in a handful of Scottish Gaelic poetical sources, all of which were arguably influenced by Alastair's use of it.

[107] See Black, "Mac Mhaighstir Alastair in Rannoch", pp. 402–3. For this aspect of Alastair's poem in praise of Gaelic (first published in his *Aiseiridh* (1751), pp. 1–7), see Thomson, *Mac Mhaighstir Alasdair*, pp. 75–82 (l. 677), in which Alastair refers explicitly to Malcolm's philological prognostications.

arises: how much might he have contributed to HB itself. More particularly, if he was, as I suspect, a major contributor to HB as we have it, could he have been the one responsible for the abecedarian element in HB, for which we have seen no early evidence? He had wider literary horizons than most, including first-hand experience of Latin, English and Scots literature. He certainly had the imagination and the inventiveness, and was willing to enrich Gaelic poetry by importing themes and forms from outside the Gaelic world. He had friends to fire up his curiosity to experiment, and to respond to his compositions.[108] The thought that he might have struck the abecedarian spark is a tempting one, to me at least.

I suppose it might be asked whether Alastair (or, if not he, someone with very similar talents) could have invented HB in its entirety. If he had been aware, say, of the sort of tradition about *brosnachadh catha* reported by Martin Martin, and had become aware of Niall Mac Mhuirich's heroicisation of Alastair Mac Colla and the 1645 campaign as the acme of Clanranald achievement,[109] could he have created HB *ex nihilo*, seeking to make Harlaw the acme of Clan Donald, or perhaps Gaelic achievement? We cannot exclude this as a possibility. Yet there are reasons to doubt such a scenario: for example, there would be something slightly odd about the echoes of HB in Alastair's *Òran nam Fineachan Gàidhealach*, if he were quoting from a work he had recently composed. An alternative is worth exploring. Supposing that we removed the whole alphabetical section but left the rest, we would still have a significant, interesting, cohesive text of sorts:[110]

---

[108] Compare the flattering Latin verses by "D. M—", headed *De auctore Testimonium*, which precede the first poem in the *Ais-eiridh*. I am most grateful to Ronald Black for identifying the author as Donald MacDonald, younger brother of Hugh MacDonald of Baleshare, who had served alongside Alastair in the Clanranald regiment in the '45. Black ("Alastair in Rannoch", p. 405) also paints a delightful picture of Alastair and Struan Robertson striking literary sparks off one another at stopovers on Alastair's journeys between Lowlands and Highlands.

[109] That is precisely how Mac Mhuirich's work was seen by Seosamh Laoide and Eoin Mac Néill, whose edition of substantial parts of it was published by Connradh na Gaedhilge (Dublin, 1914) under the title *Alasdair Mac Colla. Sain-eolus ar a ghníomharthaibh gaisge*.

[110] The following 'edition' is based on the four earliest sources. It is strictly *exempli gratia*, an attempt to reproduce the Gaelic in a fairly standard Early Modern form

A Chlanna Cuinn, cuimhnichibh
cruas a n-am na h-iorghaile,
do chosnadh chathláthrach
re bronnaibh bhar mbiodhbhaidheadh.
A Chlanna Cuinn Chéadchathaich   (5)
a-nois uair bhar n-aitheanta,
a chuiléana confadhach,
a bheithreacha bunanta,
a leómhana lánghasta,
a onchona iorghaileach,   (10)
a chruadhchraobha curanta,
(a ghasraidh sgaiteach theidhmbhearrtha)
de Chlannaibh Cuinn Chéadchathaich.
A Chlanna Cuinn, cuimhnichibh
cruas a n-am na h-iorghaile.   (15)

The remaining portion of text contains the bardic echoes (the animal images and the *dúnadh*) which Charles Dunn saw as diagnostically significant in HB. It contains a sequence of heptasyllabic lines with trisyllabic cadences–i.e. it is a plausible instance of *rosg* as postulated by Edgar Slotkin.[111] It can undoubtedly be seen as an example of a panegyric poem of incitement as described by Pádraig Ó Macháin and other modern scholars–and equally as envisioned by Seán MacCraith, the author of *Caithréim Thoirdhealbhaigh,* who included twelve poems in this metre.

On this hypothesis it would become possible to regard the alphabetical section as an excrescence, the product of a lively imagination and a mid-eighteenth-century sensibility, engrafted onto a pre-existing stock, of which we may glimpse a reflex in the concluding section of HB.

---

while retaining some Scottish features which may have been established in the language when the postulated *Ur*-text was composed. These retained features are ipv. pl. in *-ibh* (ll. 1 and 14), *-ich* for *-igh* (ll. 1, 5, 13 and 14), adjectives in *-anta* for *-ata* (8, 11), plural polysyllabic adjectives without *-a* (7, 10), and ScG *cosnadh* instead of *cosnamh* (3). I have supposed a nom. sing. **biodhbhaidh* declined like *foghlaidh* (IGT §52) on the basis of ScG *biùthaidh* (4), and admitted one somewhat dubious emendation *metri gratia* (11). Line 12 is only found in two MSS, and sits uneasily with the metre and flow of the rest; possibly, it represents a vestige of an alternative version of HB.

[111] There is also binding alliteration between lines 1–2, 11–13, 13–14 and 14–15.

This could encourage us to imagine we have caught a glimpse of a lost literary saga about *Cath Gairbheach*, or a *caithréim* of Donald of Islay, or similar. We might even be able to point to parallels, if we could relate this slimmed-down version of HB to a type of formular utterance, taking the form of "more or less rough verse",[112] which we meet in Gaelic clan legends and historical tales. The following lines are associated with the *pìobaireachd* known as *The Camerons' Gathering*, which was said to have been composed at a seventeenth-century confrontation between the Camerons and the Earl of Atholl's men:[113]

> *A Chlanna nan Con,*
> *A Chlanna nan Con,*
> *Thigibh an so,*
> *A Chlanna nan Con,*
> *A Chlanna nan Con,*
> *Thigibh an so,*
> *'S gheibh sibh feòil.*

The following words of incitement were associated with the *pìobaireachd* known as *Latha na Maoile Ruaidhe* ("The Battle of Mulroy"), a fight which took place between the MacDonalds of Keppoch and the Mackintoshes in 1688.[114]

> *'Chlann Dòmhnuill an fhraoich*
> *'Mhuinntir mo ghaoil,*
> *Luchd nan cas caol,*
> *Thugaibh am bruthach dhiu!*
> *'Chlann Dòmhnuill an fhraoich,*

---

[112] John MacInnes, "Clan sagas and historical legends", in M. Newton (ed.), *Dùthchas nan Gàidheal: Selected essays of John MacInnes* (Edinburgh: Birlinn, 2006), pp. 48–63 (58).

[113] See Whyte, *Martial Music* (note 6), pp. 1–2. "Children of the Dogs, Children of the Dogs, come here! Children of the Dogs, Children of the Dogs, come here and you will get meat."

[114] Whyte, *Martial Music*, p. 97. "Clan Donald of the heather, my beloved people, you of the slender legs, deprive them of the brae! Clan Donald of the heather, my beloved people, you of the slender legs, let us keep at them! Clan Donald of the heather, my beloved people, you of the slender legs, get them moving–the people of the kale, the people of the kale, the people of the kale and the excellent brose!"

'Mhuinntir mo ghaoil,
Luchd nan cas caol,
Cumamaid riu siud!

'Chlann Dòmhnuill an fhraoich
'Mhuinntir mo ghaoil,
Luchd nan cas caol,
Cuiribh nan siubhal iad!
Muinntir a' chàil,
Muinntir a' chàil,
Muinntir a' chàil,
'S an t-sàr bhrudhaiste.

These battle incitements–for that is what they are–raise another possibility, as we seek a way back to the late Middle Ages for HB. There could be a 'high road' involving Early Modern literary genres; but there is also the possibility of a 'low road' involving popular historical traditions. At the end of the day, the distance between the two roads may not be so great.

To sum up the results of our examination of HB and its credentials, we have seen how its eye-catching form attracted successive attempts to build it up in the late eighteenth and nineteenth centuries, and have encountered hints that that process had a longer history. We have raised questions in particular about the appositeness of its alphabetic structure to real battle situations, and suggested that this was an accretion rather than an original feature. We have raised the possibility that this accretion was the work of Alastair Mac Mhaighstir Alastair in the 1730s. We have tentatively posited the existence of an earlier text associated with the Battle of Harlaw, freed from the abecedarian dimension, and speculated what it might have looked like. There are questions remaining, of course. For example, we have assumed that a creation of the 1730s or thereby could have circulated enough to generate the surviving versions, and also a version in what could be described as an "old Galic manuscript" by the early 1770s. This does not appear implausible. Again, we have left unanswered the question of how and when the H-section was created for HB. Professor Thomson suggested that words from the already existing vowel sections were abstracted to form the new section.[115] I believe that could be the correct explanation, and would merely add that the complete absence of a H-section from MacD is perhaps an indicator of its lateness in the pre-history of HB. Again, there is doubtless more to be learned about the provenance and history of the lexicon of HB, potentially offering answers to some of the questions we have left open. We deserve a new edition; as Corpas na Gàidhlig expands and Faclair na Gàidhlig comes on stream, we will be better placed to make a realistic assault on this aspect of HB.

To revert in conclusion to our titular dilemma, I hope to have shown that the idea that HB in its present form could be a bona fide survival from the time of the Battle of Harlaw is not sustainable. On the other hand, there is definitely a bit of iceberg visible in the sub-surface; and there are just suggestions that there could be something substantial further down.

Acknowledgements

In addition to those whose help is acknowledged above, I wish to thank colleagues who suggested improvements to the Lecture as given, both at the Colloquium and subsequently. I owe a special debt to Dr. Sheila Kidd of Glasgow University and to my colleagues, Dr. Martina Ní Mheachair and Dr. Eystein Thanisch of Faclair na Gàidhlig, for assistance with regard to the MS texts of HB and Mac Mhaighstir Alastair's *Cath Fionntrágha*. I am also deeply indebted to the editors of PHCC, whose careful attention and shrewd advice has eliminated many imperfections from my text; those that remain are my own responsibility.

---

[115] Because adverb-forming *gu* becomes *gu h-* before vowels in Scottish Gaelic, all the vowel sections could be regarded in one sense as 'H-sections'; an unknown scholar must have realised that he could use this fact to complete the alphabet as he saw it. See further HBT, p. 151.

Good time(s), bad time(s): myth and metaphysics in some medieval literature?

Aled Llion Jones

Quid est ergo tempus? Si nemo ex me quærat, scio; si quærenti explicare uelim, nescio.[1]

I'll leave the Augustine without comment.

I have for a while been looking from a distance at some ideas concerning temporality in medieval Welsh literature, and when I received the invitation to give this talk, two things came immediately to mind: the Coligny calendar and the first track on Led Zeppelin's first album, 'Good Times Bad Times'. Just about then, the news came of the death of Stephen Hawking, and, reading again through A Brief History of Time,[2] I thought it would be interesting to take out of that book four or five of the main concepts of recent modern science–especially in relativity, quantum mechanics, and field theory–and look for parallels in some of the poetry and prose of the medieval manuscripts: go off, that is, in search of literary black holes.[3] This kind of thought experiment throws up endless methodological questions concerning the validity or anachronism of various heuristic or hermeneutic approaches (and a more suitable title might have been "good ideas / bad ideas"), but this is part of what is interesting. Given that 2018 was the 75th anniversary of Erwin Schrödinger's ground-breaking "What is Life" lecture series, given in February 1943 at the Dublin Institute for Advanced Studies,[4] it seemed

---

[1] Augustine, *Confessiones* lib. xi, cap. xiv, sec. 17. What is time, then? If no one is asking me, I know; if I should wish to explain it to a questioner, I don't know [editor's translation].

[2] Stephen W. Hawking (January 8, 1942 –March 14, 2018) *A Brief History of Time* (London: Bantam Press, 1988). All citations of Hawking give page numbers from this volume.

[3] By further coincidence, as this paper was being prepared for press the Event Horizon Telescope produced for the first time ever an image of a supermassive black hole, at the centre of Messier 87, a galaxy in the Virgo cluster.

[4] Erwin Schrödinger, *What is Life?* (Cambridge: Cambridge University Press, 2012 [1944]).

suitable to throw caution to the wind under the pressure of coincidence: I decided to continue in this direction hoping that, if nothing else, such an act of comparative literature would be entertaining. We will return later to address some of the methodological questions.

Time may be of many types. One could make a simple tripartite classification along the following lines: (1) External or Objective Time (usually measurable and quantifiable); (2) Internal or Subjective Time (phenomenological, psychological); and looking at these two main categories from a different philosophical perspective, we can consider (3) Metaphysical vs Immanent Time (as found, for example in Plotinus's metaphysics vs that of thinkers such as Augustine or Kant, for whom time does not exist externally or absolutely). As we move through the discussion we will have time to gesture not only to these broad distinctions, but also to play with some finer categorisations. Just to flag up some terms for the time being–many of them will be unpacked as we move along–David Brooks' useful discussion in The Deconstruction of Time[5] leads us from Cosmic Time (which is objective, linear and serial) through Dialectical Time (e.g., the kind of history found in Hegel or Marx), Phenomenological and Existential Times, and finally the Time of the Sign, being the temporality of signification itself. We shall be concerned mainly with the last three, though the Dialectical is present implicitly in a small part of my argument. This is not exhaustive: there are, of course, other times, and I shall also be referring to 'mythological' time, which I intend to leave undefined for the moment.

Modern science can be seen as a break with classical science, similarly (and in similar periodicity) to how modern literature breaks with the early modern. This is to say that classical science is roughly coterminous with the period of 'Classical Irish'. Basically, regular, predictable Newtonian science–the science of the 'clockwork universe'–is found to break down under the observational and theoretical pressures that lead to the peculiarities of Einstein and Bohr, of Relativity and of Quantum mechanics. We can say, only partially metaphorically, that realism in science breaks down into modernism and then into post-modernism.

---

[5] David Wood, *The Deconstruction of Time* (Evanston, Ill: Northwestern University Press, 2001).

The clockwork causality of Newton belongs to a physics where space is empty and homogenous: it is a neutral container in which events and objects are localised in the three dimensions of common sense, according with the geometry described already by Euclid in the fourth century BC. Time, likewise, is measurable by the clock and exists objectively, moving simply and inexorably in the direction of the future. Gurevich, in his classic study, Categories of Medieval Culture, describes how, in the shift from the middle ages to the early modern period, "European society was gradually moving from the contemplation of the world sub specie aeternitatis to an active relationship with it: a relationship measured in time." He continues with this key insight: "From being the possession of God, time had become a possession of man."[6]

In post-classical science we see time being stolen back, as Stephen Hawking describes (and it is worth noting the year mentioned here, 1915):

> Before 1915 space and time were thought of as a fixed arena in which events took place, but which was not affected by what happened in it. [. . .] The situation is quite different in the general theory of relativity. Space and time are now dynamic quantities. [. . .] Just as one cannot talk about events in the universe without the notions of space and time, so in general relativity it became meaningless to talk about space and time outside the limits of the universe. (33)

This is all simple and unsurprising, and we see similar developments in the area of culture. Walter Benjamin famously–and rightly so–borrowed from the Zeitgeist of high modernism when he railed, in his "Theses on the Philosophy of History", against the classical "empty homogenous time" of the realists;[7] similarly, for decades philosophers of history had been unpicking the objectivity of the past as representable or as

---

[6] Aron Gurevich, Categories of Medieval Culture trans. G.L. Campbell (London: Routledge and Kegan Paul, 1985 [1972]), 150.

[7] Walter Benjamin, "Theses on the Philosophy of History", in Hannah Arendt (ed.) and Harry Zohn (trans.), Illuminations (New York: Random House, 2007 [1968]), 253–264, at 261.

describable,[8] but this kind of narrative or epistemological uncertainty brings on its coat-tails connected questions concerning the ontology of the past: if it is impossible to correctly describe the past, what guarantees are there of the objective reality of that past–and by extension of the objective reality of other times? Here is Stephen Hawking again:

> *In the theory of relativity there is no unique absolute time,*
> *but instead each individual has his own personal measure*
> *of time that depends on where he is and how he is moving.*
> (Ibid.)

I do not wish to go too far into these questions here today, but–similar to those I mentioned earlier concerning anachronism–they will return in a little while.

Newton's universe was describable in terms of Euclidian geometry, and it is fair to say that in science–and not least in classical science–the *description* is considered equivalent to the reality: representation is ontology (and realist *literature* is little different in principle). Modernism–in both science and art–is more at home with the non-Euclidian, and modern science and mathematics contain any number of patterns of the non-classical, showing these to exist not merely in the sublime heights of theory and abstraction, but also in the physical world, from the endless perimeters of Chaos theory (coastlines, clouds and tree canopies occupy fractal dimensions, being chaotic and limitless) to the collapsed infinities of Big Bangs and black holes.

Space can be strange, and two of the two most commonly cited examples of non-orientable (and even non-Euclidian) shapes are the Klein bottle and the Möbius strip.[9] The Möbius strip is a curious surface used to model non-orientable two-dimensional space-time: that is, an impossible topology and, further, an impossible model of space-time. While a common loop of paper would have two surfaces–a front and a back–and

---

[8] See, for example, Paul Ricœur's discussion concerning the work of, among others, Raymond Aron, Max Weber, and the Annales school: Ricœur, *Time and Narrative* vol. 1, trans. Kathleen McLaughlin (Chicago: University of Chicago Press, 1990), 95 ff.

[9] For a discussion of the Möbius strip, and its possible limits as an empirical model of space-time, see Tim Maudlin, *Philosophy of Physics* (Princeton, Princeton University Press, 2012), 156–7.

two edges–the inner and the outer–the object under consideration has the peculiarity of being a single surface with a single edge. If you follow the outside all the way around through a single loop, you find yourself on the inside, and will have to complete a further circuit before returning to your starting point. Likewise, on tracing a route following any of the edges, you trace each part of the perimeter of the shape as you move around. This is a three-dimensional shape with a single surface and a single edge: triple but singular, three in one.[10]

It is clear to see that the Möbius strip erases the difference between inside and outside, recto and verso: the inside is only inside as we interpret it or define it thus, and the outside likewise. As a metaphor–and to anticipate somewhat a few of my conclusions–the Möbius strip, with its relational necessitation of interpretation, is one way to *visualise*–to geometrise, if you like–a type of relationship between self and other, native and foreigner, human and animal, past and future and, of course, this world and the other world.

What I aim to do here is to take a quick tour of a limited number of the impossible, non-Euclidian spaces and impossible, non-Newtonian times of Welsh and Irish medieval literature. I emphasise in advance the importance of interpretation to every step of the presentation: the concepts that emerge from the science are themselves 'merely' interpretations of the data and of the mathematics, which is why I have called this essay an exercise in comparative literature. I might have called it comparative hermeneutics. My aim is that this talk will in its own structure figuratively trace a Möbius strip: the argument, as you will see, loops back upon itself and inside itself, before coming to rest, somewhere.

Clearly literature demonstrates different attitudes to mimesis than does science, and while it may be true that particular periods are characterised by certain attitudes to temporality and spatiality, there is no need for creative authors to be entirely bound by the governing paradigms of their times: indeed, for them to be so bound would be to deny them their creativity. Elana Gomel, in her study of the representation of "impossible topologies" in recent literature insists that "[i]mpossible spaces are *unrealistic*, because realism is underwritten by the Newtonian

---

[10] This conference paper was accompanied for clarity by a single handout, a Möbius strip.

paradigm." But, she says, "they are not necessarily *unreal*." Today, she continues, "realism itself has become impossible," for the reason that "[l]ike democracy, reality has its dissidents".[11] Likewise, we need not only look for orthodox Catholic temporalities in medieval 'Christian' literature, or name as unambiguously *pagan echoes* those which seem less than clearly Christian.

Turning to Irish literature for some initial examples of non-classical space and time, John Carey's classic 1987 article, "Time, Space and the Otherworld" is an excellent place to begin, especially since it stems from his time here at Harvard, and was first published in this Colloquium's *Proceedings* just a little over thirty years ago.[12] Carey draws attention to impossible topologies and paradoxical temporalities in a number of texts, and in terms of space, he concludes, "The Otherworld [. . .] exists *in no definable spatial relationship with the mortal realm*"; indeed, it is often, he says, "as if we are separated from the Otherworld by no barrier save concealment (*díchelt*)."[13] It is hard for me here to resist the temptation to read 'concealment' and 'unconcealment' in the context of Heidegger's *aletheia*: truth and the existent world are to Heidegger precisely those things that are brought out of concealment by existential comportment, and we are here in the realm of interpretation, of hermeneutics, and even existential hermeneutics.

Concerning time and temporality, Carey says this: "Otherworld time is not only out of alignment with mortal time, but [. . .] it is fundamentally different in kind" (8). It is not simply that time flows more quickly or more slowly in the Otherworld while maintaining its linear, directed sequentiality (though it does on occasion, in keeping with the famous Twins Paradox of General Relativity); nor either that time is in any *simple* way 'out of step'; rather, otherworldly temporality itself is *of a different nature,* be that an eternal blissful present or a simultaneous presentation in

---

[11] Elana Gomel, *Narrative Space and Time: Representing Impossible Topologies in Literature* (London: Routledge, 2014), 30. See Gomel for development of many of the points in this paragraph.

[12] John Carey, "Time, Space and the Otherworld", in Brian R. Frykenberg and Kaarina Hollo (ed.), *Proceedings of the Harvard Celtic Colloquium* vol. 7 (Cambridge, MA: Department of Celtic Languages and Literatures, Harvard University, 1987), 1–27 at 7.

[13] Carey, "Time, Space and the Otherworld", 7.

the narrative moment of disparate ages. Importantly, different times permit different meanings, and types of meanings: time is far from empty and homogenous. Otherworld time, perhaps mythological time, is not simple historical cosmic time: different things happen there.

Carey gives the example of Bran mac Febail meeting Manannán driving a chariot across the surface of the sea. Mannanán, who prophesies the birth of Christ as he drives, rather than walks, on water, is on his way to effect the birth of Mongán, who, it seems, was born in the early seventh century (AD 625/6).[14] Manannán and Bran occupy different times with different landscapes, but are present to each other; and Manannán's temporality is in no way linear: he exists simultaneously before Christ as well as six centuries after him. A few years later, and two volumes of PHCC later, Carey argues that "the Irish Otherworld's characteristics are, by and large, those of the imagination itself–more specifically, of the imagination as expressed in narrative."[15] Chiming interestingly with Gwyn Thomas' unpublished suggestion that the Welsh otherworld–weird and omnipresent–is none other than the unconscious, this is another perspective which will unfurl as we continue to develop these ideas in the direction of hermeneutics (Heideggerian and otherwise).

Many of the temporally interesting texts are confusing and seem on the surface to be nonsensical. This is true in that they are impossible, as far as possibility is logical and realistic. We recall Richard Feynman's famous quip–possibly apocryphal, and possibly belonging to Niels Bohr– that "if you think you understand quantum mechanics, you don't understand quantum mechanics"–: similarly, it may be the case that if you think you understand medieval legendary temporalities, you haven't read enough.

Agallamh na Seanórach, says Carey, is "a tale preoccupied with time",[16] and beyond the glaring temporal anomalies that show "reckless"

---

[14] Carey, 'Time, Space and the Otherworld', 8.

[15] John Carey, "Otherwords and Verbal Worlds in Middle Irish Narrative", in William Mahon (ed.), *Proceedings of the Harvard Celtic Colloquium* vol. 9 (Cambridge, MA: Department of Celtic Languages and Literatures, Harvard University, 1990), 31–42, at 31.

[16] John Carey, "*Acallam na senórach*: a conversation between worlds", in Aidan Doyle and Kevin Murray (ed.), *In Dialogue with the* Agallamh [:] *Essays in Honour of Seán Ó Coileáin* (Dublin: Four Courts Press, 2014), 76–89, at 76.

divergence from comparanda, often presented as "chimerical gobbledygook", this is a story *about* the weight and pathos and consequences of time"; it is a story "in which time's *realities* are [. . .] flamboyantly made light of."[17] Carey in this article marshals the voices of Ann Dooley, Máirtin Ó Briain and Joseph Nagy among others, to unpack the texts' layers of "strangeness" (Dooley's word).[18] One main source of this temporal ambiguity, cited and discussed by Carey, is shown in Patrick's description of Caílte and Scothníam which emphasises not so much the *realities of time* but the *times of reality*–or even the *times of realities*:

> 'INgnad lind mar atchiamait sibh', ar Pátraic, '.i. inn ingen as í óc ildelbach–₇ tusa, a Cailti', ar Pátraic, 'at s(.)enoir chrin chrotach cromliath'. 'Do fuil a adhbhur sin acum', ar Cailte, '₇ ni lucht comaimsire sind, ₇ do Tuathaib dé Danann iss i, ₇ memirchradach iat sein, ₇ missi do clannaib Miled, ₇ dimbuan irchradach iat'.

> 'It is strange for me to see you thus', said Patrick: 'the girl young and beautiful–and you, Caílte', said Patrick, 'a withered stooped bent grey old man'. 'I have reason to be so', said Caílte, 'and we are not <u>folk of the same time</u> [₇ *ni* lucht comaimsire *sind*]. She is of the Túatha Dé Danann, and they are unfading; and I am of the descendants of Míl, and they are impermanent and subject to decay'.[19]

The point I wish to borrow here from Carey is that the word translated as "of the same time"–*comhaimsir*–is not to be read as "of the same age or period", but rather as "of a time which is of the same order or nature: a temporality". *Agallamh na Seanórach* presents a number of different times–different types of time–different realities of time–and those who belong to the different times–Patrick; the Fenians; the Túatha Dé Danann–belong in a clear sense to different worlds, to multiple

---

[17] Carey, "*Acallam*", 79, emphasis mine.
[18] Carey also acknowledges frequent debts to Tomás Ó Cathasaigh's work, as do I.
[19] Carey, "Acallam", 80–81. Text from Whitley Stokes (ed., tr.), "Acallamh na senórach", in Ernst Windisch and Whitley Stokes (ed.), *Irische Texte mit Wörterbuch*, Series 4: pt.1 (Leipzig: Hirzel, 1900), ll. 3904–9.

54

Otherworlds. Carey is shoulder-to-shoulder (once again) with thinkers such as Heidegger[20] when he declares that "a difference in time is also a difference in *order of being*" and, further, that the relationship between these orders of being is the argument of the text.[21]

In a notable discussion of one section of the narrative, Ann Dooley discovers, and very usefully summarises, a number of these realities:

> [T]his tale lifts a huge load; the author has combined models of cyclic and teleological historical time; he has moved the myth of the Otherworld and old heroic time into as fantastic a model as is possible; he has destabilised heroic action and eschewed a straightforward linear telling of the tale; and we have come out into an identifiable real world in the author's own time, of agricultural anxieties, their popular remedies vetted and monitored by an increasingly powerful church.[22]

These statements could, of course, almost word for word, be applied to the Welsh tales of the Mabinogi, and readers who are familiar with the Four Branches will immediately recognise the parallels (we shall explore some of them in a moment).

Carey's invocation of the imagination, and more specifically of narrative, is especially potent, and Geraldine Parsons, in her study of the narrative voice in the Agallamh (published in the same 2014 volume as Dooley's and Carey's articles) helps move the discussion towards a key ontological framework. Parson's work complicates the relationships between the past(s) and future(s) of the text, showing how they depend on the subjective narrative perspective from which these times and temporalities are considered: in analysing the narrative voice of the text, Parson shifts the focus from an external time in the world onto consciousness of time, and thus towards, I would argue, the existential experience of temporalities, that comportment towards the disclosure of

---

[20] Cf., e.g., Heidegger, *Being and Time*, trans. John Macquarrie and Edward Robinson (Oxford: Blackwell, 1962 [German orig. 1927]), or his later "Time and Being", in *On Time and Being* trans. Joan Stambaugh (Chicago: University of Chicago Press, 2002).

[21] Carey, "Acallam", 81 et passim.

[22] Ann Dooley, "The European context of *Acallam na senórach*", in Doyle and Murray (ed.), *Dialogue*, 60–75, at 64–5.

aletheia. Most importantly, these disclosures of temporality are literary: they are, Heidegger would say, ways of dwelling in poetic language.

Literature of course–as with almost any kind of writing–can show different times in the sense of different periods. Historical writing–and the writing of history–performs either the mimesis of earlier times or the description of them. Different types of writing can also describe or represent the different types of time I am more interested in here: as in the narratives described by Carey, they present on the deictic level of the story characters, events and landscapes whose spatial and temporal contexts are those of alterity. Of all literary features it may be thought that narrative is especially suitable for exploring varying and alternative temporalities, given the combination of on the one hand narrative's essential temporal nature–the fact that the reading/realising of a narrative must occur within time, as is the case with all reading and of course other types of art–and on the other, distinguishing most types of temporal literature from, say, music or even drama or cinema, the essentially verbal nature of its signification.

This last point somewhat controversially introduces the notion that a certain type of immediate meaning is present in verbal narrative at the level of the momentary unit–the word or the sentence–that is absent in visual-performative or purely aural art. A single note generally has no significance, but a single word, within a language, is a ghostly premonition of signification (to be filled and shifted by later context).

These considerations, quickly presented, to a great extent summarise most of the rest of this paper: I will mainly be developing and revisiting points such as these as we turn to Welsh prose.

The most obvious otherworldly texts (beyond explicitly Christian religious ones) are of course the Four Branches of the Mabinogi.[23] The vagaries of space and time in these have been explored often, and our conclusions for the Irish Otherworld may be applied quite well to the Welsh Annwfn,[24] the 'in-world' which exists inside and alongside this

---

[23] I acknowledge that the title is anachronous: while we certainly possess four 'branches' it is far from simple to justify considering "The Four Branches" a work. Cf., e.g., Sioned Davies, *The Four Branches of the Mabinogi* (Llandysul: Gwasg Gomer, 1993), 17–19.

[24] On the etymology and interpretation of 'Annwfn', see Patrick Sims-Williams, "Irish *Síd* and Welsh *Annwfn*", in *Irish Influence on Welsh Literature* (Oxford: Oxford University Press, 2011), 56–63.

world, simultaneously present and absent (a Schrödinger's world, even if pigs are more otherworldly than cats in Welsh medieval literature). Arawn the king of the Otherworld appears to Pwyll within Pwyll's own kingdom, as does Rhiannon, who clearly simultaneously occupies multiple spatio-temporalities as she walks her horse faster than any of Pwyll's can gallop.[25]

This simultaneous presence of different worlds, reminiscent of the Irish ontologies, is described by Elana Gomel as a "flickering" of chronotopes, and is one of five categories of impossible spaces she describes, the others being "layering", "embedding", "wormholing" and "collapsing". Gomel defines 'chronotope', after Bakhtin, as "the underlying spatial and temporal infrastructure of the story world"[26] and her categories are informed by scientific concepts (wormholing, embedding, collapsing: these are all common tropes of modern cosmology). Her argument is not that literature borrows from science, but that postmodern literature and postmodern science arise from a common conceptual background–an episteme, to borrow Foucault's word. (In parentheses I'll nod here to my question of anachronism in the context of the medieval, to be asked more fully later.)

Examples of all five types of chronotope are perhaps unsurprisingly to be found in the Mabinogi/on. (Indeed, Gomel dismisses medieval literature and folklore, since impossible spatialities and temporalities are, she says, so common here as to be uninteresting, but I shall still borrow

---

[25] See Richard Thompson (ed.), *Pwyll Pendeuic Dyuet*. Mediaeval and Modern Welsh Series (Dublin: Dublin Institute for Advanced Studies, 1957); and for English translation, "The First Branch of the Mabinogi" in Sioned Davies (trans.), *The Mabinogion* (Oxford: Oxford University Press, 2007), 3–21. The present treatment may only gesture briefly towards some few ideas in some few texts: a treatment along these lines of the multiple layered and hidden worlds of space, time and language in *Culhwch ac Olwen*, for example, is one of a large number of valuable forks in the path which I have had to ignore for the moment. Joseph Nagy has discussed *Culhwch* alongside the *Agallamh* in a manner which gives important insights into the layering of temporalities and anachronisms in both texts: 'Hearing and Hunting in Medieval Celtic Tradition' in Stephen O. Glosecki (ed.), *Myth in Early Northwest Europe* (Tempe, Arizona: Arizona Center for Medieval and Renaissance Studies, 2007), 121–152.

[26] Gomel, *Narrative Space and Time*, 28.

her vocabulary). What Gomel calls 'flickering' is perhaps most clearly found in Pwyll, as just mentioned; and 'layering' (which "places a fantastic extradiegetic space 'on top' of a realistic diegetic space"[27]—a palimpsest, in other words) is a good way of considering the general metaphorising of landscape in the tales. The 'real' landscape, either through onomastics or othering, becomes strangely impossible, and this layering of otherness has been observed many times by the Irish scholars I have already quoted: dindshenchas is precisely a layering of the extradiegetic, or metadiegetic, on top of the otherwise neutral and real landscape, and Proinsias Mac Cana (somewhat idiosyncratically) described the Fenian landscape for this reason as existing in a "fourth dimension":

> The landscape through which [the *féinnidi*] move is ostensibly that of the Irish countryside, and is generally furnished with real placenames, yet it exists in a fourth dimension where perception becomes reality, and where the secular relativities [sic] of time and space are effaced or subverted.[28]

Catherine McKenna's article on *Branwen* beautifully describes the deep layering of multiple strands of tradition in the Second Branch.[29] This 'embedding', to return to Gormel's words, "doubles the storyworld by enclosing a separate mini-universe within the diegetic chronotope"[30]: clearly, the otherworlds of the *Síd* and also those of the voyage tales are related to this mode of embedding alternative spaces and times, and in Welsh we may look to episodes such as the vanishing of Rhiannon and Pryderi to an unlocated realm beyond, or (more interestingly) to the second and fourth branches. These latter tales, while ostensibly located in the historical (at least topologically real) landscape of Wales (and, less so,

---

[27] Ibid.

[28] Proinsias Mac Cana, "The Cycle of Fionn and The Fiana", in *The Cult of the Sacred Centre: Essays on Celtic Ideology* (Dublin: Dublin Institute for Advanced Study, 2011), 243–5, at 245.

[29] Catherine McKenna, "The Colonization of Myth in *Branwen Ferch Lyr*" in J. F. Nagy (ed.), *Myth in Celtic Literatures*. CSANA Yearbook 6 (Dublin: Four Courts Press, 2007), 105–119.

[30] Gomel, *Narrative Space and Time*, 28.

Ireland) give up all pretences to be depicting a historical reality: the world of Bendigeidfran, Branwen and Matholwch is one of mythic prehistory, and that of Math, Lleu, Arianrhod and Blodeuwedd is even stranger, simultaneously expressing the mythic and the historical.

In fact, we are caught here between 'layering' and 'embedding'. 'Embedding' itself, I would argue, is often more interestingly seen to be a feature of the narrative structure of the unified Mabinogi, rather than of the landscape of any single branch: we move from chronotope to chronotope as we move from branch to branch (as temporality and spatiality themselves *branch*), and this movement is, to repeat a key point, part of the argument of the narrative. The four branches, as has been noted many times in many ways by many critics, ask what kind of comportment is most valuable and most valid: what the current argument aims to do is shift slightly the focus of the comportment.

In my mind, perhaps the most interesting episode of embedding in the Four Branches is in the Third Branch, *Manawydan*, which happens when the fog sweeps across Dyfed and erases all signs of culture, as described by Jerry Hunter in his talk at this Colloquium.[31] Patrick Ford, in his edition of this branch says this about Manawydan and Cigfa's experience following the fog (my emphasis):

> The land they subsequently rove seems clearly to be Dyfed, still rich in fish and game, but only wild animals roam where once their cultivated herds grazed. *It's as if they were in Dyfed in another, perhaps primordial, time.*[32]

This fog is pretty much the only weather that we see in the Four Branches–the only *aimsir,* or *amser*–and I mention only in passing that it is of a prophetic or even apocalyptic quality. Wales is here othered–and othered from itself–since England in this Branch functions as another other–a more 'normal', ethnic or even economic other. We have here in Dyfed a nesting, or an embedding, not of spatiality as much as of temporality.

---

[31] Jerry Hunter, "Reading Objects, Exchanging Meaning: Material Culture in the Four Branches of the Mabinogi". Unpublished paper presented at HCC 38, 5 October 2018.

[32] Patrick K. Ford (ed*.), Manawydan uab Llyr: text from the diplomatic edition of the White Book of Rhydderch*, by J. Gwenogvryn Evans (Belmont, MA: Ford and Baile, 2000), xxii. Emphasis mine.

Gomel's category of 'collapsing' 'generates chronotopes that inscribe the persistence of the past in the present through superimposition of multiple spaces within a single diegetic locus. It, e.g., "squeezes them in to the same diegetic space and uses the ensuing topological paradoxes to probe the unhealed wound of historical violence."[33] In considering the Mabinogi, there is much violence, and much of it historical, and we might be tempted to look for 'collapse' in the effects of the apocalyptic war in Ireland, where all but the few seeds of regeneration are destroyed, and the British return with the head of the twice-killed Bendigeidfran (stabbed, beheaded) to enjoy eighty-odd years of timeless bliss, before knowledge is rekindled and memory of the past drives them to London to bury the finally dead head. (Curiously, Bendigeidfran thus seems to suffer a triple death, though it is never entirely clear when he dies–and even after he is buried, he is still in a clear way undead, not fully terminated until he is dug up in the wider tradition by Arthur. Bendigeidfran's triple death is actually a triple un-death, continually deferred: it is an inverse triple death, if you like, a three-in-minus-one). The use of the term 'collapse' evokes the most extreme spatio-temporal phenomenon known to modern science, and the apocalyptic war and subsequent period of timeless bliss might be thought to be as close as the tales get to the collapse described in physics as a black hole–where the event horizon isolates the collapsed star from the surrounding space-time. (Here, it is surely relevant to remember that even the regenerated warriors of the Cauldron of Rebirth are reborn without speech: that is, without narrative capability, and by extension most likely without memory or even consciousness). If we choose to hold on to this metaphor, we are perhaps led to ask how it may be that the men managed to tear themselves away from the gravity of bliss holding them in Gwales, but it may not in fact be the case that nothing escapes a black hole. Hawking says the following:

> The existence of radiation from black holes seems to imply that gravitational collapse is not as final and irreversible as we once thought. If an astronaut falls into a black hole, its mass will increase, but eventually the energy equivalent of that extra mass will be returned to the universe in the form of radiation. (124)

---

[33] Gomel, *Narrative Space and Time*, 37.

The feast at Gwales is perhaps the ultimate impossibility of the Mabinogi (impossibility of impossibilities): a timelessness which is both a death of history (in that it is the death of memory) and enables the subsequent birth of history (as England and Wales emerge from the mythological time of Britain, and the historical provinces of Ireland are also generated): it is Black Hole and Big Bang, beginning and end, interpretatively reimagined.[34]

I acknowledge that the metaphor here is complicated, but I don't think we need to worry about unpicking it fully just now, since, as I mentioned, I would not in fact locate the real 'collapse' at any diegetic or descriptive level in the Mabinogi. Rather, as with most of the *Mabinogion* texts, it is (also) found in the way the tales embed the *different times* of history and myth, and in the way they juxtapose and superimpose the temporalities to form their arguments: this is the *branching* or the *branching off* of temporalities that I mentioned a minute ago, and, as Carey observed with the *Agallamh*, the nature of the relationship between these orders of being is the argument of the text. The narrative–the action of the plot itself, to borrow from Paul Ricœur–is the collapsing, regenerating structure. We shall return to this, after just a few more examples of interesting temporalities in Welsh medieval literature and modern physics.

Breuddwyd Rhonabwy plays with time in obvious ways: it, as well as most of the tales of the *Mabinogion*, it must be said, clearly has as one of its strategies the interrogation of how narrative constructions of the past are created; what kind of knowledge and ideologies take part–or should take part–in these creations; and whether that past has–or should have–any relevance or reality. Catherine McKenna's and Edgar Slotkin's articles on

---

[34] The idea that the universe 'itself' (i.e., the laws of physics that govern the behavior of matter) may reinterpret the heat death of the universe (expansion leading to maximum entropy and uniform zero density) as infinite compression into uniform infinite density, thus producing the conditions for an alpha-and-omega Big Bang, has been clearly expressed by Roger Penrose. See, e.g., Penrose's lecture "Before the Big Bang" given at the Isaac Newton Institute for Mathematical Sciences, 7 November 2005 and accessible at https://cosmolearning.org/ (accessed 1 November 2018); also Penrose, *Cycles of Time: An extraordinary new view of the universe* (New York: The Bodley Head, 2010). I am grateful to Samuel A. Jones for conversations concerning related ideas.

Rhonabwy[35] are superbly perceptive studies of how irony and genre are used here to cast a cloak of healthy scepticism over all interpretative strategies. The *Dream of Rhonabwy* has no final epistemological clarity (and, therefore, no ontological conclusiveness) since it is, after all, a dream—and a well-represented dream of the past at that. Waking from his vision of the surreal battling of Arthur and Owain, the dreamer has no profit from it. This dream, to paraphrase McKenna, is not a useful dream (hardly a dream at all) because it is too much of a dream. That said, it is a superb story and, vitally for us now, its chronotope is quite remarkable: it is bidirectional.

Time, according to most of particle physics, need not necessarily flow forwards: most equations work equally well either if the time variable 't' is reversed, or if 't' is entirely absent. Hawking states quite clearly that *"there can be no important difference between the forward and backward directions of [theoretical] time"* and Rovelli says this, when discussing Ludwig Boltzmann, the late nineteenth-century Austrian atomic physicist who effectively eliminated temporal directionality, even before Einstein and the others started fiddling with it:

> Boltzmann understood that there is nothing intrinsic about the flowing of time. That it is only the blurred reflection of a mysterious improbability of the universe at a point in the past.[36]

And here is Hawking's statement in context:

> *When one tried to unify gravity with quantum mechanics, one had to introduce the idea of "imaginary" time. Imaginary time is indistinguishable from directions in space. If one can go north, one can turn around and head south; equally, if one can go forward in imaginary time, one ought to be able to turn round and go backward. This means that there can be no important difference between*

---

[35] Edgar Slotkin, "The Fabula, Story, and Text of *Breuddwyd Rhonabwy*", in *Cambridge Medieval Celtic Studies* 18 (Winter 1989), 89–111; Catherine McKenna, "What dreams may come must give us pause", in *Cambrian Medieval Celtic Studies* 58 (Winter 2008), 70–99.

[36] Carlo Rovelli, *The Order of Time*, trans. Erica Segre and Simon Carnell (New York: Riverhead Books, 2018), 32.

the forward and backward directions of imaginary time. On the other hand, when one looks at "real" time, there's a very big difference between the forward and backward directions, as we all know. Where does this difference between the past and the future come from? Why do we remember the past but not the future? The laws of science do not distinguish between the past and the future. (151)

Breuddwyd Rhonabwy, as Dafydd Glyn Jones has memorably noted,[37] sees time flowing backwards and forwards simultaneously as the dreamer is taken through the landscape to meet with Arthur. While the narrative proceeds normally (the general plot seems to move from a beginning to middle and on to an end of sorts), close attention reveals that the dream begins *after* Arthur's final battle at Camlan, and it moves backwards from there. The story moves both forward and backwards in time, simultaneously, as if the chronotope of the dream were that of a *Mappa Mundi*, where movement along the spatial axis may lead backwards to the beginning of human history, as the Garden of Eden is located–or perhaps embedded–in the impossible topography.[38] Interestingly black hole theory suggests that within the event horizon of a black hole a similar reversal of time and space occurs: time becomes spatial, and space temporal. In our search for literary black holes, perhaps *Rhonabwy* is as good a candidate as any. I'm simplifying more than a little here, since I'm ignoring, for example, thermodynamics and entropy. Considering these would not alter the gist of the argument, and so I hope I may be forgiven for the moment.

Equally interesting in *Rhonabwy*–especially concerning hermeneutics and interpretation–is the event towards the close of the dream, where the poet Cadyrieith famously sings praise of Arthur, and no one present understands any of what was sung, but that it was praise. The joke here may be that its being praise is all that needed to be known for the speech act to succeed: a pragmatic theory of language tells us that words mean

---

[37] Dafydd Glyn Jones, "Breuddwyd Rhonabwy", in Geraint Bowen (ed.), *Y Traddodiad Rhyddiaith yn yr Oesau Canol* (Llandysul: Gwasg Gomer, 1974), 176–95.

[38] For useful discussion, see Natalia Petrovskaia, *Medieval Welsh Perceptions of the Orient* (Turnhout: Brepols, 2015).

what they are used to do, and Cadyrieith thus achieved his goal of praising, regardless of detailed arguments concerning semantics.

In my mind, perhaps the most interesting impossible temporalities in medieval Welsh literature are to be found in the poetry. Time (at the conference) and space (now) are predictably against me and so I will move swiftly through a mere two or three examples. I wish to stay at a distance from explicitly religious writings, and for this reason will do no more than to throw a glance in passing at the rich traditions of prophetic, apocalyptic and eschatological writings, either biblical, apocryphal or otherwise noncanonical that would be rich pickings for impossible chronotopes. In order to avoid mentioning John Carey's name again I shall mention only the other two editors, Emma Nic Cárthaigh and Caitríona Ó Dochartaigh, of the remarkable *The End and Beyond*, the massive–and massively useful–product of the *De Finibus* project into early Irish eschatological traditions recently concluded at Cork.[39] I must leave these texts to one side for now, but when the eschatological is secularised, I think that it becomes necessary to mention it, for the reason, as I have explored in *Darogan*,[40] that time and temporality become split.

Augustine had already bifurcated time with his description of the twin ontologies of the divine and the *saeculum*, where *saeculum* is human history moving linearly in the direction of end-times and reincorporation into eternity. Welsh political prophecy functions on the basis of a temporal ontology where British history–*brut*–suffers the cleaving blow of caesura when sovereignty is yielded to the Anglo-Saxons: the promised deliverer, be he Cynan, Cadwaladr, Owain or Henri VII, is to come (again) not only to kickstart Welsh self-confidence, but to restart the historical process itself. Interestingly, there is clear evidence that this prophetic discourse was alive and well far into the early modern period, with continued interest in texts as more than mere antiquarian curiosities: authors engaged with arguments considering its veracity as a valid continuation of Biblical prophecy, and as a validation, curiously enough, of Protestantism.

---

[39] John Carey, Emma Nic Cárthaigh and Caitríona Ó Dochartaigh (ed.), *The End and Beyond: Medieval Irish Eschatology* 2 Vols (Aberystwyth: Celtic Studies Publications, 2014).

[40] Aled Llion Jones, *Darogan: prophecy, lament and absent heroes in medieval Welsh literature* (Cardiff: University of Wales Press, 2013). Much of the following discussion is based on concepts and methodologies developed in the monograph.

Consider, for example, *Ymadrodd Gweddaidd*, printed in 1703.[41] The temporal split is in this discourse relocated from the Anglo-Saxons to the Catholics, with sovereignty re-established not in the figure of Henry VII but of Henry VIII and Elizabeth I, and the Reformation. I emphasise the split in the *saeculum* in this example, as a clear manifestation of the principle of good and bad time(s), whatever they are seen to be.

As well as demonstrating attitudes to temporality by means of the contents of their works, the poets, especially, used literary devices to *perform* temporalities, including impossible ones. I have discussed these things elsewhere and won't trouble you here with the details of how the the *Gogynfeirdd*–the poets of the princes, composing between around the end of the eleventh century and the end of the thirteenth–used a register of language which was purely nominal, to perform a mimesis of timelessness: that is, at key points in the poems, they produced line after line, sentence after sentence of poetry with no verbs, adverbs, prepositions or even pronouns, to speak in a voice of Adamic sublimity beyond time and space.[42] Relatedly, the later poets of the developed *cynghanedd* (in and around the fourteenth and fifteenth centuries) used tense, person, mood and spatial location (though especially the features of the verb) as poetic tropes, to be echoed from section to section of the poem in a kind of metalinguistic rhyme and metaphysical metaphor.[43] Here, to borrow Roman Jakobson's categories, it is no longer the *deictic* or the *referential* level of the language act which is doing the work, but the *metalingual* and the *poetic*. Here we have, to use Gomel's terms, examples of embedding

---

[41] *Ymadrodd Gweddaidd Ynghŷlch Diwedd y Byd Neu Tueddiad at yr amser a digwŷddo Dydd y Farn[,] Yn Cynwŷs hefyd Mwŷ na dau cant o Englynnion Duwiol; o erfynniad am drugaredd . . .* (Amwythig: Thomas Jones, 1703). I am grateful to Jerry Hunter for drawing my attention to this work.

[42] I begin to discuss the nominal sentence and its poetico-theological implications in *Darogan*. I developed these ideas quite significantly in "Poetry, Language, Grammar, Death: Reading the Gogynfeirdd with Heidegger", a paper delivered at Harvard University, Humanities Center and Department of Celtic Languages and Literatures, 26 March 2015. A published version of this developed treatment is forthcoming.

[43] For a cursory treatment of this phenomenon, see my "Cynghanedd, Amser a Pherson yng Nghywyddau Brud Dafydd Gorlech", in A. Ll. Jones and M. Fomin (ed.), *Y geissaw chwedleu*. Studia Celto-Slavica, vol. 8 (Bangor: Ysgol y Gymraeg, 2018), 139–50.

(in the case of the sublimity, embedded in the wider context of the poem) and a kind of wormholing in the case of the *cynghanedd* poetry, where times and spaces shoot back and forth across sections of the poem, communicating simultaneously across the disparate moments of the performance: a quantum action at a distance, to change the metaphor.

My final quick example is the initial poem in the oldest surviving Welsh-language compendium of poetry, the Black Book of Carmarthen. It is the opening track on the first album of Welsh poetry, if you like, and it is, suitably, a conversation–a colloquy–perhaps not necessarily of the ancients (though we do not actually know how old the protagonists are), but at least of two of our earliest poet-prophets, Myrddin and Taliesin (and do they have the blues!). The two exchange melancholic titbits concerning the fate of Wales and Britain (the good times and bad times which are to come), in a flickering of tenses past and future, until they finally reveal that there will be (and has been) the disastrous battle of Arfderydd in which many will go (and have gone) mad.

> Myr: Mor truan genhyf mor truan
> [. . .]
> Tal: Neu gueith arywderit, pan vit y deunit
> [. . .]
> Myr: Seith ugein haelon a aethan y gwyllon,
> Yg coed keliton y daruuan.
> Can ys mi myrtin guydi taliessin
> Bithaud kyffredin vy darogan.[44]

The battle of Arfderydd is of course the battle at which Myrddin himself lost (or will lose) his mind, thus obtaining the gift of prophecy. Here, if we allow the temporal ambiguity (which I think we should, following the principle of *lectio difficilior potior*), Myrddin looks forward using second sight to the future event which will give him the very power he is using to witness it.

Now, this kind of activity is clearly crazy, but it's not actually unusual, in medieval as much as in recent popular culture. You may recall Denis Villeneuve's 2016 film, *Arrival*, about a linguist employed by the US army to attempt to communicate with aliens: the climax of the film is

---

[44] A.O.H. Jarman (ed.), *Ymddiddan Myrddin a Thaliesin* (Caerdydd: Gwasg Prifysgol Cymru, 1951).

based on the premise that by learning their language, the linguist played by Amy Adams is able to access their mode of consciousness, which is unbound by human linear temporality. Adams' character is thus able to access her future and obtain a suggestion from the Chinese president concerning how she should get in touch with him back in the present, in order to save the world.

That the temporality we perceive is merely a by-product of human consciousness and has nothing really to do with the world 'as it is' is of course uncontroversial to many, from Boltzmann and later quantum theorists to Kantian philosophers, Nietzscheans or Heideggerians in their different ways. Reverse causality of the type we see in the case of Myrddin or the linguist in *Arrival* is not as entirely crazy as might be initially thought (or, at least, it is not crazy without reason). At the quantum level we only have to look in the direction of such apparent paradoxes as those thrown up by the delayed choice quantum eraser double-split experiment (DCQE). This is a development of the famous double-slit experiment which demonstrates how light on the one hand behaves as both particle and wave, and on the other, seems to behave differently depending on whether it is being observed or not. Basically, by complicating the moment and nature of the observation, the DCQE shows–or at the very least suggests very strongly–that the universe makes choices about what happened in the past based on what is about to happen in the future: that is, the physical past is formed in accordance with future choices. And this is relatively uncontroversial.[45]

As well as being relatively uncontroversial in physics, this kind of reverse causality is also entirely uncontroversial in literature. Almost everything in literature is created retroactively and retrospectively, from forewords and prefaces, created after the works they precede, just like *réamhscéalta*, to notions of periods, genres, cycles and authors, and so on, not to mention the action of the hermeneutic circle in the basic reading of any text.[46] The first line of a couplet only becomes a rhyme once the

---

[45] The reader who is perhaps unfamiliar with the experiments mentioned in this paragraph is strongly urged to seek out one or more of the many accessible descriptions available online and in print.

[46] Consider, perhaps most recently, John Carey, *The Mythological Cycle of Medieval Irish Literature* (Cork: Cork Studies in Celtic Literatures, 2018); also Catherine McKenna, "The Prince, the Poet and the Scribe: reflections on the elegiac tradition in

second is read; equally, meaning is post factum. Indeed, we might say that just as in science, fact is post factum. The future is implicit in the past. At a finer literary level, we can see (and have seen) that different genres and literary types demonstrate different temporalities: histories, chronicles, legends, sagas, poems, triads: each has a different method of organising events, and thus of showing a relationship between the events and the 'time' which reveals itself. And, of course, as we move to interpretation itself, to hermeneutics, we see basic splits in attitudes to time between synchronic and diachronic readers, from structuralist to deconstructionist, historicist to ahistoricist and new historicist and so on.

Simply put, narrative, for instance, in the unfolding of a plot–which need by no means be chronological–by definition superimposes multiple temporalities upon each other, from the linear progression of reading through the text, to the phenomenological experience of protention and retention necessarily present in the mind of the reader as he/she grasps larger and larger units of meaning, to the recursive or–to borrow from Benjamin–constellatory functioning of the plot. The hermeneutic circle is far from being a simple and unbroken Euclidian shape, and I think that Patrick Ford's "Prolegomena to a reading of the Mabinogi" is still one of the most pregnant and eloquent descriptions of this non-linear signification in the texts I'm interested in today: Ford here uses the metaphor of music–the *ceinciau* of the Mabinogi–to show how meanings arise through reading simultaneously horizontally and vertically, and how meaning is formed retroactively and recursively.[47]

Here, then, we reach David Wood's "Time of the Sign", the temporality of signification itself. Wood's argument is that structures of time are intentional structures, and that intentional structures are structures of signification. As already suggested above, words, phrases and

---

medieval Wales", in Morgan Thomas Davies (ed.), *Proceedings of the Celtic Studies Association of North America Annual Meeting 2008*, CSANA Yearbook 10 (New York: Colgate University Press, 2011), 75–95; and Jerry Hunter's discussions of the Beirdd yr Uchelwyr editions, "A New Edition of the Poets of the Nobility" in *Cambrian Medieval Celtic Studies* 41 (Summer 2001), 55–64. I touch on these issues in my *Darogan*: see, e.g., Chapter 2.

[47] P. K. Ford, "Prolegomena to a Reading of the Mabinogi: 'Pwyll' and 'Manawydan'" in C.W. Sullivan III (ed.), *The Mabinogi: A Book of Essays* (New York and London: Garland Publishing, 1996), 197–216.

sentences–that is, verbal signs–in themselves contain only ghostly premonitions of meaning when read synchronically. I think I'm correct in suggesting that Bobi Jones, the foremost Welsh literary critic, whose structuralist study of literature, *Tafod y Llenor*,[48] predated the publication of the first English-language monographs of literary structuralism, that Bobi Jones was among the first to develop the idea that the Saussurian model of the sign (signifier and signified) lacked a key feature, that feature being time. Bobi Jones of course, famously refused to publish his ground-breaking work in any language other than Welsh, and younger writers such as an upstart Jacques Derrida have somewhat stolen his thunder, while adding their own lightning (and, occasionally, fog).[49]

Central to all of Derrida's work is the notion that signification is temporal, that the access to any final meaning is ultimately and infinitely deferred, just as Bendigeidfran seems unable to die: "the sense and reference of a sign [have] the structure [if you will] of desire",[50] in David Wood's words. The point is that sense and reference can never be simultaneously present: words always stand in for the absent meaning, without mentioning the object, and the more we have one the less we can have the other. This is Heisenberg's Uncertainty Principle at the level of signification: we cannot have full textual knowledge, simply due to how things are. The post factum becomes impossible: the cheque is forever in the post and we are never able to cash in, never able to profit on't. While these are well-worn points made many times over the last decades, I shall scratch a little bit more at them for a moment.

In conclusion, I wish to raise a few small questions about the mythological, while quietly invoking Derrida's understanding of metaphysics. To anticipate a conclusion, I wish to argue that if the texts are to be read as mythological, then this should be an ironic mythology. What is to follow might calm the nerves of any who have been upset by my hitherto unquestioning use of Heidegger.

---

[48] R. M. Jones, *Tafod y Llenor* (Caerdydd: Gwasg Prifysgol Cymru, 1974).

[49] I am grateful to Jason Walford Davies for the fog joke, as I am for useful comments on an early draft of this paper.

[50] David Wood, *The Deconstruction of Time* (Illinois: Northwest University Press, 2001 [1990]), 330.

MYTH AND METAPHYSICS

What we have been looking at so far have been some very few selected depictions of temporality and spatiality. In all of them it is to be emphasised repeatedly that times and temporalities are used in the literature as literary strategies. The chronotopes used–the figuring of space and time–are exactly that: they are figures, used in the context of literary works to create complex structures of signification and to draw attention to processes of reading and understand the past. While some of the literary strategies have involved erasing time and space (at least at the deictic level: it may not be erased from the time of the work, or the time of the narrative), others have involved combining them: in these cases, the tropology of temporality has been shown to be a topology of temporality. In the words of Geraldine Parsons, in her study of the *Agallamh,* "[t]he claim that *dinnshenchas* is the gateway to all *senchas* articulates an idea which is implicit in the narrative as a whole."[51] Legend, and perhaps mythology, are brought concretely in to the landscape, thus, as we saw earlier, *othering* that landscape by making it bear "other meanings" (Wolfgang Iser's word, cited by Dooley in the article mentioned above). The meaning of space and place incorporates and supports all meaning, entirely, and space is time, just as Gaston Bachelard famously declared:

> At times we think we know ourselves in time, when all we know is a sequence of fixations in the spaces of the being's stability–a being who does not want to melt away, and who, even in the past, when he sets out in search of things past, wants time to "suspend" its flight. In its countless alveoli space contains compressed time. That is what space is for.[52]

In bringing the physically real and the 'mythological' together like this, the question arises as to which takes priority, or whether the paradox is simply that–an impossible topology. What we have here is akin to J.R. Jones' "cydymdreiddiad iaith a thir" (the mutual interpenetration of language and land), though it could easily be argued that we have not merely interpenetration but cosubstantiation. To bring things down to

---

[51] Parsons, "The narrative voice in *Acallam na senórach"*, in Doyle and Murray (ed.), *Dialogue*, 119.

[52] Gaston Bachelard, *The Poetics of Space*, trans. Maria Jolas (Harmondsworth: Penguin, 2014 [1958]), 30. Emphasis mine.

earth terminologically, we can suggest that what we have is a sign, where the land is signifier and the mythology is the signified. Therefore, by Saussurian logic, due to the fact that sign and signifier are indivisible, the mythology itself is literally brought down to earth and even secularised. I would argue that it is de-transcendentalised and, as I hope to make clear, made nonmetaphysical. My final argument involves the final twisted turn along the back (or front) of the Möbius strip.

Over the past few years I've had many conversations with colleagues at the School of Welsh at Bangor (as well as here at Harvard) concerning the role of mythology in the Four Branches–a question which has centrally informed many schools of reading. Recently a strong tendency has developed, characterised by a turn away from reading the stories as mythological, and Jerry Hunter presented at this Colloquium long-held beliefs about such complications.[53] In published work, Jessica Hemming, for example, has discussed in a series of articles aspects such as the figure of Rhiannon, often read as the Celtic goddess Epona, and the possibility of there being authentic mythological names in the Mabinogi in general: her considered conclusions are on the whole negative.[54] At a conference at Bangor in 2018, organised by the Research Centre for Arthurian Studies, Simon Rodway built on his important work in dating the texts, discussing what he called "the myth of myth" in the legends.[55] My own approach to this question is dialectical, or perhaps 'dialogic', informed by readings enabled–and even required–by the intervention in the history of Mabinogi reception of Martin Buber. I will conclude very quickly–even hastily–with a few comments in this direction.[56]

---

[53] Hunter, "Reading Objects".

[54] E.g., Hemming, Jessica, "Ancient tradition or authorial invention? The 'mythological' names in the Four Branches", in Joseph Falaky Nagy (ed.), *Myth in Celtic Literatures*, CSANA Yearbook 6 (Dublin: Four Courts Press, 2007), 83–104; *idem*, "Reflections on Rhiannon and the Horse Episodes in 'Pwyll'", *Western Folklore* 57.1 (Winter, 1998), 19–40.

[55] Simon Rodway, "The Mabinogi and the shadow of Celtic mythology" in *Studia Celtica* LII (2018), 67–85. While our aims and methodologies are quite different, our thoughts chime in important areas, especially in Rodway's insistence that these texts are not 'Celtic mythology' but rather 'Welsh literature' (68 *et passim*).

[56] For a developed discussion of the following ideas concerning Buber, see my "Martin Buber a Phedair Cainc y Mabinogi: Seioniaeth, Dyneiddiaeth a Duw", in A.

MYTH AND METAPHYSICS

Buber, the German Jewish philosopher, theologian and mystic was also a translator, most notably of Hassidic tales, mystical works of various traditions, and, with Franz Rosenzweig, of the Hebrew Bible (producing the high Modernist text, *Die Schrift*). While Buber's earlier work belonged to a romantic mysticism, he developed later a thought centred on the two concepts of Meeting (*Begegnung*), and Conversation or Dialogue (*Dialogphilosophie*). His answer to the question of how one should comport oneself towards the Absolute divine was that that the divine must be experienced in this world, through dialogue, and as the twentieth century progressed he moved further from his early fascination with negative mysticism to a developed thought that rejected a nihilating *unio mystico*. His interest in the dialogic, and in an immanent, non transcendental, nonmetaphysical, even atheistic mysticism, grew side by side with his interest in modernism, and he published his translation of the Mabinogi, *Die vier Zweige des Mabinogi*,[57] at exactly the main turning point in his thought: this was a year before Einstein published his General Theory in 1915.

For Buber, myth in the Mabinogi is circumscribed by the literary: the divine (or the mythic) *is* present, but it may not function transcendentally since it must enter into dialogue with literature. Arguing against Mathew Arnold's famous description of the Mabinogi as being created by a literary magpie who could not understand the nature of the materials he was pillaging, Buber says this:

> Und doch trifft Arnolds Gleichnis nicht völlig zu; denn
> mochten die Schöpfer der Mabinogion der heiligen

Price (ed.), *Ysgrifau Beirniadol 34* (Dinbych: Gwasg Gee, 2016), 209–38. A briefer summary may be found in my "Medieval Wales in Modern Germany: Martin Buber translates the Mabinogi", in A. Antonowicz and T. Niedokos (ed.), *Golden Epochs and Dark Ages: Perspectives on the Past* (Lublin: Wydawnictwo KUL, 2016) 181–93. While I have been unable to discuss it in this paper, I would like to stress the relevance to my current concerns of the 'conversational method' described by Joseph K. Nagy as a method of negotiation between past and present: see Nagy, "Some strands and strains in *Acallam na senórach*" in Doyle and Murray (ed.), *Dialogue*, 90–108, and also Nagy's *Conversing with Angels and Ancients: Literary Myths of Medieval Ireland* (Dublin: Four Courts Press, 1997).

[57] Martin Buber (trans.), *Die vier Zweige des Mabinogi: ein keltisches Sagenbuch* (Leipzig: Insel, 1914).

Gewalt des Mythus halb entfremdet sein, sie standen im
Dienst einer andern, die, wo sie wie hier in ihrem reinen,
starken Wesen lebt, sich als jener ebenbürtig offenbart:
der seligen Gewalt der Dichtung.[58]

And yet, Arnold's comparison is not entirely correct.
Since the creators (*Schöpfer*) of the Mabinogion could
maintain themselves half distanced from the sacred power
(*Gewalt*) of myth, they found themselves serving another
power, and that one–when one, as here, lives in its pure,
strong essence, reveals itself to be fully equal to the other.
That is, the blessed (*selige*) power of literature.

The point is, once again, that regardless of whether the Four
Branches contain 'real' mythological material or whether the audience at
the time knew this to be the case, the *performance of mythology* is what is
necessary to enable the dialogue between modes of being and time. Buber
in addition stresses in his writing the earthly and spatialised nature of the
'gods' in the Welsh texts (whether they are really gods or not is neither
here nor there), and this non-transcendent divinity clearly chimes with his
own ideas concerning the materiality of the divine encounter:

Und stärker noch als die Namen künden die Taten der
Helden, die Atmosphäre von heimlicher Macht und
Magie, die um sie ist, von ihrer instigen Natur (wobei
allerdings zu bedenken ist, daß *die keltischen Götter
niemals olympisch vom Menschlichen abgehoben waren,
sondern ihm immer wesensverwandt und verbunden
blieben*).[59]

More even than their names, the actions of the heroes and
the atmosphere of secret power and magic that surrounds
them, bears witness to their previous nature. (And yet in
doing so, it must be borne in mind that *the Celtic gods
were never Olympian, elevated above the human, but that
they remained ever essentially related to it* [*sc.* the
human], *and ever connected to it.*

---

[58] Buber, Foreword to *Die vier Zweige des Mabinogi,* 12. Translations mine.
[59] Buber, Foreword, 10–11. Emphasis mine.

Buber's Mabinogi translation places the medieval text at the heart of modernist Germany. This is a movement of which very much could be said, and it provides for me one answer to the question of whether reading the medieval literature through the lens of concepts created in the twentieth century is anachronistic. A simple answer to the question is just 'no'–no more than an archaeologist may not use dendrochronology or DNA analysis; but a slightly more complex answer is also 'no', since–to return to Walter Benjamin, the contemporary of Buber whom I referred to at the beginning of this talk–the 'afterlife' of the text (the *Nachleben*) is realised in the translation. This time of translation is the final time of signification which I shall evoke today, in order to suggest that it might be the case that while we thought we were discussing the outside of the Möbius strip—the texts themselves—we were in fact all the time on the reverse side, the side of later interpretation and translation. Having completed the reverse side now, however briefly, we are back where we started, wherever that may be, and whenever that may be, for better or for worse, for both are the same.

As an absolutely final gesture, I'd like to consider a further aspect of the indivisibility of the structure of the Möbius. If we were to try to separate out the strands of the argument, by attempting to cut through the centre, in order to break the medieval away from the modern, curiously enough what would happen would be that we would simply end up making the same journey longer and more complicated.[60]

---

[60] The Möbius strip handout should now be cut, to make the point. The cutting of the Möbius, parallel to an edge, either along its midpoint, or a third of the way from the edge, results in the formation of two intertwined strips, and also shows why Pwyll must only deliver Arawn a single blow.

Contemporary Poetry in *Llyfr Coch Hergest*: *Canu Dychan* and its Manuscript Context

Myra Booth-Cockcroft

The late fourteenth-century manuscript *Llyfr Coch Hergest* (Oxford, Jesus College MS. 111) is primarily described as a manuscript anthology–containing, as it does, a large variety of texts, both prose and poetry. Moreover, scholars have suggested that the primary impulse behind the creation of this manuscript was the antiquarian collection of texts,[1] and one of the chief explanations cited to support this argument is the near total absence of poems in the *cywydd* metre.[2] As a result of this, the manuscript's patron, Hopcyn ap Tomas, has been characterised as a traditionalist, whose primary concern in the creation of *Llyfr Coch Hergest* was to preserve the best of Welsh history and literary culture.[3]

However, alongside the historical texts, traditional narrative prose tales, and early poetry there are a substantial number of poems written by poets active contemporarily with the manuscript's construction and among these is a group of largely understudied poetry. The *canu dychan*, or 'satirical poetry' has not yet been the focus of much scholarly attention and has only recently been edited in the Welsh language series, *Cyfres Beirdd yr Uchelwyr*.[4] There is no doubt that these poems require greater

---

[1] Ceri W. Lewis, "The Literary Tradition of Morgannwg down to the middle of the sixteenth century," in *Glamorgan County History*: Vol III: *The Middle Ages*, ed. T.B. Pugh (Cardiff, 1971), 445–54 at 489; H. Fulton, "A geography of Welsh literary production in late medieval Glamorgan," *Journal of Medieval History* 41.3 (2015): 325–40, at 339.

[2] The sole exception being Iolo Goch's *cywydd* found in cols.1407–1408. Poem XXIV in Dafydd Johnston, *Gwaith Iolo Goch* (Cardiff: Gwasg Prifysgol Cymru,1988).

[3] Christine James, "'Llwyr Wybodau Llên a Llyfrau': Hopcyn ap Tomas a'r Traddodiad Llenyddol Cymraeg," in *Cyfres y Cymoedd: Cwm Tawe*, ed. Huw Teifi Edwards (Llandysul : Gomer, 1993), 4–44, at 32; Christine James, "Hopcyn ap Tomas a 'Llyfrgell Genedlaethol Ynysforgan'" in *Transactions of the Honourable Society of Cymmrodorion* 13 (2007): 31–57, at 53; Fulton, "A geography of Welsh literary production," 333.

[4] All quotations from the poems are here taken from this series of editions. Translations, unless stated otherwise, are my own.

study in order to further our understanding of the development of fourteenth-century Welsh poetry. However, the purpose of this paper is simply to illustrate that the existence of *canu dychan* in *Llyfr Coch Hergest* challenges the notion of Hopcyn ap Tomas as a traditionalist, a man with conservative tastes, and demonstrates that he was not averse to poetic innovation. In this re-examination of the characterisation of Hopcyn ap Tomas as a traditionalist, I will consider how the *canu dychan*, as contemporary (or near-contemporary) poetry, fits in to the wider manuscript context of *Llyfr Coch Hergest*. Examining the presence of this poetic corpus within the manuscript will further illuminate the organising principles that underlie the choice of texts in the manuscript, and demonstrate that these often-overlooked poems are also a valuable part of the rich literary tapestry of medieval Wales.

It is first necessary to provide an overview of the type of poetry under consideration here: the most thorough exploration of *canu dychan* to date is that of Dylan Foster Evans in his 1996 publication, *'Goganwr am Gig Ynyd': The Poet as Satirist in Medieval Wales*. In this publication Foster Evans notes that the emergence of this "thriving and vibrant genre" corresponds with the related poetic developments of the fourteenth-century, such as the innovation of *cywydd* metre—'the main poetic vehicle for the next few centuries'—and the compilation of the bardic grammars—"a mixture of native and Latin learning that was also to have a long and valuable life".[5] The *canu dychan* are usually referred to as 'satire' in English, although this does not fully encapsulate the meaning of the Welsh term. Furthermore, the poets and their contemporaries would in fact have been more familiar with the slightly older term *gogan/goganu*. It is worth noting that there appears to be a slight nuance in the meaning of these terms, and the *Geiriadur Prifysgol Cymru* definitions are as follows: *dychan*—"satire, lampoon, ridicule, sarcasm, abuse, invective; disgrace";[6] *gogan*—"defamation, slander, reproach, dispraise; ignominy, disgrace, infamy; a scoffing or jeering, raillery, derision, satire, lampoon."[7]

---

[5] Dylan Foster Evans, *'Goganwr am Gig Ynyd': The Poet as Satirist in Medieval Wales* (Aberystwyth: Canolfan Uwchefrydiau Cymreig a Cheltaidd, 1996), 1.

[6] R. J. Thomas, *Geiriadur Prifysgol Cymru* vol. 1 (1967): 1115.

[7] R. J. Thomas & Gareth A. Bevan, *Geiriadur Prifysgol Cymru* vol. 2 (1987): 1434.

The *canu dychan* is a rich genre of poetry and an array of different types of poem are represented in *Llyfr Coch Hergest*. Perhaps the most obvious subjects for this poetry are stingy patrons, such as the Hywel named in Tudur Dall's short poem "Dychan i Neuadd Hywel" who is accused of keeping both his doors and his pockets closed, as in the line "ys dôr gaead, nid rhad rhugl".[8] There are also examples of (presumably intentionally) obscene poems satirising women, such as Madog Dwygraig's "Dychan i Faald, ferch Dafydd" or Prydydd Breuan's "Dychan i Siwan Morgan o Aberteifi"–this poem is particularly unkind to its subject, one of the more tame insults being "Glwyfedig ei gwddw, a'i thin yn rhwth ac anllad."[9] Notably, these poems are directed towards specific women, rather than towards women as a population group, and so it would be interesting to consider how they fit in with the wider medieval theme of the 'debate about women'. There are also examples of poets satirising each other: the poems by Trahaearn Brydydd Mawr and Casnodyn appear one following the other in the manuscript (cols. 1343–1346 and 1346–1347, respectively) and call to mind the more famous bardic dispute between Dafydd ap Gwyilm and Gruffudd Grug. It is possible that these kinds of poems were performed at the courts of *uchelwyr* such as Hopcyn ap Tomas for entertainment–two poets making fun of each other in a performative context, the purpose being a good spirited ribbing rather than to cause actual offence. In a similar vein, there are also three poems to the same man–a Madog ap Hywel, or Madog Offeiriad, one each from Iolo Goch, Llywelyn Ddu ab y Pastard and Yr Ustus Llwyd. Perhaps this is an example of a well-known (and possibly not well-liked) figure in the community who was often the subject of derision for entertainment? Finally, there are poems to perhaps more unusual subjects, such as a Madog Dwygraig's "Dychan i'r Llo", in which he satirises a particularly underdeveloped calf: "Löe lo, leiaf–o wartheg/

---

[8] R. Iestyn Daniel, ed. *Gwaith Dafydd y Coed a Beirdd Eraill o Lyfr Coch Hergest* (Aberystwyth: Canolfan Uwchefrydiau Cymreig a Cheltaidd, 2002), 203; His door is closed, there is not ready generosity.

[9] Huw Meirion Edwards, ed. *Gwaith Prydydd Breuan a Cherddi Dychan earaill o Lyfr Coch Hergest* (Aberystwyth: Canolfan Uwchefrydiau Cymreig a Cheltaidd, 2000), 15; Bruised her neck, and her buttocks gaping and unchaste.

Eu werthu mi medraf,"[10] and Yr Ustus Llwyd's "Dychan i swrcod Madog Offeiriaid", which is addressed to the coat of the aforementioned Madog.

What we are dealing with here is clearly a multi-faceted vehicle of poetic expression. It must have been somewhat humorous, although many of the jokes are opaque to us now and the poetry is characterised by its often vulgar, and occasionally cruel, tone. As a result of this, *canu dychan* has traditionally been considered the domain of the *clêr*–the low status poets–and as embodying the death of a once-great literary tradition. There are other contributing factors to this perception of *canu dychan* as low-status poetry–one of those is the lack of examples from our earliest surviving Welsh poetry. However, as highlighted by Foster Evans, there is also a lack of praise poetry from this period; both of these genres of poetry rely mainly on people as their subject matter, and over time:

> [K]nowledge of these individuals and of the cultural and social milieu in which they lived would have decreased to the point at which the poetry devoted to them, complimentary or otherwise, would have lost much of its interest and relevance.[11]

Another contributing element is the fact that the bardic grammars, which may be regarded as "a closely contemporary literary criticism of the earliest known satire," appear to adopt a negative attitude towards this poetry,[12] as is evidenced in this passage, which states that a *prydydd* (a high-status poet) should not practice the craft of the *clerwr* (a low-status poet) since this craft is opposite to the work of the *prydydd*:

> Ni pherthyn ar brydyd ymyru ar glerwryaeth, er aruer ohoni, kanys gwrthwneb yw y greffteu prydyd. Kanys ar glerwr y perthyn goganu, ac agloduori, a gwneuthur kewilid a gwaradwyd, ac ar prydyd y perthyn kanmawl, a chloduori, a gwenuthur clod, a llewenyd, a gogonyant.[13]

---

[10] Huw Meirion Edwards, ed. *Gwaith Madog Dwygraig* (Aberystwyth: Canolfan Uwchefrydiau Cymreig a Cheltaidd, 2006), 49; Calf of the calves, the least of cattle, I am not able to sell him.

[11] Foster Evans, *"Goganwr am Gig Ynyd"*, 2.

[12] Ibid., 5–6 (quote at 6).

[13] G. J. Williams & E. J. Jones, *Gramadegau'r Penceirddiaid* (Cardiff: Gwasg Prifysgol Cymru, 1934), 35; It is not fitting for a prydydd to involve himself with the

However, there are some inconsistencies between the different manuscript versions of the bardic grammars, and in fact this passage is missing from the version contained in *Llyfr Coch Hergest*. Another passage from the version of the grammars found in this manuscript appears to imply that satire is acceptable if directed towards worthy subjects:

> Or byd kerd a deu synnwyr neu dri ystyr arnei, vn da ac
> un drwc, os kerd brydyat vyd, barner herwyd yr ystyr da;
> os kerd dychan vyd, barner herwyd yr ystyr drwc, kanys
> ny phryta neb y'r drwc, ac ny dychana neb y'r da.[14]

Further, the version of the *trioedd cerdd* from *Llyfr Coch Hergest* states that one of the three things that cause a poet to be hated is satire towards good men (*goganu dynion da*) [15]–the implication being that the satirising of bad men was allowed.[16] Although this is not the only manuscript version of the bardic grammars which employs a more lenient stance on satire, I would argue that given the volume of *canu dychan* in *Llyfr Coch Hergest*, it is likely that Hopcyn ap Tomas intentionally included a version that reflected his own poetic taste. The aforementioned "Dychan i Siwan Morgan o Aberteifi" provides a rare insight into how the poets themselves may have thought about the suitability of *canu dychan* to their status in the line "cyd bythwn bardd a phrydydd."[17] Prydydd Breuan is here invoking his status as a *prydydd*–a highly skilled and respected poet–in the penultimate stanza of a poem which cannot be described as fulfilling the criteria for a *prydydd* as it is set out in the bardic grammars.

---

art of the clerwr, in order to practice it, for it is opposite to the crafts of the prydydd. For it is fitting for the clerwr to satirise, and disparage, and cause shame and dishonour, and it is fitting for the prydydd to praise, and honour, and produce praise, and happiness, and glory. Foster Evans, "*Goganwr am Gig Ynyd,*" 6.

[14] Williams & Jones, *Gramadegau'r Penceirddiaid,* 15; If there should be a poem which has two senses or three meanings, one good and one bad, if it be a prydydd poem, judge it according to the good meaning, if it be a satirical poem, judge it according to the bad meaning, for no one composes prydydd poetry to the bad and no one satirises the good: Foster Evans, "*Goganwr am Gig Ynyd*", 9.

[15] Williams & Jones, *Gramadegau'r Penceirddiaid*, 18.

[16] Foster Evans, "Goganwr am Gig Ynyd," 9.

[17] Meirion Edwards, *Gwaith Prydydd Breuan*, 3.21; though I am a poet and a prydydd.

Clearly, he doesn't feel that composing obscene poetry of this kind and being a *prydydd* are mutually exclusive.

Adding to this notion that, despite the generally negative view of the Bardic Grammars, it was not frowned upon for a *prydydd* to compose *canu dychan*, is the context in which these poems are found. In the same manuscript in which the *canu dychan* are written there are more conventional works of eulogy, elegy and religious poetry. That these more conventional works were composed by the same poets who composed several of the *canu dychan* poems suggests that this was a more normal and accepted part of the poetic repertoire than perhaps initially thought. Further evidence to support the idea that this kind of poetry was an established part of the poetic canon in medieval Wales may be found by analogy—a significant body of similar poetry exists in the Gaelic tradition.

For this reason, I would like to briefly consider the *Book of the Dean of Lismore*; the early sixteenth-century manuscript created for the MacGregors of Fortingall which comprises a large collection of classical Gaelic verse spanning the genres of panegyric, religious, heroic, courtly and satiric poetry.[18] Although a later construction, this manuscript still provides some valuable parallels to *Llyfr Coch Hergest*. It is also viewed mainly as an anthology manuscript, with little or no organising principle. However, as noted by William Gillies this perceived lack of organisation falls apart upon closer scrutiny and 'there are some sections of [the manuscript] (for example containing sequences of bardic verse or religious exempla or Fenian lays) which have a more homogenous, planned feel to them.'[19] Furthermore, Gillies notes that "The satiric world is an intimate one; it reveals itself as being near to the personal lives and thoughts of the MacGregor brothers and their friends."[20] It is possible that the same may be said for some, though not all, of the *canu dychan* found in *Llyfr Coch Hergest*. It must be noted that the *canu dychan* poems in *Llyfr Coch*

---

[18] Martin MacGregor, "The View from Fortingall: The Worlds of the Book of the Dean of Lismore," *Scottish Gaelic Studies* 22 (2006): 35–85.

[19] William Gillies, "The Book of the Dean of Lismore: The Literary Perspective," in *Fresche Fontanis: Studies in the Culture of Medieval and Early Modern Scotland* ed. Janet Hadley Wlliams and J. Derrock McClure (Newcastle-upon-Tyne: Cambridge Scholars, 2013): 179–216 at 184.

[20] Ibid., 205.

Hergest were composed by poets who were active over the course of several decades and who came from many different regions of Wales; therefore, although it is improbable that the manuscript's patron would have understood all of the references made, it appears that these satiric poems were deemed worthy of inclusion despite the presumably obscure remarks made about individuals who were unlikely to have been known to the court of Hopcyn ap Tomas.[21] This indicates that Hopcyn appreciated the poetry for its own sake and we could speculate that it gives us a glimpse into his tastes–perhaps he was a man who enjoyed the subversive and the bawdy? Perhaps he had a wicked sense of humour? We will, of course, never be able to answer these questions with any certainty and it is unlikely that *Llyfr Coch Hergest* will be able to illustrate the social circles of Hopcyn ap Tomas in the same way that the Book of the Dean of Lismore might do for the MacGregors. But it does militate against the perception of Hopcyn as directing a conservative, antiquarian enterprise in the compilation of *Llyfr Coch Hergest.*

A further point of interest in the consideration of *canu dychan* in the manuscript is that the poets, in more than one instance, demonstrate the high degree of their own learning.[22] The most significant example of this is found in the "*Dychan i Swrcod Madog Offeiriad*" which is attributed to Yr Ustus Llwyd. Dafydd H. Evans highlighted in his edition of this poem that, in fewer than seventy lines, the poet references: two Branches of the *Mabinogi*, the Dream of Macsen, Geraint son of Erbin, Geoffrey of Monmouth, the Triads, the Thirteen Treasures, the tale of Benlli the Giant, the Life of St. Cadog, the Llywarch Hen *englynion*, the nature poem "*eiry mynydd*", genealogy, the Bible, and the body of poetry ascribed to the legendary figure of Taliesin.[23] Another poem which demonstrates a comprehensive knowledge of Welsh traditional material is Madog Dwygraig's "*Afallen Beren: Dychan i Faald ferch Dafydd*", which echoes the poem "*Afallen Beren*" from the *Myrddin* tradition. These two poems, as well as showing that the poets who wrote them were well educated in Welsh literary tradition, demonstrate coherence between the *canu dychan*

---

[21] Foster Evans, *"Goganwr am Gig Ynyd,"* 30.

[22] Ibid., 19.

[23] Dafydd H. Evans, "Yr Ustus Llwyd a'r Swrcod" in *Ysgrifau Beirniadol XVII,* ed. J. E. Caerwyn Williams (Denbigh: Gwasg Gee, 1990), 63–92.

and the wider contents of the manuscript—the poem by Yr Ustus Llwyd references several texts which themselves are found in *Llyfr Coch Hergest* and although the "*Afallen Beren*" poem to which Madog Dwygraig refers does not appear in the manuscript, two other poems from the Myrddin tradition are included: "*Cyfoesi Myrddin a Gwenddydd ei Chwaer*" and "*Gwasgargerdd Fyrddin yn y Bedd*". There is evidence, then, that the *canu dychan* were as informed by the learned tradition as some of the more conventional religious or praise poetry which has traditionally been regarded holding a higher literary value or merit.

This brings us on to the immediate manuscript context of the poetry. The majority of the *canu dychan* appears in a block together, taking up a full quire of the manuscript. The exceptions to this are six poems by Madog Dwygraig, which appear in a block of his other poetry, and two by Iolo Goch. This suggests that the inclusion of the *canu dychan* in *Llyfr Coch Hergest* was an intentional decision on the part of either the patron or the scribe, and perhaps even that the material was collected specifically with the aim of copying it into the manuscript. Grouping together poetry of a kind is not unusual in *Llyfr Coch Hergest.* Far from being haphazard, we find several such groupings: preceding the *canu dychan* the religious poetry is grouped together (and, significantly, Dafydd Johnston has demonstrated that the material between cols. 1143 and 1193 was selectively chosen by Hywel Fychan from exemplars which also contained other kinds of poetry);[24] following the *canu dychan* there is also a grouping of poetry attributed to *Beirdd y Tywysogion,* the poets of the princes. I have been focusing on the possible tastes and motives of Hopcyn ap Tomas for the majority of this paper, however I would now like to briefly consider the possibility that the manuscript's chief scribe, Hywel Fychan, is responsible for the inclusion of this material. Most of the *canu dychan* were written in his hand and given that this scribe played such a big part in the construction of the manuscript it is difficult to believe that he had absolutely no agency over the texts that were included. I would argue that it is likely that there was some element of collaboration between the scribe and the patron in this case. Hywel Fychan was a

---

[24] Dafydd Johnston, review of *Gwaith Meilyr Brydydd a'i Ddisgynyddion,* ed. J. E. Caerwyn Williams, *Llên Cymru* 19 (1996): 182–89 at 184.

prolific scribe whose work is found in seven other manuscripts,[25] and therefore would have had contacts in the scribal network involved in manuscript production; he would have been responsible for sourcing specific texts and presumably also for informing Hopcyn about the texts for which there were exemplars available. Interestingly, the section of poetry attributed to *Beirdd y Tywysogion* which follows the *canu dychan* in the manuscript is in the hand of another scribe, scribe C. This section of scribe C's work begins with Dafydd y Coed's praise poem to Hopcyn ap Tomas before turning to the older poetry, and I am grateful to Professor Dafydd Johnston for the suggestion that scribe C could be Dafydd y Coed himself, and that he copied this material, which Hywel Fychan earlier chose not to include, because it interested him as a poet. The primary evidence for the possible identification of scribe C as Dafydd y Coed derives from the presence of a poem by Dafydd y Coed earlier in the manuscript (cols. 1303–1305) written in the hand of Hywel Fychan but featuring numerous corrections in the hand of scribe C. If this suggestion is correct, then it seems to me a very clear piece of evidence in support of scribal agency in the curation of manuscript texts.

Returning briefly to the idea that *canu dychan* was considered low status poetry belonging to the domain of the *clêr*, we might view the manuscript context of this poetry in *Llyfr Coch Hergest* as a way to 'legitimize' this material—given that it is placed between two high status genres of poetry: the religious verse and praise poetry by *Beirdd y Tywysogion*. A further detail worth noting is that the *canu dychan* collected here is written either in the *englyn* or *awdl* metre–these were the more established and formal metres at the time of the manuscript's construction, with the *cywydd,* we presume, still being regarded as relatively new. Perhaps this offers another explanation for the inclusion of these poems in *Llyfr Coch Hergest*. Although the content of the *canu dychan* may be perceived as uncouth, the form is respected and, moreover, a significant number of the poems are written by well-known and established poets whose more 'respectable' work is found in the same

---

[25] These are: NLW MS. Peniarth 5 (*Llyfr Gwyn Rhydderch*, part 2); NLW MS. Peniarth 11; NLW MS. Llanstephan 27 (and its detached parts in NLW MS. Peniarth 12 and Cardiff MS. 3.242); Philadelphia Public Library Company MS. 8680.O; Oxford, Jesus College MS. 57.

manuscript. Notably, among the work of Madog Dwygraig there is a praise poem to Hopcyn ap Tomas, the manuscript patron, himself.

Despite the lack of poems in the *cywydd* metre in *Llyfr Coch Hergest,* it seems clear that the view of Hopcyn as a traditionalist and a conservative is untenable. The *canu dychan* are far from conservative and it appears that Hopcyn had a taste for these poems–perhaps he simply didn't enjoy poems in the *cywydd* metre? Perhaps he had a separate manuscript dedicated solely to poems in that form which is now lost? It is difficult to resist lapsing into pure speculation when thinking about the possible motivations of persons who were alive some seven hundred years ago, however, it is clear to me that the existence of this poetry in *Llyfr Coch Hergest*, alongside other respected and valued texts of the Welsh literary canon is significant. Furthermore, there is a strong case to be made that the existence of the body of *canu dychan* in *Llyfr Coch Hergest* reflects an intentional editorial decision on behalf of Hopcyn or Hywel (or perhaps both), appearing together, as it does, in a clearly defined section of the manuscript.

Acknowledgements

This paper arose from work towards my PhD thesis and I am grateful to the AHRC CDT in Celtic Languages for funding my project and also for enabling me to travel to America to present at HCC. I would like to thank my PhD supervisors, Professor Thomas Clancy, Professor Dafydd Johnston, and Dr. Sìm Innes for their valuable support and helpful suggestions and comments on this work.

All about the Glove: Patronage, Material Culture and the Affective Text in Dafydd ap Gwilym's *Diolch am Fenig*

Liam A. Brannelly

Diolch am Fenig is one of seven praise-poems by Dafydd ap Gwilym addressed to his patron Ifor Hael, but where the other six appear to be conventional public eulogies, this particular poem accentuates the poet's gratitude for a *specific* item: a pair of beautiful, white, deerskin gloves.[1] According to Bleddyn Owen Huws, it is a perfect example of a *cân diolch*—a thank-you poem—underscoring the interdependent set of commitments between the poet and the patron.[2] Their relationship, inflected as it is by tradition,[3] is also part of what Eve Kosofsky Sedgwick characterizes as a historically determined homosocial continuum, structurally shaped by the "articulations and mechanisms"[4] of "male friendship, mentorship, entitlement" and, sometimes, rivalry.[5] Although the French historian (and Benedictine monk) Jean Leclercq warns us "not to project on to a less erotically preoccupied society the artificially stimulated and commercially exploited eroticism of our own sex-ridden

---

[1] *Diolch am Fenig*; See Thomas Parry, ed. *Gwaith Dafydd ap Gwilym* [hereafter GDG], third edition, (Cardiff: University of Wales Press, 1979) 9; See also Dafydd Johnston, et al, *Cerddi Dafydd ap Gwilym* [hereafter CDG],, (Cardiff: University of Wales Press, 2010) 14, line 15.

[2] Bleddyn Owen Huws, *Y Canu Gofyn a Diolch, c.1350–c.1630* (Cardiff: University of Wales Press, 1998).

[3] Love-pledges between poets and patrons in medieval Welsh (as well as Irish) panegyrics are traditionally recognized elements of the bardic repertoire. Cf. Proinsias Mac Cana's famous essay "The Poet as Spouse of His Patron" in *Ériu*, volume 39 (1988), 79–85.

[4] Eve Kosofsky Sedgwick, *Between Men: English Literature and Male Homosocial Desire* (New York: Columbia University Press, 1985), 5.

[5] Ibid., 1. Sedgwick goes on to state that her use of "homosocial" as a term "describes social bonds between persons of the same sex" throughout history. Cf., also, M. J. Ailes, "The Medieval Male Couple and the Language of Homosociality" in *Masculinity in Medieval Europe*, ed. D. M. Hadley (London: Longman, 1999), 214–237.

age,"[6] it is nevertheless evident that the language used by certain medieval poets (including Dafydd) to describe the shape of their relationship with their respective patrons must be viewed through the lens of passionate, albeit uneroticized, intimacy.

In a different poem, for instance, Dafydd claims to be overwhelmed by *mawrserch*/"great love" for Ifor: *mwy no serch ar ordderch yw*/"my love for him is greater than for a lascivious woman."[7] This declaration serves as a figurative synopsis of the intimate and often lifelong commitment between poets and patrons, and even borrows some of the motifs from Dafydd's own love poetry. This may, according to Dafydd Johnston, "reflect an ideal of male bonding which was common in the late Middle Ages."[8] Like the relationship of David and Jonathan in the Old Testament, the close homosocial tie between the two men seems, finally, to hint at a kind of semi-romantic paradigm.

Declarations of love notwithstanding, the poet never loses sight of the fact that Ifor Hael is ultimately a financially enabled (as well as enabling) individual. The splendor of his court is described in loving and closely drawn detail, including a long inventory of delightful objects that rouse sentimental admiration in the poet: red gold and precious stones, falcons for hunting and, at the head of the list, bright wine to be drunk from a lustrous wineglass/*lluchwin o wydr*.[9] Although many of Dafydd's descriptions are clearly too fanciful (such as the building's floors of pure gold), it is precisely this kind of farfetched embellishment that makes this poem a characteristically "Dafyddian" text. The poet succeeds in both describing and creating a distinct and nearly *visual* experience, juxtaposing the idea of material splendor with his own emotional response to it.

In yet another poem, Dafydd alludes to his uncle Llywelyn's court in Emlyn in similar terms, describing it as *llety anghaead wastad westi*/"an

---

[6] Jean Leclercq, *Monks and Love in Twelfth-Century France: Psycho-Historical Essays* (Oxford: Oxford University Press, 1979), 100.

[7] *Basaleg* (GDG 8 | CDG 14), lines 13–14. Unless noted otherwise, all translations from the Welsh are my own.

[8] Dafydd Johnston, "The Aftermath of 1282: Dafydd ap Gwilym and His Contemporaries" in *The Cambridge History of Welsh Literature*, eds. Geraint Evans and Helen Fulton (Cambridge: Cambridge University Press, 2019), 124.

[9] *Marwnad Ifor a Nest* (GDG 11 | CDG 17), line 31, line 32 and line 29, respectively.

open house of tranquil rest"[10] and listing the qualities that make it wonderful: it is a place *lle gnawd cael gwasgawd a gwisgi—ddillad*/"where it is customary to get shelter and ready garments," a place of *fainc fancr bali*/"benches covered in silk-brocade,"[11] a place, finally, *lliwgaer yn lasgalch, llugyrn losgi*/"painted with fresh lime, with lanterns burning."[12] Incidentally, in describing this aesthetically pleasing dwelling, the poet makes use of the same kind of language he employs in describing Ifor's wife Nest and other beautiful women: Llywelyn's court is *lle dichwerw aserw o erysi—bryd*/"a bright, sweet place of wondrous form,"[13] *erwyr*/quiet and *twym*/warm.

Diolch am Fenig, meanwhile, depicts Ifor's court in similar terms; the poet spends his time

> *Yn wleddau, yn foethau, 'n faeth*
> *Yn wragedd teg, yn egin,*
> *Yn weilch, yn filgwn, yn win,*
> *Yn ysgarlad rhad rhydeg,*
> *Yn aur tawdd, yn eiriau teg.*[14]

> In revelry, in luxuries, in care/ With ladies fair [and] with young sprouts,[15] / With hawks, with hounds [and] with wine, / With scarlet, beautiful [and] gracious, / with fluid gold, with pleasant words.

Evidently, Ifor's court is a place of feasting (*gwleddau*), full of beautiful women and children, replete with wine, decked out in scarlet (a royal color), overflowing with gold; a place, finally, where "pleasant words"—i.e. words of poetry—are encouraged.

It is at Ifor's court in Basaleg that the poet receives the gift of gloves: *Menig o'i dref a gefais*/"Gloves from his dwelling I got"[16]; *deuthum o'i dai/ Â'i fenig a'i ddwbl fwnai*/"I came [away] from his house/ with his

---

[10] *Mawl Llywelyn ap Gwilym* (GDG 12 | CDG 5), line 20.

[11] Ibid., line 19 and line 29, respectively.

[12] Ibid., GDG 12, line 32 | CDG 5, line 30.

[13] Ibid., line 23.

[14] *Diolch am Fenig* (GDG 9 | CDG 14), lines 42–46.

[15] i.e. children.

[16] Ibid., line 55.

gloves and double the money"[17]; *Menig gwynion tewion teg,/ A mwnai ym mhob maneg/*"White gloves, beautiful and thick,/ With coin-wealth in each glove."[18]

The gloves appear to be beautifully made and come across as aesthetic objects in their own right; however, the poet also thinks of them as symbolic entities that tie him closer to the patron. When he puts his hand deep inside the deerskin once worn by the patron, their fingers meet, and their hands touch each other across space and time. It is a moment of staggering intimacy humorously presented as posing a challenge to Dafydd's heteronormative relationships:

> *Pob merch y sydd yn erchi*
> *Benthyg fy menig i mi;*
> *Ni châi ferch, er eu herchi,*
> *Mwy no gŵr, fy menig i.*[19]

> Every girl seeks/ A loan of my gloves. / No girl shall have them, despite begging, / Any more than a man, [these] gloves of mine.[20]

Ifor's generosity is thrown into sharp relief when compared—or, rather, contrasted—with Elen Nordd's gift of wool stockings in *Dewis Un o Bedair*.[21] If Ifor's spouse is described as *ceinlliw haf oroen/*"fair color of summer brightness,"[22] then Elen is characterized (contrariwise) as *chwannog i olud/*"greedy for wealth."[23] The poet never leaves her *heb gaffael rhyw dâl/*"without getting some payment,"[24] and their mercantile

---

[17] Ibid., lines 11–12.

[18] Ibid., lines 15–16.

[19] Ibid., lines 21–24.

[20] These lines may also be interpreted in semi-erotic terms: cf. J. E. Caerwyn Williams, *Llên a Llafar Môn* (Llangefni: Cyhoeddwyd gan Gyngor Gwlad Môn, 1963), 99, on the sexually charged colloquial definition of *maneg* as uterus/vulva. This would, of course, transform the gloves into agents of seduction. Poet and patron would then succeed in symbolically interpenetrating each other, further underscoring the utter interdependence of their relationship.

[21] GDG 98 | CDG 120.

[22] *Marwnad Ifor a Nest* (GDG 11 | CDG 17), line 24.

[23] GDG 98 | CDG 120, line 17.

[24] Ibid., line 30.

connection is highlighted even further when Dafydd refers to her as *fy anrhaith*/"my treasure," "my plunder," or "my property."[25] He produces a love-poem in praise of Elen, but the good socks he's rewarded with are nothing but a wage, paid out after he performs his customary function.

Dafydd's humorous characterization of Elen as *brenhines gwlân*/"the queen of wool" betrays the mercantile reality of their relationship, fusing together the fields of commerce and sexuality.[26] The poet suggests that Elen is in need of a loving man and that she is *hawdd ym gael*/"easy to get" on account of her useless merchant-husband Robin.[27] She becomes, to borrow a phrase from the Chaucerian scholar William F. Woods, "assimilated in metaphor" to the material possessions around her: stockings, wool or the multicolored medley-cloth with which she also apparently rewards the poet for his love-lyrics. By presenting him with the intimate gift of "good socks," Elen becomes identified in Dafydd's mind with the house of wool she inhabits: and so "[t]he merchant's wife comes to embody the quid pro quo of her thoroughly mercantile marriage."[28] Elen's romantic arrangement with Dafydd is exactly that: an arrangement. *Diolch am Fenig*, conversely, is deeply embedded within a cultural framework sensitive to the traditional poet/patron relationship.

In his recent book *Chaucer's Gifts: Exchange and Value in the Canterbury Tales*, Robert Epstein argues that "after a commercial exchange," such as Dafydd's experience with Elen Nordd, "the participants have no further obligation to each other."[29] The poem always comes first and the gold (or some other form of payment) follows. In the case of Ifor Hael, this opposition is completely reversed, and the gold is bestowed upon the poet *before* he produces the reciprocal counter-gift (i.e. the poem). Commodities, Epstein claims,

> . . . are fully alienated from the donor at the moment of transaction. Gifts are never alienated from the donor; on

---

[25] Ibid., line 18.

[26] Ibid., line 19.

[27] Ibid., line 25.

[28] William F. Woods, *Chaucerian Spaces: Spatial Poetics in Chaucer's Opening Tales* (Albany: SUNY Press, 2008), 13.

[29] Robert Epstein, *Chaucer's Gifts: Exchange and Value in the Canterbury Tales* (Cardiff: University of Wales Press, 2018), 10.

the contrary, they always retain their history. By preserving the memory of the transaction, the obligation for repayment is carried into the future, and the result is the establishment of a social bond between the transactors.[30]

Unlike Elen Nordd, who views poems as purchasable commodities, Ifor seemingly recognizes the importance of Dafydd's poetical counter-gift. The lovely white gloves bestowed on the poet are described as *pur galennig*/"a pure gift"[31] and, moreover, they are filled with silver and gold.[32] Naturally, this transforms each glove into a *purse*: a metaphorical locus of exchange in which sensuality, economic status, and poetic capital join together. The connection between poetry and pecuniary reward (perceived not as payment but as gift) is further emphasized in line 46: *yn aur tawdd, yn eiriau teg*, with "gold" and "word(s)" being directly and quite literally linked by means of rhyme: *aur = gair*.[33] Other than *maneg/menig* (occurring twelve times), *aur* or gold is the second most often-used word in the poem (as well as one of Dafydd's most cherished descriptors in general, occurring more than ninety times in the overall oeuvre). To quote the historian Joel Kaye, in another context, this serves as a recognition on the poet's part of gold's "active power to determine the circuit and direction of human exchange . . . in the monetary onsciousness of the fourteenth century."[34] In full recognition of these mercantile anxieties, the poet anticipates any possible accusation of pecuniary self-

---

[30] Ibid., 7. On the medieval concept of gift-bestowal and the (homo)-social strategy of gift-giving, see Arnoud-Jan A. Bijsterveld, "The Medieval Gift as Agent of Social Bonding and Political Power: A Comparative Approach" in *Medieval Transformations: Texts, Power, and Gifts in Context*, eds. Esther Cohen and Mayke B. de Jong (Leiden: Brill, 2001), 123–156.

[31] *Diolch am Fenig* (GDG 9 | CDG 14), line 57.

[32] The gift of a gold-filled glove is already anticipated in line 2: *o 'i lys nid âi bys heb aur*/"no finger would leave from his court without gold"—since *bys* translates either as finger or, specifically, the finger of a glove.

[33] Dafydd often refers to poetic speech as *aur mâl*/"polished gold" in his poetry.

[34] Joel Kaye, "Monetary and Market Consciousness in Thirteenth and Fourteenth Century Europe" in *Ancient and Medieval Economic Ideas and Concepts of Social Justice,* eds. S. Todd Lowry and Barry Gordon (Leiden: Brill, 1998), 371–403; 396.

interest by stressing—perhaps overstressing—that the gold and silver he receives from Ifor is not a payment but rather a gift. *Diolch am Fenig* as a whole thus serves as a poetically framed expression of gratitude, figuratively embodied in the material form of the gloves themselves.

This in no way detracts from the gloves' "narrative function" (to borrow a phrase from Jerry Hunter) as *objects*.[35] As discussed above, material objects abound in Dafydd ap Gwilym's poetry, especially in his elegies and his panegyrics: gemstones, drinking cups, articles of clothing, wine, brocade and silken cloth, and (perhaps most importantly) gold. In addition to highlighting the affective materiality of these objects (endowing them, in other words, with certain emotional qualities),[36] the poet also takes pains to present them as mediators in his relationships with others.[37] Consequently, objects serve as material manifestations of the speaker's emotional (i.e. pertaining to emotion) state of mind, as well as affective loci of tactile experience within each poem.

Diolch am Fenig, in particular, stresses the importance of material objects (in this case, gloves) as signs of affective affiliation between

---

[35] Jerry Hunter, "Reading Objects, Exchanging Meaning: Material Culture in the Four Branches of the Mabinogi" (paper presented at the 38th Annual Harvard Celtic Colloquium, Cambridge, Massachusetts, 05 October 2018).

[36] On the materiality of emotions, see Monique Scheer, "Are Emotions a Kind of Practice (and Is That What Makes Them Have a History)? A Bourdieuian Approach to Understanding Emotion" in *History and Theory* 51.2 (2012), 193–220. On the history of emotions as a discipline, see Jan Plamper, *The History of Emotions: An Introduction*, trans. Keith Tribe (Oxford: Oxford University Press, 2015). On the intersection between the study of material culture and the history of emotions, see Gerhard Jaritz (ed.), *Emotions and Material Culture* (Vienna: Austrian Academy of Sciences Press, 2003).

[37] Compare, for instance, Morfudd's birch hat and Dafydd's response to it in *Yr Het Fedw* (GDG 59 | CDG 113), as well as the emotional resonance of objects in GDG 31 | CDG 19 and GDG 32 | CDG 134. On the idea of a sentimental object, see Guy Fletcher: "something is sentimentally valuable if and only if the thing is valuable for its own sake in virtue of a subset of its relational properties, where the properties include any or all of having belonged to, having been given to or by, or having been used by, people or animals, within a relationship of family, friendship, or romantic love, or having been used or acquired during a significant experience." Guy Fletcher, "Sentimental Value" in *Journal of Value Inquiry* 43.1 (2009), 55–65; 56.

men.[38] In many ways, the gloves represent the poet's emotional attachment to his patron, initiating and quite literally materializing a kind of "sensual encounter" between the two. The poem's ultimate conceit, of course, is that gloves are objects made by hand to clothe and protect hands responsible for dispensing the gift of poetry. Thus, the affective bond between poet and patron becomes embodied in both the actual, as well as the textual (i.e. poetic), glove.[39]

In the end, *Diolch am Fenig* outlines the central role of emotions and material objects within the poet/patron relational paradigm. Both Ifor and Dafydd are portrayed as active participants in this relationship, homosocially bound together by their predetermined and culturally inflected social positions.[40] The gift of gloves, meanwhile, serves to represent, both "actually" and "textually," the emotional interaction between the two men, negotiating their relationship through the affective materiality of a traditional *cân diolch*.

---

[38] On "homo-affectivity," specifically, see Damien Bouquet and Piroska Nagy, *Medieval Sensibilities: A History of Emotions in the Middle Ages*, trans. Robert Shaw (Cambridge: Polity Press, 2018), 117–123.

[39] The anthropologist James Fernandez outlines the connection between structural and textual metaphors in the following way: structural metaphors (in this case, physical objects used representationally) highlight the "shape of [material] experience," while textual metaphors (i.e. verbal representations of physical objects) always underscore the feelings *behind* the experience. See James Fernandez, "The Mission of Metaphor in Expressive Culture (with Commentary and Reply)" in *Current Anthropology* 15.2 (1974), 119–45.

[40] Another poem addressed to Ifor, *Basaleg* (GDG 8 | CDG 14), possibly contains an ironic reference to class hierarchy. The poet describes playing *ffristiol* and *tolbwrdd* "on the same level as that powerful man"/*Yn un gyflwr â'r gŵr gwrdd*, lines 41–42. Although the rules for both games have been lost, most likely they resembled chess, presupposing (naturally) a winner and a loser. Late medieval/early modern writers often use chess "to represent the progress of an aristocratic couple's courtship." Cf. Bryan Loughrey and Neil Taylor, "Ferdinand and Miranda at Chess" in *Shakespeare Survey* 35 (1982), 113–118; 114.

"Quos edocetis fastos?": The Hisperica Famina as Productive Reading Guide

Lisabeth C. Buchelt

Reading as Practice in Medieval Ireland

The Irish secular hero extraordinaire Cú Chulainn is a character known for his ability to shape-shift into a monstrous figure capable of hyperbolic deeds of violence while in the throes of his *ríastharthae*—something Thomas Kinsella famously translated as Cú Chulainn's "Warp Spasm."[1] Cú Chulainn, interestingly enough, is also sometimes portrayed in texts as a careful, insightful 'reader,' as when he details and identifies individuals in the hosts of Connacht warriors for the Ulstermen in *Táin Bó Cuailgne*.[2] Cú Chulainn's reading prowess within this vernacular tale is so marked in this instance, that, as Ann Dooley has noted, the "textual transmission of this display fires scribe Máel Muire of the Lebor na hUidre text to add a marginal codification of his own—on the three greatest 'readings' ever made in Ireland."[3] Dooley remarks that Máel Muire is referring to the three greatest "readings" ever made in literary Ireland; but I want to remind us and more fully explore the implications of the obvious: that we get a snapshot of Máel Muire's reading technique as well. The verb in question here is *árim* from *rím*: an 'act of reckoning, relating'. Although the primary meaning of *rím* is 'reckoning' in the sense of 'enumerating', it is possible that by the twelfth century the meaning 'recounting a tale' had entered the word's semantic field.[4] Following Dooley's suggested translation of *arím*, which uses this secondary meaning, then, Máel Muire's comment could read: "This is one of the three best and most difficult readings in Ireland; that is, Cú Chulainn's

---

[1] Thomas Kinsella, *Táin Bó Cúailgne*. (Oxford: Oxford UP, 1969), 77.

[2] Throughout this essay, I use the term 'reader' to mean not only its primary sense as a reader of books, but also to describe the act of interpretation more broadly; that is, a reader can also read situations, images, feelings, ideas, etc.

[3] Ann Dooley, *Playing the Hero: Reading the Irish Saga* Táin Bó Cúailnge. (Toronto: University of Toronto Press, 2006), 37.

[4] See *Dictionary of the Irish Language* (online), s.v. 1 rímid ordil.ie/35310; also Tomás de Bhaldraithe, "Notaí ar fhocáil" in *Éigse xxv* (1991), 160–164.

reading of the men of Ireland in the *Táin*; and the reading of the Fomorian hosts in *Cath Maige Tuired*; and the reading from Ingcél of the hosts in *Togail Bruidne Dá Derga.*" If we translate the same verb using its primary meaning, the text could read: "This is one of the three best and most difficult reckonings in Ireland; that is, Cú Chulainn's counting of the men of Ireland in the *Táin*; and the counting of the Fomorian hosts in *Cath Maige Tuired*; and the counting from Ingcél of the hosts in *Togail Bruidne Dá Derga.*"[5] The exact translation choice, however, is somewhat immaterial as the important point is this: whether or not Máel Muire was thinking of 'enumerating' or 'recounting' in his deployment of *arím*, he himself is clearly engaging in an act of good reading practice. If we unpack his marginal comment a bit more, he writes that the other two greatest '(re)countings' occur in two other supreme examples of the literary conceit in Irish secular sagas known as 'the watchman device': Lúg describing the Fomorian troop in *Cath Maige Tuired* (The Second Battle of Moytura) and Ingcúil's description of the many forces arrayed against Conare in *Togail Bruidne Dá Derga* (The Destruction of Dá Derga's Hostel).[6] These are moments, like that of Cú Chulainn's in the *Táin*, in which the characters must engage in the act of 'reading' what they are 'counting' in order to perform the description; an improper and inaccurate interpretation of the enumerated objects would lead to a flawed and inaccurate description, in turn leading to a course of action based on a misinterpretation produced by inattentive and faulty 'reading'. In commenting on these moments and relating them to each other, Máel

---

[5] The texts noted by Dooley are the primary text of the tale itself: "Is assu ém damsa ol Cu Cl oldás daitsiu. air itát tri búada formsa .i. búaid roisc 7 intliuchta 7 airdmessa. ro láosa di tra ol se fomus forsaní sin;" and the marginal response in the scribe Mael Muire's hand: "Is sí seo in tres árim is glicu 7 is dolgiu dorigned I nHerind .i. árim Con Cul for feraib Herend ár Tána. 7 árim Loga for sluag Fomórach ar Cath Maigi Ted. 7 árim Ingciúil for slog Bruidni Da Dergae." Best and Bergin, *Lebor na hUidre* (Dublin: Royal Irish Academy, 1929) p. 151.

[6] For a detailed discussion on the potential origins of this literary device and its uses in both Irish and Welsh medieval literature, see Sims-Williams, Patrick, "Narrative Techniques in Irish and Welsh II: The Riddling 'Watchman Device'." In *Irish Influence on Medieval Welsh Literature.* (Oxford: Oxford University Press, 2011), 95–133.

Muire is performing good *lectio divina* techniques himself;[7] and so the line between reality and fiction blurs as he points to vernacular fictional 'readers' who do the same within the world of their sagas.

There is textual evidence that Irish monastic communities from their earliest foundations could have been familiar with the Patristic writers who most informed the reading technique of *lectio divina* and associated memory techniques of *memoria*.[8] Many of the surviving Irish monastic rules explicitly state that *lectio* be part of the daily routine for the community, and several specifically state that selections from scripture should be read while the community eats; engaging both the community's *palatum* ("palate" or "sense of taste") and the *palatum cordis* ("heart's palate").[9] Thus, it is certainly possible, likely probable, that Máel Muire is

---

[7] *Lectio divina* was a widely practiced reading technique in which a reader actively recalled other texts with which he or she was familiar and allowed them to interact with the text immediately at hand, thus enhancing their engaged, meditative reading experience.

[8] The Gospels, the Acts of the Apostles, and the Psalms all get special mention. Martin MacNamara,"Patristic Background to Medieval Irish Ecclesiastical Sources" in Thomas Finan and Vincent Twomey, eds. *Scriptural Interpretation in the Fathers: Letter and Spirit*. (Dublin: Four Courts Press, 1995), 253–281. McNamara has noted that the Irish exegetical, homiletic and theological traditions are all based on the widely read Fathers of western Christian tradition (258). McNamara also notes, in his detailed study of the possible sources for *Scéla na hEsérgi* ("Tales of the Resurrection"), that "the author is heavily dependent, whether directly or indirectly, on Augustine's *De civitate Dei*, and less so on the same author's *Enchiridion*; likewise for two sections on Gregory's *Moralia in Iob*" (264), and adds, "it goes without saying, however, that only detailed source analysis of the available material will permit us to give a full and satisfactory picture of the situation, with regard to the writings of the Fathers known and used by the Irish, and as to whether they knew them directly from full texts of the works or from excerpts and collectanea" (258). See also McNamara, *The Psalms in the Early Irish Church* (Sheffield: Sheffield Academic Press, 2000); and Gerard McGinty, "The Irish Augustine's Knowledge and Understanding of Scripture" in Thomas Finan and Vincent Twomey, eds. *Scriptural Interpretation in the Fathers: Letter and Spirit*. (Dublin: Four Courts Press, 1995) 283–313.

[9] Including the Rules of Ailbe, of Columcille, of Ciarán, of Mochuda Rathaín, of the Célí Dé, and of Tallaght. See Uinseann Ó Maidín, *The Celtic Monk: Rules and Writings of Early Irish Monks*, (Kalamazoo: Cistercian Publications, 1996). Some

not unusual in his engagement with texts; we are merely fortunate that he was enthused enough to record part of his reading process for posterity, and that the codex in which he did so survived the centuries. Although the surviving Irish monastic rules suggest only scripture for these particular reading moments, Máel Muire and his marginal comment provide us with evidence that secular literature was also an active part of the monastic reading community, and equally useful for productive *lectio divina*-style reading.

In addition to the Patristic writers, another text that was part of the general intellectual culture transmitting Classical memory techniques to the medieval world, which were then used in the practice of *lectio divina*, was *Rhetorica ad herennium* (hereafter, *RH*).[10] Within the context of medieval reading and *memoria* practices, it is a basic principle that humans are able to remember with precision and accuracy things that are especially odd or emotionally charged, as we see described in the *RH* in Book III.xvi–xxiv. In *RH* we are told that an efficient and useful "artificial memory" includes both [architectural] backgrounds and [individual] images to place against the background.[11] In other words, imagining a

---

rules even recommend the community be tested on the previous night's selection so as to be certain that they actually heard, and retained, their mental nourishment. A careful and mentally organized reader—one able to avoid *curiositas*-style mental wandering while listening to the reading and practicing good *lectio divina* technique—would, naturally, ace any next-day exam administered by his abbot over the previous night's dining entertainment. See the Rule of the Céli Dé in Ó Maidín, 88.

[10] See P. Ruth Taylor, "'Pre-History' in the Ninth-Century Manuscripts of the *Ad Herennium*." *Classica et Mediaevalia* 44 (1993): 181–254. There survive about 600 copies of this text, which represent several centuries of transmission. Of the six manuscripts of this text from the ninth to tenth centuries, four are associated with Irish or Irish-founded monasteries: one a partial copy from St. Gall; two others partial copies that have possibly been placed in the monastery of Corbie, another monastery with Irish connections in that it was founded by monks from Luxeuil who had been trained by St. Columbanus; and one other copy copied someplace in the area around St. Gall. The assumption for the idea that one of the manuscripts is from someplace around St. Gall is that it was copied from the one confidently placed in St. Gall.

[11] *Constat igitur artificiosa memoria ex locis et imaginibus. Locos appellamus eos qui breviter, perfecte, insignite aut natura aut manu sunt absolute, ut eos facile naturali memoria conprehendere et amplecti queamus: ut aedes, intercolumnium, angulum,*

house, a columnar space, a recess, an arch, or some other type of architectural space for a background against which to put images one wishes to remember, is recommended as the best way to artificially enhance one's natural memory capacity. Additionally, the best images to place within these architectural backgrounds are not "things that are petty, ordinary, and banal"; instead, the *RH* reminds its readers that seeing or hearing "something exceptionally base, dishonorable, extraordinary, great, unbelievable, or laughable," renders it something "that we are likely to remember a long time."[12] The text later suggests some ways to render one's memory images exceptional, to make them "as striking as possible":

> We ought, then, to set up images of a kind that can adhere longest in the memory. And we shall do so if we establish likenesses as striking as possible; if we set up images that are not many or vague, but doing something; if we assign to them exceptional beauty or singular ugliness; if we dress some of them with crowns or purple cloaks, for example, so that the likeness may be more distinct to us; or if we somehow disfigure them, as by introducing one stained with blood or soiled with mud or smeared with red paint, so that its form is more striking, or by assigning

---

fornicem, et alia quae his similia sunt (*RH*, III.xvi). The artificial memory includes backgrounds and images. By backgrounds I mean such scenes as are naturally or artificially set off on a small scale, complete and conspicuous, so that we can grasp and embrace them easily by natural memory—for example, a house, an intercolumnar space, a recess, an arch, or the like (*RH*, 209). (Latin text from *Rhetorica ad Herennium*, Harry Caplan, trans. Loeb Classical Library. (Cambridge, MA: Harvard University Press, 1989)).

[12] *Nam si quas res in vita videmus parvas, usitatas, cotidianas, meminisse non solemus, propterea quod nulla nova nec admirabili re commovetur animus; at si quid videmus aut audimus egregie turpe, inhonestum, inusitatum, magnum, incredibile, ridiculum, id diu meminisse consuevimus* (*RH*, III.xxii). When we see in everyday life things that are petty, ordinary, and banal, we generally fail to remember them, because the mind is not being stirred by anything novel or marvelous. But if we see or hear something exceptionally base, dishonorable, extraordinary, great, unbelievable, or laughable, that we are likely to remember a long time (*RH*, 219).

certain comic effects to our images, for that, too, will ensure our remembering them more readily (*RH*, 221).[13]

These are the types of things that help a reader locate matching images, or things, from other texts in order to properly engage with the text at hand using good *lectio divina* techniques. So, in texts about reading and the craft of memory which also discuss these notions found in *RH*, from Augustine to John Cassian, and Benedict to Gregory the Great, the metaphors used to describe the processes come from the worlds of architecture, the warrior, the kitchen, the exotic or foreign encounter, the violent, and the sensual. Within these reading contexts, good monastic readers are depicted as having memories that are in the shape of extravagant palaces; as warriors arming themselves with the spears and swords of good rhetoric and the shields of recollected texts; they sit at elaborate feasts gathering nourishment from the many proffered "dishes" at hand; they walk through an imagined countryside using the fictional landscape to help their minds plot the route they will take among the "fields"; they puncture, wound, scrape, and dismember a text in order to recombine the parts into a new learning experience; and they lovingly undress a "feminine" text to better see and experience its inner, unveiled interpretive possibilities.[14] So, perhaps in the many violent, delectable, sexual, and absurd types of images and tropes that medieval Irish texts contain in abundance—both vernacular and Latin, "sacred" and

---

[13] Imagines igitur nos in eo genere constituere oportebit quod genus in memoria diutissime potest haerere. Id accident si quam maxime notates similitudines constituemus; si non multas nec vagas, sed aliquid agentes imagines ponemus; si egregiam pulcritudinem aut unicam turpitudinem eis adtribuemus; si aliquas exornabimus, ut si coronis aut veste purpurea, quo nobis notatior sit similitudo; aut si qua re deformabimus, ut si cruentam aut caeno oblitam aut rubric delibutam inducamus, quo magis insignita sit forma, aut ridiculas res aliquas imaginibus adtribuamus, name a res quoque faciet ut facilius meminisse valeamus (*RH*, III.xxii).

[14] For more on the art and craft of memory in the Middle Ages, see the influential work of Mary Carruthers in *The Book of Memory: A Study of Memory in Medieval Culture* (Cambridge: Cambridge University Press, 1990); *The Craft of Thought: Meditation, Rhetoric, and the Making of Images, 400–1200* (Cambridge: Cambridge University Press, 1998); and with Jan M. Ziolkowski, eds. *The Medieval Craft of Memory: An Anthology of Texts and Pictures* (Philadelphia: University of Pennsylviania Press, 2002.

"secular"—another avenue of possible interpretation was suggested for their medieval audience: that of engaging in productive *lectio divina*-style reading.

These assertions that medieval intellectual culture in Ireland was aware of *lectio divina* and the reading and recollection techniques of *memoria*, *inventio*, and *oblivio* which were also necessary for good reading practices, as well as the commonplace metaphorical descriptions of reading and recollection provide a possible context in which to illuminate a famously frustrating series of Insular Latin texts, the *Hisperica Famina* (hereafter *HF*). When interpreting the *Hisperica Famina* within the framework of *lectio divina*, it becomes a type of instruction manual on productive ways to successfully integrate all the intellectual material available to a reader within Irish monastic culture—religious and secular, oral and textual, Latin and vernacular. I would like to suggest that Máel Muire's display of integrative reading techniques is a continuation of an established Irish practice of using both secular and sacred texts as catalysts for productive *lectio divina*; the endorsement of which may extend back several hundred years, and the integrative process of which is imaginatively portrayed in the *Hisperica Famina*.

The *Hisperica Famina* were most likely composed around the mid-seventh century as part of a broader intellectual phenomenon of producing intensely obscure and difficult Latin poetic texts that seems to have more or less run its course by the eighth century.[15] This work is often translated as "Western Orations"; but I prefer Ben C. Tilghman's translation of "Occidental Talkitudes" as being more in keeping with the playful spirit of these odd texts.[16] It is a series of versified texts of varying length that, although somewhat mundane and repetitive in their form and structure, as well as their subject matter, employ extraordinarily abstruse and creative Hiberno-Latin vocabulary and syntax. The most complete version of the *Hisperica Famina* is that of the A-text, Vaticanus Reginensis Latinus 81, fols. 1–12. This manuscript is believed to be from the late ninth to the

---

[15] See Michael W. Herren, *The Hisperica Famina: The A-Text.* (Toronto: the Pontifical Institute of Mediaeval Studies), 1974; also Herren, *The Hisperica Famina: Related Poems.* (Toronto: The Pontifical Institute of Mediaeval Studies, 1987).

[16] Tilghman, Benjamin C. "Writing in Tongues: Mixed Scripts and Style in Insular Art." In Colum Hourihane, ed. *Insular and Anglo-Saxon Art and Thought in the Early Medieval Period.* (Princeton: Princeton University Press, 2011) 93–108.

early tenth century, and was very possibly created at the monastery of Fleury.[17] It must be noted that one of the six surviving ninth-century copies of the *Rhetorica ad Herennium* has also been possibly placed at Fleury, potentially providing us with a very direct and material point of connection between the two texts.

The texts of the *Hisperica Famina* had mostly been dismissed by scholars as texts that were capable of driving even the most accomplished of thinkers to the depths of despair. The earliest studies from the nineteenth century were philological studies, which were successful in creating a lexicon of what came to be called 'Hisperic' language. This helped to identify a few other texts outside of the *HF* proper that deploy the same obscure vocabulary and syntax. Suggestions about the possible purpose of the *Hisperica Famina* texts range from them forming a type of intellectually exclusive encyclopedia (H. Zimmer); to not fulfilling any purpose at all other than to be types of intellectual folly (E.K. Rand). Other suggestions include: authors composing in this fashion to look to create a type of Latinate poetry that incorporated aspects of the pre-Christian Irish druidic tradition (R.A.S. Macalister); or authors creating models for students whose purpose was to convey difficult vocabulary through simplistic poetic forms and essay topics, while not being literary creations in and of themselves (P. Grosjean).[18] This last suggestion, although not without its own problems, has been called by Michael Herren, "reasonable enough", accounting "for many of their peculiarities: the subject matter, the length of the essays, the regular word order, and the use of assonance."[19] Much of the scholarship since Michael Herren's

---

[17] Michael Winterbottom also notes that the A-text of *HF* was "a Fleury book". See "On the *Hisperica Famina*", *Celtica* 8 (1968), 126–139, 128, n.17.

[18] Zimmer, H. "Neue Fragmente von Hisperica Famina," *Nachrichten d. k. Gesellschaft d. Wissenschaft zu Göttingen philol-hist., Kl.,* Heft 2 (1895), 117–65; Rand, E. K. "The Irish Flavour of the Hisperica Famina," in *Studien zur lateinischen Dichtung des Mittelalters, Ehrengabe für K. Strecker*, W. Stach and H Walther, eds. (Dresden: 1931), 134–142; Macalister, R. A. S. *The Secret Languages of Ireland.* (Cambridge: Cambridge University Press, 1937); Grosjean, P. "Confusa Caligo: Remarkques sur les *Hisperica Famina*," *Celtica* 3 (1956), 35–7. For a comprehensive bibliography of the *Hisperica Famina*, see Donnchadh Ó Corráin, *Clavis Litterarum Hibernesium*, 3 vols (Turnhout, 2017), II. 733–736 (§ 570).

[19] Herren, *The A-Text*, 19.

1974 edition and translation has agreed with his assessment of Grosjean's initial idea for the most part; since as Jane Stevenson remarks, the texts remind "almost everyone of the type of painful composition characteristic of a modern beginners' class in French or German."[20]

However, Andy Orchard, along with other scholars in some of the most recent engagements with the *Hisperica Famina*, has demonstrated that these texts are, indeed, very much literary creations. As Orchard shows, they use "such rhetorical and literary devices as repetition, parallelism, metaphor, simile, and paronomasia."[21] It should go without saying, then, that the *HF* concerns itself with using language in all its forms and that it also concerns itself with a scholar's different modes of engagement with language: creating, reciting, learning, reading, transmitting. I hope to demonstrate that much of the *Hisperica Famina* can also be interpreted as engaging with virtually every metaphoric commonplace used to describe effective and proper monastic reading habits.

The *Hisperica Famina* as a Productive Reading Guide

The overall structure of the *Hisperica Famina* consists of an opening prologue, in which the speaker asks the listener (or reader) which rhetor is to be followed and how best to improve one's reading technique. This is followed by a section called the Twelve Faults of Ausonian Diction (*De duodecim uitiis ausonicae palathi*), which details how the practice of poor Ausonian rhetoric simultaneously injures the practice of Hisperican rhetoric. Then, a narrative entitled the Rule of the Day (*Lex diei*) creates and deploys the web of commonplace reading technique metaphors as seen in other texts about the practice of *lectio divina* such as the Patristic

---

[20] Jane Stevenson, "Bangor and the *Hisperica Famina*," *Peritia* 6–7 (1987–88), 202–216; 202.

[21] Andy Orchard, "The *Hisperica famina* as Literature," *The Journal of Medieval Latin*. 10:1 (2001), 1–45; 3. See also William Sayers, "Images of Enchainment in the *Hisperic Famina* and Vernacular Irish Texts," *Études Celtiques* 27 (1990), 221–234; and Michael Herren, "The Sighting of the Host in *Táin bó Fraích* and the *Hisperica Famina*," *Peritia* 5 (1986), 197–99 for other examples of more appreciative interpretations of the *Hisperica famina*'s literary qualities; this last by Herren notes the similarities between some moments in the *HF* with the (re)counting of the warriors in this lesser-known secular tale about a cattle raid.

writers and the *Rhetorica ad herennium*. These narratives are followed by ten short essays on various topics, in which the different challenges of interpreting and transmitting knowledge are described using the metaphoric web established in the Rule of the Day. The final text is called On Deeds, or On the Doing of Deeds, or On a Deed Done (*De gesta re*), which I suggest is a 'real-time' description of the process of *lectio divina* using the combined metaphors of the whole narrative of the *Hisperica Famina*.

The opening section's questions to the reader about which rhetor is followed and which texts are recited, as well as the speaker's challenge to engage in a verbal duel, are clearly indicative of the centrality of multiple concerns about the nature of language; that is, if the text's production of creative and obscure word coinages was not enough to indicate a real engagement with, and delight in, all the possibilities of language as tool and art form. The speaker, after asking "What texts do you recite / and what rhetor do you adhere to?"; likens himself to a warrior who "unsheathe[s] [his] dexterous sword," "take[s] up [his] wooden shield," and "brandish[es] [his] iron dagger" in order to win any proposed "verbal duel."[22] Within the framework of *lectio divina* metaphors and the possible

---

[22] *Quos edocetis fastos? / Cuique adheretis rhetor? / Hinc lectorum sollertem inuito obello certatorem, / qui sophicam pla<s>mauerit auide palestram. / Nam trino antea dimicaui athletas, / inertes mactaui duelles, / ac robustos multaui coaeuos, / fortioresque prostraui in acie ciclopes; / hinc nullum subterfugio aequeuum. / Dum truculenta me uellicant spicula, / protinus uersatilem euagino spatham, / quae almas trucidat statuas;/arboream capto iduma peltam, / quae carneas cluit tutamine pernas; / ferralem uibro pugionem, / cuius pitheum assiles macerat rostrum cidones; / ob <hoc> cunctos lastro in agonem coaeuos (HF* ll. 20–36). What texts do you recite? / and what rhetor do you adhere to? / Thus do I challenge the adroit wrangler to a verbal duel, / to engage in rhetorical gymnastics with eagerness. / For previously I contended against three athletes:/I slaughtered helpless warriors, / punished powerful peers, / and brought down stouter giants in the fray; / hence I shun none of my age-mates. / When their cruel darts begin to prick me, / straightaway I unsheathe my dexterous sword, / which hacks up sacred pillars; / I take my wooden shield in hand, / which compasses my meaty limbs with protection; / I brandish my iron dagger, / whose deadly tip torments the wheeling archers; / hence I summon all my peers to the contest. All citations and punctuation, both Latin and English, are from Herren, Michael W. *The Hisperica Famina: the A-Text* (Toronto: The Pontifical Institute of Mediaeval Studies,

interaction of secular and religious texts, the speaker's reference to "Ausonian speech" and "swarms of bees" busy making honey can be read as invocations of the monastic community (monks described as bees being a very old metaphorical commonplace) and the community's basic scriptural texts ("Ausonian speech"); indeed, the speaker makes his reference plain when he provides an explanation of what he means when he comments on the "elegant assemblage of scholars" as being "dazzling."[23] The speaker engages in some verbal self-praise and in what, at first glance, appears to be 'trash-talk' against his challenger: "But with my incomprehensible keenness of mind I suspect / that you tend woolly flocks of sheep in smelly pastures"; and then suggests that the mere student in front of him can only follow "the learned hosts of savants" and that even this may be a wasted effort. The speaker provides a suggested action for this hapless student, one which scholars have interpreted as an exhortation to go back to the farm and give up trying to become learned, but which takes on a very different valence placed in the possible context of the *HF* as a how-to manual for integrating religious and secular texts through proper reading techniques.

The speaker's "marvelous plan" is for the student to "rush to the soil of your native farm / to perform your field chores with sturdy motion." If we see the "native farm" and later, "native land," as metaphors for Irish secular literature, the speaker is suggesting that the students cultivate, repair, and carefully organize the secular corpus into a productive space

---

1974.) Some translations have minor emendations of my own, and these are duly noted when they occur.

[23] *Nam aequali plasmamine mellifluam populas / ausonici faminis per guttural sparignem? / Uelut innumera apium conauis discurrunt examina apiastris / melchillentaque sorbillant fluenta alueariis, / ac solidos scemicant rostris fauos. / Hic comptus arcatorum exomicat coetus, / cui dudum per lapsa temporum stadia / parem non creuimus phalangem, / nec future temporalis globi per pagula / equiperatam fulgidi rumoris speculabimur cateruam* (*HF*, ll. 40–48). Do you produce with equal skill a mellifluous flow of / Ausonian speech form your vocal chords? / As when countless swarms of bees run to and fro in their hollow hives, / and swallow floods of honey, / and make their solid combs with their probosces. / This elegant assemblage of scholars is dazzling, / now for leagues of lapsed time / we have not seen a phalanx equal to it, / nor through future regions of the temporal sphere / shall we behold a throng to match its refulgent reputation.

from which to obtain more wisdom. Fences (divisions between genres, perhaps?) must be repaired, cattle (individual tales?) put back where they should be, families (potential relationships between texts and/or genres?) supported and reconstructed; as the speaker tells the student, "all these tasks urge you to return to your native land."[24]

This "native" literature then gets linked to a series of natural phenomena, the forcefulness and violence of which is metaphorically representative of the use the speaker makes of this material in order to "surpass your Ausonian flood" or to "vex the troublesome troop of savants."[25] The invocations of war, floods, fires, wind, and the universe at

---

[24] *[S]ed non intelligibili mentis acumine prestulor / quod lanigerosas odorosa obseruas per Pascua bidentium turmas, / qui obessa arcatorum assiduo tramite sectaris concilia, / ac cicniam gemellis bai<u>las curuanam scapulis, / rutulantem alboreis artas c[a]lamide<m> madiadis, / pexamque carneis tolibus amplecteris camisam. / Nec ophica ingenioso acumine abscultas mysteria, / sed doctoreas effeto conamine comitaris historum turmas. / Hinc mirificum tibi ingenioso libramine palo consultum: / proprigenum natalis fundi irruere solum, / ut agrica robusto gestu plasmaueris orgia. / Nam pantia ruptis astant septa termopilis, / pubescentes pecorea depascunt segetes agmina, / ueternas mesta genitrix lacrimosis irrigat genas guttis. / Nam infantilis mu<r>murat inuagitus, / ac florigera resonat clangore per arua, / externum proprifera editrix abucat marem, / placoreasque blandis concelebrat nuptias thalamis; / haec pantia natalem te stigant orgia adire limitem* (*HF*, ll. 68–86). [B]ut with my incomprehensible keenness of mind I suspect / that you tend woolly flocks of sheep in smelly pastures, / and in your persistent manner pursue the packed assemblies of the scholars, / carry a white booksack on your two shoulders, / and cast a red robe on your pale body, / and wrap an elegant cloak around your meaty limbs. / Nor do you hear the mysteries of learning with native acumen, / but accompany the learned hosts of savants with wasted effort. / And so with my natural poise I shall reveal to you a marvelous plan: / rush to the soil of your native farm / to perform your field chores with sturdy motion; / for all your fences have broken gates, / your herds of cattle are grazing on the sprouting crops, / your sorrowing mother moistens her aged cheeks with tear drops; / for loud is the wailing of your children / and the noise resounds through the flowering fields. / Your wife accepts in your place a foreign spouse / and celebrates the agreeable union with enticing embraces; / all these tasks urge you to return to your native land.

[25] *Ceu montosus scropias tranat tollus per macides, / frondeos fluctiuaga eradicate hornos deuoratio, / inormia euoluit murmure crepita, / limosam fluminio mactat crepidinem alueo, / conretas euellit uortice glarias, / pari ausonicum ex<s>ubero pululamine fluuium. / Ueluti rosea aestiui laris ueternas cremat pira[m] rubigine*

---

large foreshadows the topics of each of the short essays which follow, a point to which I shall return. Within the intellectual context of memory and reading techniques, the *HF*'s repeated concern with the interaction of, and differences between what the writer later terms the "Ausonian chain" and "Irish speech," ("*ausonica catena*" and "*scottigenum eulogium*"), as well as the fact that the reader follows the group of student-scholars who journey away from the home institution's study chamber and out into the land of the "native," we may also see, once again, a metaphor at work about the relationship between religious texts and Irish secular texts. That is, the *HF* may be read as addressing a student-scholar's access to, and desire to read and to ingest, secular texts along with religious texts. This is not to suggest that the *HF* implies that religious texts are only in Latin and secular texts are only in the vernacular; especially as the *Hisperica Famina* itself, although written in Latin, is not a religious text (though it uses monastic life to construct its metaphorical web); nor is it strictly a secular text (although as we will see, its last essay describes a battle that would be very much at home as part of the Ulster Cycle). But as this notion about the interaction between "Ausonian" and "native" is present throughout the text, it does seem to suggest that ways to integrate the two productively was a genuine concern for the reading community. As Herren notes, "the anonymous *faminator* seemed to have more in mind than the

---

amurcas, / ac aruca fauellosis minorat robora tumulis, / ciboneus torridum spirat clibanus ructum, / fra[n]gosas flectit per laquearia flammas, / aequali doctoreas torero feruore cateruas. / Ceu truculentus pecorea terret bouencus armenta, / saginatum stricta mactat iuuencum ligitur[i]a, / horribilem uisceria complet ingluuiem aruina, / sanguineum trucido hiatus sorbellat fluentum, / pari erumnosos perturbo pauore historum lochos (*HF*, ll. 87–102). As when a mountain stream passes over rocky precipices, / and the devouring flood uproots the leafy ash trees, / and unleashes thundering crashes with a roar, / destroying the mud dam in the river channel / and bearing away the hardened gravel in its whirlpool, / with equal turbulence do I surpass your Ausonian flood. / As when the red fire of the summer heat bakes the aged olive trees with its scorching / and reduces dry oaks to heaps of ashes– / as when a fiery furnace vents its torrid exhalation / and directs the crackling flames through the ceiling, / with equal heat do I scorch the learned throngs. / As when the savage water serpent terrifies the herds of cattle, / slaughters the fattened bullock with tight constriction, / and sates its horrible gluttony on the intestinal fat, / swallowing a draught of blood in a savage gulp, / with equal terror do I vex the troublesome troop of savants.

mere stringing together of hermeneutic words by class for the benefit of his Latin-composition students . . . [as] [t]he adaptation of this and other saga motifs . . . to a scholastic environment suggests . . . a more consciously literary Gestalt for the *Hisperica Famina*."[26]

The next section of the *HF*, *Lex diei*, or The Rule of the Day, also invokes many of the most common tropes and metaphors used to describe the processes and challenges of proper reading. If we continue to read while keeping the commonplace descriptions of proper reading practice in mind, and if the first sections finished with a metaphorical explanation of the importance of the principle of integrating religious and secular knowledge in theory, then the *Lex diei* section becomes a detailed metaphorical explanation on how to integrate religious and secular texts as potential reading material from which to draw in order to form a holistic intellectual community in practice.

The reader is presented with a highly detailed pastoral opening sequence, in which animals and people of all kinds are wakeful and active, which is juxtaposed with an interior scene of a scholar just stirring from sleep: "this noisy clatter incites us to stir from our bedrooms." His colleagues, however, seem to have been already up for hours reading and are irritated that his laziness infects the rest of them: "For we have devoted an entire measure of moonlight to studious wakefulness, / but you have pleasured your limbs with the corruption of sleep; / wherefore a feeling of drowsiness now overcomes us." The group of student-scholars splits up into three different groups: some "go to the warm cottages," others "traverse the leafy underwoods," and the third group "stay[s] in this ample building." We then read of one group's adventures out in the "dangerous regions" and "rough farmland" as they worry about encountering wandering bands of outlaws who "surround these highways" robbing travelers and slaughtering "armed hosts with their swords." They come across an inn, overcome an apparent language barrier, and are given what turns out to be a completely satisfactory meal. The group decides to spend the night away from their home institution and stays within "the protective walls of the town" and the inn, where they have another very fine dinner before carefully closing the "tight-fitting door, lest fierce brigands burst in" and again dividing into three groups: one to "heed their learned

---

[26] Herren, "Sighting of the Host," 399.

reading"; one to "receive the warmth of sleep"; and one to "share the night watch."[27] In the context of medieval memory and reading practices, we

---

[27] *Hic sonorous soporeis nos excitat tumultus expergesci thalamis* (*HF* l. 190): This noisy clatter incites us to stir from our bedrooms; *Totum namque nocturni ligonis lectriceis censuimus stadium excubiis; / uos soporea oblectastis pernas tabe; / ob hoc nunc somnolentus nos stigat tactus* (*HF* ll. 207–209): For we have devoted an entire measure of moonlight to studious wakefulness,/but you have pleasured your limbs with the corruption of sleep / wherefore a feeling of drowsiness now overcomes us.; *hinc caeteri apricas adeant casas, / alteri frondosa lustrent subnemora, / alii in hoc amplo stabilitent tugurio* (*HF* ll. 219–221): let some go to the warm cottages, / let others traverse the leafy underwoods,/let others stay in this ample building.; *Stricto densate tramitem colligio, / ageas astrifero statuite infolas sulco, / ne pitheis truces macerauerint mediada spiculis crudeles. / Nam talia uiperei obuallant triuia latrunculi, / multigenas degestis spoliant uiatorum turmas spiculis, / collectasque rapiunt predas, / armigera trucidant ensibus agmina. / Ob hoc stricto discriminosas irruamus cuneo per pes<s>as. / Aspera calcamus gressibus predia, / quae saxeas torrida mole glomerant statuas, / spinosasque parturient rumices. / Haec florigena exomicant arua, / quae porporeas glomerant [s]caltas, / nec lapidea artant crepita, / sed glaucicomas herbarum copulant uuas. / Caninus urbana murmurat sonitus inter nemora; / forte externus adheret moenibus latrunculus, / aut lustrantis concipiunt auribus strepitum agminis* (*HF* ll. 232–249): Crowd the path in close formation, / raise your holy headdress toward the sky, / lest cruel savages macerate our limbs with deadly darts. / For stealthy bands of brigands surround these highways, / and despoil numerous crowds of travellers with their aforesaid darts, / and slaughter armed hosts with their swords. / Therefore let us rush through the dangerous regions in a tight wedge. / We trample over the rough farmland/where parched pillars of rock are heaped / and thorny sorrels grow. / These flowery fields are a-sparkle / and replete with purple flowers; / they have no rocky parts / but contain clusters of blue grass. / The barking of a dog resounds within the woods of the town; / perhaps a foreign band of brigands is clinging to the walls, / or else they hear the din of <our> roving throng.; *Quis tales poscet poss<ess>ores / ut melchilentum concesserint opiminium? / Nam ausonica me subligat catena; / ob hoc scottigenum haud cripitundo eulogium.* (*HF* ll. 271–274): Who will ask these possessors / to grant us their sweet abundance? / For an Ausonian chain binds me; / hence I do not utter good Irish speech ; *Ob hoc alma ciuilis globi adeamus moenia, / aptam benignis poscere filoxinia<m> colonis.* (*HF* ll. 319–320): Therefore let us approach the protective walls of the town / to request suitable hospitality from the kind inhabitants.; *Stricta quadratum cludite regia [h]ostium, / ne atroces eruperint predones, / clandistimas rapere furtim gazas. / Caeteri lectoralem mentis acumine ascultent sophiam; / alteri somniosum abucent pernis fotum; / alii nocturnas librent excubias, / quatinus roseus phoebe orientis*

see here the common injunction of the need to resist fleshly indulgences (stop being lazy and wake up); the metaphor of architectural or geographic spaces as organizing containers for past reading experiences (the home institution's study hall, the woods and fields, the inn, the town); and food and feasting as a metaphor for the acquisition and "digesting" of knowledge and the process of reading.

Turning first to the martial imagery so often used in descriptions of reading and *memoria* practices and already invoked within the *HF*, the text provides reminders about how to negotiate these possibly dangerous secular-in-genre texts in its expressed fears of "cruel savages," "bands of plunderers," and "fierce brigands" that the traveling student-scholars must work to avoid. The text has already invoked the scholar-as-warrior trope, with its depiction of ideas and words as weapons and the texts already stored in his memory chambers as his shield, in the opening sequence of the entire work. In a nuanced engagement with this trope, the scholar-students are encouraged to *avoid* conflict, perhaps because they are still students and not yet masters of *memoria* and *lectio divina*. As they journey through the fields on their way to the vernacular literature outpost of the town and the inn, they must be careful to avoid that literature which will not prove to be meditatively productive, or force them away from their carefully followed route through the countryside. These deadly bands of outlaw 'texts' are contrasted with the 'neighbors' (*acculas*; *acculae*) who direct the traveling scholars to the hospitable inn and apologize for their not-so-meager victuals; the 'rustics' (*agrestibus*) who will be impressed by the line of hanging book satchels; and the 'obliging inhabitants' (*benignis colonis*) who provide the evening's hospitality. As the monastic chamber of study provides a controlled environment for proper reading and digesting of religious texts—and remember that one group of student-scholars has remained behind to read in that space—the friendly and comfortable town and inn provide an analogous controlled environment for proper use of vernacular material. It should be noted that the student-scholars have carried with them into this secular space their foundational

---

rutilauerit pruritus. (*HF* ll. 351–357): Close the square entrance with the tight-fitting door, / lest fierce brigands burst in / and stealthily carry off our hidden treasures. / Let some heed their learned reading with a keen mind; / let other receive the warmth of sleep within their limbs; / let other share the night watch, / until the rosy glow of the rising sun flashes forth.

texts and knowledge from the monastic study chamber in the form of their book satchels, which, although they do not use them, are hanging on the wall as additional organizing containers—with additional "weapons"—should they need to delve into them.

Turning now to the commonplace metaphor of text-as-food, the student-scholars are provided with two meals while they are out at the "vernacular" inn. At both meals, the food is abundant, the ale flows, but significantly the nourishment it provides is described as wholesome and beneficial (*salubrem*). In our interpretive framework, the "delicious smearing of Irish oil" on the crusts of bread becomes another image of that which is "native" or "vernacular" as good and productive of nourishment and enjoyment.[28] That is, these are not over-abundant, gluttonous "feasts" of vernacular literature; they are sweet, enjoyable, productive, and they leave the feasters ready to "scrutinize the reading assignment" and "heed their learned reading with a keen mind" before some get ready to continue

---

[28] ... *ageum esciferas reboate concentum in copias, / ut salubrem propinauerit in precordiis suxum. [...] Quae dulciora sorbuistis solamina? / Farriosas sennosis motibus corrosimus crustellas, / quibus lita scottigeni pululauit conditura olei; / carniferas pressis dentibus reminauimnus pernas, / lacteus populauit haustus, / quamuis gaudifluam bibulo ore gustauimus celiam.* (HF ll. 284–285; 297–302): ... sing out a holy harmony for the abundance of food, / so that wholesome strength may flow into our stomachs. [...] What sweeter victual have you eaten? / We munched on crusts of bread with toothy movements, / for which there abounded a delicious smearing of Irish oil. / We chomped down joints of meat with compressed teeth; / a draught of milk flowed abundantly, / <and> we thirstily drank our fill of the joy-giving ale. There has been some scholarly concern over this "Irish oil," as well as the use in the HF of "oppidum" to describe the settlement the scholars visit, especially if these descriptors are taken only literally. Thus, Eoin MacNeil and Herren ask questions about the actual care and feeding of either foreign scholars in Ireland or Irish scholars in foreign lands, or pointing out that at the time the faminators were active there were no towns in Ireland; which leads to the need to think about whether or not foreigners were visiting Irish monasteries in the seventh century, or whether or not Irish students were being educated in foreign monasteries, or whether or not Anglo-Saxon visiting scholars would feel that Irish oil was a luxurious and exotic commodity (see Herren, *Hisperica*, 33–36). I do not want to suggest that these are not worthy questions deserving of scholarly research; but sometimes if one only reads a text at the literal level, one could miss the metaphorical potential. See MacNeil, "Beginnings of Latin Culture in Ireland," *Studies* 20 (1931), 449–460.

meditating on the reading, some get ready for sleep, and some others get ready to guard them all for the night.[29] The student-scholars and lay inhabitants pass a pleasant day and evening together, keeping one another safe from the outlaw ruffians who otherwise might "burst in and stealthily carry off our hidden treasures." Metaphorically, the cultural "texts" of the religious world of the student-scholars and those of the secular world of the neighboring townspeople work together not only to provide productive reading experiences, ("hidden treasures"), but also to provide protection and guidance from encounters with "ruffian" texts.

The potential interpretive framework of *lectio divina* practice within a reading community is not limited to these two sections of the *Hisperica Famina*. In the next section, comprised of eleven short essays on various mundane topics, many of the essays could be metaphorically interpreted as meditating on the challenges of being a good practitioner of *lectio divina*. The topics of these short essays may be grouped as follows: five on different aspects of the natural world; one entitled On Many Things, but which is mostly about clothing and accessories; two on objects directly related to reading and writing; two on topics associated with religious life; and one about a violent and bloody battle. These essays are not on randomly selected topics, but instead in their stated subject matter recall

---

[29] *Inctas conditura accendite clibano tedas / ac lectoralem scrutamini fastis industriam; / soporiferam artant palpebrae grauidinem; / ob hoc blanda pecoreis uelate cubilia pratis, / rudesque serite mutatoris tapetes, / molliferos assilibus plicate puluellos gigris, / carboneas cinereo tegite strumas tumulo, / ne attigua succenderint ciscilia, / amploque arserint pirici fornacis incendio. / Stricta quadratum cludite regia [h]ostium, / ne atroces eruperint predones, / clandistinas rapere furtim gazas. / Caeteri lectoralem mentis acumine ascultent sophiam; / altteri somniosum abucent pernis fotum; / alii nocturnas librent excubias, / quatinus roseus phoebe orientis rutilauerit pruritus.* (*HF*, ll. 342–357): Kindle in the furnace your torches dipped in oil / and scrutinize the reading assignment in your books. / Our eyelids are pressed by the weight of sleep; / therefore spread the enticing couches with leather covers, / put on your coarse nightclothes, / fold soft pillows for your round heads, / cover the lumps of coal in the fire pit, / lest they ignite the kindling nearby, / and it burn with the great heat of a fiery furnace. / Close the square entrance with the tight-fitting door, / lest fierce brigands burst in / and stealthily carry off our hidden treasures. / Let some heed their learned reading with a keen mind; / let others receive the warmth of sleep within their limbs; / let others share the night watch, / until the rosy glow of the rising sun flashes forth.

the opening section of the *Hisperica Famina* and the speaker's descriptions of his verbal duel techniques and his suggested course of action for his student-challenger.

The first group of essays is focused on natural phenomena: On the Sky (*De caelo*); On the Sea (*De mari*); On Fire (*De igne*); On the Field (*De campo*); and On the Wind (*De uento*). Although diverse in the types of natural phenomena addressed, each of the essays provides a fuller description of the natural phenomena to which the warrior-speaker compared his verbal dueling abilities in the opening section of the *HF*, thus providing a type of closing thematic frame for some of the metaphors invoked throughout the text. But perhaps more telling than the subject matter, especially in terms of the practice of good reading technique, are shared conceits throughout all the essays centered on the transmission of knowledge, which do not prove the speaker to be the perfected verbal warrior he describes himself to be in the opening sequence, but instead a reader very cognizant of the fact that these techniques need to be constantly reviewed and rehearsed in order for a reader to stay at 'the top of his game'. The first is a repeated motif of being careful and judicious in the type of language used. Thus, in On the Sky, the speaker informs us that he "shall produce an abundance of words in measured tones"; in On the Sea, the speaker "shall attempt to forge a wheel of words"; and in On Fire, the speaker will "describe [this element] in rigorous tones."[30] The descriptive terms of "measured" and "rigorous," along with the qualifier of "attempt," all provide reminders to the reader that language is a technology to be used with careful thought and focused application. If we categorize these opening poetic essays further, there are two associated with human manufacture: On Fire and On the Field. The other three—On the Sky, On the Sea, and On the Wind—are all items that are beyond human manufacture, and the simultaneously productive and destructive potential of each are part of their depictions. This recognition that many

---

[30] *De hoc amplo olimpi firmament / loquelosas depromam lento murmure strues.* (*HF*, ll. 358–359): Regarding the huge firmament of the heaven / I shall produce an abundance of words in measure tones.; *De hoc amplo anfitridis licumine / loquelosum cudere nitor tornum.* (*HF*, ll. 381–382): Concerning the vast water of the ocean / I shall attempt to forge a wheel of words.; *Natalemque flammiuomi laris depromam lento murmure rigorem*: (*HF*, l. 339): I shall describe in measured tones the original hardness of hot fire:

natural elements have the capacity to be both productive or destructive may connect to a second theme linked to language technologies.[31]

This second theme is a version of what is commonly known as the 'unspeakability' motif, often seen in medieval apocalyptic literature or in descriptions of visions of hell or heaven.[32] So, in On the Sky, the speaker will not attempt to describe formations in the apex of Heaven: "which I shall not struggle to explain within the allotted time"; nor will he describe the formations in the field in On the Field: "which I shall not endeavor to explain in the course of my speech." In On Many Things, the speaker "cannot describe in the allotted time" all the many things carried by the scholars; nor can the speaker "explain with speech the rest of the objects" that go into making up the contents of a book satchel; and in On the Chapel, the speaker says that it "contains innumerable objects, / which I shall not struggle to unroll from my wheel of words."[33] The deployment of

---

[31] William Sayers takes a different tack when discussing the metaphorical possibilities of the texts' introduction of the natural world. He remarks, "[t]he metaphors in the *Hisperica Famina* that are employed for the acquisition and exercise of rhetorical skill are, we have seen, of two types: cultural (turning, forging, encatenation, warfare), and natural (aquatic flow and flood, fire). The discipline and strenuous effort of the former eventually yield to the accrued freedom and power of the latter, as the binding chain is succeeded by the unbound flood," concluding that the use of metaphors "is symptomatic of the larger Irish conception of artistic activity in its relation to divine forces" ("Enchainment" 233).

[32] This motif is clearly related to the Latin rhetorical device of *praeteritio*, which is also very likely to be playing a role in the construction of the text of the *HF*. Discussion of *praeteritio*'s place in the *HF* is, however, beyond the scope of this essay.

[33] *Innumera caeli cacuminis astant schemata, / quae temporeo propiamine explicare non famulor.* (*HF*, ll. 379–380): "Innumerable formations stand at the peak of heaven, / which I shall not struggle to explain within the allotted time."; *Plurifica campaneus nectit scemicamina fundus, / quae loquelari tramite haud explicare nitor, / ne doctoreas rhetorum grauauerit uena<s>.* (*HF*, ll. 474–476): "The country estate contains many formations, / which I shall not endeavor to explain in the course of my speech, / lest it vex the learned abilities of our rhetoricians."; *Innumeri quadrigonas captant scutilibus peltas, / ferriales uibrant idumis pugiones, / ac altera glomerant plasmamina, / quae temporali propiamine non exprimo.* (*HF*, ll. 509–512): Many grasp square shields in their shield hands, / brandish iron daggers in their hands, / and possess other objects, / which I cannot describe in the allotted time.; *Caetera non*

this motif may be seen as a reminder to the reader that a good practitioner of language technologies can recognize when the technology is inadequate, and will clearly indicate such moments so that the reader may perhaps fill in the gaps with his or her application of *memoria*. In other words, although a good reader is aware that, ideally and theoretically, language has an infinite number of words with which to express its ideas, he or she is also aware that once language moves into the physical world it, by necessity, becomes finite and is bounded by time.

This simultaneous recognition of the need to be careful in the production of content as well as the apparently innate inability to do so completely is said to be the result of two constraints: not having enough time, and not wanting to "vex" or bore the "learned rhetoricians." So, although the individual essays appear to be related in only the most superficial of ways through their outward content, they are shown to be more complexly related through the speaker's relationship to his ability or inability to create text *about* the content, and through the attendant reader's ability or inability to *interpret* that content given the same constraints of "time" and as a fellow member of the "community of rhetoricians" invoked. Indeed, in his expressed desire not to irritate the community of rhetoricians, the speaker seems to imply that they must finish the task that he can only begin. He helps with the new project of creating a community capable of finishing his text, and then interpreting it, through the overall narrative arc created by the next few essays. Starting with the essay On Many Things, the texts describe a community of imagined scholar-readers and the items they need to be successful intellectuals.

On Many Things (*De plurimis*) is a discussion of splendid clothing worn by persons with curly yellow hair who "carry booksacks on their necks." It describes them as also carrying shields and brandishing iron daggers in their hands, before stating that "[they] possess other objects, /

---

explico famine schemata, / ne doctoreis suscitauero fastidium castris. (*HF*, ll. 529–530): I cannot explain with speech the rest of the objects, / lest I bring forth weariness in the camps of the learned.; *Innumera congellat plasmamina, / quae non loqueloso explicare famulor turno.* (*HF*, ll. 559–560.): The chapel contains innumerable objects, / which I shall not struggle to unroll from my wheel of words.

which I cannot describe in the allotted time."[34]   This may be read as a description of the potential reader-scholar: the sartorial splendor representative of the extent of their well-educated minds, in much the same way as the invocation of purple cloaks and crowns is in the *Rhetorica ad herennium*; the weaponry representative of their ability to deploy their knowledge efficiently, which is a repeat of the words-as-weapons theme seen in both the opening section and the *Lex diei*. The next essay, On the Book Container (*De taberna*) focuses on what is arguably the most important accessory for an elegantly dressed scholar-reader: the book satchel mentioned as being "on the necks" of these appropriately attired people.

On the Book Container speaks of the gleaming white satchel itself and of the time-consuming work that goes into creating it. The essay first describes the finished product as being square and carefully sealed with no less than twelve cords, a fitting protection for the powerful "weapon" which it contains for the scholar-readers who carry it around their necks.[35] The text then describes in detail the somewhat violent tasks involved in constructing book satchels (and books, for that matter) as it speaks of the "fattened sheep" that had to be slaughtered and then butchered in order to "flay the hairy hide with a sharp knife"; the subsequent stretching of it to dry it with "fiery smoke"; and the cutting and shaping of the satchel by a

---

[34] *Plurifici storn<in>os carnali compage globant amictus, / ostreas pastricant armellosas, / giluas uerticibus alunt mitras, / crispososque sedant cincinnos, / ac librosas copulant tricarias / nitentes ceruicibus gestant curuanas. / Innumeri quadrigonas captant scutilibus peltas, / ferriales uibrant idumis pugiones, / ac altera glomerant plasmamina, / quae temporali propiamine non exprimo.* (*HF*, ll. 503–512): Many heap up motley raiment around their fleshy frames, / gather together purple vestments, / support yellow caps on the crowns of their heads, / smooth their curly locks, / tie their yellow braids, / and carry bright booksacks on their necks.

[35] *Haec alborea exomicat taberna, / quae spissas breuiusculo tegmine artat setas; / quadrigono degestum sutum est figment archimium, / unicam superna amplectitur ianuam ora, / quae stricto asilibus poligonis rotis cluditur operculo, / ac bis senis alligatur adeo restibus, / flexaque a<r>catorum ceruicibus uehitur sarcina.* (*HF*, ll. 513–519): This white satchel gleams, / it has thick bristles that provide a rather small cover; / the aforesaid container is sewn in the shape of a square; / the upper rim surrounds a single opening, / which is closed by a tight covering with many-angled turning knobs, / then is bound by twelve cords, / and the curved load is born on the necks of the scholars.

"proud craftsman" with "tight laces" before finishing the satchel with the final touch of a "choice strap."[36] The essay does not detail the other accessories mentioned in On Many Things, instead deploying the 'unspeakability' motif about them: "I cannot explain with speech the rest of the objects, lest I bring forth weariness in the camps of the learned."[37] We can perhaps read this again as a reminder to the reader that the "weapons" contained within the well-constructed "*armarium*" held within the mind of the appropriately "dressed" scholar-reader is nearly infinite and the possible combinations to produce a truly productive reading experience unique to each scholar-reader. Interestingly, the next essay seems to suggest that the imagined scholar-reader does not pull out a book from his book satchel, with its somewhat static textual contents. Instead, it is about the medieval equivalent of a personal slate, or chalkboard, or white board: a wax writing tablet, a purposefully impermanent way in which to record texts and to transmit knowledge.

Within our interpretive framework of reading techniques and language technologies, On the Writing Tablet (*De tabula*) is arguably the most complex of the series of essays to this point. The poet combines the nature imagery already encountered in the *Hisperica Famina*'s initial sections and integrates it with the description of the construction of a writing tablet in such a way as to echo the description of the construction of the book satchel in the previous essay. The wood used to make the tablet frame is connected to the "leafy oak of a green field" of which it

---

[36] *Huius inclitum depromam curuanae ductum: / saginatas pecodis dudum tegebat pernas, / hirtumque acuto framine decoriauit carnifex corium, / densaque tensum est parieti inter uimina, / ac igneo aruit fumo. / Obansque edictum lacerauit opifex archimium, / astrictis corialem pastricauit corregiis tegulam, / bis binos plasmauit angulos, / lectoque pellicium gestamine perfecit armarium.* (*HF*, ll. 520–528): I shall describe the excellent construction of this book satchel: / not long ago it protected the fattened flesh of a sheep; / a butcher flayed the hairy hide with a sharp knife; / it was stretched on the wall between thick stakes / and dried with fiery smoke. / A proud craftsman cut out the aforesaid container, / drew taut the skin covering with tight laces, / fashioned the four angles, / and finished the leather container with a choice strap.

[37] *Caetera non explico famine schemata, / ne doctoreis suscitauero fastidium castris.* (*HF*, ll. 529–530): I cannot explain with speech the rest of the objects, / lest I bring forth weariness in the camps of the learned.

was a living part before "the artisan cut off a growing branch." These "kindling pieces" are then joined together, embellished with carvings and painted designs, and rubbing wax "from another region" is placed inside to "contain the mysteries of rhetoric in waxen planes."[38] All the components of this wax table are connected to integrated movement, rather than stasis: the dynamism of a frame made of kindling wood that was recently growing; that it is carried rather than held; that its wax comes from far away. All these elements underscore the ephemeral quality of knowledge placed on a wax tablet. As when a teacher or student uses a chalkboard or white board, the knowledge is recorded, read, rubbed out, and something new is written on it: the "mysteries of rhetoric" are constantly in motion if the tablet is in the hands of an engaged scholar-reader. This metaphor of movement is continued in this essay's particular

---

[38] *Haec arborea lectis plasmata est tabula fomentis, / quae ex altero climate caeream copulat lituram. / Defidas lignifero intercessu nectit colomellas, / in quis compta lusit caellatura. / Aliud iam latus arboretum maiusculo ductu stipat situm, / uaria scemicatur picture, / ac comptas artat oras. / Haec olim frondea glaucicomi creuit inter robora fundi. / ferrialique crescentem amputauit opifex secure stipitem, / quadrigonum ligneo dolauit incrementum neruo, / micram eruit ascia margeriam, / ornatamque perfecit tabulam, / quae dexterali historum gestatur iduma, / ac sophica caereis glomerat misteria planetis.* (*HF*, ll. 531–544): This wooden tablet was made from choice pieces; / it contains rubbing wax from another region; / a wooden median joins the little divided columns, / on which lovely carving has played. / The other side has a somewhat larger area of wood; / it is fashioned with various painted designs / and has decorated borders. / This once grew among the leafy oaks of a green fields; / the artisan cut off a growing branch with his iron axe, / hewed the square product out of the fibre of the wood, / carved a small border with his knife, / and finished the embellished tablet, / which is carried in the right hand of the scholars / and contains the mysteries of rhetoric in waxen [planes]. I have chosen to use "planes" for "planetis," as this choice seems more descriptive of the immediate object than Herren's choice of "spheres." That said, metaphorically the notion of the planets as "wanderers" equally underscores the essay's theme of movement (many thanks to the anonymous reader at *PHCC* for pointing out this possibility). Also, Herren notes for "*fomentis*" on line 531, "quite clearly not 'kindling wood,' but simply 'wood.'" I would like to suggest, however, that including the additional possible meaning of "kindling wood" works metaphorically within our framework if a reader thinks of his intellect being ignited or sparked by the "mysteries of rhetoric" that he encounters on this wax tablet.

formation of the 'unspeakability' motif: "Now I shall retreat along my course of words in a trice, / lest I perturb the superior abilities of the rhetoricians."[39] The speaker does not simply stop speaking, but rather must move back—perhaps we should think of him as erasing—his "course of words," in order to create space for those scholars of "superior ability." When placed within our interpretive framework of reading and language technologies, *De tabula* emphasizes active movement and creation of both the tablet itself and its way of containing and transmitting knowledge that is different from that of a book satchel or a book. The reading or acquisition of knowledge is by necessity a communal activity in which the reader-scholar must not only actively engage with the text(s) at hand, but should also be engaging with other reader-scholars, whether those are physically present with him during the reading moment or spiritually with the community that is formed in his memory. The next essay tells the reader that he now has all his tools—physical and mental—at the ready, and it is time to engage actively with the community of ideas that is created when practicing proper *lectio divina*.

There follows the essay On the Chapel (*De oratorio*) which seems to participate in the pattern established by the previous three essays of describing individual elements necessary to a scholarly reading experience. On the Chapel describes the structural and architectural elements of a wooden oratory, and this has led many scholars to use it as evidence for the presence of actual wooden oratories in early medieval Ireland.[40] And it is certainly possible that the poet is writing from life

---

[39] *Nunc loquelarem celery flexu retraho tramitem, / ne ingeniosas rhetorum grauauero domescas.* (*HF*, ll. 545–546): Now I shall retreat along my course of words in a trice, / lest I perturb the superior abilities of the rhetoricians.

[40] *Hoc arboretum candelatis plasmatum est oratorium tabulis, / gemellis conserta biiuguis artat latera; / quadrigona edicti stabilitant fundamenta templi, / quis densum globoso munimine creuit tabulatum, / supernam compaginat camaram, / quadrigona comptis plextra sunt sita tectis. / Ageam copulat in gremio aram, / cui collecti cerimonicant uates missam. / Unicum ab occiduo limite amplectitur ostium, / quod arborea strictis fotis cluditur regia. / Extensum tabulosa stipat porticum collectura, / quaternas summon nectit pinnas. / Innumera congellat plasmamina, / quae non loqueloso explicare famulor turno.* (*HF*, ll. 547–560): This wooden oratory is fashioned out of candle-shaped beams; / it has sides joined by four-fold fastenings; / the square foundations of the said temple give it stability, / from which springs a solid

experience, as have many poets before and after him, and that we do indeed have a description of the material culture present in an early Irish church in much the same way that the few surviving wax writing tablets are indeed made of wooden frames around wax panels. But I would like to follow through on a suggestion made by Niall Brady by placing it within the context of our current interpretive framework. Brady remarks that the word used for "center" or "middle" to indicate the physical location of an altar, *gremium*, can be read metaphorically. Brady writes that *gremium* "is a word with diverse meanings and [. . .] 'centre' and 'middle' are only the most usual translations. The 'bosom' of a church or community can also substitute, along with 'heart' or even 'womb'."[41] This notion of the altar as the "heart," or "womb," or protective "lap," combined with the poet's continued emphasis on wood as a framing device, may suggest that

---

beamwork of massive enclosure; / it has a vaulted roof above; / square beams are placed in the ornamented roof. / It has a holy altar in the centre, / on which the assembled priests celebrate the Mass. / It has a single entrance from the western boundary, / which is closed by a wooden door that seals in the warmth. / An assembly of planks comprises the extensive portico; / there are four steeples at the top. / The chapel contains innumerable objects, / which I shall not struggle to unroll from my wheel of words."

[41] Niall Brady, "*De orotoria*: *Hisperica famina* and Church Building." *Peritia* 11 (1997): 327–335, 330. Brady's essay is another example of looking at the descriptions provided in the *HF* literally, in this case mining the text for what it might tell us about early medieval church construction in Ireland. He notes the multiple meanings for another word, *pinna*, which is usually translated as "steeple" since the building described is a church—though steeples in the modern architectural sense do not seem to have been a part of the early medieval Irish architectural visual vocabulary. Brady suggests, "if 'wing, feather, fin' is substituted a more reasonable solution [to the material interpretation of roof decoration] quickly emerges" (333). Brady connects the use of *pinna* to the wing-like flourishes depicted on the church shown on f. 202v of the Book of Kells (TCD MS 58). Elizabeth Boyle has discussed the allegorical use of feathers as fanciful and absurd roof thatching in *Echtra Cormac i Tir Tairngiri* (see her "Allegory, the *aes dána* and the liberal arts in medieval Irish literature." In *Grammatica, Gramadach and Gramadeg: Vernacular Grammar and Grammarians in Medieval Ireland and Wales*, Deborah Hayden and Paul Russell, eds. (Amsterdam, Philadelphia: John Benjamins Publishing Company, 2016), pp. 11–34). This again suggests that the text of the *HF* demands of its readers the retention of the broadest semantic field possible for even its quotidian vocabulary.

we are to read the wax tablet of the previous essay and this wooden church as analogous to each other. On the most superficial level, both the writing tablet and the church are "square" (*quadrigon-a; -um*), and they are both wooden. But there are important differences between these superficial similarities. The notion of the square form lends a solid foundation to both objects. But, as we have seen, the wood in *De tabula* is associated with dynamic movement: the kindling of ideas, its growth while still out in nature, the carved and painted designs decorating the frame. In contrast to this, the wood of *De oratorio* is associated with protected containment: the "enclosure" is constructed of "solid beamwork"; the roof is vaulted and ornamented; the wooden door at the single entrance "seals [in] the warmth"; and there is the additional protection at the entrance of "an assembly of planks [comprising] the extensive portico." Thus, read metaphorically, the descriptors associated with the wood of each object echo the essential purpose at the "heart" of each object. That is, as the erasable wax at the center of the tablet forms a dynamic medium for the communal exchange of ideas through active ingestion of the text temporarily written on its surface, the warm and attended altar at the center of the church provides the calm thoughtful center from which to perform proper *lectio divina*. Additionally, another deployment of the 'unspeakability' motif that finishes *De Oratorio*, in contrast to that deployed at the end of *De tabula*, emphasizes quiet containment rather than dynamic engagement: "The chapel contains innumerable objects, / which I shall not struggle to unroll from my wheel of words." Here, the poet merely silences his language—he simply will not allow his "wheel of words" to move—rather than actively go back and "erase" his words.

If the previous nine poetic essays are read as forming an interlocking series, rather than as random one-offs, the tenth, On Prayer (*De oration*), may be interpreted as a prayer that a scholar-reader would recite before beginning his meditative reading practice.[42] On Prayer recalls imagery

---

[42] *Supernum uasti posco herum poli– / qui mundanam almo numine condidit molem, / tithico terrestrem obuallat limbo crepidinem, / humanos lecto restaurant uernaculos increment, / glaucicomas folicia strue tegit amurcas, / florigeros alit de tellure culmos, / almi gibrarum turmis collocate premia throni– / mihi aestiuum nauiganti fretum / robustam concede puppim, / ut furibunda euadam discrimina.* (*HF*, ll. 561– 570): I pray the Ruler of the boundless sphere– / Who has created the mass of the world with His benign power, / envelops the rim of the earth with the sea's girdle, /

from all of the preceding poetic essays: "sea's girdle," humanity, trees and their "abundance of leaves," as well as more destructive natural forces in "the stormy strait" through which the speaker says he must "sail." The speaker is clearly about to begin a journey, as the purpose of the prayer is to ask for a "stout ship" in which to safely sail through the storm in order to "escape the baneful judgment." Unlike the other essays, there are no self-conscious asides about attempting to use language to describe something, no invocation of the 'unspeakability' motif, no humility tropes about not wishing to offend superior rhetoricians or scholars. Apparently, this scholar-reader, having described his tools and his potential relationship to them, is now ready and confident in his ability to deploy them. Again, thinking of the poetic essays as a series and within the interpretive framework of *lectio divina* as a practice, On Prayer becomes the metaphorical centering deep breath before beginning a properly executed reading experience. And *De gesta re* becomes a description in "real time" of that reading practice: not a description of the content of the experience (*what* is being read), but of the reading experience itself. As has been shown, if viewed from within our framework, these essays are not on randomly selected topics, but instead in their stated subject matter recall the opening section of the *Hisperica Famina* and the speaker's descriptions of his verbal duel techniques and his suggested course of action for his student-challenger. The final essay about a violent and bloody battle, *De gesta re*—"On Deeds," "On the Doing of Deeds," or "On a Deed Done"—invokes again virtually all the metaphors for the process of reading as a battle or a feast. *De gesta re* becomes a description of what would ensue if the "brigands" of the *Lex diei* broke through the safety of the hostel and the scholars needed to access the additional weapons in their book bags, all of which have been so carefully detailed in the preceding essays.

The opening lines of On the Doing of Deeds (*De gesta re*) mark this essay as very different in tone from the others in that the narrative voice changes to third person and its "once upon a time" signals to the reader

---

restores the human race with a select increment, / covers the grey olive trees with an abundance of leaves, / fosters the shoots as they flower from the earth, / and establishes for masses of men the rewards of His holy kingdom– / grant a stout ship/to me as I sail through the stormy strait, / that I may escape the baneful judgement.

that we have moved into the genre of epic.[43] We read a graphic, bloody description of a hunt for wild boar and the ensuing barbequed pork feast. But unlike the pleasant communal meal between scholars and townsfolk at the hostel in the *Lex diei* section, this meal is indeed a food orgy, with "raw flesh" that drops "liquid gore" and these are "brigands" led by a "powerful chieftain" who "swilled the porky fodder down their throats."[44] The "native inhabitants" then work to protect their "ancestral ploughfields," once they see the brigands out in "the oaks of the forest" and seemingly attack them. There is a battle in which it appears the natives best the brigands, but then the "savage band of robbers" apparently bests the natives.[45] The natives then seem to go home and tell stories; an

---

[43] *Lapsis olim annosae uoraginis stadiis, / rutilante foebei orientis aurora, / quidam furibundus armatorum latrunculus, / externas inimicosae telluris adiit metas.* (*HF*, ll. 571–574): Once upon a time, leagues ago in the whirlpool of the years, / When Phoeban dawn was flashing in the East, / a certain rampaging band of armed brigands / approached the outer boundaries of an enemy land.

[44] *Hinc quadrigona inserta ueribus statuitur craticula, / setosasque roseis torrent toles flamm[e]is, / ac arboreis crudas insuunt sudibus pernas. / Ostrea sanguinei licuminis decidunt inter faces stillicidia, / assataque carnei ponderis gustant armatores frusta, / suillum sorbent faucibus pastum.* (*HF*, ll. 585–590): Then a square gridiron was made from crossed spits, / and they roasted the bristly flesh in the red flames / and attached the raw flesh to wooden stakes. / Purple drops of liquid gore fell among the sticks, / and the brigands tasted roasted morsels of the fleshy mass / and swilled the porky fodder down their throats.

[45] *Hinc progeny istius telluris acculae / extremas natalis soli obuallabant assidue oras, / ne inimicale paternis polleret discrimen sulcis. / Iamque solitis finalis globi lustrantes anfractibus / edictum siluestrea prospectant latrunculum inter robora. / Tum frondens irruente caterua fra[n]goricat saltus, / ac proteruus clamat ilico coetus / quod ex crudely strage non euaderent de agmine superstites, / priusquam atroces alitum ueherent in aethera ungues. / Hinc strictan furibundi densant aciem tyranny, / ac armifera ferunt in cidones rostra. / Alboreum aereo spargitur chimentum sulco, / truces reciproco libramine penetrant dolones, / degestaque carneas terebrant spicula toles, / ac carnifera porporei serpent per latera riui. / Inormes ruunt in obello gigantes / ac assiles soluunt ensibus gigras. / Dum toxicus irruentem certandi robore frangit latrunculus phalangem, / morifera spoliant uestium strue cadauera, / horrendoque iubilant crudeles tumult. / Hinc reduce tramite paternum remeantes in solum / fabulosam exprimunt accolade soriam.* (*HF*, ll. 591–612): Then the native inhabitants of that land / busily began to fortify the outer boundaries of the native soil, / lest a hostile attack prevail over their ancestral ploughfields. / And now traversing

oddly productive note on which to end a description of a battle, which the natives seem to have lost. Herren notes that the hunt scene is very reminiscent of the *Aeneid*, with which I certainly agree. But it and the gluttonous feasting scene following it are also reminiscent of analogous scenes from Irish secular sagas: *Scéla Muicce Meic Dá Thó, Fled Bricrend, Mesca Ulad*, and *Togáil Bruidne Dá Derga* are only a few examples. That said, if we simply read the brigands here as representing "Hisperic," disorganized secular texts and the natives representing "Ausonian," organized sacred, then we are stuck with the sacred texts "losing" the battle against the secular texts.

But if we maintain our framework in which we read the *HF* in general as being about the interrelated skills necessary for proper reading practice and the integration of "sacred" with "secular" textual materials, and that On the Doing of Deeds (*De gesta re*) is a 'real-time' description of that *process*, then we can note that the essay moves from a space of gluttonously excessive, indeed chaotic, actions to one of controlled interaction. The natives first establish boundaries and then attack in an organized fashion. The brigands are nearly routed until they, along with the natives, respond with "battle lines" and engage each other with more control and order. The hunt and unmannerly feast are what happens when a reader allows any type of texts, whether secular or sacred, to run amok, rather than to be controlled through proper *lectio divina* practice. But when properly read and contained—penetrated, decapitated, stripped through a *curiositas* controlling theme or motif—the robbers and natives both retreat "to their home soil on a backward course" and both are victors

---

the familiar bypaths of their boundary-land, / they espied the aforesaid band of brigands among the oaks of the forest. / Then the leafy woodland resounded with the onrushing horde, / and instantly the audacious troop cried out/that no survivors of the force would escape from the cruel slaughter / before the savage claws of birds would bear them into the sky. / Next the raging leaders drew tight their battle lines / and turned their armed faces against the archers. / White stone is shot into the sky, / cruel darts penetrate alternately; / the aforesaid darts pierce meaty limbs, / and rivers of purple wind through fleshy flanks. / Enormous giants rush forward in battle / and sever round heads with their swords. / When the savage band of robbers broke the attacking phalanx with the strength of their fighting, / they stripped the dead bodies of their clothing / and heartlessly rejoiced with terrible shouts. / Then retreating to their home soil on a backward course / the natives poured out a wealth of tales.

who become "the natives [who] poured out a wealth of tales." The gory battle imagery returns us to the same imagery used at the beginning of the Occidental Talkitudes: to the prologue in which the speaker describes himself as a word-warrior, and to the stated fear of "brigands" in the *Lex diei* section, which are kept out of the hostel by the book satchels along the wall. After the description, and assembling, of the tools necessary to engage in organized mental battle in the essays, On the Doing of Deeds provides us with an example of a successful outcome of engaging secular and sacred texts with each other. If the reader follows the advice given in the Prologue, the Twelve Faults of Ausonian Diction, and the Rule of the Day, and then assembles the proper meditative reading tools as described in the ten short essays, the readers' experience will be like the successful battles of On the Doing of Deeds: as both sides retreated to their "homelands" with new "tales" to integrate into their community's existing intellectual culture, so the reader will productively integrate his "Ausonian" knowledge with his "Hisperican."

Setting the *Hisperica Famina* within this interpretive framework, which suggests that this series of poems and poetic essays metaphorically describes the medieval practice of *lectio divina*, is not to suggest that this is the definitive meaning of these texts. Indeed, the multitude of excellent potential interpretations of the *HF* which have been posited over many years by many scholars seems to underscore that these texts were constructed in such a way as to be highly malleable and versatile pieces of literature, and thus useful to many readers for many different purposes. Scholars from diverse disciplines within medieval studies have been able to propose various interpretations of these texts, but the one thing they all share is the drive to construct an interpretive framework that is intertextual in its methodology.

So, in addition to those potential interpretations already mentioned, a linguist and philologist can argue that "the inventiveness shown in these texts is so clearly deliberate that it seems to have constituted one of the main reasons for writing them: it seems that often an obvious word is not used if a neologism can be coined."[46] Anthony Harvey then demonstrates

---

[46] Anthony Harvey. "Blood, Dust and Cucumbers: Constructing the World of Hisperic Latinity." In Emer Purcell, Paul MacCotter, Julianne Nyhan and John Sheehan, eds. *Clerics, Kings, and Vikings: Essays on Medieval Ireland in Honour of Donnchadh Ó Corráin.* (Dublin: Four Courts Press, 2015), 352–362; 353.

how the texts of the *HF* have taken their inspiration for how to coin those neologisms from the work of Virgilius Maro Grammaticus and the methods by which he builds his neologisms. A Celtic Studies scholar who specializes in literature, religion, and mythology can do a comparative intertextual study of the two radically different versions of the essay On the Doing of Deeds as it appears in the A-text and the B-text of the *HF* as he looks to answer the question, "[c]ould this, then, be a case in which a bare 'theme' rather than a textual model was the faminators' starting point?" After John Carey presents several ideas about the different potential sources for the two stories, he suggests that the B-text could be borrowing from oral tradition rather than "learned borrowing."[47] Or Sarah Corrigan, a specialist in Medieval Latin literature, can argue: "that the intention of the authors is to present the reader with *enigmata*, but also with more. [. . .] *Hisperica Famina* incorporates source texts in such a way that prior knowledge of the sources themselves is required of readers if they are to understand fully what they are reading." Corrigan clearly demonstrates that "[t]he complex language in which simple subjects are described contains encoded references to passages in the sources . . . [and] [f]rom these the reader must puzzle out the literary references conjured up from the unnamed sources by playful adaptation and borrowings" by showing the intertextual links between the *HF* and its sea creatures and

---

[47] John Carey, "The Obscurantists and the Sea-Monster: Reflections on the *Hisperica Famina*." *Peritia* 17/18. (2003/04), 40–60; 44; 55. Carey writes, "[w]e shall be looking at the content of these two stories [*De gesta re* as they appear in A-text and B-text] [. . .]Far from there being any such close correspondences of word and phrase as we have been considering up until this point, there is not even any real unity of subject: the A-text describes a swine-poaching foray which provokes a battle, while the B-text speaks of a naval expedition whose climax comes when the entire fleet is swallowed by a sea-monster. The heading *De gesta re* is appropriate enough to both, but this is about all that they have in common." I agree with Carey's assertion that the radical differences between the content of the two texts of *De gesta re* is likely an example of two different rhetoricians working with the same theme but producing very different narratives. I am less certain about the source study aspects of Carey's work, especially since he mentions indigenous Canadian narratives, but neglects to mention the (much closer to home) *immrama* narratives as potential sources for inspiration.

those sea creatures in Pliny's *Naturalis historia.*[48] Each one of these scholars-readers has interpreted the *Hisperica Famina* from within the range of their knowledge and previous reading experiences. And though each has produced a reading quite different from previous readings, each scholar-reader has arguably produced a "correct" interpretation. So perhaps that is where the complexity of language and the multiplicity of possible sources for which the *Hisperica Famina* is justly famous performs its most basic work. It is not only a text that potentially *describes* good *lectio divina* reading practices; it is also one that inspires them.

Acknowledgments

Many thanks to the anonymous reader(s) at *PHCC* for the thoughtful and insightful comments, corrections, and suggestions; this article is much improved because of them. Any remaining errors or oversights are entirely my responsibility.

---

[48]Sarah Corrigan. "Hisperic Enigma Machine: Sea Creatures and Sources in the *Hisperica Famina.*" *Peritia* 24/25. (2013/14), 59–73; 63.

Dom Yann Derrien's Journey to "Sant Jakez an Turki:" European Pilgrimages in Breton Ballads

Éva Guillorel

Dom Yann Derrien is one of the most interesting *gwerzioù* evidenced in Breton oral tradition. It tells how a young priest undertakes a journey to the shrine of Saint James of Compostela. At the beginning of the song, Dom Yann Derrien sees a new star in the sky, which starts to speak to him: it is the penitent soul of his mother. She asks him to carry out on her behalf a pilgrimage she had promised to make when alive: without having accomplished it she cannot gain entry to heaven. The ballad then recounts the long voyage of the priest to Spain in order to save his mother's soul. Among the many Breton ballads dealing with pilgrimages, this one has very distinctive characteristics. A detailed textual and melodic analysis shows that it belongs to the oldest corpus of *gwerzioù* rooted in medieval inspiration whereas most of the other ballads known by ethnographic investigations are not older than the sixteenth or seventeenth centuries.

The characteristics of an ancient *gwerz*

Several criteria support this idea, whether it be the number and distribution of versions, the metric structure, the places of pilgrimages mentioned or other narrative elements.

Twenty-six versions of this song are known, either heard and written down by nineteenth-century folklorists or sound recordings made later from informants having learnt it from oral tradition. Others certainly exist but belong to unavailable private collections. The song is particularly well attested in Vannetais, Upper Cornouaille and Trégor: this cartography reflects first of all the intensity of field recordings made in these areas in the last two centuries.[1] Others are also found in the less prospected Léon,

---

[1] For a French presentation of this song and a map locating the different versions see: Éva Guillorel, *La complainte et la plainte: Chanson, justice, cultures en Bretagne (XVIe–XVIIIe siècles)* (Rennes-Brest: Presses universitaires de Rennes-Dastum-Centre de Recherche Bretonne et Celtique, 2010), 368–376. Four new versions have been found since that publication and have been integrated to the analysis proposed in this article. See also the many versions of songs and folktales gathered by Jean Gauter,

with a version even recorded on the island of Ouessant[2] at the extreme north-west of Brittany in 1906.[3] Although some *gwerzioù* have not circulated beyond a very local perimeter, or are known in a very limited number of versions,[4] a broad geographical circulation associated with a textual and linguistic adaptation to local dialects is the sign of a long period of transmission. This reality, which applies quite well to the case of *Dom Yann Derrien*, is nevertheless common to a large number of *gwerzioù* and we must turn to other features to measure its richness.

Many versions of the song keep traces of a structure in octosyllabic tercets, considered the most ancient metrics of Breton ballads. Some of them alternate tercets with distics whose second verse is repeated; another is structured in quatrains–sometimes deriving in sestets, equivalent to two tercets–with a repetition of the second verse, which corresponds to a structure in three verses remodeled on a four-phrase tune. In a masterly study, the ethnomusicologist Donatien Laurent has described the same metrical structure in *Skolan*, a *gwerz* whose text has great similarities with the Welsh poem *Yscolan* written down in the thirteenth-century *Black book of Carmarthen*.[5] *Dom Yann Derrien* is also well documented in regard to its music, with nine known tunes: their analysis mostly confirms the use of tercets for the melody, sometimes in the form of distics whose second verse is repeated, although simple distics or quatrains are also found.

Mémoire contée et chantée du chemin de saint Jacques en Bretagne (Association bretonne des amis de Saint-Jacques-de-Compostelle, 2015).

[2] In order to facilitate the understanding of place names, they are given from their French form rather than their Breton form throughout this article.

[3] The version from Ouessant is published in: Éva Guillorel, *Barzaz Bro-Leon: Une expérience inédite de collecte en Bretagne* (Rennes-Brest: Presses universitaires de Rennes-Centre de Recherche Bretonne et Celtique, 2013), 336–337.

[4] Two examples are developed in: Donatien Laurent, *Aux sources du Barzaz-Breiz: La mémoire d'un peuple* (Douarnenez: ArMen, 1989), 287–296; Daniel Giraudon, "Itron a Gerizel," *Bulletin de la Société d'Émulation des Côtes-du-Nord* 112 (1984): 60–77.

[5] Donatien Laurent, "La gwerz de Skolan et la légende de Merlin," *Ethnologie française* 1 (1971): 28 and notes p. 44.

DOM YAN DERRIEN

The place names

If we focus now on the text, the place names related to pilgrimages provide an additional clue to place the ballad in a vein of medieval inspiration. The song refers almost always to Saint James of Compostela, except a version mentioning "*Sant Gelvestr Allemang,*" that is Saint Servatius in Maastricht. Both locations correspond to European sanctuaries that attracted Breton pilgrims in the Middle Ages. *Hent sant Jakez*, the 'road to Saint James,' actually designates the Milky Way in Breton as in many other European languages.[6] The twelfth and thirteenth centuries correspond to the golden age of the pilgrimage, although a Breton nobleman undertaking a journey to Compostela is already evidenced as early as the beginning of the eleventh century in the abbey Sainte-Croix-de-Quimperlé's cartulary.[7] By contrast, the *Ancien Régime* period corresponds to a severe decline, so that the historian Georges Provost concludes to a "true indifference of the early modern Breton-speaking people to long distance pilgrimages."[8]

The name of Compostela is never found in ballads and more ancient names are preferred: a song collected in Goudelin by Yann-Fañch Kemener evokes, with some confusion, a journey "*da Sant-Jakez e koste Spagn, / Da Sant-Jakez en Alemagn / Ha da Sant-Jakez Galile*" (To Saint James in Spain, / To Saint James in Germany / And to Saint James in Galilee).[9] Other versions mention '*sant Jakez e Galis*' ('Saint James in

---

[6] René Couffon, "Notes sur les cultes de saint Jacques et de saint Eutrope en Bretagne: Contribution à l'étude des chemins de Compostelle au Moyen-Âge," *Mémoires de la Société d'Histoire et d'Archéologie de Bretagne* 48 (1968): 31–75; Henri Gaidoz and Eugène Rolland, "La voie lactée," *Mélusine* 2 (1884–85): 151–154; Martial Ménard, "Notennoù a-zivout un nebeud anvioù brezhonek a ya da envel ar c'halaksienn Lacteus Orbis," in *Breizh ha Pobloù Europa. Bretagne et Peuples d'Europe: Mélanges en l'honneur de Per Denez*, ed. Herve Ar Bihan (Rennes: Hor Yezh-Klask-Presses universitaires de Rennes, 1999), 457–467.

[7] Herve Bihan, "Un notennoù hag un evezhiadennoù bennak a-zivout Breizh ha Santiago-de-Compostela," *Hor Yezh* 220 (1999), p. 19–41.

[8] Georges Provost, *La fête et le sacré: Pardons et pèlerinages en Bretagne aux XVIIe et XVIIIe siècles* (Paris: Le Cerf, 1998), 123.

[9] This song and a detailed survey of the references to Saint James in dictionaries and literature printed in Breton from the end of the Middle Ages are presented in: Bihan, "Un notennoù."

Galicia') and most of all *'sant Jakez an Turki'* ('Saint James in Turkey') which is the common designation. We find all these names in the Breton written sources, whereas the reference to Compostela appears only in the second half of the eighteenth century. Turkey may be an approximate geographical evocation for Judea, where Saint James's martyrdom is located according to the Acts of the Apostles (12, 1), but it is more certainly a stereotyped place name often used in Breton songs to refer to exotic largely unknown destinations.

The narrative elements

The narrative elements found in *Dom Yann Derrien* are also in favor of a medieval inspiration for this *gwerz*. The return of the penitent soul (Breton *anaon*) of the hero's mother, who cannot find rest before having repaid a debt of two *sous* (a ridiculously small amount of money) owed to her aunt, and most of all before having realized the pilgrimage she had promised, recalls *post mortem* pilgrimages mentioned in late medieval wills, in Brittany or elsewhere: in such documents, the testator required a third person to be paid to undertake the journey instead of him for the repose of his soul. A will written down in 1411 by Jean du Berry, prosecutor in Paris Parliament court, provides that several pilgrimages promised but never made by his wife should be realized, including one to Santiago de Compostela.[10] Many legends and traditions about the *anaon* have been collected by folklorists like Anatole Le Braz in Western Brittany (and published in his famous *Légende de la mort* in 1893) or Albert Poulain in Eastern Brittany in the second half of the twentieth century.[11] A folktale collected earlier by François-Marie Luzel in Plouaret, entitled *Sant Jakes a Galis*, also shows strong similarities with the *gwerz*: the story deals about the penitent soul of a dead husband who asks his

---

[10] "Pour ce que m'a donné à entendre que mad[ite] compaigne avait dévotion de faire un voyage à Saint-Jacques en Galice, combien qu'elle ne m'avait rien déclairé et que je n'y feusse point consenti, toutes voies je veux que l'on y envoye messager certain qui de ce rapportera lettre de certification," cited in: Philippe Ariès, *L'homme devant la mort* (Paris: Seuil, 1977), 77.

[11] Anatole Le Braz, *La Légende de la mort chez les Bretons armoricains* (Paris: Laffont, 1994), 325; Albert Poulain, *Sorcellerie, revenants et croyances en Haute-Bretagne* (Rennes: Ouest-France, 1997), 209–210.

wife to go to Compostela to realize the pilgrimage he had promised when he was alive.[12]

Other unusual motives must be pointed out. Several Vannetais versions of *Dom Yann Derrien* justify the mother's request by the fact that without external help she only progresses the length of her coffin every day on the road to Compostela and will have to stay in the purgatory until she arrives at the sanctuary instead of going to heaven. This reference to purgatory, necessarily later than the twelfth century when this new Christian concept started to be developed,[13] appears only in five versions. Others mention a red rooster or a black dog, corresponding to two different forms of the devil which try to prevent the priest from reaching his destination.

After a journey rife with difficulties, some versions end with the description of the edifying and holy death of the pilgrim once his task has been accomplished. In the song collected by Yann-Fañch Kemener in Laniscat (Upper Cornouaille), the priest's sister approaches him in order to wipe the sweat from his brow–a gesture which recollects that of Veronica wiping the face of Jesus as he climbs up to Golgotha.[14] But the Breton priest replies: "*Ma c'hoer Vari, 'ma zorchit ket; / Glizh ar maro a dorchihet*" (My sister Mari, do not wipe my face; / It is the dew of death you would wipe away).[15] Another text has the pilgrim return with a handkerchief which he gives his sister, saying that she must never wash it for "*goad hon Zalver a zo enn-han*" (the Saviour's blood is on it). When the young woman, unbelieving, dips the cloth in the river where she is doing her washing, the water dries up miraculously.[16] All these narrative elements, very uncommon in the repertoire of *gwerzioù*, reinforce the

---

[12] Published in: François-Marie Luzel, *Contes inédits: Carnets de collectage III*, ed. Françoise Morvan (Rennes: Presses universitaires de Rennes-Terre de Brume, 1996): 414–417. The pilgrimage to Compostela is also mentioned in other folktales collected by Luzel; for this aspect see: Bihan, "Un notennoù," 27–28.

[13] Jacques Le Goff, *La naissance du Purgatoire* (Paris: Gallimard, 1981).

[14] This scene does not appear in the episodes of the Passion in the New Testament but has been nonetheless largely spread in the occidental Christianity.

[15] Yann-Fañch Kemener, *Carnets de route* (Morlaix: Skol Vreizh, 1996), 95.

[16] Collected by Jean-Marie de Penguern and published in *Dastumad Penwern. Chants populaires bretons de la collection de Penguern* (Rennes: Dastum, 1983), 327–330.

impression of a song more ancient than most of the ballads collected in the nineteenth or twentieth century.

The account of a distant journey

The *gwerz* about *Dom Yann Derrien* is also of interest for its account of the different steps of a distant pilgrimage characterized by a long and risky journey. One verse repeated at various points gives rhythm to this narration: "*hir eo an hent ha pell mont di!*" (the way is long and it is far to go).[17] The priest goes away for a voyage of several months, if not several years, and the travel preparations are detailed with very concrete details: persuading family and friends to let him go, finding money for the journey (400 or 500 *écus* that he has to borrow from his father or brothers and sisters) and choosing the right attire (a dozen of shirts and surplices as well as "*un daou pe dri boned kare, / Gollin ket ma ano 'veleg*'" ('two or three square caps / So that I won't lose the name of priest). One version collected in Upper Cornouaille notes that he should learn "*seiz sort langach*" (seven kinds of languages), a symbolic number which underlines the difficulty of the enterprise but which is not that far of the reality if we count the number of different linguistic areas one must cross between Lower Brittany and Galicia.[18]

The journey begins by land to reach the Breton coasts and then continues by sea. The obstacles, both natural and supernatural, are legion. Dom Yann Derrien is harassed by evil beasts. His ship is then attacked and he is taken prisoner by Moorish or Turkish pirates who reproach him for his Catholic faith. All these elements echo the maritime insecurity linked to mostly Muslim piracy on the European coasts, although Christian ships also participated in such attacks in the context of political rivalries between kingdoms. Written sources corroborate the descriptions of the song: in 1417, during the One Hundred Years' War, the ship of Jean Moisan, from Western Brittany, was captured by pirates from Plymouth as he returned from Santiago de Compostela, in a situation very similar to the Breton pilgrims from Dol who were attacked in 1379 by a ship from Exeter. The contrary is also true: in the fifteenth century, Breton pirates

---

[17] A variant tells: "*Hir é en hent, en dud zo kri*" (the way is long and the people are cruel).
[18] Kemener, *Carnets de route*, 95.

lashed out at ships conveying English pilgrims by order of the Duke of Brittany.[19] Similar dangers appear in another less often collected *gwerz* evoking the same destination through the story of a young female pilgrim abducted by Sarracens on the road to Compostela.[20]

It is only thanks to a sequence of miracles that Dom Yann Derrien achieves his goal: as he lies at the bottom of sea, Saint James answers his prayers and sends him to Turkey in an instant. There he can celebrate the requested masses and returns safe and sound to Brittany by the same miraculous process. Some versions specify that he returns from Compostela on the very day his family, thinking him dead after many long months away, is holding his funeral: he actually makes his last sigh after gaining the certainty that his mother can now reach paradise.

The pilgrimage to Saint James of Compostela among the repertoire of *gwerzioù*

Beyond the analysis of this song, the contextualization of *Dom Yann Derrien* in the wider repertoire of *gwerzioù* allows further measurement of its specificity, especially with regard to pilgrimage practices. These are very often mentioned in songs: such an abundance reflects particularly prevailing practices in Lower Brittany until today, well-documented thanks to many written and iconographic sources and usually called '*pardon.*'

Sanctuaries outside of Brittany are very rarely mentioned, Saint James of Compostela being by far the most frequent: Rome and the Jordan Valley also appear anecdotally. Breton destinations are clearly privileged, especially four major sanctuaries: Le Folgoët in Léon, Le Yaudet and Saint-Jean-du-Doigt in Trégor as well as Sainte-Anne-d'Auray in Vannetais. This geography corresponds to cultural practices that can be

---

[19] Couffon, "Notes," 37; Guillaume Mollat, *Études et documents sur l'Histoire de Bretagne (XIIe–XVIe siècles)* (Paris: Champion), 191–192. Other historical examples of Breton pilgrims going to Compostela are listed from ducal archives in: Agnès Le Lay, "Le pèlerinage des Bretons à Saint-Jacques de Compostelle," in *Bretagne et religion*, ed. Christian Brunel, vol. 2 (Rennes: Travaux de la section Religion de l'Institut culturel de Bretagne, 1997), 121–134.

[20] See among others the version published by François Marie-Luzel, *Chants et chansons populaires de la Basse-Bretagne: Gwerziou II* (Paris: Maisonneuve & Larose, 1971), 20–23.

precisely dated: these places are the most frequented sanctuaries in the seventeenth and eighteenth centuries. After a medieval period under the sign of openness to the great circuits of European pilgrimages, the devotional mobility in Western Brittany was then characterized by a local transposition of these, encouraged by the Catholic Reformation and paving the way for a phase of geographical retreat on Breton pardons between the end of the Middle Ages and the sixteenth century: this 'Low-Breton autarky'[21] originates in cultural particularities specific to Breton-speaking Brittany. The *pardon* to Le Yaudet, very often mentioned in *gwerzioù*, peaked in the second half of the seventeenth century and in the first decades of the eighteenth century, before a significant decline also perceptible in the sanctuary of Le Folgoët, well established since the fourteenth century.[22] All written archives also coincide in affirming that the seventeenth century is the golden age of Sainte-Anne-d'Auray, a pilgrimage established from 1625 after the local peasant Yves Nicolazic discovered a statue of Saint Anne in a field.[23]

All these pilgrimages do not lose their prestige after the end of the eighteenth century, and their great vitality is still widely attested by the folklorists of the nineteenth century.[24] However, the rarity of mentions in *gwerziou* to pardons that were booming in the nineteenth century, such as Bulat or Sainte-Anne-la-Palud, pleads in favor of a cultural dating of these songs during the *Ancien Régime*.[25]

The internal analysis of *Dom Yann Derrien* (structure, text, tune, narrative motives) based on the comparison between the multiple known variants recorded in oral tradition, as well as the parallel between this *gwerz* and others evoking the theme of pilgrimages and pious devotions,

---

[21] Georges Provost, "Le pèlerinage en Bretagne aux XVIIe et XVIIIe siècles" (Rennes: Ph.D., 1995), 269.

[22] Louis Kerbiriou, *Notre-Dame du Folgoët: Un grand sanctuaire marial en Bretagne. Notice descriptive, historique et archéologiqu*e (Brest: Louis Le Grand, 1938), 12–16.

[23] J. Buléon and E. Le Garrec, *Sainte-Anne d'Auray, Histoire d'un village: Ses origines, son histoire au XVIIe-XVIIIe siècle* (Vannes: Lafolye, 1924), 37–68.

[24] Especially in: Anatole Le Braz, *Au Pays des Pardons* (Rennes: H. Caillière, 1898).

[25] For a developed approach to the methodology of cultural dating of *gwerziou* and a detailed study on the geographical distribution of pilgrimages in Breton songs see: Guillorel, *La complainte.*

allow to underline its originality and antiquity. Although it is impossible to give a precise date for this cultural production having circulated orally–no written trace is known until the nineteenth century, as is the case for almost all Breton ballads–there are many arguments for medieval inspiration, whereas most of the *gwerzioù* collected since the first ethnographic investigations relate to the end of the sixteenth century and more broadly to the seventeenth and eighteenth centuries. *Dom Yann Derrien* thus presents a very interesting mix between literary motives relating to the supernatural dimension in Christianity and narrative details that are historically credible in the context of the central and late Middle Ages, developed through a metric structure bearing the trace of archaisms. All this gives this *gwerz* a feeling of strangeness that surrounds it with a special atmosphere around the topic of a religious practice–pilgrimages–deeply rooted in Breton history and culture over time.

ÉVA GUILLOREL

Appendix: Dom Jean Derrian, two versions of the *gwerz*

Version A: Version collected by Augustin Guillevic in Melrand (Morbihan) in 1883.

Dom Jean Derrian, through glass (x2) Noticed a star (x2)	*Dom Jean Derrian dré ur huiren* (x2) *E remerkas ur stireden* (x2)
And it was like a woman Suffering great pain.	*Hanval mat e oé d'oh ur voéz* *E vehé bet é creis er gloéz.*
Dom Jean Derrian swiftly went To talk with her, and said	*Dom Jean Derrian aben e yas* *De gonz dehi, hag e laras :*
– Star, tell me now What is it that you represent?	*– "Stireden, d'ein é larehet* *Petra é représantehet ?*
– My darling boy, do you not know? I am the one who gave birth to you.	*– Me mabig peur, ne ouiet ket* *Mé-é en hani dès hou kaññet.*
– If you are the one who gave birth to me Where do you come from, and where are you going?	*– M'ar d'oh en hani dès me gaññet* *A b'ban é tet, ha men é het ?*
– I'm going to Santiago in Galicia Where God in his justice has sent me.	*– E han de San Jacque é Galice,* *Léh me has Doué en é justis.*
My son, pity me – I only progress The length of my coffin every day.	*D'oh ein, me mab, hou péet truhé* *Ne rhan meit hèd me hleur bamdé.*
– O mother dear, please tell me If I may go on your behalf.	*– Me mammig peur, d'ein larehet* *Eit oh m'ar don mad de vonnet.*
– Yes, my son, but I say to you now, It will take you all the time you have:	*– Ya, mès, me mab, me larou d'oh,* *Ol hou ç'amzér e riñkehoh.*
And, in addition, four hundred *écus* Which you will also have to find.	*Hag eit hou tispãgn piar hant scouët,* *E vehé hoah ret d'oh cavet.*

135

DOM YAN DERRIEN

– Mother dear, go no further
I will make the journey on your behalf.

– If you make this journey for my sake
Sleep at night, walk during the day

Or else a wicked beast will find you
And tear you to pieces on the spot.

– My dear mother, I will not fail
To do everything just as you have said.

– Go then, and say to your brothers
'I have a voyage to make'.

Soon after, his brothers gathered round,
Dom Jean Derrian said

– I have to go on a long journey
But I will need four or five hundred écus.

No-one replied to this
But his sister Mari, who said

– Now that you are a priest
You want to travel the world.

– I am not travelling the world
I want to go to Santiago

To Santiago, my sister Mari
For my mother and yours

And there I will say the mass
That she has long been asking for.

– Me mammig peur, n' det ket pelloh,
Me hrei er voyaj aveit oh.

– M'ar groet eit on er voyaj-sé
Kousket de noz, kerrhet d'en dé.

Pé ur loñnig vil hou kavou
Ha kent pêl, hi hou tispennou.

– Me mamig peur, sur ne vankein
D'hobér er peh e laret d'ein.

– Kerrhet enta, ha d'hou preder,
Laret: "M'ès hur voyaj d'hobér."

Kent pêl, d'hé verdér dastumet
Dom Jean Derrian en doé laret :

"D'hobér ur voyaj pêl é han
Mès piar, pemb kant scouët e rinkan."

Hañni dehou ne reskondas
Mès é hoér Mari e laras :

– "Berman m'en d'oh hui beléguet,
Guelet bro aben é klasket.

– Dé ket de redek bro é han
Monnet de Sant Jacque é houlennan.

Monn't de Sant Jacque, me hoèr Mari,
Aveit me mam hag hou ç'hani.

Laret enou en overen,
E ma guerço d'oh é goulen."

Scarcely had he finished speaking When his eyes filled with tears.	*N'oé ket achiùet hoah é lar,* *P'oé lan é zeulegad a zar.*
– Go, brother mine, oh yes go Make that journey you have promised.	*– "Kerrhet, mem brér, oh ya, kerrhet,* *Groeit er voyaj e huès grateit.*
– Mother dearest, I will redeem you Heaven's gate will open for you.	*– Me mamig peur, m'hou télivrou,* *Hag en néan d'oh me zigourou.*
Brothers, I bid you farewell Pray God that I will return	*Mem berder, d'oh hui kenavo,* *Pedet Doué eit ma t'ein én dro*
If I do not return within seven years Hold my funeral mass, and my octave.	*Ben seih vlé m'ar n'arrihuant ket* *Groeit m'interr'mant ha me eihved."*
And so Dom Jean Derrian set about His voyage with great joy	*Nezé Dom Jean Derrian e yas* *D'hobér er voyaj get joé bras.*
Often he was seen reciting The prayer for the departed.	*Liés é oé guélet é laret* *Pedenneu er ré trémenet.*
But when he arrived at the coast He had a terrible fright	*Ar vord er mor p'oé arriùet,* *En hum gavas skontet meurbet.*
A little red cock appeared And said to him at once	*Hur hogic ru hum brezantas* *Ha dehou aben e laras :*
– Where are you going, night-traveller Disturbing me in my sleep?	*– "Men é het-hui, filajour noz,* *Deit d'em jeînein é me repoz ?*
Retrace your steps, return whence you came Or I will fling you into the sea.	*Troeit hou rodeu, kerrhet en dro,* *Pé é kreis er mor m'hou taulo.*
– Oh Lord, give me your aid I wish I were at Santiago.	*– Tré Doué, nehoah, emb sekouret,* *É Sant Jacque é karehen bet."*

Scarcely had he spoken these words When he found himself at the entrance to Santiago.	*N'oé ket hoah é gonz reih laret Pe oé ar drézen Sant Jacque rantet.*
– *Monsieur* priest, give me, I beg Permission to hold a mass	– *"Eutru Person, m'hou ped, reit d'ein Permission d'overennein,*
To say my mass here As my poor mother asked.	*De laret amen m'overen, E ma m' mam peur d'oh é goulen."*
With great devotion for his mother's sake He paid God his ransom.	*Eit é vam get dévotion Ean bayas de Zoué é ranson.*
As Dom Jean Derrien made his way home He found himself wrapped in a brightness	*Dom Jean Derrian é tonn't d'er gér, Hum gavas groñnet a sklerdér.*
Shining in brilliance above his head He saw a star,	*Ligernus bras a drest é ben Ean e huélas ur stireden.*
And it was like a woman Who might be in the very midst of joy.	*Hanval mad d'oh ur voés e oé, E vehé bet é kreis er joé.*

ÉVA GUILLOREL

Version B: Unsourced version written down in Jean-Marie de Penguern's
manuscript collection of songs, mid-nineteenth century.[26]

– Dom Iann Derrien, you are lying On a bed of soft feathers, and I am not!	– *Dom Iann Derrien te a zo kousket War ar plun fin, me ne maon ked !*
– Who is here right now? It is already late at night.	– *Piou zo aze d'ar poent ma ? Pellik en noz e zeo dija.*
– Dom Iann Derrien, I am your mother Who is in the purgatory amid the flames	– *Dom Iann Derrien me eo ta vam Zo er Purgator e kreis ar flam*
And who will stay there forever I you don't help me, Dom Iann Derrien	*Hag a vezo da virviken Ma nem sikoures, Dom Iann Derrien !*
When I lived on earth And pregnant with you, my son priest, I promised to go to Saint-Jean,	*Pa voan war an douer o kerzet Eus ho tougen ma mab Belek Da Sant Iann moa laret monet.*
To Saint-Jean, Le Yaudet, and to the blessed Saint James	*Na da Sant Iann, a dar Ieodet, A da Sant Jakes viniget*
To Saint James in Turkey The way is long and it is far to go!	*A da Sant Jakes a Durki Hir eo an hent, pel eo mont di !*
The poor soul in pain was sighing, Dom Iann Derrien comforted her:	*An anaön kes a hirvoude, Dom Iann Derrien, en konsole :*
– Keep quiet, mother, don't cry, I will make sure you are rescued.	– *Tewet, ma mam, na voelet ket, Me reï ma veet sikouret.*
My poor mother, tell me, What is your mind still concerned about?	*Ma mammik paour din a leret Petra c'heus c'hoas war ho speret ?*

---

[26] Bibliothèque nationale de France, Coll. Penguern, ms. 95, f. 102v–110v. Unknown tune. English translation by Éva Guillorel.

139

– I owe your aunt two *sous*,
Those are still concerns of mine.

– Keep quiet, mother, don't cry,
These two *sous* will be paid.

Dom Iann Derrien said
To his eldest sister three days later:

– Prepare me in a small travel bag
A little money, some laundry

To wipe away sweat and tears,
I will now go across the country.

– What crime did you commit,
If you have to leave the country?

– I am going to Saint-Jean, Le Yaudet,
and to the blessed Saint James

To Saint James in Turkey
For your mother and mine,
The way is long and it is far to go!

– If you obeyed me,
You would send a messenger.

– I will certainly not send a messenger,
I alone have to go.

Dom Iann Derrien said
When he came out of the house:

– If I don't come back in six months,
Say my octave and my service

– *Daou guennek e klefoant d'ho moëreb*
Reze c'hoas so war ma speret.

– *Tewet ma mam na welet ket*
An daou guennek se vo pêet.

Dom Iann Derrien a lavare
D'he c'hoar henan tri de goude :

– *Dastum din en eur fakik veac'h,*
Eun toullet arc'hant, a lienach,

Da sec'hi ar c'hoëz hag an daëro,
Me a ia breman da foëta bro.

– *Petra an torfet o c'heus gret*
Ma er mes ar bro e renket monet ?

– *Me a ia da Saint Iann, a d'ar Ieodet,*
A da Sant Jakes viniget,

A da Sant Jakes a turki,
Evit ta vam a ma hini
Hir eo an hent, pel eo mont di !

Ma vije ouzin e sentjac'h
Vije kas kannad e rajac'h.

– *Kannadet sur ne gasinn ket,*
Me ma hunan renko monet.

Dom Iann Derrien a lavare
Deus er ger na pa sortie :

– *Ma na retornan varben c'hoec'h mis*
Gret ma eïsvet ha ma servis

Say my octave and my service And my anniversary mass according to custom.	*Gret ma eïsvet ha ma servis* *A ma de-a-bla herve er his.*
When he came to the coast He found a ship.	*Pa erruaz e bord an od* *Kavas eur batiment war flod.*
– Master of the ship, tell me, Would you take me in your boat?	*– Na mest al lestr, lerit-hu diñ* *Ha c'houi em c'hemerfe n'ho ti ?*
I am going to Spain You will be paid as you wish.	*Petek bro Spaign ma stremenet,* *Peet vefet vel ma keret.*
When they were at sea The master said:	*Pa woant war ar mor em lestret* *Ar mest en deveus lavaret :*
– Climb on the highest mast To find out where we are here.	*– Pignet da vek 'r wern huelan* *Da c'hout pelec'h ez omp aman ?*
The sailors said On the ship's deck when they went down:	*Ar verdidi a lavarent* *War bont al lestr pa ziskennent*
– We went up as high as we could And we saw nothing	*– Huelan ma hellemp e zomp bet* *Na netra na momp bed gwelet*
Except for three large masted ships We fear they will be Moors!	*Nemet taer lestr bras a gwerniet* *Aon momp e zint moroet !*
The big Moor said To the master of the ship after saluting him:	*Ar Moro bras a lavare* *D'ar mestr al lestr p'hen salude :*
– Master of the ship, tell me, What do you hide in your ship?	*– Na mestr al lestr, larest-te din* *Petra e t'eus kuzet n'ez ti ?*
– Poor Dom Iann Derrien Who is here to do penance	*– Na n'eo ar paour Dom Iann Derrien* *Zo aze c'hober pinijen*

DOM YAN DERRIEN

Who does a hard penance For his dead mother.	*O c'hober pinijen garo* *Evit he vamm a zo maro.*
The big Moor said To Dom Iann Derrien that day:	*Ar Moro bras a lavare* *Da Dom Iann Derrien an de se :*
– You will renounce your god Or I will throw you overboard.	*– Pe renonç a ri d'as toue* *Pe me stollo war da ben, aze.*
– Throw me anywhere you want, I will not renounce my god.	*– Va zollit e lec'h ma keret,* *Evit dam Doue ne renonçin ket.*
Scarcely had he finished talking When he was thrown overboard in the sea.	*Ne wa ket e c'her peurlavaret* *War he pen er mor ne voa tolet.*
We could hear Dom Iann Derrien At the bottom of sea that said:	*Dom Iann Derrien a we klevet* *Er goelet ar mor e lavaret :*
– Blessed Saint James, I have seen your church and your cemetery.	*– Otro Sant Jakes viniget* *Goël a ren ho iliz hag ho veret.*
I just wanted to go, I had three masses to say	*Din me a moa c'hoant da vonet* *Teïr offern em boa da lavaret.*
One for the Holy Spirit, Another for the one who is in pain	*Unan evit ar spered glan,* *Unal evit an eb zo en poan*
Another for the one who is in pain And one for myself.	*Unal evit an eb zo en poan* *Hag unal evit on va hunan.*
Scarcely had he finished talking When he entered the church of Saint James.	*Ne woa ket he c'her peurlavaret* *En Iliz Sant Jakes e c'heo antreet.*
– Could I not have water and white wine And anyone to attend my mass?	*– Ma mije me dour a gwin gwen,* *Unan da respont va offern ?*

Scarcely had he finished talking When water and white wine were brought to him	*Ne voa ked he c'her peurlavaret* *Dour a gwin gwen dean zo rentet*
Water and white wine were brought to him And someone to attend his mass.	*Rentet eus dean dour a gwin gwen,* *Unan da respont he offern.*
When he had said his masses He threw himself at the foot of the saint:	*Pa voa he offerenou laret* *Da dreid ar Sant eo n'em strinket :*
– Blessed Saint James, You have worked miracles for me	*– Otro Sant Jakes viniget,* *Miraklo em andret o c'heus gret ;*
Would you work another one By sending me home among mine?	*A c'hoas e raffer eur burzud* *Va renter er ger e touës va zud.*
Dom Iann Derrien asked At his parish church, when he arrived:	*Dom Iann Derrien a c'houlenne* *Ne Iliz parrous pa n'arrue :*
– What is new in this village That I see people who mourn?	*– Para neve bars er bourg man* *Ma welan tud en kaon hennan ?*
– A young priest has left, He has not been back in two years, His parents are grieving in the cemetery.	*– Eur Belek iaouank zo sortiet,* *Boë daou vla ne ket retornet* *E dud zo n' kaon bars er verret.*
– Change the bells, The priest has returned.	*– Leket er kleïer da chanj son,* *Arru er Belek bars er c'hanton.*

William Rooney: The Celtic Literary Society and the Gaelic League?

Brian Ó Conchubhair

> The name William Rooney has long been familiar to historians of Ireland . . . yet he remains an elusive figure.[1]

> Rooney is indeed an important figure who is rarely considered, . . .[2]

Now largely effaced from the collective memory, the Celtic Literary Society, as distinct from the Irish Celtic Society,[3] provides a useful point of reference to critique Conradh na Gaeilge/The Gaelic League's radicalism, conservatism, growth and influence. Ultimately, the Celtic Literary Society's willingness to integrate with other cultural and political groups, rather than form strategic alliances, damaged it. The decision to merge with other organizations such as Maud Gonne's radical Inghinidhe na hÉireann and affiliate with Cumann na nGaedheal, founded in September 1900,[4] is no less important. The combination of these factors saw the Society lose its distinctive identity and specific focus; simultaneously, it rendered the Gaelic League the primary Irish-language organization not only in Dublin, but in Ireland and further afield. It also solidified the League's position as defender and voice of the some one million Irish speakers on the island. Its slippage from cultural memory may be attributed to a combination of factors including, in no small part, the early death of its founding member, William Rooney. This essay traces Rooney's short life and the rise and fall of the Celtic Literary Society. In

---

[1] Matthew Kelly, ". . . and William Rooney spoke in Irish." *History Ireland* 15, no. 1 (Jan/Feb. 2007): 30–34. https://www.historyireland.com/20th-century-contemporary-history/and-william-rooney-spoke-in-irish/

[2] Nelson Ó Ceallaigh Ritschel, "William Rooney," *History Ireland* 15, no. 2 (Mar/Apr. 2007): 8.

[3] Founded in Dublin in 1845 with a view of cultivating and more widely diffusing a knowledge of the language, history, antiquities, bardic remains, &c. of Ireland.

[4] "Basically a front for the IRB (Irish Republican Brotherhood)" see Brian Maye, *Arthur Griffith* (Dublin: Griffith College Publications, 1997), 94–95.

sketching the Society's arc, it illuminates the complexity, interdependency and overlapping agendas that existed during the Irish Revival. Rooney and the Celtic Literary Society, nonetheless, are essential to understanding how the Gaelic League rationalized itself within the wider Irish-Ireland cultural nationalist project. As an alternative to the vision offered by Douglas Hyde, D.P. Moran and W.B. Yeats, Rooney is essential to appreciating the Irish Revival's complexity and diversity. Reintroducing the Celtic Literary Society into the narrative of the Irish Revival not only disturbs the simple narrative proposed by Yeats and long favored by historians but also reconstructs the internal rivalries, tensions and alliances between various organizations–the Society for the Preservation of the Irish Language, Gaelic League, Gaelic Union, Celtic Literary Society and the Leinster Literary Society.

The Celtic Literary Society is indistinguishable from William Rooney. Writing of Cumann na nGaedheal in 1967, T.P. O'Neill wrote that Rooney was "a guiding spirit in its activities . . . It was not a cultural society alone for it also had a political policy, . . ."[5] Some fifty years later, in 2007, Ó Ceallaigh Ritschel posited that "Arthur Griffith's papers, especially *The United Irishman* (1899–1906) and *Sinn Féin* (1906–14), may have been more radical had the working-class Rooney lived and remained at Griffith's side."[6] Best known in popular culture as the author of once-popular songs such as "The Men of the West", "Ninety Eight", and "An tSean Bhean Bhocht", Rooney, at the time of his premature death in 1901, represented the great hope of nationalist Ireland. Had he lived, he may well have become a central figure in Irish cultural and nationalist politics. As Shovlin speculates, "[w]hat role he might have played in the new Ireland must remain moot, but it is likely that he would have become a significant actor in the move towards independence: his best friend Griffith, after all, became the Free State's first leader in 1922."[7]

---

[5] T.P. O'Neill, *Irish Press*, 6 September 1967, 8.

[6] Ó Ceallaigh Ritschel, "William Rooney," 8.

[7] Frank Shovlin, "Who Was Father Conroy?: James Joyce, William Rooney, and 'The Priest of Adergool,'" *James Joyce Quarterly* 47, no. 2 (Winter 2010): 257.

The 1901 census records his father, Patrick (59 years old and a speaker of Irish and English), as a Dublin tradesman and coachbuilder.[8] He had also participated in the 1867 Fenian uprising and served as a leader of the veterans' Old Guard Union.[9] William Rooney was apparently born in October[10] 1873 at 39 Mabbot Street, a tenement building in Dublin's Monto district.[11] Rooney, according to Connolly, was the eldest of a family of seven, with four brothers and two sisters.[12] In 1901, the family resided at Leinster Avenue, North Dock, Dublin and consisted of Patrick (58); Theresa (53); Patrick[13] (20); John (24); Luke (18)[14] and Judith (22). Educated by the Christian Brothers in Dublin's Great Strand Street, and for a short period at the Brothers' Richmond Street School,[15] he became a junior clerk in a solicitor's office in Dame Street,[16] according to Bradley, when he was about twelve years of age. Nonetheless, he continued nighttime education to complete the Intermediate Examination, Junior Grade in 1887.[17] He achieved honors in English, Algebra, and a pass in

---

[8] Tomas S. Cuff, "The 40th Anniversary of the Death of William Rooney occurs in this month," *Irish Press*, 17 May 1941, 2.

[9] David Connolly, "'The real founder of Sinn Féin' William Rooney (Liam Ó Maolruanaidh), 1873–1901," 1 June 2017 http://www.anphoblacht.com/contents/ 26896. Pádraic Óg Ó Conaire, in *Liam Ó Maolruanaidh 1897–1901* (Dublin: Clódhanna Teo., 1975, reprinted from the Capuchin Annual), suggest the family originated in Mayo, hence Rooney's attraction for the country and frequent trips there.

[10] Connolly suggests 29 September 1873, while Bradley suggests 20 October 1873.

[11] See Matthew Kelly, http://www.generalmichaelcollins.com/life-times/1905-founding-sinn-fein/william-rooney-sinn-fein/

[12] Connolly, "'The real founder of Sinn Féin' William Rooney (Liam Ó Maolruanaidh), 1873–1901." While several sources list Mabbot Street, Ó Conaire, states that Rooney's birthplace was 23 Leinster Avenue, North Strand.

[13] Participated in the 1916 Rising in St. Stephen's Green. See Ó Conaire, *Liam Ó Maolruanaidh 1897–1901*, 7.

[14] Also participated in the 1916 Rising in Finglas. See Ó Conaire, *Liam Ó Maolruanaidh 1897–1901*, 7.

[15] Patrick Bradley, "William Rooney–A Sketch of his Career," *Poems and Ballads: William Rooney* (Dublin: *The United Irishman*, 17 Fownes Street, n.d.), xiv.

[16] Ibid., xiv.

[17] Connolly, "'The real founder of Sinn Féin' William Rooney (Liam Ó Maolruanaidh), 1873–1901."

Arithmetic, Chemistry, Philosophy and Drawing.[18] Reluctant to apply for a position in the Civil Service in case of an overseas posting, he also rejected, allegedly at his mother's behest, a position with a Limerick newspaper.[19] Soon after commencing work in Dame Street, he switched to a new clerical position with the Midland Great Western Railway and worked in a North Strand office. Later, he unsuccessfully applied for a position as a schools' attendance officer.[20]

Typical of his generation, he joined the Fireside Club,[21] "the largest children's association in Ireland in the late 1880s."[22] Cultural nationalism shaped its teachings: the academic study of the Irish language, history, and literature, as well as social instruction concerning equality of the sexes, self-sufficiency, independence, and unity as a prerequisite for social progress.[23] These activities introduced him to Arthur Griffith, who become his confidant.[24] With Henry Egan Kenny ("Sean-Ghall"), Rooney established the City of Dublin Branch of the Irish Fireside Club in late 1888.[25] Their meetings convened initially at Dame Street and later at Clarendon Street.[26] The club decided to establish an Irish-language class and wrote to the Society for the Preservation of the Irish Language (SPIL) seeking an instructor. Consequently, Richard Joseph O'Mulrennin became the club's Irish-language instructor. O'Mulrennan, who wrote for *Irisleabhar na Gaedhilge* as "Clann Conchubhair," had previously taught

---

[18] Ó Conaire, Liam Ó Maolruanaidh 1897–1901, 4.

[19] Ibid., 3.

[20] Ibid., 9. It is also suggested that Rooney worked at Wallis's (carriers for the Post Office). See J.J. O'Kelly ('Sceilig'), Bureau of Military History, Witness Statement 384, 4–5.

[21] Nollaig Mac Congáil, "Weekly Freeman agus Irish Fireside Club ag Cothú an Náisiúnachais agus an Ghaelachais. Bealach na hÓige?" *Seanchas Ardmhacha: Journal of the Armagh Diocesan Historical Society* 21, no. 2 & 22, no. 1 (2007/2008), 278–318.

[22] Ríona Nic Congáil, "'Fiction, Amusement, Instruction': The Irish Fireside Club and the Educational Ideology of the Gaelic League," *Éire-Ireland* 44, no. 1&2 (2009), 91–117.

[23] Ibid.

[24] Ó Conaire, 5.

[25] Nic Congáil, 104.

[26] Bradley, xvi.

Irish in Louvain in Belgium. Returning to Ireland in 1876, he worked as the "Agricultural Editor" for the *Freeman's Weekly* and is frequently presumed to be the source for Joyce's famous line in *A Portrait of the Artist as a Young Man* that "John Francis Mulrennan has just returned from the west of Ireland. European and Asiatic papers please copy." Rooney proved an able student and O'Mulrennan a competent teacher. Within a few short years, Rooney delivered a speech in Irish at the laying of the foundation stone for the Wolfe Tone statue. In 1889, Rooney read two papers to the Club on the topics of "Some Minor Irish Litterateurs" and "Illustrious Irishmen," which, according to Bradley, "both in style and treatment, and in the evidence they exhibit of research and wide reading, were far above the average work of a boy who had not yet completed his sixteenth year."[27] In 1890, Bradley's account sees Rooney joining the Leinster Literary Society where he also read papers, and in June 1891 he published his first poems in *United Ireland*.[28] His earliest collaborations with Griffith appeared in the *Evening Herald* in early 1892 when they co-authored a series of articles on "Notable Irish graves in and around Dublin."[29]

In addition to participating in the pro-Parnell Young Ireland League and leading excursions to sites of national importance, he featured prominently in the '98 Committee, established in early 1897 to commemorate the centenary of the 1798 Rebellion. This project took Rooney throughout Ireland and, as Bradley claims,

> [T]o him the greater credit is due for the impetus which the Irish Language movement received in the country districts during those years. He would frequently leave his work on a Saturday evening, take a train West or to some other portion of Ireland, address a meeting in Irish on Sunday, travel back to Dublin again by the night train, and return to work as usual on Monday morning.[30]

---

[27] Ibid., xvii. The style here is typical of Bradley's tone when lauding his wife's former intended.

[28] Ibid., xviii

[29] Ibid., xviii–xix.

[30] Ibid., xxiii.

Presumably, it was on such a trip that newspapers selectively reported his comments much to the detriment of the Gaelic League as Eoin Mac Néill recalls in his memoir:

> In the early days of this movement there was a society in Dublin called the Celtic Literary Society. It also took the Irish language under its wing, especially to the extent of passing resolutions condemning persons and parties for not doing enough for Irish. I did my best to attract the young people of this society into the working scheme of the G.L. and was partly successful. Among those that came over and joined us was William Rooney who is well remembered for his poems and writings on national subjects. He attended a meeting somewhere in Connacht [,] I'm not now certain where but I think it was in the neighbourhood of Ballaghaderreen [,] and he made a speech there of which of course only the most combative parts got into the newspapers. He denounced the inactivity of the Irish Parliamentary Party in the matter of the language. There were other parties with a nationalistic programme who were quite as open to the same denunciation. His speech had the effect of causing some of the leading members of the Parliamentary Party to regard the G.L. as a hostile political force and I have good reason to know that that notion lasted within the Irish party though not among all its members as long as the Party itself existed. Among those who had this notion of G.L. hostility were John Dillon and William O'Brien and later Joseph Devlin. . . . When Mr. Devlin came to the front with his organization of the revived A.O.H. the Irish language appeared (1900) as an article in their programme. But I had no difficulty in recognizing a very thorough hostility toward the whole Irish language movement within the Hibernian organization."[31]

---

[31] *Eoin MacNeill: Memoir of a revolutionary scholar*, ed. Brian Hughes (Dublin: Irish Manuscripts Commission, 2016), 28–29.

In addition to proselytizing for the language in the Irish-speaking districts, Rooney's lasting legacy may be the prominence of the Irish language on 1798 memorials.[32] Typical in this regard is the 1798 memorial in Graigue, Carlow, where the majority of the 53-word inscription is in Irish followed by a 22-word English translation.

> *I gcuimhneamh ar sé céid fear agus dá fhichid d'fhearaibh Éireann d'imir a n-anam agus do dhoirt a gcuid fola ag troid mórchatha ar an láthair seo in aghaidh gall an dá ficheadh do Bhealtaine san mbliadhain d'Aois an Tighearna Míle Seacht gCéid nócha a hocht. Suaimhneas síorruidhe go dtugaidh Dia dhóibh.*

> Amen. In memory of the 640 United Irishmen who gave their lives for their country at the Battle of Carlow May 25th 1798.[33]

Other bilingual monuments include the Ann Devlin statue in St. Michan's Park, Dublin. Such Irish-language inscriptions in the Gaelic font represent the first manifestations of the Irish Revival in the public sphere. While SPIL, the Gaelic Union, and the Gaelic League published academic and popular materials, these permanent structures erected in public places were highly visible and elegant in design and execution. They mark the reappearance of the Irish language in post-famine Ireland and its reemergence in the public sphere, as well as its introduction into the cultural politics of commemoration.[34]

When the Belfast-based newspaper, *The Shan Van Vocht*[35] closed, to be replaced by the Dublin-based *United Irishman*, the directors offered Rooney the editorship. He declined, hoping instead to tempt Griffith back

---

[32] Bradley, xxiv. See also Turpin, John. "1798, 1898 & The Political Implications of Sheppard's Monuments." *History Ireland* 6, no. 2 (1998), 44–48.

[33] Editor's Note: The inscription is not in italics, but it is our stylistic practice to give the primary language in italics when it is followed by an English translation.

[34] See Senia Paseta, '1798 in 1898: The Politics of Commemoration,' *The Irish Review*, no. 22 (1998), 46–53.

[35] Established in Belfast in January 1896 by Alice Milligan ("Iris Olkyrn") and Anna Johnson ("Ethna Carberry").

from South Africa.[36] The *United Irishman* first appeared on 4 March 1899—the same time that Conradh na Gaeilge replaced *Fáinne an Lae*, (first issued on 8 January 1898 by Bernard Doyle) with *An Claidheamh Soluis*—and ran until 1906. But the *United Irishman*, under Rooney's guidance, offered a different perspective toward literature written in English than *An Claidheamh Soluis*.[37] Between leading excursions, editing the *Seanchuidhe*, working for the Midland Great Western Railway Company[38] and being the *United Irishman*'s "most prolific writer"[39] from March 1899 to March 1901, he became engaged to Máire Ní Chillín/Máire Killeen (1874–1956).[40] Their marriage, scheduled for May 1901, never occurred. A 'serious cold' contracted in March 1901 led to a serious deterioration of his health.[41] Tuberculosis caused his death on 6 May 1901; a death, according to Yeats, that "plunged everybody into gloom."[42] His friend Griffith "was desolate and for many weeks his pen recorded little but his grief. His family and Rooney's had lived in the same

---

[36] Ó Conaire, 6. See Owen McGee, *Arthur Griffith* (Dublin: Merrion Press, 2015), 40 and see also Seán Ó Luing, *Art Ó Gríofa* (Dublin: Sáirséal agus Dill, 1953), 53–55. Rooney is often named as the *United Irishman*'s joint editor.

[37] Andrew Murphy, *Ireland, Reading and Cultural Nationalism, 1790–1930: Bringing the Nation to Book* (Cambridge: Cambridge University Press, 2018).

[38] As a railway employee, he traveled for free on weekends.

[39] Bradley claims that he refused two offers of editorship from different regional newspapers, see Bradley, xxxiii.

[40] "Deirtear go raibh lámh agus focal idir í féin agus Liam Ó Maolruanaidh a d'éag ar 6 Bealtaine 1901. Is inspéise gur tugadh Craobh Fhear na Muintire ar chraobh den Chonradh i gConga (*An Claidheamh Soluis* 2 Bealtaine 1903)—bhí 'Fear na Muintire' ar cheann d'ainmneacha cleite Uí Mhaolruanaidh. Bhí sí ina ball den Choiste Gnó i 1902 agus 1904 nuair nach raibh ach beirt bhan eile ina mbaill: Úna Ní Fhaircheallaigh agus Máire Ní Aodáin. Tuairiscíodh (idem 30 Aibreán 1904) go raibh sí ag moltóireacht ag Feis Shligigh. Bhí éirithe as an gCoiste Gnó aici toisc, b'fhéidir, go raibh sí imithe abhaile go Conga. Phós sí Pádraig Ó Brolcháin, duine de chairde móra Uí Mhaolruanaidh, ann 30 Meitheamh 1904. Art Ó Gríofa a sheas le Pádraig. Bhí seachtar mac acu agus is le Gaeilge a thóg siad iad." https://www.ainm.ie/ Bio. aspx?ID=699.

[41] Ó Conaire, 12.

[42] Letter to Lady Gregory, 21 May 1901 *Collected Letters* third ed. John Kelly and Ronald Schuchard (Oxford: Oxford University Press, 1994), 72.

house . . ."[43]   He was buried at Glasnevin, where allegedly more than thirty floral wreaths garnished his coffin,[44] and the national newspapers mourned his premature death. The *Southern Star* lamented that:

> [I]n the death of William Rooney at the age of twenty-seven, Ireland has lost, as a contemporary well puts it, 'The Davis of the National Revival.' For the past two years his contributions to the Gaelic and extreme Nationalist journals, under the signatures of a.k.a.–Fear na Muintire, Criadhaire, Sliabh Ruadh, Clann an Smoil, Shel Martain, Knocksedan, Killester, Feltim, Ballinascorney have awakened true nationality in the hearts of thousands.[45]

Máire Ní Chillín/Máire Killeen, his Mayo-born fiancée, was a leading member of the Ard-Chraobh of Conradh na Gaeilge, among the most active female members of the Gaelic League, and a vice-president of Inighidhe na hÉireann. In June 1904, three years after Rooney's death, she married the Dongeal-born Patrick Bradley/Pádraig Ó Brolcháin (1876–1934), who had edited Rooney's ballads and poems and provided a highly hagiographic account of his wife's former lover in a volume entitled *Poems and Ballads: William Rooney* (1902). On Lady Gregory's advice, *The Daily Express* editor E.V. Longworth offered this volume for review to a young Irish writer. The volume and damning review might well have sunk into the mists of time had the reviewer not been James Joyce. Griffith, among others, never forgave him for his slight on their dear dead friend.

Though Rooney's poetry had been acclaimed in patriotic circles, it didn't warrant such honours according to Joyce. Rooney "has no care . . .

---

[43] Younger, 21.

[44] Ó Conaire, 13.

[45] *Southern Star*, 11 May 1901, 5; *Freeman's Journal*, 18 September 1901. In a similar vein, *The Freeman's Journal* grieved that the death of William Rooney in the dawn of his manhood deprived the society of its bravest laborer. While his hand held the helm we knew all was safe, but now that we are to know him no more, that we are never to hear his voice again urging us to be confident of the future, it behooves us all to persevere more determinedly in the work to which he devoted his life is to be carried to fruition.

to create anything according to the art of literature," Joyce wrote, because "patriotism has laid hold of the writer." Instead of literature, all Joyce found was "a weary succession of verses, 'prize' poems–the worst of all." "[T]hey have no spiritual or living energy, because they come from one in whom the spirit is in a manner dead . . . a weary and foolish spirit, speaking of redemption and revenge, blaspheming against tyrants, and going forth, full of tears and curses, upon its infernal labours." Though he admired a translation Rooney had made from a poem by Douglas Hyde, Joyce found there was "no piece in the book which has even the first quality of beauty, the quality of integrity, the quality of being separate and whole . . ." Joyce's sense that patriotism made bad poetry was made explicit in his comment that Rooney "might have written well if he had not suffered from one of those big words which make us so unhappy." Arthur Griffith, on the other hand, saw Rooney's patriotism as that which made his poetry significant, and used this line of Joyce's in an advertisement for the book, inserting the word patriotism in brackets after "one of those big words."[46]

As Ó Luing interprets Joyce's action as:

> *Éireannach ag scríobh i bpáipéar Sasanach ag lochtúchán ar shaothar náisiúnta Éireannaigh eile, ba leor san chun Art Ó Gríofa a ghríosadh chun feirge, ach nuair b'é a chara ionmhain a bhí i gceist ina theannta san ba dheacair dó an gníomh a mhaitheamh agus is rud cinnte nár mhaith.*[47]

> An Irishman writing for an English paper faulting the nationalist work of another Irishman, such was sufficient to enrage Arthur Griffith, but the fact that the other Irishman was his dear friend made it difficult for him to forgive the deed, and he certainly never did.

Given Joyce's disparagement of Rooney's verse, it is ironic, as Frank Shovlin convincingly argues, that the title character of Rooney's poem "The Priest of Adergool: An Incident of the Connacht Rising"—a poem

---

[46] See James Joyce, *Occasional, Critical, and Political Writing*, edited with an Introduction and Notes by Kevin Barry (Oxford: Oxford University Press, 2000). http://jamesjoyce.ie/on-this-day-11-december/
[47] Ó Luing, *Art Ó Gríofa*, 98, (translation by author).

that won a prize offered in 1898 by the *Weekly Freeman* for the best poem written on an incident in the 1798 rebellion—is the origin for Fr. Conroy, Gabriel's brother and a senior curate in Balbriggan, in Joyce's story famous 'The Dead".[48]

The Celtic Literary Society: A Political Gaelic League?

Rooney, shaped by the Fireside Club, joined the pro-Parnellite Leinster Literary Society that assembled at Marlborough Street,[49] where Griffith, as President and Vice-President, was to the fore in issuing statements of support for Parnell. Rooney began attending meetings in early 1891, before joining as a member on 13 February 1891. On 27 February, he read a paper on "Art M'Morrough O'Kavanagh," and soon became editor of *Eblana*, the Society's manuscript journal, As Vice-President he signed the minutes. Despite his claim that he was "never a supporter of Parnell but an indifferent nationalist," Griffith issued an "Address to C.S. Parnell," that Rooney also signed in 1892. The 1892 split ruptured the Society, which dissolved on 9 December 1892.[50] Some members reconstituted themselves as *Comh-Chumann Gaedhilge Éigseach*/The Celtic Literary Society, and convened for the first time in September 1893 at No. 32 Lower Abbey Street.[51] The decision to establish this Society apparently occurred at a meeting at Rooney's North Strand home on 3 February 1893.[52] Its most active members, other than Rooney, as Seamus McManus recalled included Griffith, Denis Devereax, Peter White, Pádraig Ó Brolcháin and Tom Cuffe.[53]

---

[48] "Our first encounter with Father Conroy in Joyce's writing comes in the early pages of 'The Dead' where, as Gabriel Conroy's brother, he is mentioned in order to illustrate their mother's upwardly mobile and snobbish nature." Shovlin, 257.

[49] Ó Conaire states that he was heavily involved in the production of *Eblana*, the Leinster Literary Society's magazine. See *Liam Ó Maolruanaidh 1897–1901*, 9.

[50] For details of the Leinster Literary Society's final meeting, see McGee, *Arthur Griffith*, p. 18. M. Seery and J. Boland, two IRB leaders, managed this premises. See McGee, note 31, p. 396.

[51] Joseph Edmundson Masterson, writing in the *Irish Press* (7 September 1935, 8) argues that the Society initially met at his residence (15 Sinnott Place) until another premises was procured.

[52] Ó Luing, 31.

[53] Seamus MacManus, Bureau of Military History, Witness Statement S0283, 173.

Rooney served as the Society's president and the editor of its manuscript journal, *An Seanachuidhe*. The Celtic Literary Society aimed "to educate every inhabitant to the errors of the past; the needs of the present and the possibilities of the future."[54] *The Freeman's Journal* reported the Society's objectives were "to spread as much knowledge of their own country amongst the working youth of Dublin, as the utilitarianism of the time had obliged them to know about others, and by creating an appetite for native literature[,] prepare the way for the works promised by the projectors of an Irish Library."[55] Its goals were fourfold: 1) The study and cultivation and support of the Irish language, 2) The extension of the knowledge of the Irish language, history and antiquities, 3) The popularizing of Irish music and 4) The encouragement of Irish industries. The stated principles of the Society were "broadly National, being Non-Sectarian and Non-Partisan." The key words 'broadly National' and 'non-partisan' were of tremendous significance. They distinguish the Society from the Gaelic League, which was both non-political and non-sectarian. This distinction allowed the Society to discuss and engage in politics—and the overlap between the Society and the Pro-Boer Transvaal Committee is marked—while simultaneously allowing the Gaelic League to declare itself as non-political and above politics. Accordingly, it made the Society a natural fit for Griffith's An Comhairle Náisiúnta/National Council and, later, Sinn Féin. It also marked the Gaelic League as a more appealing proposition for Irish-language Unionists, Irish-speaking Protestants and Quakers, and consequently allowed the League to present itself as a non-sectarian organization whose members practiced a diversity of religions.

With Rooney elected president for the first season[56], the inaugural meeting occurred on 4 October 1893 at Costigan's Hotel, 38 Sackville Street/Upper O'Connell Street, where Rooney delivered the opening

---

[54] *Western People*, 10 July 1971, 18.

[55] *Freeman's Journal*, 25 September 1893, 6. Also present at the meeting were John O'Leary, Joseph T. Doyle, James Murphy, John H. M. Derby, T. Thompson, James Ryan, John Clogg, John Doran, Wm Valentine, T. Wilson, T. P. Fox, John Nolan, Kevin O'Toole, Thomas Tallon, P. O'H Nally, J. A. Meyrick, and John A. Whelan.

[56] *Freeman's Journal*, 25 September, 1893, 6. Vice-President Joseph T. Doyle; treasurer, Mr. William Fanning; Secretary, Mr. John E. Whelan; librarian, Mr. John Clogg; and Messers Murphy, Graham, Ryan, and Doran as committee.

address entitled "Sir Samuel Ferguson."[57] The Society subsequently announced its meetings were "open to ladies, who do not require tickets."[58] Relevant here is the issue of timing. The Gaelic Literary Society formed late September 1893 at 38 Sackville Street, Dublin. On 16 June 1892, Douglas Hyde had delivered a version of his "The Necessity for De-Anglicising Ireland" to the Gaelic Society of New York. This speech "fully reported in Dublin"[59] convinced several Civil Servants in the Four Courts to approach Hyde about forming a new popular Irish-language organization.[60] Hyde revisited his topic at the Irish National Literary Society on 25 November 1892. The lecture led to the creation of the Gaelic League / Conradh na Gaeilge at Martin Kelly's civil service academy at 9 Lower Sackville Street, Dublin, on 31 July 1893. Two months later the Gaelic Literary Society, shaped by different aims and goals to the Gaelic League, appeared. Nonetheless, these two organizations, formed within months of each other on the same Dublin Street offer a fascinating and revealing window into the politics, tensions and concerns that animated the times.

The League's aims were twofold: 1) The preservation of Irish as the national language of Ireland and the extension of its use as a spoken language and 2) The study and publication of existing Gaelic literature and the cultivation of a modern literature in Irish. In addition to the Roscommon-born and university-educated Hyde, the founding members included Charles Percy Bushe (Dublin-born civil servant in the Four Courts); Thomas Walker Ellerker (Yorkshire-born senior official at the Four Courts); Rev William Hayden S.J. (Waterford-born Jesuit, university

---

[57] *Freeman's Journal*, 25 September, 1893. McGee contends, "The disgruntled Griffith and his cousin Edward Whelan would not join Rooney's Celtic Literary Society for some time, however. Instead, they took the opportunity to become members of the executive of the Young Ireland League (YIL), which was a far more influential body that campaigned for changes in the Irish educational system." See McGee, *Arthur Griffith*, p. 18. Brian Maye suggests that Griffith had joined the Society before emigrating to Africa, and on his return to Dublin was elected vice-president in September 1899 and president the following year. Cf. Maye, *Arthur Griffith*, p. 15.

[58] *Freeman's Journal*, 4 October 1893, 5.

[59] *Eoin MacNeill: Memoir of a Revolutionary Scholar*, 21.

[60] Ibid., 21.

educated); Martin Kelly (native speaker from Clare, civil servant in the Four Courts); John McNeill (Antrim-born civil servant in the Four Courts); Patrick O'Brien (Cork-born native speaker, printer); T. O'Neill Russell (West-Meath-born Quaker and commercial traveler in the U.S.A.); James Michael Cogan (Dublin-born civil servant in the Four Courts) and Patrick J. Hogan (Limerick-born barrister and civil servant in the Four Courts).

While Rooney and Griffith were working-class Dublin Catholics and largely self-educated, the League's founders were an assortment of Catholics and Protestants, rural and university-educated men. In accounts of Society meetings, the absence of clerics, Catholic or Protestant, is striking and in stark contrast to the ubiquitous presence of Catholic priests and conservative Catholics at all levels of Gaelic League activity. The League embraced women as full members at all administrative levels including the national executive.[61] It also established an impressive network of branches throughout urban and rural Ireland as well as overseas. Despite annual elections, Hyde retained the presidency from 1893 until 1915, and the League's leadership structure remained largely stable. Hyde served as President for 22 years from 1893 until 1915 when the I.R.B.-inspired coup led him to resign on the grounds that the League was no longer non-political.[62] Such stability in leadership ensured continuity in procedures and consistency in policy. The League had become "Hyde's League" and as such linked the League in the public mind and media to a particular individual who came to personify the organization. The Society, on the other hand, never achieved that consistency of leadership or national profile.

Having expanded membership to women in 1894, the Society admitted non-Dublin members in 1895. Such corresponding members paid a fee of 2s 6d per year that entitled them "to all the privileges of ordinary

---

[61] "… the first Irish national society which accepted women as members on the same terms as men ... From the beginning, women sat on its Branch Committees and Executive." See Jennie Wyse Power in W.G. Fitzgerald (ed.), *The Voice of Ireland* (Dublin: Virtue, 1924), 158.

[62] Brian Ó Conchubhair, "Capturing the Trenches of Language: World War One, the Irish Language and the Gaelic League," *Modernist Cultures* 13, no. 3, 382–398.

membership" whenever they were in Dublin.[63] This would later rise to 4p per week for Dublin-based members and a half crown per year for country members. In terms of membership fees, the Gaelic League's annual fee was five shillings;[64] ($2 for Americans); SPIL charged 10 shillings (Associates 1 shilling); the National Literary Society also charged 10 schillings; the Irish Texts Society requested 7s 6d ($2 for Americans) while the London-based Irish Literary Society required 21 shillings.[65] The Society evidently saw itself initially as Dublin-based rather than following the Gaelic League or GAA model of numerous local branches scattered throughout the provinces. The lack of a geographical spread not only reduced its overall influence, but limited membership and restricted revenue.

The 1900 report testifies to close links between the Society and the Gaelic League. The Society's choral class, "as well as assisting on all occasions in the gaiety, aided the Central Gaelic League in making the evening concert of the Feis Laighean a success, rendering the choruses in Gaelic, and assisting also later on in the chorus organized for the Oireachtas."[66] The Society also boasted that its language classes "have all but outgrown the facilities provided, and are amongst the best attended in the city," and congratulated itself that "many of the classes at present held in connection with the Gaelic League branches are being taught by scholars who gained their knowledge of Irish mainly in the society's classes, and point to the fact that we possess the only class which has existed without a week's interruption for the past seven years."[67] Not only did the Society maintain a productive relationship with SPIL, but also "the relations of the society with the League have been most friendly, and will, we trust, remain so while one enemy of an Irish-Ireland remains to be

---

[63] *Freeman's Journal*, 27 December 1895, 5. This would later rise to 4p per week for Dublin-based members and a half crown per year for country members.

[64] *Scientific and Learned Societies of Great Britain: A Handbook Compiled from Official Sources* (London: Allen & Unwin, 1901).

[65] Ibid.

[66] *Freeman's Journal*, 12 September 1900. The choir leader was a man named Lawless according to Henry C. Phibbs, See Bureau of Military History, Witness Statement 0848, 3–4.

[67] *Freeman's Journal,* 12 September 1900.

combatted. The committee desire to thank the Society for the Preservation of the Irish language for the gift of prizes for the classes."[68]

Given his engagement to a leading Gaelic Leaguer, Rooney's interaction with Gaelic League officials and the lack of hostility between the Celtic Literary Society and the League, why did Rooney never become a senior figure or official in the Gaelic League of which he was a member or, more pertinent, why did the Celtic Literary Society never affiliate with the League and become a branch? The answer, it appears, is politics:

> Of the Gaelic League he was always an enthusiastic supporter and worker, though with its policy in some respects he was not in agreement. He thought the term 'non-political' was too narrowly construed by the League, and that its policy, to really raise the enthusiasm of the people, must be strongly national in its highest sense— must, in fact, recognize Ireland's claim to complete nationhood, and work with the idea before and towards that ideal.[69]

Kelly discerns that most revivalist organizations "tended to identify themselves as politically non-aligned, but it would be a mistake to equate this with the apolitical principles of the Gaelic League."[70] Unsurprisingly, given the overlap between the Gaelic League and the Society, Rooney was coopted as a Gaelic League member in May 1896.[71] When he was nominated for the Gaelic League Executive, his bid proved unsuccessful.[72] McGee suggests "[a]lthough Rooney had been co-opted as a member of the League's committee for organizing Oireachtas meetings, he was always denied membership of its executive council."[73]

---

[68] Ibid.

[69] Bradley, xxv. Nonetheless, the impact of politics on the Leinster Literary Society was not forgotten. The Celtic Literary Society, according to McGee, "wisely resolved not to allow contemporary party politics to be discussed at its meetings." See McGee, *Arthur Griffith*. p. 18.

[70] See Matthew Kelly, http://www.generalmichaelcollins.com/life-times/1905-founding-sinn-fein/william-rooney-sinn-fein/

[71] *Freeman's Journal*, 26 May 1896, 4.

[72] Ó Conaire, 9.

[73] McGee, *Arthur Griffith, p.* 63.

The Gaelic League's refusal, in early 1897, to participate in the 1798 centenary because it violated its non-political, non-sectarian policy led to tensions with the Celtic Literary Society. While Kelly argues "much of Rooney's thought derived from Hyde's brilliant intervention,"[74] Rooney believed "that a Gaelic League agenda without an explicit separatist dimension would prove to be yet another 'West British' illusion."[75] Yet, Bradley, in keeping with the glorification of his subject, stated "while holding these views, and giving expression to them when occasion arose, [Rooney] ardently supported the League, and during his tours in the West he placed a large number of branches on a foundation."[76] On the other hand, the Celtic Literary Society and the Gaelic League found themselves in direct opposition when competing for funds in 1894 from the Mullen Bequest,[77] a considerable amount of money an Irish gun maker had left for the promotion of Irish in Ireland.[78]

By early November 1893, the Young Ireland League and the Celtic Literary Society successfully petitioned the Governors of the City of Dublin Technical Schools to provide Irish-language class in their schools and to appoint a professor of Irish.[79] That same month, the Society opened membership to ladies.[80] The catalyst for this enfranchisement appears to have been Maud Gonne, whose request for membership was initially rejected.[81] The report from November 1893 provides a taste of the weekly meetings:

---

[74] Kelly ". . . and William Rooney spoke in Irish."

[75] Ibid.

[76] Bradley, xxvi.

[77] See *The Monthly Review* 17, (1904), 128.

[78] *The Nation*, 13 March 1897, 13.

[79] *Freemans Journal*, 13 November 1893, 6 and *Freeman's Journal,* 7 November 1893, 2.

[80] *Freeman's Journal*, 13 November 1893, 6.

[81] Maud Gonne, *The Autobiography of Maud Gonne: A Servant of the Queen*, eds. Anna Bride McWhite and A. Norman Jeffares (1938; Reprint, Chicago: University of Chicago Press, 1995), 94. She had attempted to join the Celtic Literary Society who "produced a Manuscript Journal *An Seanachie* which I found very interesting. I was so delighted with the Club and its activities that I told the secretary I wanted to become a member. He looked embarrassed. Willie Rooney was called to explain, as politely as he could, that the rules of the Club excluded women from membership."

The routine business having been disposed of the chairman called on the editor to read the current number of the *Seanachie*, the society's MS journal. The contents were numerous and varied, and were very warmly received. They included articles on 'Ellen O'Leary, poetess and Fenian,' by Ossian; 'National Education, Here and Elsewhere,' by Sliabh-Martin; 'Spranger Larry,' by Shanganus; 'Inspiration from Mitchel,' by Shawn Duin; 'Can the Orangemen be Converted?' by Fireghan; 'Nationality v Cosmopolitanism,' by Kilmaeanogne; and 'Wolfe Tone," by Los; 'Three Songs–The Little Brown Berry, Rosie Flaherty, and To Die for Motherland,' by Anemoe, Ballynagois and Glendhu respectively; 'Connaught,' a piece of verse, by Hi Fiachra; 'Found,' some verses by Shemus; the third and fourth chapters of the society's composite novel. 'The Sons of Cain,' and two sketches, 'On the Long Car' (Cluain Tarbh), and 'A Beautiful Legend' (Kilgobbin) . . . On Wednesday next Mr. John R. Whelan will read a paper entitled 'From Freedom to Serfdom' dealing with Ireland from the landing of St. Patrick to the English invasion.[82]

Matters of a political nature frequently appeared as topics for debate. December saw the Society discuss the motion "Could the Irish Nation exist independent?,"[83] while other topics included "Will the Celtic become the Ruling Race"[84] and "That English Rule has benefited Ireland."[85] Such subjects conform to Kelly's contention that cultural nationalism offered separatists opportunities to disseminate ideals of Irish self-reliance and the

---

For more on women in Cumann na nGaedheal, see J. MacPherson, *Women and the Irish Nation: Gender, Culture and Irish Identity, 1890–1914* (Springer, 2012).

[82] *Freeman's Journal*, 13 November 1893, 6.

[83] *Freeman's Journal*, 13 December 1893, 6.

[84] *Freeman's Journal*, 4 April 1894, 7.

[85] *Freeman's Journal*, 28 January 1896, 3.

incompatibility of British state authority with Irish progress and prosperity.[86]

Debating was not the Society's sole activity. By early November, Michael Cusack (1847–1906) conducted an Irish language class every Monday evening at 8 pm, after the regular meeting. Pádhraic Óg Ó Conaire contends that this class, taught initially by Pádraic Mac An Fhailinghe/P. Nally,[87] and subsequently Michael Cusack, existed from the beginning.[88] Cusack's role offers a fascinating crossover between the

---

[86] M.J. Kelly, *The Fenian Ideal and Irish Nationalism, 1882–1916* (Woodbridge, Suffock: The Boydell Press, 2006), 10.

[87] Patrick Nally (1868–1911), lived with his parents at 56 Eccles Street, Dublin. A founding member of Cumann na bPíobairí in February 1900, he published *An Modh Réidh leis an nGaedhilge do mhúnadh* (An Cló-Chumann, 1904. 71 pages), the first textbook to use the direct method in Irish. He edited *An Gadaí Dubh Ó Dubháin*, which tale he sourced from Máire Ní Chillín. Micheál Ó Maoláin claimed Nally was the first person to teach Irish in Dublin as living language. A cousin of Patrick was William Nally (1857–1891), a member of the Supreme Council of the Irish Republican Brotherhood, who was imprisoned in 1881 and also died in prison in 1891. See Pádraig Ó Baoighill, *Nally as Maigh Eo* (Dublin: Coiscéim, 1998), 347–352. See also See Seán Ó Luing, *Art Ó Gríofa* (Dublin: Sáirséal agus Dill, 1953), 32. Regarding An Modh Díreach, the preface explained its aim as follows: "Seo leabhar ar shlighe nua chun na Gaedhilge a mhúineadh. Tá ana-chuid suime á chur i múinteóireacht an Gaedhilge le déidheannaighe; táthar ag aighneas is ag díospóireacht go héachtach i dtaobh na ceiste seo. Ní héan droch-chomhartha é sin mar taispeánann go bhfuilimíd dáríribh chun na Gaedhilge a leathadh ar fuid na tíre go léir agus gur mhaith linn fios d'fhagháil ar an gcuma b'fhearr chuige. Ná síltar go mbeidh éin cheann díobh ag déanamh cumhangthais ar an gceann eile. Beidh slighe a ndóthain dóibh go léir ann. Leabhairín ana-thairbheach is eadh an leabhairín seo an Mhodh Réidh. Ní labhartar éin-nídh ó thosach bárra leis na scoláirí acht Gaedhilg. Ní bhíd i bhfad ag foghluim ar an gcuma so nuair bhíonn a gcluasa oilte go leór ar fhuaim na teangan, agus as cuma dhóibhcad do bhuailfidh umpa as soin amach. Do réir deallraimh, is deacair rudaí simplidhe a sholáthar chun tosnughadh ar theangaidh ar an gcuma so. Bheidh cuid de na habairtibh go crapathe agus go haindeis i n-indeóin díchill duine. Tá rudaí crapaithe san leabhairín seo; acht ní fhágann soin é gan bheith n-a áise mhaith chun na Gaedhilge a mhúineadh acht é chur i láimh dhuine go bhfuil a fhios aige cad do bhaineann le múinteóireacht. Is iad muinntir An Cló-Chumainn a chuir i gcló é, agus go deimhin ní holc a chuireadar chuige."

[88] Ó Conaire, 9. When Nally was ill, 'Sceilig' (J.J. O'Kelly) taught the class. See Bureau of Military History, Witness Statement 848, 6.

BRIAN Ó CONCHUBHAIR

Celtic Literary Society, the Gaelic League, the SPIL, and the Gaelic Athletic Association, and shows how interconnected these disparate Revivalist organizations were. A nominal charge for membership–2d per week–met expenses.[89] The commitment to the Irish language featured again in early 1894 when representatives of the Young Ireland League, the Gaelic League, and the Celtic Literary Society met at 15 D'Olier Street. With Griffith presiding, they discussed an Irish-Language Congress based on the 1882 Irish-Language Congress.[90] Among the bodies represented at the 27 March Easter Congress that convened in the 'new' ballroom of the Mansion House were clergymen and members of the Christian Brothers' community, and a large number of National schoolteachers.[91] Several of the speakers addressed the meeting in Irish as well as in English. The Lord Mayor presided, and among those present were representatives of St. Patrick's Training College, Marlborough Street Training College, Christian Brothers, and teachers from Clare, Kerry, Galway, Tipperary, Cork, Mayo, Carlow and Sligo, as well as representatives of the Sheridan Literary Society,[92] the Young Ireland League, the Gaelic League and the Celtic Literary Society.

The Gaelic League representatives included Michael Cusack, J. MacNeill, T. O'N Russell, J.J. Barrett, William Byrne, J. Casey, Thomas Corless, P. Conway, P. Nally, J. Nally, H.A. MacNeill, Miss O'Donovan, Rev. P. O'Leary, P.P., William Colbert, Patrick O'Brien and J. Burgess. The Celtic Literary Society representatives included Wm. Rooney, Joseph Doyle, John R Whelan, M.J. Quinn, P. Morgan, T. Wilson, J. Tinnains, J. M'Cally, P. Nally, John Doras, John Clegg, P. J. Gregan and S.J. Barrett.[93] The crossover in membership is striking: Cusack (the Society's teacher and G.A.A. founder) and P. Nally (publisher of the Society's textbook) both represented the Gaelic League, while S.J. Barrett (SPIL member, and

---

[89] *Freeman's Journal*, 5 November 1894, 4.
[90] 'Irish Language Congress Committee,' *Freeman's Journal*, 16 February 1894, 4. See also *Report of the Proceedings of the Congress Held in Dublin on the 15, 16 and 17th of August, 1882 by the Society for the Preservation of the Irish Language, to consider the present position of the Irish Language as a Vernacular, and how its use might be prompted.*
[91] See Ó Luing, *Art Ó Gríofa*, 30–32.
[92] See Kelly, *The Fenian Ideal and Irish Nationalism, 1882–1916*, 103.
[93] *Freeman's Journal*, 28 March 1894, 2.

future Gaelic League treasurer) represented the Society. The interconnectivity and fraternization of people in the Gaelic League, the Celtic Literary Society, as well as the Gaelic Union and the SPIL, is remarkable.

The Lord Mayor in the course of his address referred to the circular issued from the 1882 Congress. He expressed his regret that at their few victories which included Irish could now be taught, outside school hours, in national schools; Irish now had a status, along with the dead languages, on Royal University and Intermediate Education curricula, and Irish-language Professors had been appointed at Maynooth College, at Clongowes College, and at the St. Stephen's Green University College. As ever, the Christian Brothers provided classes in many of their schools for the study of Irish. Yet, he noted:

> [W]hile the advances were so few the deficiencies, which still existed in making the Irish language a useful and a living language, were numerous, and, as far as he could see, they were practically pretty much in the same condition in the year '94 as in the year 1882. No professors had been appointed in the teaching colleges. Out of 8,500 National schools, only 50 schools taught Irish. Prizes were not given in the National schools, and no class books were published. No diocesan colleges, grammar schools, or collegiate institutions, with the exception of Maynooth, Clongowes, Blackrock College, St. Jarlath's College, Rockwell College, and a few others, taught the language . . . no arrangements had been issued for training teachers or for securing that the various persons holding public appointments throughout the country should have that knowledge of Irish which in some parts of the country at all events would be of great use in communicating with a large section of the people. [He] hoped that the Congress of '94 would be attended with a greater need for success than that which followed the Congress of '82.[94]

---

[94] Ibid., 2.

BRIAN Ó CONCHUBHAIR

In the summer of 1894, the Society's language class met at 81 Great Britain Street/Parnell Street.[95] A history class was added in the fall of 1894 to teach "Irish history to the youths of the city."[96] In December 1894, Joseph Doyle, the Society's president proposed a motion at the annual general meeting "that the teaching of Irish in the primary schools is the surest sign of making its use universal through the country, and as that can only be accomplished by the teachers being thoroughly acquainted with the language, that we call on the managers of the Training Colleges to take immediate steps to make Irish an essential item in their curricula."[97] The language class, using O'Growney's books, continued to meet on Monday evenings in 1895 with attendance "open to non-members of the society, of both sexes, on the payment of 1d weekly."[98] In September 1901 the *Freeman* reported that the Society's Irish classes continued "their success of previous years, and the numbers attending have so largely increased that it is now considered advisable, if not imperative, to assign two nights for the teaching of Gaelic. Perfect unanimity exists between the Gaelic League and the society . . . The committee have again to express their gratitude to the SPIL for their gift of book prizes to our Irish classes."[99]

This collegiality is at odds with the animosity frequently on display between the Gaelic League and SPIL regarding orthography, syntax, grammar and the very nature and purpose of the Irish language. The Celtic Literary Society seemingly navigated a steady path through the choppy linguistic and socio-linguistic waters of the early revival. In 1899 Bernard Doyle, based at 9 Upper Ormond Quay, published P. Nally's *Gaduidhe Dubh Ó Dubháin* on behalf of the Celtic Literary Society.[100] Described as "Gaelic texts, Vol I.," this slim folktale, "edited for the Society, with a complete Vocabulary of all the words in the Text," appeared in 1899 in Gaelic font and in dialectical, rather than classical, Irish. The anonymous

---

[95] *Freeman's Journal*, 11 June 1894, 4.
[96] *Freeman's Journal*, 21 November 1894, 8.
[97] *Freemans Journal*, 22 December 1894, 4.
[98] *Freeman's Journal*, 11 November 1895, 7.
[99] *Freeman's Journal*, 18 September 1901. Now the site of the Gate Hotel.
[100] The text featured as a prescribed examination text for Scholarship Examination in 1907 as described in the *Annual General Report of the Department* 6, Parts 1905–1906.

preface explains the desire to meet "the want of a reading book and vocabulary, at a low price, which would be suitable for students who had mastered the four books written for the Gaelic league by Father O'Growney, or the three books of the Society for the Preservation of the Irish language." Once again, we see the Society to the fore in editing and publishing vernacular Irish-language texts and providing textbooks that address the needs of those not met by O'Growney's *Simple Lessons. An Claidheamh Soluis* kindly reviewed the publication in December 1899 glossing over errors for which the Society for the Preservation of the Irish language might have been excoriated. "There are a few errors in the spelling, and one or two in the parsing, but not such as to seriously interfere with the usefulness of the book. We make the criticism in view of the fact that the book is brought out as the first of a series—a most commendable and creditable undertaking for the Celtic Literary Society. The printing is excellently done by Bernard Doyle."[101]

A heated debate in 1895 concerning the role of Young Ireland League members led to accusations that the Society was only that organization's fag end. After the resignation of one member, the committee strove to increase membership and, consequently, Rooney recommended Griffith, who was duly elected in November 1895.[102] If the Society limited itself initially to the metropolitan center, by the turn of the century it was diversifying. In 1900, the committee congratulated the Society on the starting of kindred organizations in Cork,[103] Limerick,

---

[101] *An Claidheamh Soluis* 1, no. 41, 23 December 1899, 651.

[102] See Ó Luing, *Art Ó Gríofa*, 33.

[103] Among the founding members of the Cork Celtic Literary Society were Terence MacSwiney, Tomás MacCurtain, Seán O'Hegarty and Daniel Corkery. See http://www.corkarchives.ie/media/U271web.pdf . *The Irish Independent* refers to David O'Conor as a member of the Cork Celtic Literary Society, who later in 1906 founded Sinn Féin in Cork. "Under the late Arthur Griffith, he was Foreign Editor of the *Sinn Fein Daily*, in 1909. Later he returned to Germany as Managing Editor of the *German Export Review*, and while there, he contributed many informative industrial articles to the Irish newspapers. On the outbreak of the War he went to America and was appointed national organizer of the Friends of Freedom for the United States during the visit of President de Valera to that country. Returning to Ireland in 1922 he was arrested and kept for six months in Cork prison. On his release he went again to Germany, where he received an important post in the German Foreign Office." He

Derry and Mountmellick (Laois) within the previous year, and expressed the desire to cordially co-operate with them in all their undertakings.[104] The Celtic Literary Society in Castlebar also produced a version of *O'Donnell's Cross*, a dramatic adaption of L. McManus' novel *In Sarsfield's Days*.[105] The issue of politics featured prominently at the Society's seventh annual general meeting. The president and chair T.P. Fox remarked that while the Boers' struggle had commanded members' attention, the literary programme of the session had been adhered to with fidelity.[106] He recalled how the session opened on Friday 6 October 1899, with an inaugural lecture on "The Definition of an Irish Nation" presided over by Maud Gonne, and reported that

> . . . [t]he National anniversaries of the session were fittingly honoured. Through the courtesy of the Committee of the Workmen's Club, York street, the Davis anniversary was celebrated there by a lecture and concert of Davis' songs, rendered by members of the society's choral class. The Mitchell anniversary was commemorated by a lecture delivered by Mr. W.J. Ryan: the Manchester Martyrdom was commemorated by a lecture also delivered in the hall of the Workmen's Club, and the birth of Emmet was commemorated by the usual lecture and concert of songs associated with his memory. . . . The society, through its members, has taken an active part in the informing of public opinion on the merits of the war against the Transvaal, and has been instrumental

---

returned to Ireland shortly before his death in 1934. See *Irish Independent,* 8 May 1934, 9. For Fr. Kavanagh's role in the Cork Celtic Literary Society, see McGee, *Arthur Griffith*, pp. 48–49.

[104] *Freeman's Journal,* 12 September, 1900.

[105] Major John MacBride (1868–1916) was a CLS member. In 1900, when Michael Davitt resigned his Mayo seat in the British House of Commons, in protest at the Boer War, Arthur Griffith nominated John MacBride as a by-election candidate. The play, published in 1908 by Sealy, Bryers and Waker (Middle Abbey Street, Dublin) notes the National Players' Society in Dublin staged the play in Samhain (November) 1907 as well as the Catholic Young Men's Society, Dundalk in February 1908 and the Celtic Literary Society, Castlebar in February 1908.

[106] *Freeman's Journal*, 12 September, 1900.

in exhibiting to the world the opinion of Dublin on the question. Similarly, in the organisation and management of the Patriotic Childrens' Treat, the members of the various classes of the society were unsparing in their efforts to prove that Irish Nationality has an abiding place in the hearts of Dublin's boys and girls. The committee congratulate the ladies' committee on the magnificent success of its undertaking.[107]

Yet the Society's independent days were numbered. On 30 August 1900, Griffith and Rooney, following up on Griffith's article in the *United Irishman* in March 1900 that called for an association to unite disparate nationalist groups, established Cumann na nGaedheal as a political organization and umbrella cultural and educational society for advanced nationalist/separatist groups. In October 1900, Inghinidhe na hÉireann affiliated themselves with Cumann na nGaedhael and accepted representation on the governing council. If the lines between the Celtic Literary Society and politics were previously somewhat blurred, the Rubicon had now been crossed: the Society joined the new umbrella group on 19 October 1900 to "advance the cause of Ireland's National independence."[108]

Further integration, and a blurring of identities, followed on 2 January 1901 when the newly founded Cork branch of Cumann na nGaedhael titled itself the Cork Celtic Literary Society. Its attitude on political neutrality was clear and several of its members would figure prominently in subsequent Irish history. Seven of the young men who had been in the Young Ireland Society met to form a new society, as a branch of the National Organisation, Cumann na nGaedheal. It was decided to call the Society 'The Cork Celtic Literary Society.' So that there would be no ambiguity regarding its aim, it put as its object: 'To Strive For The Establishment Of An Irish Republic.' Immediate means proposed were: 1 A. Adopting and propagating the principles of the United Irishmen. 1 B. Working for the restoration of the national language. 2. The study and teaching of Irish History. In another matter the Society adopts the objects of Cumann na nGaedheal. The seven young men were: Terence

---

[107] Ibid.

[108] *Freeman's Journal*, 18 September, 1901.

MacSwiney, Dan Tierney, Batt Kelleher, Fred Cronin, Bob Fitzgerald, Michael Radley, Liam Roche.[109]

Griffith informed the Celtic Literary Society Branch on 6 September 1901 that:

> [T]he society has sustained the heaviest blow that could possibly have been inflicted on it by the death of its founder and inspirer, William Rooney . . . . The death of William Rooney in the dawn of his manhood deprived the society of its bravest labourer. While his hand held the helm we knew all was safe, but now that we are to know him no more, that we are never to hear his voice again urging us to be confident of the future, it behoves us all to persevere more determinedly in the work to which he devoted his life if it is to be carried to fruition.[110]

In 1902, The Celtic Society was operating in Cork city at rooms in Great George's Street where a very large attendance, including many members of Inghinidhe na hÉireann discussed the tenth number of *Éire Óg*, the Celtic Literary Society's manuscript journal.[111] By now the Society was clearly integrated into Cumann na nGaedheal. In 1903, the Liverpool Cumann na nGaedheal branch advertised a series of lectures on Irish history and culture organized by the Celtic Literary Society. *The Southern Star* reported that the "Celtic Literary Society of Cumann na nGaedheal" passed a resolution calling on "Cork Country Council, Cork Corporation, and other public bodies, to reject any address to the English King."[112] In 1904, the usual Dublin weekly meeting learned that Seamus MacMannus would deliver the 1905 inaugural address on the topic of "Idealism in Ireland."[113] In 1907, Cumann na nGaedheal merged with the Dungannon Clubs and An Comhairle Náisiúnta/the National Council to

---

[109] Bureau of Military History 1913–21. Witness Liam de Roiste No. 2 Janemount, Sunday's Well, Cork. B.S.M. 2. Part 1, 4.

[110] *Freeman's Journal*, 18 September, 1901.

[111] *Irish Examiner*, 23 April 1902, 6. Described as "Irisleabhar míosamhail chun cabharughadh leis an ndream athá a d'iaraidh Éire dhéanamh Gaedhealach."

[112] *Southern Star*, 4 July, 1903, 7.

[113] *Freeman's Journal*, 24 October 1904.

form a new political party called Sinn Féin.[114] An Comhairle Náisiúnta/The National Council's founding manifesto was a bilingual document with the name of the organization in Irish only, but with a subtitle in parenthesis as "The National Committee"—indicating that Rooney's legacy was not forgotten. This political organization represented Griffith's policy of national economic, cultural and political self-reliance and aimed "to establish in Ireland's capital a national legislature endowed with the moral authority of the Irish nation." Despite securing 27% of the vote in the 1908 North Leitrim by-election, it failed as a political party until 1916 when the British authorities mistakenly named the IRB Easter Rising a Sinn Féin rebellion. In 1917, republicans rallied under the banner of Sinn Féin and the party, in various guises, has participated in Irish and British politics ever since. The same cannot be said of the Celtic Literary Society. Now forgotten, its role in the Irish-language and cultural revival is overlooked—as is often the fate of minor parties when they merge with larger entities in the pursuit of power.

The Celtic Literary Society sheds critical light on the Gaelic League. Not only were Catholic priests and curates over-represented, for obvious reasons, in rural and provincial League branches, the League actively cultivated Catholic bishops and Cardinals as shapers of public opinion. Nonetheless, members of different religions did occupy leading roles within the League especially at the national level. But recognition of, and respect for, formal religion appears lacking in the Society where priests, ministers, parsons and nuns were markedly absent. While the Society accepted women after Maud Gonne's intervention, women do not appear to have held leadership roles; the League, however, not only accepted women from the start, but before long had numerous branches across the provinces and beyond.[115] With Hyde constantly re-elected as president from 1893 to 1915, the League benefitted from a high-profile leader who commanded respect and authority. The university-educated Hyde shrewdly took advantage of his network of academic contacts at the 1898 Commission on Intermediate Education to challenge and embarrass

---

[114] Griffith published "The resurrection of Hungary: a parallel for Ireland" in *The United Irishman* in 1904.

[115] MacPherson, 127–129. Working-class women appear conspicuously absent from both organizations.

Trinity College. In the process, he raised the League's profile nationally and internationally. Recognizing the importance of publicity, the League established a weekly newspaper, a publishing house, and issued propaganda and promotional pamphlets. Hyde's social origins, academic education and scholarly reputation facilitated the 1905–1906 American fund-raising tour that involved public academic lectures at Harvard, Yale, the University of California, Berkeley, and two visits to the White House. The League's ambitions were always national and preserving the language in the Irish-speaking districts was critical. It initiated several successful high-profile events such as Oireachtas na Gaeilge, Irish-Language Week and the Irish-Language Fund. While the League allied itself with other organizations (GAA, cycling clubs), it retained its own distinctive identity and particular goals.

In contrast, the Celtic Literacy Society's legacy included bilingual 1798 memorials, the Irish-language component of Cumann na nGaedheal and the early Sinn Féin, and the establishment of the Irish Literary Theatre in as much as the Society was instrumental in Alice Milligan's writing "The Deliverance of Red Hugh," a play to celebrate Samhain.[116] The production apparently inspired W.B. Yeats to see his own plays performed with a Dublin accent; the result was *Cathleen ni Houlihan*.[117] The Society was a Dublin-based organization that made little effort initially to expand beyond the capital or create a network of rural branches. Its Dublin members were regarded as Pro-Parnell and pro-IRB. Its rotating presidency, while democratic, prevented the emergence of a strong dominant leader—such as Hyde—who could shape the organization over time and become its public face. Comprised largely of Dublin-based working-class males, the absence of Catholic clerics in the minutes and newspaper accounts is striking and underlines by contrast how comfortable the League was with Catholic clergy. In addition to being urban and working-class, the Society's membership tended to be non-university educated. While widely read and well informed, they tended in large part to educate themselves through extensive use of public libraries. The decision to be 'non-partisan,' rather than 'non-political,' allowed for

---

[116] Henry C. Phibbs, Bureau of Military History, Witness Statement 848, 4–5.

[117] Richard J. Finneran and George Mills Harper (eds.) *The Collected Works of W.B. Yeats*, Vol II: The Plays (New York: Simon and Schuster, 2010), 834.

cooperation with political groups but also made it sympathetic to the IRB. Critically, the League's non-partisan clause allowed it, and Hyde, to assert their 'non-political' status–a distinction they stressed often and frequently, even after the Society's demise.

Whereas the Gaelic League influenced dancing, music, singing, folklore, and place names as well as fashion and design, the Society offered a vision of an Irish-language organization that quickly abandoned its specific agenda and merged with other groups following a broader, vaguer, more generalized objective. This policy is very similar to that which the League ultimately adopted in 1915 when the IRB forced Hyde's resignation.[118] Yet, we may ponder what would have happened had the League abandoned its non-sectarian, non-political stance much sooner? What if it had participated in the 1798 commemorations and merged with the National Council and, later, with Sinn Féin? How dissimilar were the later P.H. Pearse's attitudes toward Synge, and Rooney's attitudes toward literature in English? What would have been lost in terms of the Irish-speaking districts and the production of Irish-language literature? Had the League merged with the Society and Inighidhne na hÉireann, what role would Hyde, MacNeill, and Peter O'Leary have played? Had Rooney lived, would he have been the IRB's choice to replace Hyde as president in 1913 and 1915, as it sought control of the League? What role would Rooney have played in the Irish Volunteers or in the cultural politics of the Free State?

---

[118] See Timothy G. McMahon, "Douglas Hyde and the Politics of the Gaelic League in 1914," *Éire-Ireland* 53, no.1 (2018), 29–47.

The *Annals of Ulster* and Anglo-Saxon Kingship: a Preliminary Discourse

Calum Platts

. . . ₇ þy ilcan geare geeode Ecgbryht cyning Miercna rice ₇ al þæt besuþan humbre wæs ₇ he wæs se ealhteþa cyning se þe bretwalda wæs.[1]

. . . and in the same year King Ecgberht conquered the kingdom of Mercia and all that was to the south of the Humber and he was the eighth king who was *Bretwalda.*

This entry in the A recension of the *Anglo-Saxon Chronicle* (better known as the *Parker Chronicle*) contains what is probably the most controversial word in Anglo-Saxon historiography: *Bretwalda.* It has traditionally been interpreted as meaning 'Britain-ruler' and indicating a king who had achieved supremacy throughout Southumbria—the name for the Germanic-controlled region south of the Humber.[2] The Chronicler lifted the significance of controlling this region from Bede's *Historia Ecclesiastica,* in which its apparent importance has its origins.[3] As such

---

[1] Cambridge, Corpus Christi College MS 173, f. 12r.

[2] The position of Northumbria within this is curious. Neither the *Historia Ecclesiastica* nor the *Anglo-Saxon Chronicle* suggest that holding Northumbria was necessary to be marked as an especially powerful king. However, this did not preclude three Northumbrian kings: Edwin, Oswald and Oswiu, from being included by Bede in his list of kings who had *imperium* throughout Southumbria and by the Chronicler (who based his list upon Bede's) in his list of *Bretwaldas.*

[3] Bertram Colgrave and R. A. B. Mynors ed. and trans., *Bede's Ecclesiastical History of the English People* (*HE*) (Oxford: Clarendon Press, 1969), 148–50. Bede's *Historia Ecclesiastica* is the major source available to Anglo-Historians historians, studying the seventh and early eighth centuries. The *Historia Ecclesiastica* is famed for its clarity and use of source material to construct arguments. For centuries Bede's authority was unquestioned, hence his importance to early proponents of the *Bretwaldas.* Recent studies have sought to emphasize Bede's agenda and his sometimes telling silences, although his importance remains undiminished. A good and fairly recent introduction to Bede, his history and his other works is Scott Degregorio ed., *The Cambridge Companion to Bede* (Cambridge: Cambridge Univesity Press, 2010).

the existence of the *Bretwaldas* ostensibly has the authority of Bede, but not only is he vague in describing the significance of these men, the word *Bretwalda* is completely absent from his work. Consequently, since the mid-nineteenth century a debate has raged as to the significance of the *Bretwaldas*. Many have contended that *Bretwalda* was a title; a title signified an office, which in turn must have had powers, privileges and responsibilities.[4] The simple fact that all other recensions of the *Anglo-Saxon Chronicle* use the term *brytenwealda*—meaning 'wide rulers'—has led to more cautious assessments. Indeed, Barbara Yorke, Steven Fanning and above all Simon Keynes have led the way in querying the basic

---

[4] This maximalist interpretation finds support from: Francis Palgrave, *History of England, Vol. I: Anglo-Saxon Period* (London: W. Clowes, 1831), 76–7; Johann Lappenberg, *A History of England under the Anglo-Saxon Kings, Vol. I*, trans. Benjamin Thorpe (London: John Murray, 1845), 125–6; Edward Freeman, *The History of the Norman Conquest of England: its Causes and its Results, Vol. I* (Oxford: Clarendon Press, 1867), 549; H. Munro Chadwick, *The Origin of the English Nation* (Cambridge: Cambridge University Press, 1907), 12; Frank Stenton, *Anglo-Saxon England* (Oxford: Clarendon Press, 1971), 34–6; Eric John, *Orbis Britanniae and other studies* (Leicester: Leicester University Press, 1966), 6–14.

[5] Barbara Yorke, "The Vocabulary of Anglo-Saxon Overlordship," in *Anglo-Saxon Studies in Archaeology and History* 2 (1981): 171–200 at 172–8, 184; Steven Fanning, "Bede, Imperium and the Bretwaldas," in *Speculum* 66 (1991): 1–26 at 15–17; Simon Keynes, "England, 700–900," in *The New Cambridge Medieval History, Vol. II, c. 700–c. 900*, ed. Rosamond McKitterick (Cambridge: Cambridge University Press, 1995), 18–42 at 39; Simon Keynes, "Rædwald the Bretwalda," in *Voyage to the Other World: The Legacy of Sutton Hoo*, ed. Calvin B. Kendall and Peter S. Wells (Minneapolis, MN: University of Minnesota Press, 1992), 103–124 at 109. Other papers that tend towards a minimalist interpretation include: John Mitchell Kemble, *The Saxons in England: A History of the English Commonwealth till the Period of the Norman Conquest, Vol. II* (London: Longman, Brown, Green and Longmans, 1849), 10–18; William Stubbs, *The Constitutional Development of England, Vol. I* (Oxford: Clarendon Press, 1892), 180–1; Charles Plummer, *Venerabilis Baedae, Opera Historica: Tomus Posterior* (Oxford: Clarendon Press, 1896), 85; I. Maier, "The Bretwalda King," in *Melbourne Historical Journal* 6 (1966): 53–61; Patrick Wormald, "Bede, the *Bretwaldas* and the Origins of the *Gens Anglorum*," in *Ideal and Reality in Frankish and Anglo-Saxon Society: Studies presented to J.M. Wallace-Hadrill*, ed. Patrick Wormald, Donald Bullough and Roger Collins (Oxford: B. Blackwell, 1983), 99–129 at 117–19.

historicity of the *Bretwaldas*.[5] However, despite these more recent and compelling critiques the idea of supreme kingship amongst the Anglo-Saxons and therefore the *Bretwaldas* has remained alluring and persists.

A hitherto unused source for this debate is the *Annals of Ulster* (*AU*); based on earlier exemplars, the *AU* contain the best continuous record of early medieval Irish history. It contains occasional entries concerning the Anglo-Saxons (see Appendix, Table 1), amongst them a series of notes, running from the seventh to the ninth century, recording the deaths of Anglo-Saxon kings, who are accorded the title *rex Saxonum*.[6] This title could be translated as either 'a king of the Saxons' or 'the King of the Saxons.' The latter translation might suggest contemporary, independent evidence of some form of supreme kingship amongst the Anglo-Saxons. The interpretation and significance of this title is not the purview of this paper. This paper simply seeks to prove the validity of the Irish annals to Anglo-Saxon history and thereby set up these annals, not least this question about the *reges Saxonum*, for future study from an Anglo-Saxon perspective. Consequently, there is a focus upon existing scholarship concerned with the Irish annals and Anglo-Saxon-Irish links, utilising it to demonstrate that the Anglo-Saxon entries are contemporary and reliable. The annal entries are also placed alongside the Anglo-Saxon corpus of material to demonstrate their independence. Overall, this study seeks to demonstrate the utility of the Irish annals to Anglo-Saxon history and highlight an important question about Anglo-Saxon kingship that emerges from such a study.

The Question of Contemporaneity

Establishing the contemporary nature of the seventh-, eighth- and ninth-century entries of *AU* is a twofold task. The first task is the demonstration that *AU*, themselves the product of the fifteenth century, contain entries written over eight hundred years earlier. The second is to

---

[6] This title appears intermittently with figures in the tenth century onwards, but the death of Æthelwulf arguably ends the consistent, essentially generational, use of the title by the annalists. Moreover, its potential significance is diminished by the triumph of the House of Wessex and the consolidation of the Anglo-Saxon kingdoms into a single kingdom.

show that the Anglo-Saxon entries form part of that early tradition. The former issue is relatively straightforward, understanding a contemporary annalistic record to mean that on an annular basis a person summarised the key events of the past year, thereby building up a record. Indeed, there has been a general acceptance of Smyth's seminal article arguing that the annalistic record becomes contemporary in the mid-sixth century.[7]

Mc Carthy alone rejects this view, preferring a record dating back to Patrick's evangelisation of the Irish, with the record being transmitted to St. Columba by Finnian of Movilla.[8] The basis of his theory is derived from Ó Buachalla's work. He established that the entries, which lack indications that they are retrospective, all derive from Leinster.[9] However, Ó Buachalla was very cautious, merely commenting that these six entries "are possibly genuinely contemporary records."[10] Mc Carthy assumes that these entries are contemporary and surprisingly asserts that he will take as contemporary any entry unless there is positive proof to reject it as an insertion or part of a reconstructed record.[11]

There are two principle problems with this. Firstly, the context of the fifth-century annals would strongly militate against a contemporary record; the vast majority are demonstrably derived from other sources. Indeed, numerous entries explicitly note this fact.[12] As such, the fifth-century annals read as a reconstructed record and this creates the second problem: six possibly contemporary entries for an entire century does not make an annalistic record, which is fundamentally an annular record. Mc

---

[7] Alfred P. Smyth, "The Earliest Irish Annals: Their First Contemporary Entries, and the Earliest Centres of Recording," in *Proceedings of the Royal Irish Academy* 72C (1972): 1–48; Thomas Charles-Edwards, *The Chronicle of Ireland: Volume One* (Liverpool: Liverpool University Press, 2006), 8.

[8] Daniel P. Mc Carthy, *The Irish Annals, Their Genesis, Evolution and History*, (Dublin: Four Courts, 2008), 163.

[9] Ibid., 154.

[10] Liam Ó Buachalla, "The construction of the Irish Annals, 429–466," in *The Journal of the Cork Historical and Archaeological Society* 63 (1958): 103–16 at 115.

[11] Mc Carthy, *Irish Annals*, 159.

[12] Seán Mac Airt and Gearóid Mac Niocaill ed. and trans., *The Annals of Ulster (to A.D. 1131) (AU)* (Dublin: Dublin Institute for Advanced Studies, 1983), s.a. 432, 435, 436, 438, 439, 440, 446, 449, 451, 456, 457, 458, 459, 460, 461, 467, 468, 469, 470, 471, 475, 481, 482, 483, 485, 486, 490, 491, 493, 494, 495, 496, 497.

Carthy is aware of this problem and seeks to address it by arguing that other genuine fifth century entries have been edited out by Ecgberht of Iona due to his hostility to the Dionysiac method of calculating Easter and a desire to emphasise papal and Patrician supremacy.[13] At the outset, this is an argument *ex silentio* and as such is unverifiable. Moreover, there is positive evidence against Mc Carthy's arguments. Firstly, his evidence that Ecgberht altered the early annalistic record lies in a misreading of Bannerman's article on the Scottish entries. Mc Carthy states that Bannerman described a Northumbrian Chronicle that was inserted into the Irish record.[14] Bannerman in fact did no such thing, instead arguing (and this is what Mc Carthy misunderstood) that an *Iona Chronicle* served as the means of transmission to an *Ulster Chronicle* that co-existed with it in Ireland.[15] The Anglo-Saxon and Scottish entries were always part of Bannerman's *Iona Chronicle*, thereby depriving Mc Carthy of the physical evidence that Ecgberht had tampered with them. Secondly, *AU* record the change to Iona's method of calculating Easter; Ecgberht of Iona's great triumph.[16] It is hardly credible that Ecgberht would carefully delete the fifth-, sixth- and seventh-century references to the Easter controversy and

---

[13] Mc Carthy, *Irish Annals*, 141–4, 154.

[14] Ibid., p. 141.

[15] John Bannerman, *Studies in the History of Dalriada* (Edinburgh: Scottish Academic Press, 1974), 9–10, 20–22.

[16] *AU*, s.a. 716.

leave this smoking gun.[17] As such, the origins of the Irish annalistic tradition need to be placed later in time.[18]

This is not to say that Smyth's arguments are beyond reproach; there are certain flaws with his approach and so the argument can be further honed. He noted a shift in the style of *AU*: there is a notable change in the tone of the annals, shown by the nature of the entries, the number derived from other sources and the shift to more local, internal record keeping. As part of this shift in style, three types of entries become markers of contemporaneity: astronomical events; natural disasters (*i.e.* plagues and famines) and the weather.[19] This argument is ostensibly very compelling: astronomical data can be checked to see whether an Irish annalist could have observed the noted phenomenon and natural disasters and the weather suggest the annalist is reacting to immediate events in the society around them. However, the problem with astronomical events is that they attracted especial attention from medieval people. As a result, annalists took care to note them, even if they could not have been observed in

---

[17] It is worth querying whether there has to be an editor of the early annals. While it is surprising that 716 is the only reference to the Easter controversy, the history of the controversy is the history of Iona's defeat. As such, would an Ionan annalist (see below) choose to record it? If there is indeed an editor (and this debate all revolves around negative evidence), it seems to me more credible to identify Adomnán, the abbot of Iona. His own opposition to the Dionysiac method could be a motive, but the threat of Armagh to Iona's claims to primacy seem more likely. Adomnán's *Vita Columbae* is, in part, a refutation of Armagh's claims and Adomnán may have sought to obscure evidence of Iona's divergence with the papacy over Easter by editing such references (such as a hypothetical one concerned with the Synod of Whitby of 664) out of the annals.

[18] For other critiques of Mc Carthy's arguments, consult: Thomas Charles-Edwards, "Review of The Irish Annals: Their Genesis, Evolution and History, by D. P. Mc Carthy," in *Studia Hibernica* 36 (2009–10): 207–10; Denis Casey, "The Irish Annals: Their Genesis, Evolution and History, by Daniel P. Mc Carthy," in *Early Medieval Europe* 18 (2010): 126–8; Nicholas Evans, *The Present and the Past in Medieval Irish Chronicles*, (Woodbridge: The Boydell Press, 2010), 145–70.

[19] Smyth, "The Earliest Irish Annals," 9–11; Francis Ludlow, "Assessing non-climatic influences on the record of extreme weather events in the Irish Annals," in *At the Anvil: Essays in Honour of William J. Smyth*, ed. Patrick Duffy and William Nolan (Dublin: Geography Publications, 2012), 93–133 at 100–1.

Ireland—an eclipse noted for 496 demonstrates this.[20] As such, while eclipses visible in Ireland are present at the start of the sixth century and can be used as likely proof of some form of record keeping, they cannot be used as evidence of a contemporary annalistic record.[21] Turning to natural disasters, annals are disproportionately concerned with political and religious events (especially in the fifth century). The burgeoning evidence of natural disasters, appearing in 536, 539 and 545, is an interesting style change and suggests that the annals were existing within a social landscape, to which an annalist was responding.[22] However, natural disasters can create long memories; they are events of great moment and profound impact and thus get remembered. It is the weather that is crucial; weather, even unusual, violent weather, loses its significance quickly—the consequences are remembered, not the causes, as in 536 and 539; famines which can probably be attributed to climactic cooling caused by a volcanic eruption.[23] The first entry concerned with weather is 564, followed by further references in 588 and 589.[24] This strongly suggests that the annals are contemporary by no later than 564.

The annals are therefore contemporary records from the mid-sixth century and so can be used for the period with which we are concerned. Proving individual entries are contemporary is less straightforward, however one can turn to a different set of annals for comparison. The *Annals of Tigernach* (*AT*) and *AU* are remarkably similar before diverging

---

[20] *AU*, s.a. 496; *Nasa Eclipse Website* (*NEW*), "Eclipse of 22nd October 496," accessed 25 September, 2018, https://eclipse.gsfc.nasa.gov/SEsearch/SEsearchmap .php?Ecl=04961022; Daniel Mc Carthy and Aidan Breen, "An evaluation of the astronomical observations in the Irish Annals," in *Vistas in Astronomy* 41 (1997): 117–38 at 127.

[21] *AU*, s.a. 512; *NEW*, '5th January 512', accessed 25 September, 2018, https://eclipse.gsfc.nasa.gov/ SEsearch/SEsearchmap.php?Ecl=05120105; '29th June 512', accessed 25 September 2018, https://eclipse.gsfc.nasa.gov/SEsearch/ SEsearchmap.php?Ecl=05120629; '24th December 512', accessed 25 September, 2018, https://eclipse.gsfc.nasa.gov/SEsearch/SEsearchmap.php?Ecl=05121224.

[22] *AU*, s.a. 536, 539, 545.

[23] Francis Ludlow, "The dating of volcanic events and their impact upon European society, 400–800 CE," in *The European Journal of Post-Classical Archaeologies* 5 (2015): 7–30 at 13–16.

[24] *AU*, s.a. 564, 588, 589.

in the mid-eighth century, when *AT* have a lacuna before beginning again in the tenth century. The degree of commonality suggests they both have the same underlying text, generally called the *Iona Chronicle*.[25] Naturally, the editing over centuries and *AT*'s composition partially in Irish means that discrepancies in phrasing and dating are to be expected.[26] Furthermore, where *AT* have entries not found in *AU*, a majority stand at the end of an annal or within one that is blank in *AU*. This is quite strong evidence for such material for the fifth to eighth centuries being added by a later redactor, working no earlier than the tenth century.[27] Consequently, emphasis must be on points of comparison between the two annals and whether unique entries conform to verifiable patterns that are in common between the two.

The Anglo-Saxon references show remarkable similarities (see Appendix Table 1). There are, nevertheless, still some interpolations to be noted and corruptions to be cleaned up. It is doubtful that the reference to Augustine's mission is contemporary.[28] Edwin's death in *AT* in 634 is probably also an insertion.[29] 633 is probably a corrupted reference to Edwin, as it reads in *AU*, and the corruption confused a scribe, who thought Edwin's death had been overlooked.[30] However, 633 in *AT* is significant because the Irish form of *rex Saxonum—rí Saxan*—appears, suggesting Edwin was the first *rex Saxonum* of the Irish annals.[31] The 650 annal concerning Penda's and Oswiu's battle is problematic, especially in *AT*'s account, which accords with the battle of Winwæd and which it

---

[25] Kathryn Grabowski and David Dumville, *Chronicles and Annals of Mediaeval Ireland and Wales: The Clonmacnoise-group Texts* (Woodbridge: The Boydell Press, 1984), 53–6, 111–12; Bannerman, *History of Dalriada*, 8.

[26] Eoin MacNeill, "The Authorship and Structure of the Annals of Tigernach," in *Eriu* 7 (1914): 30–111 at 65–74; Grabowski and Dumville, *Chronicles and Annals*, 118–19.

[27] Grabowski and Dumville, *Chronicles and Annals*, 119, 127.

[28] *AU*, s.a. 598; Gearóid Mac Niocaill ed. and trans., *Annals of Tigernach*, (*AT*) (unpublished manuscript), accessed 20 September, 2018, http://celt.ucc.ie/published/T100002A/index.html, s.a. 597.

[29] *AT*, s.a. 634.

[30] *AU*, s.a. 631; *AT*, s.a. 633.

[31] *AT*, s.a. 633.

correctly records five years later.[32] *AU* simply record a battle.[33] This suggests *AT* have become corrupt. It is, however, unlikely to be an insertion; Penda campaigned frequently into Northumbria and once attacked Bamburgh. Bede does not provide a date for this event in the *Historia Ecclesiastica* but mentions it just before Aidan's death in 651; 650 is then a plausible date.[34] Bede's births in 650 and again in 654 are obviously insertions; one cannot have two births.[35] Moreover, births were simply not recorded in this period, due to succession to lands and thrones not being automatic and neither date appears in *AT*. The reference in *AT* to Æthelwald Moll as *ríg Saxan* is concerning, given the lack of such a reference in *AU* and the fact that it stands at the end of the annal entry.[36] However, it forms part of the verifiable earlier pattern common to both *AU* and *AT* of the *reges Saxonum*. Moreover, Dumville does specifically note that this entry might be an example of an early annal because it uses the king's nickname (Moll) and conforms to a trope present in more reliable entries about royal *clericatus*.[37] On balance, it is probably authentic. The final problematic entry, which the lacuna prevents comparison with *AT*, is in 780 and concerns "*Eilpin, rex Saxonum*."[38] This is presumably a corruption, as it refers to Alpín, king of the Picts, who died in 780. With these exceptions apart, a comparison of *AT* and *AU* shows a remarkable concordance. This strongly suggests therefore that by the divergence of *AT* and *AU* in the mid-eighth century the Anglo-Saxon entries were already present in the annalistic record.

The Question of Reliability

The answer to the question of the reliability of the annals rests upon the location of the annalist and, for the purposes of this discussion, the links between the Anglo-Saxons and the Irish, which would facilitate the exchange of information, such that the Irish might interpret and record

---

[32] *AT*, s.a. 650, 655.

[33] *AU*, s.a. 650.

[34] *HE*, 262.

[35] *AU*, s.a. 650, 654.

[36] *AT*, s.a. 764.

[37] Grabowski and Dumville, *Chronicles and Annals*, 115 n. 20.

[38] *AU*, s.a. 780.

what they had heard. At the outset, in the period from the sixth to the ninth centuries there were at least two places in which the annals were written. In 676 "Failbe returns [reveritur] from Ireland"[39] while Adomnán in 697 "proceeded [ad . . . pergit] to Ireland."[40] Both entries imply the annalist was outside of Ireland. By contrast, in 754 Sleibéne, abbot of Iona, "came [venit] to Ireland,"[41] this time placing the annalist within Ireland.

The recognition of this distinction in the record of travel aids the identification of the earlier location. The early annals must have been written in an Irish context but outside of Ireland, which logically points towards Dál Riata. This inference is corroborated by the focus upon the affairs of Dál Riata throughout the sixth and seventh centuries. The obits or abdications of Dál Riatan kings are, uniquely, consistently recorded.[42] This interest in one kingdom is complemented by an interest in one monastery: Iona. The first reference to weather, intriguingly, occurs one year after Iona's foundation in 563.[43] There is also a complete record of the foundation and abbots of Iona; no other ecclesiastical institution has such a complete record in the early annals.[44] Crucially Iona was also within Dál Riatan territory, eliding the Ionan and Dál Riatan purview perfectly. Furthermore, the geographic spread of entries up to *c.* 740 match areas with which Iona would have had easy lines of communication: Scotland and the northern kingdoms and eastern seaboard of Ireland.[45] This all suggests that the annals were written by the monks of Iona at this point in time; hence the name: the *Iona Chronicle.*[46]

From the mid-eighth century there is slightly more equivocation. The consensus is on a location somewhere in the midlands of Ireland, although whether they were housed at a monastery in Brega, at Clonmacnoise or at

---

[39] *AU*, s.a. 676; *AT*, s.a. 676.

[40] *AU*, s.a. 697; *AT*, s.a. 697.

[41] *AU*, s.a. 754; *AT*, s.a. 754.

[42] Bannerman, *History of Dalriada*, 8; *AU*, s.a. 507, 538, 574, 606, 629, 642, 654, 660, 689, 697, 698, 700, 707, 721, 723, 733, 741; *AT*, s.a. 506, 537, 573, 629, 643, 654, 659, 689, 697, 698, 700, 721, 723, 733,

[43] *AU*, s.a. 563, 564; *AT*, s.a. 562; Smyth, "The Earliest Irish Annals," 34.

[44] Abbots of the sixth and seventh centuries: *AU*, s.a. 563, 595, 598, 605, 623, 652, 657, 669, 679, 704; *AT* s.a. 562, 593, 596, 603, 624, 652, 656, 669, 679, 704.

[45] Smyth, "The Earliest Irish Annals," 36.

[46] Bannerman, *History of Dalriada*, 9.

Clonard is a matter of opinion.[47] Mac Niocaill is slightly less certain in his interpretation, arguing for two annalistic streams, identifying a northern one, perhaps centred on Armagh, and, in keeping with general opinion, a midlands one.[48] These arguments are based, as with Iona, on assessing the geographic focus of the entries. Suffice it to say that an Irish midlands location is secure, with less agreement concerning a northern recension.

For the earlier location of Iona, there is significant evidence of direct contact with the Anglo-Saxons. The earliest demonstrable link is the flight of Æthelfrith of Northumbria's family north after the victory of Rædwald of East Anglia at the battle of the River Idle and Edwin's succession to the throne of Northumbria in 616.[49] In exile, Æthelfrith's sons Oswald and Oswiu were educated and baptised at Iona, which proceeded to send missionaries to Northumbria at Oswald's request when he ascended the throne.[50] This makes the two entries concerning Æthelfrith potential retrospective additions to the text, heard from the royal and noble exiles in Dál Riata.[51] It is telling that the first entry after these that appears in both *AU* and *AT* concerns the death of Edwin, which led, after a brief delay, to the return of the exiles.[52] This link with Iona became formalised with the establishment of Lindisfarne, of which Iona was the mother house. Despite this formal connection ending at the Synod of Whitby in 664 links remained.[53] Adomnán of Iona visited Northumbria and seems to have had close ties with the king, Aldfrith.[54] Sufficiently close ties endured into the 730s such that Bede knew the date of death of Ecgberht of Iona to include it in the *Historia Ecclesiastica*.[55]

---

[47] Charles-Edwards, *Chronicle of Ireland*, 7–8; Mc Carthy, *Irish Annals*, 7; Mac Airt and Mac Niocaill, *Annals of Ulster*, xi.

[48] Gearóid Mac Niocaill, *The Medieval Irish Annals*, (Dublin: Dublin Historical Association, 1975), 22.

[49] *HE*, 180.

[50] Ibid., 212, 218–20.

[51] *AU* s.a. 600, 613; *AT* s.a. 598, 611.

[52] *AU*, s.a. 631; *AT*, s.a. 633; *HE*, 212–14.

[53] *HE*, p. 298–308; Betram Colgrave ed. and trans., *The Life of Bishop Wilfrid by Eddius Stephanus*, (Cambridge: Cambridge University Press, 1985), 20–2.

[54] *HE*, 504–6.

[55] Ibid., 554.

Beyond Northumbria, the letters of Aldhelm, a West Saxon, are invaluable. Not only may he have studied at Iona, but his letters testify that his pupils had journeyed to study in Ireland.[56] Moreover, he also bears witness to Irish students arguing with Theodore of Canterbury about computistics. These students would have been from the northern parts of Ireland, perhaps even Iona itself, given their opposition to the Alexandrine method of calculating Easter (southern Ireland having already adopted this method).[57] This is a crucial bit of evidence, because it reveals contact with the north of Ireland and indeed Iona was not confined to Northumbria, which might have limited viable interpretations of the meaning of *rex Saxonum*.

There were also palpable links beyond Iona. Anglo-Saxon ecclesiastics, as Aldhelm's letters show, travelled to Ireland to study. *Mag nÉo*, founded by Colmán of Lindisfarne, was famous, attracting comment from both Bede and Alcuin as to the number of Anglo-Saxons who went there.[58] *Rath Melsigi* is another famous example, having attracted St. Willibrord, while others, such as the Glen of Aherlow and *Tulach Léis na Saxan* also attracted students.[59] The connections of *Rath Melsigi* serve to highlight the close connections of the Anglo-Saxon and Irish Churches. Firstly, Willibrord's mission to Frisia had its origins within, and likely

---

[56] Michael Lapidge, "The Career of Aldhelm," in *Anglo-Saxon England* 36 (2006): 15–69 at 22, 48, 64; "Letter III: To Wihtfrith," in Michael Lapidge and Michael Herren ed. and trans., *Aldhelm: The Prose Works* (Ipswich: D.S. Brewer, 1979), 154–5 at 154.

[57] "Letter V: To Heahfrith," in Lapidge and Herren ed. and trans., *Aldhelm*, 160–4 at 163; Clare Stancliffe, *Bede, Wilfrid and the Irish* (Jarrow: St Paul's Church, 2003), 3.

[58] *HE*, 348; *Epistolae Karolini Aevi* II, E. Dümmler ed., MGH Epist. 4 (Berlin: Weidmann 1895), 445–6 (no. 287); Fiona Edmonds, "The Practicalities of Communication between Northumbrian and Irish Churches, *c.* 635–735," in *Anglo-Saxon/Irish Relations Before the Vikings: Proceedings of the British Academy* 157, James Graham-Campbell and Michael Ryan ed. (Oxford: Oxford University Press, 2009), 129–47 at 143.

[59] Alcuin, "The Life of St Willibrord," in *The Anglo-Saxon Missionaries in Germany: Being the Lives of SS Willibrord, Boniface, Sturm, Leoba and Lebuin, together with the Hodoeporicon of St Willibald and a Selection from the Correspondence of St Boniface* (London: Sheed and Ward, 1954), 3–22 at 5–6; Edmonds, "Practicalities of Communication," 143; D. Ó Cróinín, "Rath Melsigi, St Willibrord and the Earliest Echternach Manuscripts," in *Peritia* 3 (1984), 17–44, at 32.

derived its manuscripts from, an Irish milieu.[60] Within this, the evidence of the Echternach manuscripts, which possess a Hiberno-Saxon style, reflect the intermingling of the two cultures and the exchange of ideas that the connections of the schools allowed.[61] Secondly, Ecgberht of Iona, who ultimately converted Iona to the Alexandrine Easter, spent much of his career at *Rath Melsigi*, possibly heading it given that he was able to dispatch Willibrord and his companions to Frisia.[62] Indeed, Ecgberht's career is a testament to the inter-connections of the Insular World. Not only does he show how influential an Englishman could become in the Irish Church, but he counselled Ecgfrith against attacking the Irish in 684. Despite spending much of his life in Ireland, he still had the connections to possess an intimate knowledge of affairs in the Northumbrian court and provide his advice.[63]

In similar fashion, Irish ecclesiastics, who lack ties to Iona in the evidence, are to be found in various Anglo-Saxon kingdoms. In the early eighth century, an Irish priest named Ultán was a scribe associated with Lindisfarne.[64] There is also a letter to Offa from Charlemagne, which provides some intriguing evidence. Charlemagne wrote to Offa about

---

[60] *HE*, 480; Ó Cróinín, "Earliest Echternach Manuscripts," 33.

[61] Ó Cróinín, "Earliest Echternach Manuscripts," 38–9. In addition to this example, one could cite the evidence for Irish influences upon Anglo-Saxon texts. The Codex Amiatinus, for example, follows a corrupt Irish text for its psalter. More famously, there is the influence of the penitentials, with Irish echoes clearly present in the Penitential of Theodore. Kathleen Hughes, "Evidence for Contacts between the Churches of the Irish and English from the Synod of Whitby to the Viking Age," in *England before the Conquest: Studies in Primary Sources Presented to Dorothy Whitelock*, Peter Clemoes and Kathleen Hughes ed. (Cambridge: Cambridge University Press, 1971), 49–67, at 59–64.

[62] *HE* 312–14, 474–80.

[63] *HE*, 428. Ó Cróinín hypothesises that the "Ecg" in Ecgberht's and Ecgfrith's names might suggest they were related and that Ecgberht consequently was a member of the Northumbrian royal family, which could explain Ecgberht's knowledge of the attack. D. Ó Cróinín, *The Kings Depart: The Prosopography of Anglo-Saxon Royal Exile in the Sixth and Seventh Centuries*, Quiggin Pamphlets on the Sources of Gaelic History 8 (Cambridge: Department of Anglo-Saxon, Norse and Celtic, 2007), 15–17.

[64] *Aethelwulf De Abbatibus*, A. Campbell ed. (Oxford: Clarendon Press, 1961), 19; Hughes, "Evidence for Contacts," 56; Ó Cróinín, "Earliest Echternach Manuscripts," 37.

"Your [*i.e.* Offa's] Scottish priest"[65] in order to acquire aid in returning him to his homeland. On a straightforward level the letter is evidence of the movement of Irish ecclesiastics through the Anglo-Saxon kingdoms. However, the "your"[66] implies that the priest was at Charlemagne's court through Offa's patronage, suggesting in turn that he had spent time at Offa's court. This implies that Offa was known in Ireland such that he could attract Irish ecclesiastics into his service. The scale of this Irish clerical presence amongst the Anglo-Saxons may be reflected in the fifth canon of the Synod of Chelsea. It heavily criticised the Irish episcopacy and prohibited Irish priests from baptising or celebrating the Eucharist.[67] A single disruptive Irish priest in Francia, even a few of them, would scarcely have elicited a synodal response.

Clearly there were excellent contacts with Iona to allow the facilitation of information-exchange. While the uncertain location of the annals after they moved from Iona means that direct links cannot be proved, the evidence of the Irish schools and of Offa's priest and the Synod of Chelsea still points to good, wide-spread connections.[68] As such, there is no reason to doubt the reliability or authenticity of the Anglo-Saxon entries preserved in *AU* and *AT*; Irish observers would have had access to information concerning the affairs of Anglo-Saxon England and, while naturally they would have placed their own interpretation on it, this does not detract from the utility of the information they record.

---

[65] "27. Charles the Great to Offa, king of Mercia, 793–6," in *The Reign of Charlemagne: Documents on Carolingian Government and Administration*, H. R. Loyn and J. Percival ed. (London: Edward Arnold, 1975), 112–13 at 113.

[66] Ibid.

[67] Hughes, "Evidence for Contacts," 56–7, 64–5; Arthur Haddan and William Stubbs, ed., *Councils and Ecclesiastical Documents Relating to Great Britain and Ireland Vol. III* (Oxford: Clarendon Press, 1871), 581.

[68] This was a brief survey of some of the more noteworthy evidence of links between the Anglo-Saxons and Irish in this period; a subject which could be a paper in itself. An excellent work on the topic, including both historical and archaeological papers on the subject, is Graham-Campbell's and Ryan's *Anglo-Saxon/Irish Relations Before the Vikings*. Another good survey is Kathleen Hughes, "Evidence for Contacts" 49–67.

The Independence of the Annalistic Record[69]

The final step in demonstrating the credibility of the annals as a source for the Anglo-Saxons is proving the independence of these entries from an Anglo-Saxon source, such as Bede's works, the *Anglo-Saxon Chronicle* and the Anglian genealogies. Firstly, very simply, there is no concordance between either *AU* and *AT* or Bede's chronicles: the *Chronica Maior* and the *Chronica Minor*.[70] Moreover, the annalist occasionally supplies independent information. Concerning the Battle of Caer Legion in 613, the king of the Britons is named as Solon, a detail appearing in no Anglo-Saxon source.[71] The entry for 685, referring to Ecgfrith's attack on Ireland in 684, uniquely provides both a month and a place for the invasion: June and Mag Breg.[72] In 698 the patronymic for the ealdorman Behrtred is given—*filius Bernith*—which is absent from the *Historia Ecclesiastica* and the battle referenced is overlooked in the *Anglo-Saxon Chronicle*.[73] Overall, the fact that the annals can supply independent evidence that supplements the Anglo-Saxon record is, in itself, strong evidence to suggest that they are not dependent on either Bede's works or the *Anglo-Saxon Chronicle*.

This argument is further strengthened by the phrasing of the entries. One example is the title accorded Archbishop Theodore of Canterbury. The title "*episcopus Britannie*"[74] appears in neither the *Anglo-Saxon Chronicle* nor the *Historia Ecclesiastica*, both of which consistently call Theodore archbishop.[75] Furthermore, the Irish typically provide patronymics within their obits, which occurs with the Anglo-Saxon entries

---

[69] See Table 1

[70] Faith Wallis ed. and trans, *Bede: The Reckoning of Time* (Liverpool: Liverpool University Press, 1999), 157–237; Calvin B. Kendall and Faith Wallis ed. and trans, *Bede: On the Nature of Things and on Times* (Liverpool: Liverpool University Press, 2010), 126–31.

[71] *AU*, s.a. 613; *AT*, s.a. 611.

[72] *AU*, s.a. 685; *AT*, s.a. 685.

[73] *AU*, s.a. 698; *AT*, s.a. 698; *HE*, 564.

[74] *AU*, s.a. 691; *AT*, s.a. 691.

[75] *HE*, 31, 335, 353, 369, 471, 563; G. N. Garmonsway ed. and trans., *The Anglo-Saxon Chronicle* (*ASC*) (London: Dent, 1954), 34–5, 37–41.

in 631, 671, 675, 680, 686, 698, 704, 713, 716, 718 and 731.[76] This is a style that is largely absent when either Bede or the *Anglo-Saxon Chronicle* record deaths.[77] There are two exceptions within the *Anglo-Saxon Chronicle*. It provides a patronymic and name for Wulfhere in 675 (although his patronymic is separate from his death) and provides a genealogy for Ceolwulf in 731.[78] As regards Wulfhere's obit, it is difficult to countenance the idea of dependence on the *Anglo-Saxon Chronicle* principally because the entry, as it appears in *AU* and *AT*, fails to name Wulfhere; a scribe copying a record of someone's death it unlikely to forget such a detail. Ceolwulf is simpler to deal with because the genealogy supplied by the *Anglo-Saxon Chronicle* describes him as "the son of Cutha, the son of Cuthwine,"[79] not as *AU* and *AT* have it: "Cuthwine's son."[80] This lack of agreement between the *Anglo-Saxon Chronicle*, Bede and the annals would suggest that they are unrelated.

The patronymics could lend themselves to a dependence upon the Anglian genealogies.[81] This is immediately a rather limiting proposition because it could only explain nine out of the forty-two entries. There is also no dependence upon these genealogies for Behrtred son of Bernith's obit.[82] This fact alone is fairly convincing evidence for annalistic independence. Patronymics form part of the native annalistic style, as such one could question why there is a need to seek an explanation for their appearance. Nevertheless, there are two points that are worth emphasising. The first is that the genealogies are written in Old English with the Old English patronymic style. As such, to give an example, Oswiu is noted as "*Oswio Æðelfriðing*"[83] as opposed to the annalistic Latin: "*Ossu filii*

---

[76] *AU*, s.a. 631, 671, 675, 680, 686, 698, 704, 713, 716, 718, 731; *AT*, s.a. 671, 675, 680, 686, 698, 704, 713, 716, 718, 731.

[77] *HE*, 202–3, 348–9, 400–1, 565–7; *ASC*, 24–5, 34–5, 38–9, 40–5.

[78] *ASC*, 34–5, 44.

[79] *ASC*, 44.

[80] *AU*, s.a. 731; *AT*, s.a. 731.

[81] The genealogies have been published in: David Dumville, "The Anglian Collection of Royal Genealogies and Regnal Lists," in *Anglo-Saxon England* 5 (1976): 23–50 at 30–7.

[82] *AU*, s.a. 698; *AT*, s.a. 698.

[83] CCCC 183 65*r*, col. 2: Dumville, "Anglian Collection," 32.

Eitilbrith"[84] or Irish: "*Ossu maic Etilbrith.*"[85] Consequently, direct comparisons cannot be made between the two sources, although this cannot be proof of independence. Secondly, the patronymics appear in the annalistic record as obits. As such, a crucial element to this record is the year of death. The genealogies and regnal lists lack this information. Occasionally the lengths of the reigns of the kings of the various kingdoms are given but no dates, although admittedly it would not be difficult for a copyist to find a reference date and calculate the years of the kings' deaths.[86] Nevertheless, placing the annals and the genealogies and the regnal lists side by side does reveal these distinctions which create problems for arguments of dependence. This is underscored by the highly limited amount of genealogical information in the annals. There is no compelling answer to the question of why an annalist with these tables in front of him would copy such a small amount of information. Given that the Anglian Collection can explain so few of the annalistic entries and none of them particularly convincingly, it is far simpler to argue that the annals are independent of them.

The final point of comparison is the Latin of the annalist and that of Bede. This too would suggest independence. Bede's entries are all longer and more detailed than the annalists' (see Table 1). Moreover, specific words are often different. Bede names Lindisfarne "*insula Lindisfarnensi*"[87] while the annals use "*Insola Med Goet*"[88] and "*Inis Metgoit.*"[89] Osred's death is noted by Bede with "*occiso*"[90] and "*interfectus,*"[91] contrasting strikingly with the annalistic "*iugulatio,*"[92] which could be the first compelling evidence Osred was assassinated— *iugulatio* implying that his throat was cut. A similar point can be made for

---

[84] *AU*, s.a. 671.

[85] *AT*, s.a. 671.

[86] These are the Tiberius B. v and CCCC 183: Dumville, "Anglian Collection," 32–3, 35–6.

[87] *HE*, 218.

[88] *AU*, s.a. 632.

[89] *AT*, s.a. 635.

[90] *HE*, 552.

[91] *HE*, 566.

[92] *AU*, s.a. 716.

the obits of Oswald and Penda. As the entries survive in *AU*, there is no mention of their deaths. *AT* can supplement *AU* here, because it does explicitly note that fact and so the record of their deaths may have been in the original text of the *Iona Chronicle*. For both Oswald and Penda, the word "*cecidit*"[93] is used in *AT* to note that they had died in battle. Bede uses "*occisus est*"[94] and "*occisus*"[95] when recording Oswald's death, "*occisionem*"[96] and "*periit*"[97] for Penda. The different vocabulary used by these two accounts would indicate independence. Even if it is claimed that the references to these kings' deaths were inserted into *AT*, the lack of explicit reference to death in *AU* still points to differences between Bede and the original *Iona Chronicle* as it is preserved in later texts. Furthermore, in 671 and 675 the deaths of Oswiu and Wulfhere are noted in *AU* and *AT* by use of the noun "*mors*."[98] Bede expresses this with verbs: in the case of Oswiu "*mortuus est*"[99] and "*obit*;"[100] Wulfhere's death is noted with "*defunctus*."[101] A final example may be given for the Battle of Nechtansmere. The references to the high casualties and Ecgfrith's death differ. Bede wrote "*cum maxima parte copiarum extinctus*,"[102] using "*occisus est*"[103] in the closing chronicle. *AU*'s entry reads: "*magna cum caterua militum suorum interfectus est*,"[104] with *AT* following this exactly: "*magna cum caterua militum suorum interfectus est*."[105] There is therefore no evidence to suggest that the Latin of the Ionan annalists and Bede is related, lending support to the idea that the annalistic material was not interpolated from an Anglo-Saxon source. Ultimately, there is nothing

---

[93] *AT*, s.a. 641, 655.
[94] *HE*, 240.
[95] *HE*, 564.
[96] *HE*, 294.
[97] *HE*, 564.
[98] *AU*, s.a. 671, 675; *AT*, s.a. 671, 675
[99] *HE*, 348.
[100] *HE*, 564.
[101] *HE*, 564.
[102] *HE*, 428.
[103] *HE*, 564.
[104] *AU*, s.a. 686.
[105] *AT*, s.a. 686.

compelling about the annalistic Anglo-Saxon records to suggest that they are insertions from other texts. As such, I would posit that it is perfectly legitimate to ask questions of the annals concerned with what *rex Saxonum* means.

Conclusion

The Irish annals are therefore a contemporary, reliable and independent witness to Anglo-Saxon history and the *Annals of Ulster*, with the most complete record, is the best exemplar for this. The internal evidence of the annals suggests an *Iona Chronicle* was in existence from the 560s, before giving way to a chronicle being kept on the Irish mainland, most likely somewhere in the midlands. By a comparison of the Anglo-Saxon entries in *AU* with those in *AT*, it is clear that they form a part of these earliest phases of the annalistic tradition. Alongside this, the evidence of close and sustained communication between the Irish and Anglo-Saxon worlds provides a context in which the information could have made its way into the *Iona Chronicle* and its successors. Moreover, a comparison of the annalistic entries and Anglo-Saxon sources suggests that there is no relation between the two corpora of material. Consequently, there is potential in future studies of the annalistic material from an Anglo-Saxon perspective. Above all, the significance of the *reges Saxonum* is a clear topic that emerges for future study. The Irish context of the title needs to be analysed in order to understand how best to interpret the title, as does its relationship to Anglo-Saxon kingship and the historiography of the *Bretwaldas*.[106]

Acknowledgements

Thanks are due to Immo Warntjes, who supervised my MPhil dissertation, from which this article has been developed, as well as Patrick McAlary, Brittany Hanlon, Stephen Connelly and Joe Mc Carthy for commenting upon various drafts of this paper.

---

[106] How the annalistic references to Anglo-Saxon kings compares to Bede's list of kings possessing *imperium* in Southumbria, which in turn informs the *ASC*'s list of *Bretwaldas* is tabulated in Table 2. There is a curious overlap with Bede's list but the annalistic list is more extensive, even for the seventh century.

Table 1 Comparison of annual entries 597/8–858 with HE

Year	AU entry	AU translation	Year	AT entry	AT translation	Iona Chronicle (Y/?/N)	Historia Ecclesiastica [Bede]	Anglo-Saxon Chronicle
598	Augustinus venit in Angliam	Augustine came to England	597	Saxanaigh do dul cum credmi	The Saxons came to the faith	N (the difference between the two suggests both are retrospective additions after they diverged)	Augustinus cum familis Christi…rediit in pus Verbi perventique Brittaniam AND Anno DXCVII venere Brittaniam praefati doctores	Her Gregorius papa sende to Brytene Augustinum. mid wel manegum munecum. þe Godes word Engla ðeoda godspelledon
600	Bellum Saxonum in quo uictus est Aedan	The battle of the Saxons in which Aedan was vanquished	598	Cath Saxonum la h-Aedan, ubi cecidit Eanfraith frater Etalfraich la Mael Uma mac Baedan, in quo uictus erat	The battle of the Saxons by Aedan, where Eanfraith brother of Aethelferth fell by Mael Uma son of Baetán, in which he was vanquished	Y (although where the text diverges ?)	Unde motus eius profectibus Aedan rex Scottorum, qui Brittaniam inhabitant, venit contra eum cum immense et forti exercitu; sed cum paucis victus aufugit. Siquidem in loco celeberrimo, qui dicitur Degastan, id est Degsa lapis, omnis pene eius est caesus exercitus. In qua etiam pugna Theodbald frater Aedilfridi cum omni illo, quem ipse ducebat, exercitu peremtus est	
613	Bellum Caire Legion ubi sancti occisi sunt et cecidit Solon m. Conaen, rex Britanorum	The battle of Caer Legion, in which holy men were slain, and Solon son of Conaen, king of Britons fell	611	Cath Caire Legion ubi sancti occissi sunt, et cecidit Solon mac Conain rex Bretanorum et Cetula rex cecidit. Etalfraidh uictor erat, qui post statim obit	The battle of Carleon where saints were killed, and Solon son of Conan king of the Britons fell, and Cetula the king fell. Etalfraidh was victor, who thereafter soon died	Y (although where the text diverges ?)	Siquidem post haec ipse, de quo diximus, rex Anglorum fortissimus Aedilfrid collecto grandi exercitu ad Civitatem Legionum, quae a gente Anglorum Legacaestir, a Brettonibus autem rectius Carlegion appellatur, maximam gentis perfidae stragem dedit	
627			627	Babtismum Etuin maic Elle, qui primus credidit in reghionibus Saxonum	The baptism of Etuin son of Elle, who first believed in the regions of Saxons	?	Igitur accepit rex Eduini cum cunctis gentis suae nobilibus ac plebe perplurima fidem et lauacrum sanctae regenerationis anno regni sui undecimo AND Anno DCXXVII Eduini rex baptizmus cum sua gente in pascha	Her Edwine kyning wæs gefulwad mid his þeode on Eastron

Year	AU entry	AU translation	Year	AT entry	AT translation	Iona Chronicle (Y/?/N)	Historia Ecclesiastica [Bede]	Anglo-Saxon Chronicle
			631	Cath Fedha Eoin, in quo Mael Caith mac Scandail, rex Cruithniu, uictor erat. Dal Riada cecidit. Condadh Cerr ri Dal Riada cecidit, & Dicuill mac Eachach ri ceneoil Cruithne cecidit, et Nepotes Aedan ceciderunt, id est Rigullan mac Conaing & Failbe mac Eachach & Oisric mac Albruit rigdomna Saxan cum strage maxima suorum	The battle of Fid Eoin in which Mael Caith son of Scannal, king of cruithniu, was the victor. Connadh Cerr king of Dal Riada fell, and Dicuill son of Eachach king of Cenél Cruithne fell and the nephews of Aedan fell, that is, Rigullan son of Conaing and Failbe son of Eachach and Oisric son of Albruit, king worthy Saxon, with their utmost destruction	?		
631	Bellum filii Ailli	The battle of Aille's son	633	Bas Ailli rig Saxan	The death of Aelle, king of the Saxons	Y – Bellum filii Ailli regis Saxonum	Concerto gravi proelio in campo qui vocatur Haethfelth occusus est Eduini AND Anno DCXXXIII Eduini rege peremto	Her Edwine wæs ofslægen, 7 Paulinus huerf eft to Cantwarum, 7 gesæt þæt biscepsetl on Hrofesceastre
			634	Cath Etuin maic Ailli reghis Saxonum, qui totam Britanniam regnauit, in quo uictus est Catgualiaun rege Britonum et Panta Saxano	The battle of Edwin son of Elle, who ruled the whole of Britain, in which he was conqured by Cadwallon, king of the Britons, and Penda Saxon	N		

Year	AU entry	AU translation	Year	AT entry	AT translation	Iona Chronicle (Y/?/N)	Historia Ecclesiastica [Bede]	Anglo-Saxon Chronicle
632	Insola Med Goet fundata est	The island of Medgote was founded	635	Inis Metgoit fundata est	Inis Metgoit was founded	Y	Venienti igitur ad se episcopo, rex locum sedis episcopalis in insula Lindisfarnensis, ubi ipse petebat, tribuit	
			637	Congregacio Saxonum contra Osualt	The congregation of the Saxons against Oswald	?		
639	Bellum Osualdi regis Saxonum	The battle of Oswald, king of the Saxons	641	Cath Osualt contra Panta, in quo Osualt cecidit	The battle of Oswald against Panta in which Oswald fell	Y	Quo complete annorum cirriculo occisus est, commisso gravi proelio, ab eadem gente paganoque rege Merciorum, a quo et predecessor eius Eduini peremtus fuerat, in loco quo lingua Anglorum nuncupatur Maserfelth AND Anno DCXLII Osuald rex occusis	Her Oswald Norþanhymbra cyning ofslægen wæs
642	Bellum Ossu contra Britones	The battle of Oswy against the Britons	643	Cath Ossu inter eum et Britones	Oswy's battle between him and Britons.	Y	Quo post annum deveniuns cum exercitu successor regni eius Osuiu abstulit ea[1]	
650	Bellum Ossu fri Pante	The battle of Oswy against Penda	650	Cath Ossu fri Pante, in quo Panta cum .xxx. regibus cecidit	The battle of Oswy against Penda in which Penda with thirty kings fell	Y – Bellum Ossu fri Pante	Nam tempore episcopatus eius hostilis Merciorum exercitus Penda duce Nordanhymbrorum regions impia clade longe lateque devastans perventi ad urbem usque regiam	
650	Hoc anno Beda natus est	This year Bede was born				N		
651	Quies Aedain episcopi Saxonum	Repose of Aedán, bishop of the Saxons	651	Quies Aedain espuic Saxan	The rest of Aodán bishop of the Saxons	Y	Obiit autem septimo decimo episcopatus sui anno, pridie kalendarum Septembrium AND Anno DCLI...Aidan episcopus defunctus est	Her Oswine kyning wæs ofslægen, 7 Aidan biscep forþferde
654	Beda hoc anno natus est	This year Bede was born				N		

[1] Whether this Bedan event is the same as the annalistic entries is uncertain; the dating of the event suggests they might be, but the information contained within the respective works is too dissimilar to be certain of a link. This could, however, be taken as further proof of the independence of the annals.

Year	AU entry	AU translation	Year	AT entry	AT translation	Iona Chronicle (Y/?/N)	Historia Ecclesiastica [Bede]	Anglo-Saxon Chronicle
656	Bellum Pante regis Saxonum. Ossu uictor erat	The battle of Penda, king of the Saxons; Oswy was victor	655	Cath Pante regis Saxonum, in quo ipse cum .xxx. reigibus cecidit. Ossiu uictor erat	The battle of Penda the king of Saxons in which he with thirty kings fell. Ossiu was the victor	Y (although the reference to the thirty kings might be an insertion in AT)	Inito ergo certamine fugati sunt et caesi pagani, duces regi xxx, qui ad auxilium venerat, pene omnes interfecti AND Anno DCLV Penda periit²	Her Penda forwearp
660	Obitus Finnani episcopi filii Rimedo	Death of bishop Finnán son of Rimid	659	Obitus Finain maic Rimedha, espuic	The death of bishop Finan son of Rimid	Y	Defuncto autem Finano, qui post illum fuit, cum Colmanus in episcopatum succederet	
668	Nauigatio Columbani episcopi cum reliquis sanctorum ad Insolam Uacce Albae, in qua fundauit aeclesiam; & nauigatio filiorum Gartnaidh ad Hiberniam cum plebe Sceth	The voyage of bishop Colmán, with the relics of the saints, to Inis Bó Finne, where he founded a church; and the voyage of the sons of Gartnaid to Ireland with the people of Sci	668	Nauigatio Colmani episcopi cum reliquiis sanctorum ad Insulam Vacce Albe in qua fundauit eclesiam. Et nauigatio filiorum Gartnaith ad Iberniam cum plebe Scith	The journey of bishop Colmán with the relics of saints to the island of Vacca Alba, in which he founded a church, and the journey of the sons of Gartnaith to Spain with the people of Scith	Y	Colman videns spretam suam doctrinam sectamque esse dispectam, adsumtis his qui se sequi voluerant, id est quo pascha catholicum et tonsuram coronae (nam et de hoc quaestio non minima erat) recipere nolebant, Scottiam regressus est, tracturus cum suis quid de his facere deberet AND Anno DCLXIIII ... Colman cum Scottis ad suos reversus est	Colman mid his geferum for to his cyöðe
671	Mors Ossu filii Etilbrith regis Saxonum	Death of Oswy son of Aethelfrith, king of the Saxons	671	Mors Ossu maic Etilbrith rig Saxan	The death of Ossu son of Aethelfrith, king of the Saxons	Y	Osuiu rex Nordanhymbrorum presses est infirmitate, qua et mortuus est AND Anno DCLXX Osuiu rex Nordanhymbrorum obit	Her forþferde Osweo Norþanhymbra cyning
675	Mors filii Pante	Death of Penda's son	675	Mors filii Panntea	The death of the son of Panntea	Y	Anno DCLXXV Uulfheri rex Merciorum, postquam xvii annos regnaverat defunctus, Aedilredo fratri reliquit imperium	Wulfhere forþferde

² It is reasonable to suppose that the reference to thirty kings, which appears only in AT, is an interpolation from Bede.

Year	AU entry	AU translation	Year	AT entry	AT translation	Iona Chronicle (Y/?/N)	Historia Ecclesiastica [Bede]	Anglo-Saxon Chronicle
676	Columbana, episcopus Insole Uacce Albe, & Finain filii Airennain pausant	Colmán, bishop of Inis Bó Finne, and Finán, son of Airennán, rest	676	Columban espoc Insole Vacce Albe & Finan mac Airennain pausant	Columban the bishop of the island of Vacca Alba and Finan son of Airennan rested	Y		
680	Bellum Saxonum ubi cecidit Ailmine filius Ossu	The battle of the Saxons, in which Aelfwine son of Oswy fell	680	Bellum Saxonum ubi cecidit Almuine filius Osu	The war of Saxons in which fell Almuine son of Osu	Y	Occisus est Aeluini frater regis Ecgfridi AND Anno DCLXXVIIII Aelfuini occisus	Her Ælfwine wæs ofslægen
685	Saxones Campum Bregh uastant et aeclesias plurimas in mense Iuni	The Saxons lay waste Mag Breg, and many churches, in the month of June	685	Saxones Campum Breg uastauerunt, et eclesias pluriamas, in mense Iuni	The Saxons laid waste Campus Breg, and several churches, in the month of June	Y	Anno dominicae incarnationis DCLXXXIIII Ecgfrid rex Nordanhymbrorum, misso Hiberniam cum exercitu duce Bercto, vastavit misere gentem innoxiam et nationi Anglorum semper amicissimam, ita ut ne ecclesiis quidem aut monasteriis manus parceret hostilis	
686	Bellum Duin Nechtain uicisimo die mensis Maii, Sabbati die, factum est, in quo Etfrith m. Ossu, rex Saxonum, x.u. anno regni sui consummata magna cum caterua militum suorum interfectus est	The battle of Dún Nechtain was fought on Saturday, May 20th, and Egfrid son of Oswy, king of the Saxons, who had completed the 15th year of his reign, was slain therein with a great body of his soldiers	686	Cath Duin Nechtain uicesimo die mensis Maii, sabbati die factum est, in quo Ecfrith mac Osu, rex Saxonum, quinto decimo anno reighni sui consummato, magna cum caterua militum suorum interfectus est Ia Bruidhi mac Bili regis Fortrenn	The battle of Dún Nechtain was carried out on the twentieth day of the month of May, a Sunday, in which Ecfrith son of Osu, king of the Saxons, in the 15th year of his rule completed, with a great body of his soldiers was killed by Bruide son of Bile king of Fortriu	Y (although where the text diverges ?)	Siquidem anno post hunc proximo idem rex, cum temere exercitum ad vastandam Pictorum provinciam duxisset, multum prohibentibus amicis et maxime beatae memoriae Cudbercto, qui nuper fuerat ordinatus episcopus, introductus est simulantibus fugam hostibus in angustias inaccessorum montium, et cum maxima parte copiarum, quas secum adduxerat, extinctus anno aetatis suae XLmo, regi autem XVmo, die tertio decimo kalendarum Iuniarum AND Anno DCLXXXV Ecgfrid rex Nordanhymbrorum occisus est	Ecgferþ cyning mon ofslog

196

Year	AU entry	AU translation	Year	AT entry	AT translation	Iona Chronicle (Y/?/N)	Historia Ecclesiastica [Bede]	Anglo-Saxon Chronicle
691	Theodorus, episcopus, Brittanie, quieuit	Theodore, bishop of Britain, rested	691	Teodorus episcopus Britaniae quieuit	Theodore bishop of Britain rested	Y	Id est DCXCmo incarnationis dominicae, Theodorus beatae memoriae archiepiscopus, senex et plenus dierum, id est annorum LXXXVIII, defunctus est AND Anno DCXC Theodorus archiepiscopus obiit	Her Þeodorus ærcebiscop forþferde
693	Bellum contra Pante	Battle against Penda				N		
698	Bellum inter Saxones & Pictos ubi cecidit filius Bernith qui dicebatur Brectrid	A battle between the Saxons and the Picts, in which fell Bernith's son, called Brectrid	698	Cath eter Saxones et Pictos, uibi cecidit filius Bernith, qui dicebatur Brechtraidh	A battle between Saxons and Picts, where the son of Bernith, who was called Brechtaidh, was killed	Y	Anno DCXCVIII Berctred dux regius Nordanhymbrorum a Picts interfectus	
699	Bouina strages in Saxonia	A murrain of cattle in the land of the Saxons	699	Bouina straghes in Saxonia	A murrain of cattle in the land of the Saxons	Y		
704	Aldfrith m. Ossu sapiens, rex Saxonum, moritur	The learned Aldfrid, son of Oswy, king of the Saxons, dies	704	Altfrith mac Ossa .i. Fland Fina la Gaedhelu, ecnaidh, rex Saxonum fuit	Altfrith son of Oswu, called Flann Fina by the Gaels, a wise man, was the king of the Saxons	Y (although where the text diverges ?)	Anno dominicae incarnationis DCCV Aldfrid rex Nordanhymbrorum defenctus est, anno regni sui vicesimo necdum impleto AND Anno DCCV Aldfrid rex Nordanhymbrorum defunctus est	Her Aldferþ Norþanhymbra cyning forþferde
712	Beda librum magnum hoc anno fecit	Bede composed a great book this year	712	In hoc anno fécit Béda librum magnum .i. Berba Béid	In this year Bede made a great book i.e. Berba Béid	Y (although one might query how quickly a work could be distributed and critiqued)		

Year	AU entry	AU translation	Year	AT entry	AT translation	Iona Chronicle (Y/?/N)	Historia Ecclesiastica [Bede]	Anglo-Saxon Chronicle
713	Filia Ossu in monasterio Ild moritur	Oswy's daughter dies in the monastery of Hilda	713	Filia Osu in monasterio Hild moritur	The daughter of Osu in the monastery of Hild dies	Y	...donec conpleto unde LX annorum numero, ad complexum et nuptias sponsi caelestis virgo beata intraret.	
716	Iugulatio regis Saxonum, Osrit filii Aldfrith, nepotis Ossu	The killing of the king of the Saxons, Osred, son of Aldfrid, grandson of Oswy	716	Guin rig Saxan .i. Osrith mac Aldfrith nepotis Osu	The slaying of the king of the Saxons i.e. Osrith son of Aldfrith grandson of Osu	Y	Siquidem anno ab incarnatione Domini DCCXVI, quo Osredo occiso Coenred gubernacular regni Nordanhymbrorum suscepit AND Anno DCCXVI Osred rex Nordanhymbrorum interfectus	Her Osred Norþanhymbra cyning wearþ ofslægen
718	Filius Cuidine, rex Saxonum, moritur	Cuthwine's son, king of the Saxons, dies	718	Mac Cuitin rex Saxonum mortuus est	The son of Cuthwine, king of Saxons, died	Y		
730	Beda claruit	Bede became famous	729	Andsa bliadain-si ró scuir Beda don croinic .i. lebur oirisen, do scribad	In this year Bede finished the chronicle, that is, the book of history which he was writing	?/N		
731	Filius Cuidini, rex Saxan constringitur	Cuthwine's son, king of the Saxons, is imprisoned	731	Mac Cuitine rex Saxan constringitur	The son of Cuthwine, king of the Saxons, is imprisoned	Y	Anno DCCXXXI[3] Ceoluulf rex captus et adtonsus et remissus in regnum	
735	Beda, sapiens Saxonum, quieuit	Bede, a learned man of the Saxons, rested	735	Beda sapiens Saxonum, quieuit	Beda the wise man of the Saxons rested	Y	Anno DCCXXXV . . . Baeda presbyter obiit	forþferdon Tatwine ⁊ Bieda
757	Edalbald, rex Saxonum, moritur	Ethelbald, king of the Saxons, dies	757	Édalbald ri Saxan mortuus est	Aethelbald king of the Saxons, died	Y		mon ofslog Eþelbald Miercna cyning

[3] From hereon the *Historia Ecclesiastica* entries derive from the continuations.

Year	AU entry	AU translation	Year	AT entry	AT translation	Iona Chronicle (Y/?/N)	Historia Ecclesiastica [Bede]	Anglo-Saxon Chronicle
780	Eilpin, rex Saxonum, moritur	Eilpin, king of the Saxons, dies				Y (corrupted) – probably Eilpin, rex Pictorum, moritur		
796	Offa, rex bonus Anglorum, moritur[4]	Offa, the good king of the English/Angles, dies				Y (because it forms part of a verifiable earlier pattern)		Her Adrianus papa ⁊ Offa cyning forþferdon
821	Comulf, rex Saxonum, moritur[5]	Coenwulf, king of the Saxons, dies				Y (because it forms part of a verifiable earlier pattern)		Her wearþ Ceolwulf his rices besciered
858	Adulf rex Saxan, mortui sunt	Ethelwulf, king of the Saxons, died				Y (because it forms part of a verifiable earlier pattern)		he gefór

[4] This is a fascinating change of style. There has long been debate as to whether Offa called himself *rex Anglorum*. None of his charters with such a title are original single sheets and while the numismatic evidence might suggest he did it is not conclusive. Offa's obit seems to fit within the series of the *reges Saxonum* and as such the change in style strongly suggests that the annalist was reacting to a known practice at Offa's court. Whether it should be translated as 'King of the English' is a vexed question.

[5] The *Chronicon Scotorum* is closely related textually to *AT* and covers part of *AT*'s lacuna. CS replicates this entry suggesting, as with *AT* and the earlier entries, that these Anglo-Saxon entries form part of the early annalistic record. *Chronicon Scotorum*, 821.

Table 2

Kings who achieved supremacy throughout Southumbria (*HE*)	*Bretwaldas* listed by the *Parker Chronicle*	*Reges Saxonum* (*AU* and *AT*)
Ælle	Ælle	
Ceawlin	Ceawlin	
Æthelberht	Æthelberht	
Rædwald	Rædwald	
Edwin	Edwin	Edwin
Oswald	Oswald	Oswald
		Penda
Oswiu	Oswiu	Oswiu
		Ecgfrith
		Aldfrith
		Osred
		Coenred
Æthelbald[107]		Æthelbald
		Æthelwald Moll
		Offa
		Coenwulf
	Ecgberht	
		Æthelwulf

[107] Æthelbald is not included in the list in Book 2 Chapter 5 but Bede describes his power in very similar terms in his summary of the state of Britain at the end of Book 5. *HE*, 148–50, 558.

Failed Ritualized Feasts and the Limitations of Community in *Branwen ferch Lŷr*

Melissa Ridley Elmes

Early prose narratives of the medieval North Atlantic world demonstrate a preoccupation with kinship and kingship, often featuring marriages meant to bring communities into alliance, and even more often focusing on the fallout when those marriages fail to keep the peace and violence erupts at or following a feast.[1] As Alfred Nutt argued long ago, and Alaric Hall and Brent Miles have more recently reiterated, there are significant parallels between the Middle Welsh *Branwen ferch Lŷr* (hereafter, *Branwen*), known more colloquially as the Second Branch of the *Mabinogi*, and Norse and German narratives similarly featuring marriages gone awry.[2] However, where Germanic texts like the Old Norse *Saga of the Volsungs* and Old English *Beowulf* use such literary events to discuss the positive and negative aspects of women's influence and the importance of heroic action and above all, loyalty to one's lord, in establishing a more lasting peace,[3] the reading I present in this article

---

[1] This paper has been modified from the version presented at the Colloquium through addition of some brief literary context, critical context, and explanatory notes, and with expanded discussion of the stakes of the reading for the characterization of Efnysien as recommended by the audience, for which suggestion I would like to offer many thanks.

[2] Alfred Nutt, "Mabinogion Studies I.–Branwen, the Daughter of Llyr," *Folk-Lore Record* 5 (1882), 1–32; Alaric Hall, "Gwŷr y Gogledd? Some Icelandic Analogues to *Branwen ferch Lŷr,*" *Cambrian Medieval Studies* 42 (Winter 2001), 27–50; Brent Miles, "*Branwen*: A Reconsideration of the German and Norse Analogues," *Cambrian Medieval Studies* 52 (Winter 2006), 13–48. Note that while the full text is most often published in English translation as *The Mabinogion*, and earlier scholarship refers to it as such, this is almost certainly due to a transcription error and more recently scholars have shifted to *Mabinogi*, the form I employ accordingly in this article.

[3] Studies that showcase the role of women as peace-weavers and inciters in the Germanic literary tradition include Jana K. Schulman, "'A Guest is in the Hall': Women, Feasts, and Violence in Icelandic Epic," in *Women and Medieval Epic: Gender, Genre, and the Limits of Epic Masculinity*, edited by Sara Poor and Jana Schulman (New York: Palgrave, 2007), 209–233 and Michael J. Enright, *Lady With a*

suggests that for its medieval Welsh audience the story of *Branwen* held a different focus.

Scholars of this Second Branch of the *Mabinogi* have engaged in a wide range of approaches—seeking to plumb its lost origins in the mythic and legendary tradition; consider its analogues and parallels in Germanic, Norse, and Celtic literature and international folk and popular story types; establish its position in the overall collection of stories with which it is bound; critique it as an impressively unified or, alternately, a disjointed and faulty, collection of story elements; examine it as a Mirror for Princes[4]; and consider the psychological effects of shame on the characters and the physical effects of violence on the family and nation.[5] All of these

---

Mead Cup: Ritual, Prophecy, and Lordship in the European Warband from La Tene to the Viking Age (Dublin: Four Courts Press, 1995).

[4] A literary genre popular throughout the medieval and early modern periods, consisting of advice, instructions for correct conduct, and models of good rulership on which to meditate, serving essentially as a textbook for young rulers.

[5] Classic studies on the mythological origins of the *Mabinogi* include John Rhys, *Lectures on the Origin and Growth of Religion as Illustrated by Celtic Heathendom[The Hibbert Lectures, 1886],* second edition (London: Williams and Norgate, 1892); Edward Anwyl's series of essays on "The Four Branches of the Mabinogi" in *Zeitschrift fur celtische Philologie* I (1897), 277–93; 2 (1899), 124–133; and 3 (1901), 123–134 (which also comment on the story's origins as fragments of earlier sagas); and W. J. Gruffydd, *Rhiannon: An Inquiry Into the Origins of the First and Third Branches of the Mabinogi* (Cardiff: University of Wales Press, 1953). More recent scholarship on the mythology and legendary elements include Proinsias Mac Cana, *The Mabinogi* (Cardiff: University of Wales Press on behalf of the Welsh Arts Council, 1977). Mac Cana also examines the Irish affinities in the *Second Branch* and discusses the textual relationships between the various branches; Patrick K. Ford, "Prolegomena to a Reading of the *Mabinogi*: 'Pwyll' and 'Manawydan,'" in *Studia Celtica* 16/17 (1981–1982), 110–125; John Carey, "A British Myth of Origins?" in *History of Religions* 31.1 (1991), 24–38; and Sioned Davies, "Venerable Relics? Revisiting the *Mabinogi*," in *Writing Down the Myths*, edited by Joseph Nagy (Turnhout: Brepols, 2012), 157–179. Scholars who have examined the tale's affinities and parallels with Germanic and Norse texts include Nutt, Hall, and Miles (See: n. 1 above); Patrick Ford focuses on *Branwen*'s position in Celtic literature in "Branwen: A Study of the Celtic Affinities," *Studia Celtica* 22/23 (1987–1988), 29–35; and Andrew Welsh examines *Branwen*'s place in the international and popular folk tale traditions in "Branwen, Beowulf, and the Tragic Peaceweaver Tale," in *Viator* 22 (1991), 1–13. The relationship of the *Branches* to one another is discussed by J. K.

readings offer important insights and showcase *Branwen*'s broad interpretive potential and historical and critical interest; I seek not to argue with or overturn any of these earlier findings but to contribute another reading that enhances what has already been said and opens a new avenue of critical exploration into this tale. My approach centers on close reading the feasts in this narrative and their aftermath in a practice constituting what Patrick Ford calls paying "narrative attention."[6] This approach reveals that in *Branwen*, the feasts serve as a cause-and-effect series of events that lead to the destruction of a community that is articulated as inevitable because it is tied to that most unstable thing—the construct of human honor. Understanding that, as Catherine McKenna warns us, "with no other version against which we can read it, [the *Mabinogi*] we have no instrument with which to analyze the particular ways in which our text is the product of the cultural milieu in which it was produced,"[7] and thus face the "difficulties of recuperating with any precision the clerical and/or aristocratic community in which the Four Branches were written—its tastes, experiences, ambitions, and anxieties"[8] yet, at the same time, the Four Branches are "the product of . . . the world of the Welsh princes of Gwynedd, Deheubarth, and Powys"[9] and it is possible to read "the texture

---

Bollard in "The Structure of the Four Branches of the Mabinogi," in *The Mabinogi: A Book of Essays*, edited by Charles William Sullivan (New York: Garland, 1996), 165–196, and in that same volume, Jeffrey Gantz, "Thematic Structure of the Four Branches of the Mabinogi," pp. 265–276; also, Matthieu Boyd in "Why the *Mabinogi* Has Branches," *Proceedings of the Harvard Celtic Colloquium* 30 (2010), 22–38. The *Mabinogi* read as a Mirror for Princes is treated in Helen Fulton, "The *Mabinogi* and the Education of Princes," in *Medieval Celtic Literature and Society*, edited by Helen Fulton (Dublin: Four Courts Press, 2005), 235–247. The centrality of shame to the text is most recently examined in John K. Bollard, "Meuyl ar uy maryf: Shame and Honour in *The Mabinogi*," *Studia Celtica* 47 (2013), 123–47; and Lesley Jacobs examines the centrality of kinship in "Trouble in the Island of the Mighty: Kinship and Violence in *Branwen ferch Lŷr*," *Viator* 40.2 (2009), 113–133.

[6] Ford, "A Study of the Celtic Affinities," 103–104.

[7] Catherine McKenna, "The Colonization of Myth in *Branwen ferch Lŷr*," *Myth in Celtic Literatures,* edited by Joseph Falaky Nagy, *CSANA Yearbook* 6 (Dublin: Four Courts Press), 105–120, at 107.

[8] McKenna, "Colonization of Myth," 108.

[9] Ibid.

of the tale as written"[10] through the lens of that world: "The texture of *Branwen* speaks of the losses, anxieties, and uncertainties of Wales during the period of the Norman incursion."[11] Attentive reading yields evidence that within this texture, while questions of kinship and kingship are certainly a major focus, the element of personal honor is the source of those losses, anxieties, and uncertainties in *Branwen*. While critical focus has heretofore (and profitably) been placed on insult and shame, then, I argue that by looking explicitly at the notion of honor in this tale we can find that, whether real or perceived, the violation of honor and its ramifications is the shaping and driving narrative force of the Second Branch of the *Mabinogi*. In addition to revealing something of the cultural preoccupation with honor that this tale highlights, this reading also has important ramifications for our understanding of the character of Efnysien, who has long been read as a trickster figure, simply malicious, or senselessly violent—a foil to Bendigeidfran's good kingship—but proves to be far more complex, narratively important, and interesting.

The Second Branch of the *Mabinogi* begins with a wedding uniting Matholwch, King of Ireland and Branwen, daughter of Llyr and sister to Bendigeidfran, the King of Britain, "*ymrwymaw Ynys y Kedeirn ac Iwerdon y gyt, ual y bydynt gadarnach.*"[12] (to bind the Island of the Mighty and Ireland together, so that they may be stronger.) A feast marks the occasion. The feast itself is not described, but careful attention is paid to where each of the main figures is seated, both according to Welsh law,

---

[10] McKenna, "Colonization of Myth," 111.

[11] McKenna, "Colonization of Myth," 112.

[12] *Branwen Uerch Lyr:the second of the four branches of the Mabinogi*, edited by Derick S. Thomson (Dublin: Dublin Institute for Advanced Studies, 2010), 2:37–38. While Ifor Williams, *Pedeir Keinc y Mabinogi* (Cardiff: University of Wales Press, 1951; rpt. 1996) is the standard scholarly edition, it is not as readily or widely available as Thomson's; for the purposes of accessibility, then, all quotations from the Second Branch of the *Mabinogi* are taken from Thomson's edition and cited by page and line numbers. Translations of *Branwen* are my own except where indicated, cross-referenced with Sioned Davies, *The Mabinogion: A New Translation* (Oxford: Oxford University Press, 2007); Jeffrey Gantz, *The Mabinogion* (Harmondsworth, Middlesex: Penguin, 1976), and Gwyn Jones and Thomas Jones, *The Mabinogion* (London: J. M. Dent, 1993).

which prescribed where everyone sat according to status;[13] a significant social display at an occasion also representing the binding together of the new community:

> *Yn Aberfraw dechreu y wled, ac eisted. Sef ual yd eistedyssant: brenhin Ynys y Kedeirn a Manawydan uab Llyr o'r neill parth idaw, a Matholwch o'r parth arall, a Branwen uerch Lyr gyt ac ynteu. (2.52–3.55)[14]*

---

[13] Sioned Davies notes this legal aspect to the seating arrangements in her explanatory notes for "The First Branch," *The Mabinogion*, 229 n.5.

[14] The formulaic presentation of feast-scenes in which the placement of the main figures takes precedence over and eclipses in detail any other aspect of the event echoes throughout the *Mabinogi,* repeatedly calling attention to their importance in establishing both character rank and relationship: in "Pwyll, Lord of Dyved" for example we are told of the first feast: "*Ac ar hynny e ymolchi yd aethant, a chyrchu y bordeu a orugant, ac eisted a wnaethant ual hynn–y urenhines o'r neill parth idaw ef, a'r iarll, debygei ef, o'r parth arall.*" (4.84–8): Then they went to wash, and went to the tables, and sat in this manner—the queen on one side of him and the earl, as he supposed [him to be] on the other side. This seating description is followed by a brief statement that Pwyll converses with the queen, finds her enchanting, and is amazed at the opulence of the court: "*O'r a welsei o holl lyssoed y dayar, llyna y llys diwallaf o uwyt a llynn ac eurlestri a theyrndlysseu.*" (4.91–92): Of all the courts he had seen on earth, that was the court best provided with food and drink and golden plates and royal jewels. But, aside from describing the rich strangeness of Arawn's court, there are no details of the actual feast. At the second feast in *Pwyll*, "*Kyweiryaw y neuad a wnaethpwyt, ac y'r bordeu yd aethant. Sef ual yd eistedyssont, Heueyd Hen ar neill law Pwyll, a Riannon o'r parth arall idaw; y am hynny pawb ual y bei y enryded. Bwyta a chyuedach ac ymdidan a wnaethont.*" (12.305–309): The hall was prepared, and they went to the tables. This is how they sat, Hyfaidd Hen on one side of Pwyll, and Rhiannon on his other side; and then the rest of the company according to rank. They ate and amused themselves with games and conversed. There is again no description of the feast, but rather a focus on the interruption of the event by a visitor, then leading us into the tale's next episode. Finally, in the third feast in *Pwyll*: "*Y neuad ynteu a gyweirwyt y Pwyll a'e niuer ac y niuer y llys y am hynny, ac y'r bordeu yd aethont y eisted; ac ual yd eistedyssant ulwydyn o'r nos honno yd eistedwys paub y nos honno. Bwyta a chyuedach a wnaethont, ac amser a doeth y uynet y gyscu.*" (16.423–427): The hall was prepared for Pwyll and his retinue, and for the men of the court as well, and they went to the tables and sat; and as they had sat the year before, they each sat [again] that night. They ate and reveled, and the time came to go to sleep. Here, again, the focus is on seating location and status, and not the feast, itself.

> *In Aberffraw the feast began, and they sat down. This is how they sat: the king of the Island of the Mighty with Manawydan son of Llyr on the one side of him, and Matholwch on his other side, and Branwen daughter of Llyr next to him [Matholwch].*[15]

There is a clear sense of hierarchy involved in this seating arrangement that can be read beyond merely following the prescribed laws of rank at the table to consider the symbolic tableau presented as well. The two kings sit side-by-side, but the King of Britain, as the more prestigious figure, is accompanied by a high-ranked member of his own family— perhaps as a symbol of the family's unified stance in the arrangement of the marriage, but also almost certainly as a precaution against any potential threat or harm to the king's person. Branwen is seated on the other side of Matholwch, symbolically representing her separation from her own family and impending union with the Irish king. With only the four figures present at the table, this should not be read as a moment of demotion for Branwen, but rather of re-association. She is still the sister of the princes of Llyr, and still royal in her own right; but now her physical placement at the side of Matholwch is a visual marker of her role as the unifying member of both families. Her placement at Matholwch's other side binds him physically to the Llyr family while also indicating Branwen's new position in both families.[16] This placement of the newly-

---

All quotations for the First Branch taken from R.L. Thomson, *Pwyll Pendeuic Dyuet* (Dublin, 2010), with my own translations again cross-referenced with Davies, Gantz, and Jones (See: n. 11 above).

[15] To avoid confusion, I have elected to fully Anglicize "Llyr" in my translations, omitting the circumflex and retaining the "Ll" rather than preserving the orthographic mutation present in the Welsh.

[16] This position of the married woman as a bridge between two families with ties to each is discussed by many scholars, including Morfydd E. Owen, who writes in his essay on the legal aspects of women's shame and honor that: "her [the woman's] links were dual. They lay both with the kin into which she was born and with the kin with which she was associated through her husband after marriage." Owen, "Shame and Reparation: Women's Place in the Kin," in *The Welsh Law of Women: Studies Presented to Professor Daniel A. Binchy On His Eightieth Birthday*, edited by Dafydd Jenkins and Morfydd E. Owen (Cardiff: University of Wales Press, 1980), 40–68, at 40. Michael Enright provides a socio-historical look at this same phenomenon in the

allied family members is a visually symbolic representation of the ideal work of the wedding feast, which is supposed to result in a clear union between two people that in turn forges an alliance between their communities. Branwen's clear continued importance as a subject member of the Llyr family as well as a symbolic figure unifying them with the Irish royal family is the central point around which my argument concerning the second, violent feast in the story develops; this ideal union is not always the reality. Even when such a union is achieved, it can prove fragile enough to be dismantled by the actions of a single individual who disapproves of the union and whose disapproval and corresponding belief that he has been dishonored is not registered and dealt with before the wedding takes place.

Efnysien, a half-brother to Branwen who was not invited to the wedding feast, disapproves of the match and is insulted at not having been consulted in the matter: "*Ay yuelly y gwnaethant wy am uorwyn kystal a honno, ac yn chwaer y minheu, y rodi heb uyghanyat i? Ny ellynt wy tremic uwy arnaf i.*" (3.70– 73) (Is it thus they have done with so good a maiden, and a sister of mine at that, given her away without my permission? They could not have insulted me more.) No reason is given for his omission in the decision to marry Branwen to Matholwch, or for why he was not invited to the feast, although Lesley Jacobs reads it as competition between the brothers brought about by the limits of the Welsh legal system to account for half-siblings,[17] a reading to which I add that just beneath the surface of his statement that he could not have been insulted more lies the perceived attack upon Efnysien's personal honor that serves as the inciting incident for the escalating conflict that comprises the rest of the narrative. Efnysien's response to this slight upon his honor is a violent one; he brutally flays the horses of the Irish contingent so that they cannot be ridden:

Celto-Germanic warbands in *Lady with a Mead Cup* (See: n. 3 above) and, for comparison, Elizabeth Cox treats the parallel concept of the *friðusibb* in "'Ides gnornode/geomrode giddum': Remembering the Role of a *friðusibb* in the Retelling of the Fight at Finnsburg in *Beowulf*," in *Reconsidering Gender, Time and Memory in Medieval Culture*, edited by Elizabeth Cox, Liz Herbert McAvoy, and Roberta Magnani (Cambridge: D.S. Brewer, 2015), 61–78.

[17] Jacobs, "Trouble in the Island of the Mighty," 116–118.

*Ac yn hynny guan y dan y meirych, a thorri y guefleu wrth
y danned udunt, a'r clusteu wrth y penneu, a'r rawn wrth
y keuyn; ac ny caei graf ar yr amranneu, eu llad wrth yr
ascwrn. A gwneuthur anfuryf ar y meirych yuelly, hyd nat
oed rym a ellit a'r meirych. (3.73–77)*

And then he went up to the horses, and cut their lips to the
teeth, and their ears down to their heads, and their tails to
their backs; and where he could grasp the eyelids, he cut
them to the bone. And thus he maimed the horses, so that
they were no good for anything.

Both insulted and hamstrung politically by the damage done to their
horses, the Irish do not interpret this as an act performed by an individual,
but as an insult perpetrated by the British ruling family, and they
determine that it is in their best interests to leave. Bendigeidfran, insulted
in turn by their breach of protocol in leaving his court without his
permission, sends messengers to learn why. Matholwch informs the
messengers of his understanding of the situation:

*Rodi Bronwen uerch Lyr ym, yn tryded prif rieni yr ynys
honn, ac yn uerch y urenhin Ynys y Kedeyrn, a chyscu
genthi, a gwedy hynny uy gwaradwydaw. A ryued oed
genhyf, nat kyn rodi morwyn gystal a honno ym y gwneit y
gwaradwyd a wnelit ym. (4.95–99)*

I was given Branwen, daughter of Llyr, one of the Three
Chief Maidens[18] of this Island, and a daughter to the king
of the Island of the Mighty, and I slept with her, and
afterwards I was insulted. And it is strange to me, that [the
insult] was not done before such a fine maiden was given
to me.

The messengers assure him that he has misread the situation:

*Dioer, Arglwyd, nyt o uod y neb a uedei y llys . . . na neb
o'e kynghor y gwnaet(h)pwyt y gwaradwyd hwnnw yt. A
chyt bo gwaradwyd gennyt ti hynny, mwy yw gan*

---

[18] I use Davies' translation of "yn tryded prif rieni yr ynys honn" here; *The
Mabinogion*, 24.

Uendigeituran no chenyt ti, y tremic hwnnw a'e guare.
(4.99–103)

God knows, Lord, neither on the part of the ruler of this
court . . . nor any one of his council was this insult done
to you. And while you view this as a disgrace, the insult
and trick are worse for Bendigeidfran than for you.

From the perspective of the British as conveyed by these messengers,
the feast's function as a unifying event has not been violated in an official
capacity. This message reinforces the point that Efnysien was not
welcome at the feast, that he is not considered a member of the king's
council, and that he acted on his own recognizance. The statement that the
insult and deception are worse for Bendigeidfran underscores the
significance of the feast's outcome for him, as well. Efnysien's attack,
carried out against a political and familial ally without his knowledge or
consent, is a direct challenge to Bendigeidfran's authority as the high king.
The political instability this action reveals should have been dealt with at
or before the feast; the evident attempt to avoid such dishonor by
excluding Efnysien from that event has failed.

Bendigeidfran's response is exactly what it should be both personally
and as a king; upon hearing that Matholwch remains dissatisfied, he
declares that "*nyt oes ymwaret e uynet ef yn anygneuedus, ac nys gadwn.*"
(4.107–108) (it is no good if he goes away angry, and we cannot allow
it.)[19] This declaration has the effect of unifying his court in a single
purpose—to bring Matholwch back and make amends—and demonstrates
Bendigeidfran's keen understanding of the situation on both a personal
level—*it is no good if he goes away angry and we cannot allow it*, because
he is now a member of our family through this union—and also,
politically: *it is no good if he goes away angry and we cannot allow it*,
because the Irish may find it necessary to retaliate for the insult and thus,
to enact violence upon the British people. Bendigeidfran proposes a
settlement intended to reaffirm his commitment to Matholwch and to re-
establish honor: the replacement of all the maimed horses, and more
besides.

---

[19] I use Davies' translation of "nyt oes ymwaret e uynet ef yn anygneuedus, ac nys
gadwn" here; *The Mabinogion*, 25.

Matholwch agrees to the terms, and Bendigeidfran binds their settlement, as he did the union of their houses, by again placing Matholwch at the high table between the family members in a show of unity: *"Ac ual y dechreuyssant eisted ar dechreu y wled, yd eistedyssant yna."* (5.128–29) (And as they had begun to sit at the start[20] of the feast, so they sat then.) Noting that Matholwch still seems downhearted, Bendigeidfran offers to increase his compensation, offering him in addition to the price of the mutilated horses a magic cauldron with the power to bring dead warriors back to life, save that they return mute. Matholwth accepts the enhanced settlement, and takes Branwen back to Ireland, where *"dirwawr lywenyd a uu wrthunt"* (8.204) (they were greeted with great happiness) and *"Ny doey wr mawr, na gwreic da yn Iwerdon, e ymw(e)let a Branwen, ni rodei hi ae cae ae modrwy ae teyrndlws cadwedic ydaw"* (8.204–206) (No great man nor good gentlewoman in Ireland came to visit Branwen to whom she did not give a brooch or a ring or a treasured royal jewel.) Branwen performs her duties as queen with aplomb, so that *"y ulwydyn honno a duc hi yn glotuawr, a hwyl delediw a duc hi o glot a chedymdeithon."* (8.207–209) (that year brought her fame, and she flourished in honor and companionship.) Finally, she becomes pregnant and gives birth to a son, Gwern. By giving gifts, cultivating relationships, and producing an heir, Branwen engages in precisely the behaviors that signal good queenship, and the union appears successful. However, the narrative takes a darker turn, tied to the same initial point of dishonor caused by Efnysien's action:

> *A hynny yn yr eil ulwydyn, llyma ymodwrd yn Iwerdon am y guaradwyd a gawssei Matholwch yg Kymry, a'r somm a wnathoedit idaw am y ueirch . . . A nachaf y dygyuor yn Iwerdon hyt nat oed lonyd idaw ony chaei dial y sarahet. (8.213–218)*

> In the second year, lo there was murmuring in Ireland concerning the insult that Matholwch received in Wales, and the shameful trick played against him and his horses . . . And behold an uprising in Ireland that left no peace for him until he avenged the insult.

---

[20] I have elected to replace "beginning" with "start" here to avoid the awkward repetition of "begin" in English.

The text does not explicitly state it, but an either/or outcome is clearly indicated: either Matholwch satisfies his people's desire that he exact revenge for the insult, or there will be civil unrest and a challenge to his kingship. The people of Ireland respond to the reports of the insult sustained by Matholwch in Britain by clamoring for immediate nullification of the union between the countries. And despite Branwen's irreproachable activity as queen, because she is also a member of the house that purportedly insulted Matholwch and thus a symbol of that house's union with Ireland, the people call for the dissolution of their marriage as well; further, she is stripped of her honor and dignity, beaten, and forced to cook for the court. While on the surface this could be read simply as Branwen's being reduced to the status of a non-noble woman, reading this scene against the medieval Welsh laws of women reveals that in fact, she is being treated as harshly as the law permits a queen to be treated. The triad discussing the insult of a queen reads as follows: "*O teyr ford e serheyr e urenhynes; o torry e naud, neu o'y tharau, neu o grybdeyllau peth o'y llau.*" (In three ways the queen is insulted, namely by breaking her protection, or by striking her or by snatching something from her hand.)[21] Significantly, Branwen's shaming is conducted not along the lines of Irish law, but of Welsh law—the law of the culture in which this story was developed and written down. This may simply have been a reflexive choice on the part of the (almost certainly) Welsh author, but it also permits a Welsh audience of the story to understand the full degree of dishonor to which Branwen has been subjected and, because of this shaming of his wife, the depths of dishonor to which Matholwch has fallen in the eyes of his people, reinforcing the centrality of honor to this story.

This moment in which Branwen is punished by the people of Ireland for her British kinsman's insult against them highlights the limitations of kingship, of queenship, and of the power of the ritual of feasting as union: in this literary representation of Welsh culture, it can all be endangered by a single insult, because no one is considered blameless in the giving and receiving of an insult. The insult enacted upon the Irish king and, by association, his people, by Efnysien as a result of his own exclusion from the wedding feast—an insult that also implicates Bendigeidfran, as the one who excluded Efnysien from the feast—results in the symbolic dissolution

---

[21] As cited in Owen, "Shame and Reparation," 46.

of the nations' union through Branwen's humiliation, and a three-year embargo physically marking the political breakdown by shutting down communication entirely between Ireland and Wales.[22]

When Branwen smuggles a message to her brother detailing her current state, Bendigeidfran invades Ireland. Although the Irish try to prevent the invasion, in the end they are forced to offer hospitality to Bendigeidfran's army. An Irish contingent informs Bendigeidfran that Matholwch has decided to give the kingship of Ireland to *"[G]wern uab Matholwch, dy nei ditheu, uab dy chwaer, ac yn y ystynnu y'th wyd di, yn lle y cam a'r codyant a wnaethpwyt y Uranwen."* (11.302–304) (Gwern son of Matholwch, your nephew, the son of your sister, and will invest him in your [Bendigeidfran's] presence, to requite the disgrace and injury that was done to Branwen.) Bendigeidfran agrees to this plan, unaware that at this point neither he nor Matholwch is privy to what is really going on; like Efnysien before them, the Irish, insulted at the invasion of their land without their consent, have taken matters into their own hands. They counsel Matholwch to build a hall that can contain Bendigeidfran, who has never before been able to fit into a building, in order to secure peace between the countries, a plan to which Matholwch readily agrees.

When the hall has been built, Efnysien enters it and grows suspicious at the bags hung on hooks around the walls. There is no sense that he is acting on behalf of Bendigeidfran in a protective capacity, such as conducting surveillance for possible dangers to the king's person; yet, this is precisely what he uncovers. In a particularly gruesome scene, he walks around the room asking the Irishmen *"Beth yssyd yn y boly hwnn?"* (13.334) ('what is in this bag?') When the Irish respond, *"Blawt, eneit"* (13.335) ('Flour, friend') Efnysien prods the bag with his hand and, feeling a man's head, squeezes it until he feels the skull bone. He then goes around the room performing this act over and over again, until the Irishmen hanging in the bags are all dead. The Irish set up a premeditated death-feast, but Efnysien has thwarted their efforts. Initiated nominally to bring about peace, this feast is corrupted from its inception because the intention was never reconciliation in the first place, but rather, continuation of the honor-centric pattern of insult-injury-retaliation.

---

[22] See Thomson, 8.221–225.

Rendering the hall safe for the British visitors seems like a strange move for a character who has already proven himself to be against the union between Branwen and Matholwch, Britain and Ireland. However, that this is not an act of reconciliation on his part but rather a re-framing of the scene for other premeditated actions becomes chillingly clear. The feast begins according to plan: "*y dothyw y niueroed y'r ty . . . Ac yn gyn ebrwydet ac yd eistedyssant y bu duundeb y rydunt, ac yd ystynnwyt y urenhinaeth y'r mab.*" (13.350– 353) (the retinue entered the house . . . and as soon as they sat down there was concord between them, and the boy was invested as king.) This feast is thus revealed to be both a scene of reconciliation between the nations, and the coronation feast for the new Irish king, Gwern. Gwern, as the son of Matholwch and Branwen, is the physical manifestation of their union. That both parties have agreed to uphold his right to the throne and are in attendance at this coronation feast should bring stability to the situation, and indeed this seems to be the case; we are told that Bendigeidfran calls Gwern to him, from him, Gwern travels to Manawydan and then to Nysien, and "*a phawb o'r a'e guelei yn y garu.*" (13.356) (all those who saw him loved him.) Like his mother before him, Gwern wins the hearts of the people with his correct, ritualistic behavior.

Although present at this feast, as opposed to his omission from the first one, Efnysien is again in the position of feeling slighted, this time by Gwern: "*Paham . . . na daw uy nei, uab uy chwaer, attaf i? Kyn ny bei urenhin ar Iwerdon, da oed genhyf i ymtiryoni a'r mab.*" 14.358– 360) (Why doesn't my nephew, the son of my sister, come to me? . . . Even were he not king of Ireland, I would like to be friendly with the boy.) He couches his request in seemingly harmless terms, but Efnysien's next actions betray his true purpose in calling the boy to him as a violent one. "*'Y Duw y dygaf uyg kyffes,' heb ynteu yn y uedwl, 'ys anhebic a gyflauan gan y tylwyth y wneuthur, a wnaf i yr awr honn.*" (14.361– 363) ('I make a confession to God,' he said to himself, 'I will now commit an unimaginable crime in the eyes of the household.') Before anyone in the house can intervene, he hurls Gwern into the fire. No motivation is given for this sudden act of regicide. In the absence of evidence to the contrary, this act must therefore be read either as a random act of cruelty, or as an act intended to follow up his other efforts at retaliation for the initial insult and loss of honor he suffered in not being consulted on the union of

Matholwch and Branwen. If the latter, and most probable, explanation is true, then what he has done—destroying the fruits of that initial union and, in so doing, also destroying the foundation of the newly reconciled union—is further evidence that this narrative is particularly concerned with the tenuous nature of unions forged through ritualistic acts such as the feast. Neither the wedding feast, nor the coronation feast, is sufficient to guarantee safety and stability within the community, unless all members of that community are both included and in accord with the feast's function. If Efnysien had not killed the Irishmen in the sacks, then the outcome of this coronation feast was still destined to be a bloody one. The hall was erected for the purpose not of building or reiterating a community, but of permanently destroying one. It is not a hall intended to restore peace, but to respond to perceived dishonor. With so many individuals now actively engaged in a struggle to avenge and reclaim their honor, there is no peaceful way to leave.

Gwern's death by regicide is followed in short order by the re-animation of the Irish corpses using the magic cauldron; Bendigeidfran's own death and Branwen's death of a broken heart; and finally, viewing the many dead and dying men of the Island of the Mighty, Efnysien determines that now the only way for him to recoup his honor is to end this violent altercation that he initiated: "*Oy a Duw . . . guae ui uy mot yn achaws y'r wydwic honn o wyr Ynys y Kedyrn; a meuyl ymi . . . ony cheissaf i waret rac hynn.*" (14.380– 382) (Alas to God . . . woe is me that I am the cause of this funeral pile of men of the Island of the Mighty; and shame to me . . . if I do not strive to deliver them from this.) With this statement, Efnysien permits himself to be thrown into the cauldron, and there "*Emystynnu idaw ynteu yn y peir, yny dyrr y peir yn pedwar dryll, ac yny dyrr y galon ynteu*" (14.384– 385) (he stretches himself out in the cauldron, until the cauldron bursts into four pieces, and his heart bursts too.) Reading Efnysien's character through the lens of honor—its perceived loss, and his subsequent efforts to avenge it, prior to this point in the tale and into this moment—renders him more than merely a trickster, or a malevolent being, an allegorical "un-Peace," or even a man bent on revenge against all costs, which are the usual readings of his character. Instead, he becomes a cautionary figure; a man who realizes only when things have gone irredeemably too far, that the cost of his honor is too much to pay—and who then pays that cost in his final effort to recoup it. He dies honorably enough, but while his death paves the way for the men of the Island of the Mighty to win this battle, it is a hollow victory. The narrator is careful to underscore the devastating outcome of this failed coronation feast: "*Ny bu oruot o hynny eithyr diang seithwyr, a brathu Bendigeiduran yn y troet a guenwynwaew.*" (14.387– 15.388) (There was no real victory even so except that seven men escaped, and Bendigeidfran was wounded in the foot with a poisoned spear.) This statement demonstrates an emphasis on the impermanence of human community, by highlighting the futile nature of attempts at stabilizing a community gone spectacularly awry. Later, we learn that the seven men return to the Island of the Mighty, only to find that those left behind and charged with the island's keeping have been overrun and there is a new king. The narrative continues with a new community rising from the ashes of these failed earlier communities.

The feasts in *Branwen* therefore showcase the power that literary feasts have to provide hope and support towards building a stable society, and also how just as easily they can serve as catalysts of violence when not everyone involved in a given community agrees with the feast's purpose and outcome. Perhaps more chillingly, this narrative reveals cultural anxieties tied to the idea that no number of unifying feasts is sufficient to compensate for one man's slighted honor. The feasts and their aftermath in the *Mabinogi* show that in the Welsh imaginary from which this tale arose, when the fate of a community depends primarily upon the honor of its individual members, that community is inherently unstable and, ultimately, unsustainable: any change in one's state of honor will result in a correspondent change in the community, and sometimes catastrophe ensues.

Acknowledgments

I wish to express thanks to this article's anonymous reviewer for helpful and encouraging feedback, and I extend particular gratitude to Stephen Hopkins for reviewing my quoted passages and translations in and from Welsh for infelicities; any errors that remain are my own.

Beards and Barbarians: Marginal Illustrations in Gerald of Wales' *Topographia Hibernica*

Fabienne Schwizer

Gerald of Wales was a late twelfth and early thirteenth-century cleric in Anglo-Norman England who wrote on a myriad of topics, spanning from hagiography and ecclesiastical matters to politics and history writing.[1] Part Welsh himself, he wrote extensively on the Irish and Welsh, dedicating two works each to these Celtic peoples—his portrayal of the Irish especially is considered scathing. His *Topographia Hibernica* (known in English as *The History and Topography of Ireland*) especially is a curious text. As a Simon Mittman describes it as being "part miracle story and part topography . . . a mass of amorous goats, ox-man, bearded ladies, werewolves, gold-toothed fish, speaking crosses and eternally burning hedges," a quote that, although biased from a monster-focused viewpoint, summarizes the work well.[2] Gerald presented it in Oxford in 1188, where he read it aloud over three consecutive days.[3] It consists of three books, one each on the geography and creatures of Ireland, its wonders and miracles, and, lastly, its inhabitants.[4] Based on the number of surviving manuscripts, it must have been the high medieval equivalent of a bestseller.[5] Four of those surviving manuscripts are illustrated,[6] two of

---

[1] The most influential work on Gerald and his writings remains Robert Bartlett's *Gerald of Wales* (Oxford: Oxford University Press, 1982), while excellent newer research can be found in Georgia Henley and A. Joseph McMullen, eds., *Gerald of Wales: New Perspectives on a Medieval Writer and Critic*, (Cardiff: University of Wales Press, 2018). Gerald's known works have been edited in the Rolls Series as *Giraldi Cambrensis Opera* (8 vols, ed. J. S. Brewer, James F. Dimock and George F. Warner. (London: Various Publishers, 1861–1891)).

[2] Asa Simon Mittman, "The Other Close at Hand: Gerald of Wales and the 'Marvels of the West,'" in *The Monstrous Middle Ages*, ed. Bettina Bildhauer and Robert Mills (Toronto and Buffalo: University of Toronto Press, 2003), 97–112, at 97.

[3] James F. Dimock, "Preface," in *Giraldi Cambrensis, Opera* Vol. V, ed. James F. Dimock (London: Kraus Reprint (1964), 1867), ix–lxxxix, at li.

[4] Breen, "Embellishing History," 106.

[5] Ibid.

[6] Michelle P. Brown, "Marvels of the West: Giraldus Cambrensis and the Role of the Author in the Development of Marginal Illustration," in *Decoration and Illustration in*

216

which are of especial interest: MS Royal 13 B VIII, kept in the British Library in London, and MS 700 of the National Library of Ireland in Dublin. Both of these manuscripts contain marginal illustrations in pen and color showing scenes mentioned in the text, often drawing from Irish life and nature.[7] While it is "intended as a description of Ireland, its land, climate and people," most of it seems based on hearsay rather than observations from Gerald's travels to Ireland in 1183 and 1185.[8] From a political viewpoint, the *Topographia* shines a light on the representation of the Anglo-Norman invasion of Ireland happening at the time, utilizing different genres to convey its pro-settler worldview.[9] This article aims to show how the marginal illustrations of human figures in these two early manuscripts of the *Topographia Hibernica* interpret the text. It will specifically look at two episodes related in the *Topographia*, the stories of the werewolves and St. Brigid's fire, for evidence of how the illustrations contained in these manuscripts express anti-Irish bias.

The exact dating of the manuscripts in question has been under debate: Michelle P. Brown dates the London manuscript to c. 1200 due to its script, and argues that the Dublin manuscript was created soon after.[10] Catherine Rooney, on the other hand, believes that the relationship between these two manuscripts is more complicated, as the text seems to

---

Medieval English Manuscripts, ed. A.S.G. Edwards (London: The British Library, 2002), 34–59, at 37.

[7] Antonia Gransden, "Realistic Observation in Twelfth-Century England," *Speculum* 47 no. 1 (1972): 29–51, at 49.

[8] Thomas O'Loughlin, "An Early Thirteenth-Century Map in Dublin: A Window into the World of Giraldus Cambrensis," *Imago Mundi* 51 (1999): 24–39, at 24; Gransden, "Observation," 48.

[9] Rhonda Knight, "Werewolves, Monsters and Miracles: Representing Colonial Fantasies in Gerald of Wales's Topographia Hibernica," *Studies in Iconography* 22 (2001): 55–86, at 55.

[10] Brown, "Marvels," 39–40. While earlier scholars had dated these manuscripts to the mid-thirteenth century, Brown's argument is more convincing. She argues that the script is "above top line", i.e. less compressed than it was to become, as well as lacking details commonly seen in early thirteenth-century textualis script, such as e.g. the dotting of i's. She also believes the decoration of the initials to be more reminiscent of twelfth- than thirteenth-century manuscripts.

be more advanced in one or the other at different points of the text.[11] A third opinion is voiced by Amelia Sargent, who has recently argued for five distinct versions of the *Topographia* authored by Gerald. She sees the London manuscript as part of the third recension of the *Topographia*, which she dates to the early 1190s, with this specific manuscript being a late itineration of the same–its marginal additions bring it from the third to the fourth recension, where she believes the illustrations to originate. The text of the London manuscript was copied from a slightly earlier manuscript, MS Rawlinson B188, housed in the Bodleian Library in Oxford, where the illustrations are not yet present.[12] She therefore dates this recension, and with it, the London manuscript to Gerald's first sojourn in Lincoln.[13] The Dublin manuscript is considered part of the fifth recension, with part of the changes characterizing this revision found in its margins. Sargent dates this version of the text to 1207–1209.[14]

As these dates set the creation of the manuscripts during a period where Gerald himself had still been alive, and actively working on his texts, as well as these manuscripts both being placed at the heart of revisions by Sargent, this allows for theories that Gerald had been connected to the creation of these manuscripts.[15] There is no clear evidence for the manuscripts' origin, but scholars have argued that they originated in Lincoln using paleographical evidence, as well as, in Sargent's case, intertextual evidence.[16] The London manuscript contains 147 folios,[17] the *Topographia* taking up folios 1 recto to 34 verso. It is

---

[11] Catherine Rooney, "The Early Manuscripts of Gerald of Wales," in *Gerald of Wales: New Perspectives on a Medieval Writer and Critic*, ed. Georgia Henley and A. Joseph McMullen (Cardiff: University of Wales Press, 2018), 97–110, at 108 (Note 9).

[12] Scott, "Introduction," xxxv.

[13] Amelia Borrego Sargent, "Gerald of Wales' Topographia Hibernica: Dates, Versions, Readers," *Viator* 43:1 (2012): 241–262; at 253.

[14] Ibid., 243; 258.

[15] Scott, "Introduction," xlvi; Sargent, "Dates, Versions, Readers," 254; 259.

[16] As it is known that Gerald spent time there between 1192 and 1198, this would support the assumption that it originated in his workshop. Brown, "Marvels," 46; Nigel Morgan, *Early Gothic Manuscripts* I (London: Harvey Millar, 1982), 105; Sargent, "Dates, Versions, Readers," 253; 259.

[17] Morgan, Manuscripts, 104.

bound together with Gerald's *Expugnatio Hibernica* and *Itinerarium Kambriae*, as well as Henry of Sawtry's *Purgatory of St. Patrick*.[18] It contains around 45 colored illustrations accompanying the text of the *Topographia*, none, however, for the other texts.[19] The Dublin manuscript is purely made up of Gerald's two Irish texts, with the *Topographia* filling pages 5 to 97. It contains 39 illustrations for the *Topographia*, in slightly simpler colors than the earlier manuscript, as well as some (though much fewer) for the *Expugnatio*.[20] This might be the copy that Gerald is known to have sent to Hereford in 1218.[21]

Sixteen of the illustrations contained in both manuscripts show human figures. These images are at the center of this research, as these marginal illustrations are not merely decoration, but contain interpretations of the text. Although the images in the above-mentioned manuscripts are often thought of as mere supplements to the text, they interact with it to produce their own version of the events related.[22] As Knight argues, they are also imbued with colonial ideology, which is especially visible in the illustrations of the werewolves and the fire of St. Brigid, two of the scenes that are of central importance to this argument and will be explored in detail below.[23] In both those cases, the illustrations show clear discrepancies in the treatment of the Irish between the two manuscripts. Through their very different interpretations of the same stories, these manuscripts imply clear political statements on the perception of the Irish people.

While the addition of marginal illustrations is an unusual occurrence, these manuscripts are by no means anomalies. Brown lists examples for such illustrations throughout the Anglo-Saxon period, and half a century after Gerald, Matthew Paris famously both wrote and illustrated his own work with marginal illustrations.[24] Marginal illustrations then reached the

---

[18] Dimock, "Preface," xx.

[19] Morgan, *Manuscripts*, 105.

[20] Morgan, *Manuscripts,* 106.

[21] Breen, "Embellishing History," 105–6.

[22] Knight, "Werewolves," 56.

[23] Ibid., 57.

[24] Many examples for this can be found in Brown, "Marvels," 49–50; Morgan, *Manuscripts*, 105; Brown, "Marvels," 35.

apex of their importance between the late twelfth and late fourteenth century,[25] becoming increasingly important as a place for additional information and decoration.[26] Michael Camille interprets marginal images as a variation of the written gloss, interacting with and reinterpreting a text.[27] This makes sense when one considers that the reader usually cannot separate text and images if he is used to perceiving them as one entity.[28] While they are separated, but still on the same page, according to A. Kibédi Varga's concept of *interreference*, they will always interact.[29]

Due to the close correspondence between the text and the illustrations, it is thought that Gerald himself had been involved in the development of the canon of images.[30] Although no autograph manuscript exists, it has been assumed that he is connected to the creation of a model which would have formed the basis for the later surviving manuscripts.[31]

Nigel Morgan explains that this would most likely have been developed during Gerald's stay in Lincoln (1192–1198), as the style of the illustrations shows similarities to the Leningrad Bestiary, which was produced in the Lincoln region at the time.[32] This is also where Sargent places the London manuscript.[33] The fact that many of these illustrations are clearly different iterations of the same image supports the theory that both manuscripts might originate from the same workshop, and if this workshop is taken to be Lincoln, where Gerald spent most of the 1190s, it seems plausible that Gerald himself was involved in their creation and therefore influenced the images. A factor pointing in this direction is that the illustrations show details that indicate firsthand knowledge of Irish culture: Brown argues that the illustration of an Irish musician, present in

---

[25] Michael Camille, *Image on the Edge: The Margins of Medieval Art* (London: Reaktion Books, 1992), 160.

[26] Mary C. Olson, *Fair and Varied Forms: Visual Textuality in Medieval Illuminated Manuscripts* (London and New York: Routledge, 2003), 156.

[27] Ibid., 20.

[28] A. Kibédi Varga, "Criteria for Describing Word-and-Image Relations," *Poetics Today* 10 no. 1 (1989): 31–53, at 33.

[29] Ibid., 39.

[30] Brown, "Marvels," 42; 45; 47.

[31] Knight, "Werewolves," 60.

[32] Morgan, *Manuscripts*, 105.

[33] Sargent, "Dates, Versions, Readers," 253.

both manuscripts, show an instrument that seems to be a Celtic harp, similar to the late medieval "Brian Boru's harp," which is kept at Trinity College Dublin.[34] The illustrations also depict Irish dress and culture to a more detailed extent than is given in the text.[35]

Nevertheless, the idea of Gerald as the direct creator of the illustrations has been previously discounted, though Morgan suggests he might have sketched the subjects himself.[36] This is because Gerald does not mention artistic talents in his works (in which he does not hesitate to praise himself) while also lamenting the limitations of written descriptions.[37] If we apply Gerald's own idea of an angel assisting in in the creation of a book mentioned in the *Topographia*, where the angel instructs and assists the scribe in the design of the illustrations, to the creation of these manuscripts, Gerald could be seen as taking the role of the angel, telling his scribes and illustrators what to depict.[38] This fits in with Paul Binski's argument on authorship of the "higher power" (in this case the angel, or Gerald) as the original *auctor*, the "unmoved mover", and the scribal *auctor* as both "moved" by the higher power and "mover", through the physical creation of the work.[39] Furthermore, as only the original "mover" understands the reasoning and causality behind the work while the others involved are merely following his instruction, he would take the role of the true author.[40] While this would be a rather obvious conclusion to come to when looking at the verbal component of the manuscript, the text itself, Binski's interpretation of this concept, which he mainly applies to architecture, allows the author to surpass the verbal boundaries and be applied to non-verbal authorship as well—such as, in this case, the illustrations accompanying a text, which may have been authored by a man who never drew a single image.

---

[34] Brown, "Marvels," 47.

[35] Scott, "Introduction," xliv.

[36] Morgan, *Manuscripts*, 105.

[37] Bartlett, *Gerald of Wales*, 103–119; Brown, "Marvels," 40–1.

[38] Ibid., 42.

[39] Paul Binski, "'Working by Words Alone:' The Architect, Scholasticism and Rhetoric in Thirteenth-Century France," in *Rhetoric Beyond Words: Delight and Persuasion in the Arts of the Middle Ages*, ed. Mary Carruthers (Cambridge: Cambridge University Press, 2010), 14–51, at 21.

[40] Ibid., 22.

BEARDS AND BARBARIANS

Example 1: Werewolves

In book II of the *Topography*, Gerald tells the story of a priest encountering a pair of speaking wolves in a forest in Meath while travelling through Ireland.[41] The wolves declare themselves to be humans from Ossory, victims of an old curse by Natalis, a sixth-century monk and saint. This curse has caused two natives of Ossory at a time to be turned into wolves for seven years each since the time of Natalis. One of the two wolves, the female, is ill, and they ask the priest for the sacrament, who is hesitant to share this with creatures he does not perceive as Christian. Ultimately, the priest reluctantly agrees. This passage has been the subject of study, for example by Catherine E. Karkov, who argues that the story can be seen as a metaphor for the conquest of Ireland.[42] The priest is travelling from Ulster to Meath, that is travelling between two Anglo-Norman held areas which are divided by the Irish-ruled Airgialla, which John had been trying to carve up during his 1185 expedition, setting the story in a contested "wild" area. This allows for the parallel to be drawn from the redemption of the wild werewolf to the absorption of this previously Irish area into the fold of civilized, Anglo-Norman rule.[43] Karkov further suggests that the incorporation of a female werewolf in what she sees a traditionally male role could be connected to the idea of the personification of Ireland's sovereignty as an old woman roaming the wilderness, needing to be tamed by a man through sex or marriage (which is prevalent in early Irish pseudohistorical tales), further linking Gerald's werewolves to the colonialization of Ireland.[44] Lindsay Zachary Panxhi shows how this is one of the passages Gerald kept emendating throughout

---

[41] This story can be found in book two, chapter 19 of the *Topographia Hibernica*. (*Giraldus Cambrensis: Opera* Vol. 5, ed. James F. Dimock (London: Longmans, Green, Reader, and Dyer, 1867), 103.)

[42] Catherine E. Karkov, "Tales of the Ancients: Colonial Werewolves and the Mapping of Postcolonial Ireland," in *Postcolonial Moves: Medieval through Modern*, ed. Patricia Clare Ingham and Michelle R. Warren (Houndmills and New York: Palgrave Macmillan, 2003), 93–109.

[43] Ibid., 97.

[44] "[. . .] werewolves in the Celtic, Germanic, and Classical traditions are almost all male, although there are more wolfish women in the Irish tradition than elsewhere." Karkov, "Tales of the Ancients", 99.

the five recensions of the *Topographia*, turning it into a nuanced theological discussion of human nature, and warning against the danger of moral decay.[45]

This passage is depicted in very different ways in the two manuscripts: In the London manuscript (Figs. 1A and B)[46], the priest is approached by one wolf, taken along and brought to the other wolf in order to provide the sacrament. This shows a tale of redemption, explained step by step, from the approach of the wolf to the sacrament, and is consistent with the story told in the text.

Figure 1A : **Werewolves, BL MS Royal 13 B VIII, f. 17v © British Library**

---

[45] Lindsay Zachary Panxhi, "Rewriting the Werewolf and Rehabilitating the Irish in the *Topographia Hibernica* of Gerald of Wales," *Viator* 46:3 (2015): 21–40, esp. at 39–40.

[46] Figures 1A and B are one illustration spanning over the gutter in the original.

Figure. 1B: Werewolves, BL MS Royal 13 B VIII, f. 18r © British Library

Figure 2: Werewolf, NLI MSS 700, p.49. Reproduced courtesy of the National Library of Ireland

By contrast, the Dublin manuscript (Fig. 2) only has simple images of the priest sternly talking to the wolf, with the boy accompanying him

224

staying by the fire. This looks like the act of denying the wolf's request for salvation for his mate, emphasizing the priest's reluctance to share the viaticum with the wolves. It seems that the London manuscript attributes a desire for Christianity and therefore civilization to the wolves, whereas the Dublin manuscript disregards the redemption aspect of the written story, and is therefore less clear if separated from the text. If considered along Karkov's reading of the wolves as an allegory of the conquest, this lack of redemption gains another dimension: the conquest cannot be completed. Thus, the very different images provided give an utterly contrary interpretation of the tale, especially to any illiterate viewers, starting a pattern that continues on throughout the manuscript, presenting the Irish, here represented through the wolves, in a more critical light than the text requires.

In the middle of the twelfth century, the historian William of Malmesbury wrote the following on the English perspective on the Norman Conquest:

> [Harold Hardrada] did, however, send scouts on ahead to spy out the numbers and strength of the enemy. [. . .] On their return Harold asked them what tidings they brought with them. After enlarging at great length on the leader's superb self-confidence, they added in all seriousness that almost every man in William's army seemed to be a priest, all their faces including both lips being clean-shaven; for the English leave the upper lip, with its unceasing growth of hair, unshorn, which Julius Caesar describes as a national custom of the ancient Britons too in his book on the Gallic War.[47]

This use of facial hair as a social denominator is fascinating. Throughout the Middle Ages, facial hair was used to identify social groups, be that based on faith, lifestyle, or nationality. For example, Christopher Oldstone-Moore reports that crusaders purposefully shaved in order to be distinguishable from the Muslims they were fighting, and that in Spain, Muslims were required to wear their beards long so that they

---

[47] William of Malmesbury, *Gesta Regnum Anglorum* Vol. I, ed. and trans. R.A.B. Mynors, R.M. Thompson, and Michael Winterbottom, Oxford Medieval Texts (Oxford: Clarendon Press, 1988), 450.

could be easily identified.[48] This is echoed in further references to invaders making the people of England shave after the Norman conquest, likely as a marker of cultural identity, by writers such as Matthew Paris or Aelnoth.[49] Similar to William of Monmouth's description of the beards of the English, Gerald describes the Welshmen as follows: "The men are in the habit of shaving their beards, except for the moustache alone."[50] The Irish, by contrast, supposedly display their lack of civilization and culture in both their dress and their beards, as Gerald claims in Book Three of the *Topographia Hibernica*.[51] This statement, found among the many negative ideas about the Irish in the *Topographia*, shows that Gerald uses beards as a cultural identifier for the Irish, visually separating them from the Anglo-Normans. This theme had also spread into the *Expugnatio Hibernica*, where the beards of the Irish had presented enough of a source of wonderment that John and his men famously pulled their beards: "But our newly arrived Normans treated them with contempt and derision, and showing them scant respect, pulled some about by their beards which were large and flowing according to their native custom."[52] Taken together with the role of the marginal illustrations in the manuscripts of the *Topographia* described earlier, these preconceptions about facial hair bring about interesting implications, as the beards of the figures associated with passages of the texts present a political statement. This becomes especially clear in the story of St. Brigid's Fire.

---

[48] Oldstone-Moore, Christopher, *Of Beards and Men: The Revealing History of Facial Hair.* (Chicago: University of Chicago Press, 2015), 99.

[49] Stafford Pauline, "The Meanings of Hair in the Anglo-Norman World," in *Saints, Scholars and Politicians: Gender as a Tool in Medieval Studies*, ed. Mathilde van Dijk and Renée Nip (Turnhout: Brepols, 2005), 153–71, at 159.

[50] *Giraldus Cambrensis: Opera* Vol. 6, ed. James F. Dimock (London: Longmans, Green, Reader, and Dyer, 1868), 185. Translation by author.

[51] *Giraldus Cambrensis: Opera* Vol. 5, ed. James F. Dimock (London: Longmans, Green, Reader, and Dyer, 1867), 150.

[52] Giraldus Cambrensis, *Expugnatio Hibernica*, ed. and trans. A.B. Scott and F.X. Martin (Dublin: Royal Irish Academy, 1978), 237 (II.36).

Figure. 3: Brigid's fire
BL MS Royal 13 B VIII,
f. 23v © British Library

Figure 4: Brigid's fire, NLI MS
700, p. 65. Reproduced courtesy of
the National Library of Ireland

Example 2: Brigid's Fire

Brigid's Fire is a holy place in Kildare still active today, which contains a perpetual fire. It is guarded in turn by twenty nuns, nineteen of which are living nuns from the Kildare community and, during her lifetime, Brigid was the twentieth. After her death, Brigid is said to have kept the watch through her saintly powers. This fire is surrounded by a hedge, which men cannot pass–and it is said that if one should find his way inside, he will not be able to escape divine wrath. In a story about the Fire in the *Topographia*, an archer of Strongbow's household breaches the sanctity of Brigid's fire by jumping over the hedges and blowing on the fire. In consequence, he goes mad and disturbs the town. When he is

227

eventually captured, he requests to be brought to a stream, from which he then drinks until he dies of it. Similar to the illustrations of the werewolf story, the London manuscript (Fig. 3) contains a more narrative illustration, featuring the archer first over a fire, then by a stream. The image's significance is very clear in the context, although it could be taken to be something utterly different without the accompanying text, as the fire is not presented as particularly "holy" and the man seems to be merely lying by the side of the stream on his own. Furthermore, through his depiction as a clean-shaven individual, it is made clear that the culprit is of Anglo-Norman heritage rather than Irish. By contrast, the Dublin manuscript (Fig. 4) shows only a very schematic drawing of the man inside the hedge, blowing on the fire. Just as the man in the first image is clearly a member of the colonizing society, the man here is clearly depicted as Irish, as he sports a long beard. As this person is a member of Strongbow's household and thus associated with the colonial power, it would seem more likely for the tale to be interpreted as discussing a member of the Anglo-Norman society, ignorant of the local traditions and legends. By marking the man as Irish, the illustration avoids such implied criticism of the Anglo-Normans, while depicting the Irish in a more negative way.

With this tale as well as the aforementioned story of the werewolves, there is an obvious discrepancy between the text and image. While the London manuscript shows action and consequences and thus tells the story as it was written, the Dublin Manuscript only shows one aspect of it. Given that the Dublin manuscript's werewolf is only shown to be talking to a defensive cleric and its archer is merely shown while desecrating Brigid's fire, the Irish are portrayed in a much worse light in this manuscript. They lose their ability for redemption and justice, which is still present in in the London manuscript, where the wolf receives the sacrament and the soldier receives divine punishment for his heretical act. This focuses on their humanity rather than their difference from the English. When looking at the illustrations that are contained in both manuscripts, they are often incredibly similar, differing only in minute details and stylistic choices, as mentioned before.

Figure 5: Scribe BL MS Royal 13 B VIII, f. 22r
© British Library

Figure 6: Scribe, NLI MS 700, p. 61. Reproduced courtesy of the National Library of Ireland

Example 3: The Scribe

In the illustration of an Irish scribe, these changes can easily be recognized in the chair that the scribe is sitting on, for example. The faces are drawn differently, with the London manuscript (Fig. 5) featuring a completely shaved individual, whereas Dublin's scribe (Fig. 6) has a slight beard. This fits in well with the two earlier examples, where the illustrations clearly show a stronger bias against the Irish in the Dublin manuscript. We can assume that this scribe was a monk, and monks were supposed to shave throughout the Middle Ages. The Dublin scribe's facial hair therefore shows him to be insufficiently cultured and likely Irish, whereas the London manuscript's scribe looks more properly shaved, and therefore more sophisticated.

These examples present a consistent political statement exhibited in both manuscripts, with the Dublin manuscript implying a stronger anti-Irish bias than the London manuscript. It is fascinating that this is a pattern that is visible throughout the manuscripts, and it begs to be mentioned that in the illustrations accompanying the text of the *Expugnatio Hibernica* in the Dublin manuscript, the Anglo-Norman leaders are consistently depicted as clean-shaven, except for Henry II, who is portrayed as a bearded ruler. This portrayal of Henry II might hint at his later criticism of the Angevin dynasty voiced in the *De Principis Instructione*, however the style of beard given to Henry in this image is very different to the beards associated with the Irish, and therefore might not be significant at all.

The editorial choices made in the illustrations of both of these manuscripts lead to the conclusion that these illustrations must have been elaborated separately from an earlier exemplar. In both the examples of the werewolves and Brigid's fire discussed in detail in this article, the Dublin depiction is much simpler, while most of the remaining images that appear in both manuscripts are kept the same. This is especially the case when looking at the passage discussing the werewolves, where Lindsay Zachary Panxhi's careful textual reconstruction has shown that Gerald kept returning to this passage, rendering it far more elaborate and nuanced. It would not make sense that the illustration simplifies over time to depict a more critical reading. As Panxhi's analysis of the werewolf tale shows, Gerald became less preoccupied with subjugating the Irish people over the course of his later recensions: "Gerald again emphasizes his conviction that the Irish are not a race set apart due to inferiority or bestiality. Instead, people of every ethnicity, Normans included, have the same propensity to sin, and must beware lest they fall."[53] It seems convincing that Gerald was the originator of a programme of illustration, which both manuscripts have independently been based on. While scholars have convincingly argued Gerald's potential connection to these copies based on textual evidence, the illustrations could have been separate additions at a different date. It seems that at least the Dublin manuscript must have been illustrated independently of its author.

---

[53] Panxhi, "Rewriting the Werewolf," 39.

The Story of Mog Ruith: Perceptions of the Local Myth in Seventeenth-Century Ireland

Tatiana Shingurova

The seventeenth century in Ireland was a turning point for the traditional Gaelic learned classes. The dynastic validation provided by Irish *seanchaithe* and their lucrative role in the articulation of a Gaelic ideology led to their particular denigration by the crown-administration in Dublin from the mid-sixteenth century onwards.[1] After the defeat of the Gaelic Irish at Kinsale in 1601 and the subsequent Flight of the Earls in 1607, more and more of the elite-class became anglicised and less space was left for the traditional relationships between a lord and a poet. With the spread of English common law throughout the country, especially primogeniture, the legitimizing role of the learned class lost its importance.[2] Henceforth, the Irish learned classes found themselves in a severe situation, lacking the traditional patronage of the Gaelic aristocracy and being persecuted by English laws against poets. This overall decline of traditional Gaelic society and the traditional functions of the *seanchaithe* and poets in the face of anglicisation and Reformation led to their attempts to adapt their learning to socio-political and economic changes in their country. This found its expression in the raising of an Irish identity which fused Roman Catholicism with Gaelic consciousness, uniting those of both Gaelic and Anglo-Norman descent under a common religion and culture.[3] The poets and historians took a new role in articulating a collective sense of identity and cultural consciousness, which became important in the face of early modern colonialism.

In the seventeenth-century Ireland, this task was undertaken by Geoffrey Keating, Dubhaltach Mac Fhirbhisigh, and Mícheál Ó Cléirigh;

---

[1] Marc Caball, Karina Hollo, "Later medieval Ireland, 1200–1600", in *The Cambridge History of Irish Literature*, ed. by Margaret Kelleher, Philip O'Leary (Cambridge: Cambridge University Press, 1982), 74–139, at 82.

[2] Mícheál Mac Craith, "Literature in Irish, c.1550–1690", in *The Cambridge History of Irish Literature*, ed. by Margaret Kelleher, Philip O'Leary (Cambridge: Cambridge University Press, 1982), 191–281, at 219.

[3] Ibid., p. 220.

and it found expression in poems by Lughaidh Ó Cléirigh, Dáibhí Ó Bruadair, and many others. Working under the framework of *Lebor Gabála Érenn,* "The Book of the Invasion of Ireland", they achieved a common identity for both Gaels and Sean-Ghall–Éireannaigh, with Catholicism, Counter-Reformation, and loyalty to traditional Gaelic institutions, as essential components.[4] Scholars and bards took fragmentary pieces of Irish history and fitted them together, adapting and reworking different stories and mythological characters according to their aims and the needs of their society as they understood it. Many medieval myths and characters received a new interpretation, and Mog Ruith, the legendary druid of Munster, the executioner of John the Baptist and the ancestor of Fir Maige Féne, was a colourful example.

According to mediaeval Irish historiography, Mog Ruith was a famous druid from Munster, *dia ndruidechtae* (a god of druidism)[5] in Ireland during the reign of king Fiacha Muillethan, as well as during the reign of nineteen kings, as one text tells us.[6] The last fact once again emphasizes his mythological character.

In the paternal line, he belonged to the descendants of Fergus Mac Róich, and was conceived during the exile of the latter from Ulster. His mother–Cacht daughter of Cathman, king of Britons from the Isle of Man– was a slave in Ireland in the house of Roth mac Rigoill. In some genealogical records[7] Mog Ruith was the son of Fergus and Cacht, in others[8] he was the son of Cuindesaig mac Fer Glan from the people of Fergus, a royal poet of the Ulaid.

---

[4] Ibid., p. 220.

[5] John Carey, "An Old Irish poem about Mug Ruith", *Journal of the Cork Historical and Archaeological Society* 10 (2005), 113–134, at 118.

[6] Ibid., 121.

[7] Genealogies in Oxford, Bodleian Library, MS Laud Misc. 610, ed. Kuno Meyer, "The Laud Genealogies and Tribal Histories", *Zeitschrift für celtische Philologie* 8 (1912), 291–338 at 332; and in Oxford, Bodleian Library, Rawlinson B 502, ed. Michael O'Brian, *Corpus Genealogiarum Hiberniae* (Dublin: Dublin Institute for Advanced Studies, 1962), 279.

[8] Parentage given in *Imtheachta Moga Ruith* in Royal Irish Academy (hereafter RIA) MS 23 P 12, The Book of Ballymote, P. 265, b65; and Trinity College Dublin (hereafter TCD) MS 1318, The Yellow Book of Lecan, p.190 a10.

To learn his magic, Mog Ruith went to the East and became a student of Simon Magus. That was when he beheaded John the Baptist according to the Irish apocryphal tradition. This episode of his life was known only in Ireland and appears only in medieval Irish Apocrypha. There is a group of texts mentioning the execution:

1.) A poem from Leabhar Uí Maine The Book of Uí Maine (f 123 recto col. b).[9] Incipit "Clanna Israel uili scailseat fon mbith mbharrbuidi . . ."

2.) A poem from the The Book of Uí Maine (f 211 verso col. a).[10] Incipit "Absdolon adba na righ".

3.) A prose text from Leabhar Buidhe Leacáin The Yellow Book of Lecan (p. 159 col. 849 ff) concerning the adventures of Mogh Ruith.[11]

4.) Six quatrains from National Library of Scotland, Adv. MS 72.1.1(1–2).[12]

This Irish reimagining of the biblical story of John the Baptist's execution, with Mog Ruith as an executioner was well-known in Ireland by the end of the eleventh century.[13] Being contemporary with other misfortunes of Ireland of that period (destructions caused by long-term Viking-invasion, bad weather-conditions in 1095–96, crop failure, the following famine and plague at the end of 1096), it could contribute to a

---

[9] Edited by Annie M. Scarre, "The Beheading of John the Baptist by Mog Ruith", *Ériu* 4 (1910), 173–181. For manuscript citations to facsimiles, see bibliography following this article.

[10] Brian Ó Cuív, "Two Items from Irish Apocryphal Tradition", *Celtica* 10, (1973), 87–113, at 104–110.

[11] Ed. and tr. Kate Müller-Lisowski, "Texte zur Mog Ruith Sage", *Zeitschrift für celtische Philologie* 14 (1923), 145–163, at 145–153.

[12] Ed. and tr. Brian Ó Cuív, "Two items from Irish Apocryphal Tradition", *Celtica* 10 (1973), 87–113, at 104–110. The poem from the latter manuscript also mentions the curse put on the Irish by John the Baptist once he discovered the race of his murderer. Ibid., 109.

[13] Aideen O'Leary, "Mog Ruith and apocalypticism in eleventh-century Ireland", in *The individual in Celtic literatures, CSANA Yearbook, 1,* ed. J. Nagy (Dublin: Four Courts Press, 2001), 50–60, at 59.

general fear of the upcoming apocalyptic events[14] and waiting for God's punishment at the end of the century, which is reported by The Annals of Ulster (1096,3)[15] and The Annals of the Four Masters (1096.9).[16]

The Annals of the Four Masters (1096.9) gives us the following note:

> *Feil Eóin for Aoine isin m-bliadhain-si. Ro ghabh imeagla mhór Fiora Ereann reimpi, conadh i comhairle ar-riacht lá cleirchibh Ereann im comarba Phátraicc dia n-imdhiden ar an tedhmaim ro tircanadh dóibh ó chéin a forchongra for chach a c-coitchinne tredhenos ó Chedaoin go Domhnach do dénamh gacha mís, et trosccadh gach laoi go cenn m-bliadhna[.]*
>
> The festival of John fell on Friday this year; the men of Ireland were seized with great fear, and the counsel taken by the clergy of Ireland, with the *comarba* of St. Patrick at their head, in order to save them from the mortality which had been predicted to them [. . .] and was to command all in general to observe a three days total fast, from Wednesday to Sunday, every month, and a fast every day till the end of the year[.][17]

The reason for this extraordinary panic could be that all the tribulations of Ireland aligned with the fact that in 1096 the feast of the decollation of John the Baptist (29 August) fell on a Friday, which probably echoed Good Friday, the day of Jesus's crucifixion.[18] The fear could be also related to the tenth-century text "The Second Vision of

---

[14] O'Leary, "Mog Ruith and apocalypticism", 59.

[15] Ed. and tr. Seán Mac Airt and Gearóid Mac Niocaill, *The Annals of Ulster* (Dublin, 1983), accessed December 7, 2018, http://www.ucc.ie/celt/online/T100001A/, at 529.

[16] Ed. and tr., John O'Donovan, *Annála Rioghachta Éireann. Annals of the Kingdom of Ireland by the Four Masters, from the earliest period to the year 1616* (Dublin,1856), accessed December 7, 2018, http://www.ucc.ie/research/celt/published/T100005B/index.htm, at 953.

[17] Ibid.

[18] O'Leary, "Mog Ruith and apocalypticism", 58.

Adamnán" which predicted great plague and the mortalities one after another until the mortality of the feast of John (the Baptist).[19]

The crisis had a deep impact on political and ecclesiastical governments.[20] There is evidence that councils and synods were undertaken in all parts of Ireland to discuss the ecclesiastical reform afterward.[21] The universal hysteria, which was caused by human and by natural factors together and kindled by the legend of Irish national guilt for the deed of Mog Ruith, led to the reform-movement and finally to the Gregorian reform in twelfth-century Ireland.

The killing of John the Baptist was not, however, the main story of Mog Ruith's biography. At least, it was not the earliest one. The oldest surviving text mentioning the druid is *De fabulis Moga Ruith,* which is datable to the sixth or seventh century.[22] It has come down to us in Leabhar Leacain, The Book of Lecan;[23] in the manuscript it follows the genealogical record of Mog Ruith's descendants and precedes the text *Mog Ruith rígfile gan gai*[24] "Mog Ruith a royal poet without a falsehood".[25] *De fabulis* gives a short outline of the druid's participation in the conflict between the king of Tara Cormac mac Art, and the king of Munster, Fiacha Muillethan, which is known as *Forbhuis Droma Damhghaire* or "The Siege of Knocklong". The later copy of *De fabulis* is a part of the genealogies of *Síl Ír* from The Book of Uí Maine.[26] The most extensive version of the *Forbhuis Droma Damhghaire* came down to us in the fifteenth-century manuscript known as the Book of Lismore and is roughly dated to the Middle Irish period.[27] The same manuscript contains another reference to the same story in the topographical document

---

[19] Ed. and tr. Stokes, Whitley, "Adamnan's Second Vision", *Revue Celtique* 12 (1891): 420–43, at 423.

[20] O'Leary, "Mog Ruith and apocalypticism", 58–9.

[21] Ibid., 60.

[22] Donnchadh Ó Corráin, *Clavis Litterarum Hibernensium. Medieval Irish Books & Texts (c. 400–c. 1600)*, (Turnhout: Brepols, 2017), p. 1389.

[23] RIA MS 23 P 2, The Book of Lecan, f. 124 recto col. b lines 31–47.

[24] Ibid., f. 124 verso, (37qq).

[25] John Carey, "An Old Irish poem about Mug Ruith", 113–34.

[26] RIA MS D ii 1, The Book of Uí Maine, f. 72 verso col. a-b.

[27] Ed. and tr. M.-L. Sjoestedt, "Forbhuis Droma Damghaire", *Revue Celtique* 43 (Paris, 1926–7), 1–123.

Críchad an Chaoilli "The boundary of Caoille".[28] and in the poem *Bai fáidh an feinnidh bai sinn* "The warrior who dwelt here was a prophet".[29]

Forbhuis Droma Damhghaire describes a siege led by the king of Tara, Cormac mac Art against the Munster king Fiacha Muillethan at the place *Druim Damhghaire,* later known as Knocklong, because Fiacha refused to pay him tribute. To succeed in this campaign, Cormac took five powerful druids with him, who blocked up the water and milk of the household from Munster, so they had to drink blood from their cows. Since arms were useless against the druids, the men of Munster decided to seek the help of the druid Mog Ruith who, as the narrative says, was a foster-father to the king of Munster, Fiacha. As his reward, Mog Ruith chose the fertile land of Fermoy for his descendants as well as a lot of privileges and nobility for Fir Maige Féne. As soon as the reward was agreed upon, the wizard released the streams of Munster with the power of his druidic spear, killed Cormac's druids, and banished Cormac together with his troops from Munster.

The killing of John the Baptist and the druid's participation at *Forbhuis Droma Damhghaire* were two of the most common stories about Mog Ruith in the Middle Ages, as one can judge from numerous surviving texts. Other texts provide us also with fragmentary pieces of his further biography, for example about his long life during the rule of nineteen kings[30] or about his death.[31]

Texts on Mog Ruith, apart from the genealogical record, are preserved mainly in the following manuscripts:

---

[28] Ed. and tr. J.G. O'Keeffe, "The Ancient Territory of Fermoy", *Ériu* 10 (1926/1928), 170–89.

[29] Ed. R. A. S. Macalister, *The book of Mac Carthaigh Riabhach, otherwise The Book of Lismore.* Facsimiles in Collotype of Irish Manuscripts, 5 (Dublin 1950), 73. 189 c 34.

[30] John Carey, "An Old Irish poem about Mug Ruith", 121.

[31] Ibid., 121. Also *Lebor gabála Érenn: The Book of the Taking of Ireland,*ed. R. Macalister, in 5 volumtes, Irish Texts Society vols 34-35, 39, 41, 44 (Dublin: Irish Texts Society, 1932–42), vol.5 (44) 199-200.

The Book of Uí Maine (late fourteenth century)[32]

An account of the descendants of Mog Ruith, begins "Mogh Ruith mac Feargusa a quo Fir Muigi",[33]
A poem on Tlachtga the daughter of Mog Ruith in *Dindschenchas*, begins "Tlachtga tulach ardan uas*",*[34]
Two poems on the killing of John the Baptist by Mog Ruith.[35]

The Yellow Book of Lecan (fourteenth-fifteenth centuries)[36]

An account of the beheading of John the Baptist, begins "Bai ri aingid etrocair isin domun"[37]
Imtheachta Moga Ruith (legend about the Irish druid Mog Ruith, said to have assisted Simon Magus in opposing the Apostle Peter).[38]

The Book of Lecan (early fifteenth century)[39]:

Síl Moga Ruith meic Fergusa[40]
Mog Ruith rígfile gan gai,
De fabulis Moga Ruith.
An account of the birth of Fiacha Muillethan son of

---

[32] RIA MS D ii 1, The Book of Uí Maine. For description, see *Catalogue of Irish Manuscripts in the Royal Irish Academy* (hereafter *RIA Catalogue*) fasc. XXIV, Kathleen Mulchrone (Dublin: Royal Irish Academy, 1942) 3314.

[33] RIA MS D ii 1, The Book of Uí Maine, f. 72 verso, col. a.

[34] Ibid., f. 166 verso col. b.

[35] Ibid., f. 123 recto col b; f. 211 verso col. a.

[36] TCD MS 1318 (The Yellow Book of Lecan). For description see J. Gwynn, ed. *Catalogue of Irish Manuscripts in the Library in the Trinity College Dublin*, (Dublin, 1921), 94. On a date of the manuscript see Nollaig Ó Muraíle, *The Celebrated Antiquary Dubhaltach Mac Fhirbhisigh (c. 1600–1671): His Lineage, Life and Learning* (Maynooth, 1996), 19.

[37] TCD MS 1318, f .159 col 849.

[38] TCD MS 1318, f. 190 col. 906 line 90; Müller-Lisowski, "Texte zur Mog Ruith Sage", 145–53.

[39] RIA MS 23 P 2, The Book of Lecan. For description see *RIA Catalogue* , fasc. XIII, Kathleen Mulchrone (Dublin: Royal Irish Academy, 1933) 1551.

[40] The Book of Lecan, f. 124 a.

Eogan Mór and of the Siege of Druim Damghaire, begins "Doluid Éogan Mór mac Aililla Uluim"[41]

The Book of Lismore (fifteenth century)[42]

Forbhuis Droma Damhghaire,
Críchad an Chaoilli,
A poem beginning Bai fáidh an feinnidh bai sinn.

The Book of Fermoy (mainly fifteenth century)[43]

Domnall Chnuic an Bhile. A poem on David O'Keefe, introducing the story of *Forbhuis Droma Damhghaire.* [44]

Egerton 92 (a fragmentary copy of the Book of Fermoy, fifteenth century)[45]

Boile Moga Ruith "The rage of Mog Ruith",[46]
Accalaim Mogha Ruith ocus escub Cairpre "The Colloquium of Mog Ruith and the bishop Cairpre",[47]
A short poem, beginning Se fichit bliadan "120 years".[48]

---

[41] Ibid., f. 167 r recto; Ed. and tr. Whitley Stokes, "A note about Fiacha Muillethan", *Revue Celtique* 11 (1890): 41–5.

[42] Brian Ó Cuív, "Observations on the Book of Lismore", *Proceedings of the Royal Irish Academy: Archaeology, Culture, History, Literature*, Vol. 83C (1983), pp. 269–292, at 269.

[43] RIA MS 23 E 29, The Book of Fermoy. See description in *RIA* Catalogue, fasc. xxv Gerald Murphy and Elizabeth FitzPatrick (Dublin: Royal Irish Academy, 1940) 3091.

[44] RIA MS 23 E 2923 E 29, f. 26 col. a. Ed. and tr. E. Knott, "Address to David O'Keefe", *Ériu* 4 (1910): 209–32.

[45] British Library MS Egerton 92, fragment of the Book of Fermoy, cf. *RIA Catalogue*, fasc. xxv by Gerald Murphy and Elizabeth FitzPatrick (Dublin: Royal Irish Academy, 1940) 3096.

[46] MS Egerton 92, f. 9 col. b.

[47] MS Egerton 92, f. 8 col. a–b.

[48] Ibid.

MS 72.1.1(1–2) National Library of Scotland (fifteenth century)[49]

A poem about the execution of John the Baptist by Mog Ruith and on further curse put by the saint man on the Irish).[50]

The Psalter of Tara (seventeenth century)[51]

Boile Moga Ruith.[52]

This list, though not complete, shows us which legends on Mog Ruith had spread by the Early Modern period in Ireland and could have been available to seventeenth-century scholars. However, we should bear in mind that they may have had access to other stories regarding the druid's biography, from manuscripts now lost.

In this seventeenth-century context we should accentuate the following works: *Iomarbhágh na bhFileadh* "The Contention of the bards"[53] (Mog Ruith is mentioned mainly in the poems by Tadhg Mac Bruaideadha and Lughaidh Ó Cléirigh); *Foras Feasa ar Éirinn* "The History of Ireland" by Geoffrey Keating;[54] the poem *Iomdha scéimh ar chur na cluana* by Daibhi Ó Bruadáir;[55] *Leabhar na nGenealach* "The Great Book of Irish Genealogies" by Dubhaltach Mac Fhirbhisigh.[56]

---

[49] National Library of Scotland; prior to 1925 Library of the Faculty of Advocates, Adv. MS 72.1.1(1–2). Black, Ronald, "Catalogue of Gaelic manuscripts in the National Library of Scotland: Adv. MS 72.1.1", *Irish Script on Screen–Meamrám Páipéar Ríomhaire*, accessed May 2019, https://www.isos.dias.ie/libraries/NLS/NLS Adv MS 72 1 1/english/index.html.

[50] Brian Ó Cuív, "Two items from Irish Apocryphal Tradition", 87–113.

[51] Gwynn, *Catalogue of Irish Manuscripts the Trinity College Dublin*, 50.

[52] TCD, MS 1289, p. 939.

[53] Ed. and tr. Lambert McKenna, *Iomarbhágh na bhfileadh: The contention of the bards*, 2 vols, Irish Texts Society 20, 21 (London, 1918).

[54] Ed. and tr. David Comyn, and Patrick S. Dinneen, *Foras feasa ar Éirinn: The History of Ireland by Geoffrey Keating D. D.*, Vol. 2 (London: Irish Texts Society, 1908), 320–21.

[55] Ed. and tr. MacErlean, John C*., Duanaire Dháibhidh Uí Bhruadair. The poems of David Ó Bruadair*, Irish Texts Society, Vol. 1 (London, 1910), 88–119.

[56] Ed. Nollaig Ó Muraíle, *Leabhar mór na ngenealach: The great book of Irish genealogies, compiled (1645–66) by Dubhaltach Mac Fhirbhisigh*, 5 vols (Dublin: DeBúrca, 2003).

Iomarbhágh na bhFileadh "The Contention of the bards" (c.1616–1624)

The first work in the list is "The Contention of the bards," a curious literary controversy which lasted approximately from 1616 till 1624 and ran to thirty contributions.[57] It was initiated by the Southern poet Tadhg Mac Bruaideadha who was working under the patronage of Donnchadh Uí Briain, the fourth Earl of Thomond and president of Munster since 1605. Uí Briain had been known at the time for its loyalty to the English crown and for this reason, was flourishing, in comparison with many other Irish aristocratic families of that period. Therefore Tadhg had reasons to view the prospects for the future with more satisfaction and optimism than his fellow-poets from other parts of Ireland, especially those from Ulster,[58] whose earls Hugh Uí Néill, Earl of Tyrone and Rory O'Donnell, first Earl of Tyrconnell had recently defeated in the battle of Kinsale by the English and had to flee to the Continent in the hope of obtaining help for their war against the English crown.

The framework of the Contention follows the customary rivalry between *Leth Moga* and *Leth Cuinn*, the "Southern" and "Northern" Halves of Ireland, where Tadhg represents the Southern part or "Eberians", descendants of Míl's son Eber, to whom Donnchadh Uí Briain, the patron of Tadhg, traced his origins. The most furious opponent of Tadhg was Lughaidh Ó Cléirigh, who belonged to the family which provided bards to Ó Domhnaill, the main rivals of the English crown during the Nine Years' War. Ó Domhnaill in their turn belonged to the offspring of Niall Noígíallach, descendant of Míl's son Éremón, and therefore to "Eremonians", who conflated with the Northern Half, *Leth Cuinn*. This mythical rivalry between the dynasties of *Leth Moga* and *Leth Cuinn* received a new interpretation during the sixteenth century when all Ireland was shired and Co. Clare in Connacht became a disputed territory between Munster and Connacht. In the end, Co. Clare was promised to the fourth earl of Thomond as the reward for his military support of the crown

---

[57] Joseph Leerssen, *The contention of the bards (Iomarbhágh na bhFileadh) and its place in Irish political and literary history*, (London: Irish Texts Society, 1994), 5–6. McKenna, *Iomarbhágh na bhfileadh*, Vol.1., viii.

[58] Ibid., 11.

during the rebellion of Uí Neill and Ó Domhnaill.[59]   In 1615 Co. Clare was recognized as part of Munster and Donnchadh Uí Briain was appointed to be president of that province. Around the same time Tadhg Mac Bruaideadha, working under Thomond's patronage writing the first poem of Contention, *Olc do thagrais a Thorna,* "Poor spite of your good learning, O Torna", to celebrate the dominance of the South over the North.[60]

In this poem Tadhg attacked the semi-historical poet, Torna Eigeas, *file* to Conn Cétchathach, blaming him for historical inaccuracy and for partiality in favour of Ireland's "Northern Half" and the Eremonian branches of the Gael. To prove his argument Tadhg mentions many great deeds of the Eberians and of all Munster kings who were known to him over the ages. Among these, he referred to the Siege of Knocklong and to the victory of Fiacha Muillethan over Cormac mac Airt:

> *Níor mhaoidh tú i dtrát a mhaoidhimh, Cur Cormaic mic Airt Aoin-Fhir d'Fhiacha fo ghabhail coire iar maidhm Dhroma Damhgaire.*

> You mention not, when you should have done so, the putting of Cormac son of Art Aoinfhear by Fiachaidh under the hook of a cauldron after the battle of *Druim Damghaire.*[61]

This poem provoked some of his contemporaries with Northern, Eremonian affiliation and turned into the famous literary dispute invoking the participation of 13 different poets.[62] Answering Tadhg's poem and his statement about the story of *Forbhuis Droma Damhghaire,* Lughaidh Ó Cléirigh, who was working under the patronage of Ó Domhnaill, the enemy of the Uí Briain in the battle of Kinsale, recalled Mog Ruith's role in the conflict and argued that, since Mog Ruith was from *Síl Ír,* the victory over Cormac could not be attributed to Eberians.[63] However, Tadhg in the poem *Éisd a Lughaidh rem Labhra,* "Listen Lughaidhh to my

---

[59] Ibid., 22.

[60] Ibid.

[61] McKenna, *Iomarbhágh na bhfileadh,* Vol. 1, 16–17.

[62] Ibid., Vol. 1, ix–xiii.

[63] Ibid., Vol. 1, 26–27.

words", disagreed, saying that Lughaidh was not familiar with the true version of the story of the Siege, and told the story of the Siege as it was known to him:

> *Cormac féin thug leir a tuaidh draoithe d'iarraidh beirthe buardh*
> *Dár thráighsead uisge Mumhan ceathrs is daoine ar dtiormughadh*
> *Dealbhaid mar shearamh dá spairnn caoire ris nach gabhdaoir airm*
> *Már maiseach an iarraidh neirt dod rig onórach oirdheirc.*

It was Cormac himself who came from the North to conquer the druids
At whose word Mumha's waters ebbed away, and cattle and men were parched.[64]
As a resource for their fight, the druids formed the fire-balls against which arms availed not
If that be for your honourable noble king, a creditable means of getting power![65]

> *Coisgis Mogh Ruith ceird na druadh 's ar a shon do ghlac a luach Fiacha Muimhneach do chlaoi a neart níor chlaoi Mogh Ruith ach draoidheacht.*

Moghruith baffled the druids' arts and got the reward for that. Fiacha of Mumha broke the strength of the Northerns. Mogrhruith only destroyed their wizardry.[66]

> *Ann ngach ionadh thear is thuaidh í bhfuil sgríobhtha sdair an tsluaigh ar a n-abraim an-oise tógbhaim íman fhiadhnaise.*

---

[64] Ibid., § 175.
[65] Ibid., § 176.
[66] Ibid., 52–53 §178.

I take the story of that hosting where it is found written
everywhere North or South to witness to the truth of what
I say.[67]

In his poem, Tadhg tries to distance King Fiacha from Mog Ruith,
pointing out that the druid had no relation to King Fiacha and participated
on behalf of Munster only because of the reward promised to him.
Moreover, he justified Fiacha's seeking help from the druid, claiming that
arms were useless against Cormac's druids and that it was Cormac himself
who was first to rely on the help of druids. The poet's description of
wizardry is like the one from The Book of Lismore. However, while in
The Book of Lismore Mog Ruith is called foster-father of Fiacha,[68] there
is no mention of this in the Contention. Tadhg, as Lughaidh did not
recognize Mog Ruith as one of the men of Munster and tried to avoid the
discussion about the druid's participation in the battle as much as possible.

Another curious piece of information from the passages above is
Tadhg's statement that the version of the Siege known to him was
widespread "everywhere from North or South". The versions of the story
which came down to us in different manuscripts do not confirm his
statement. There is no version earlier than the seventeenth century in
which Mog Ruith would only assist Fiacha and not be the main character
of the story. The only version which would suit Tadhg's description is
presented in Keating's "History of Ireland".[69] However, it was written
after the time of *Iomarbhágh na bhFileadh*. Therefore, it is difficult to
confirm that the version of the story referred to by Tadhg had ever existed.
It might be that in this passage of the poem, Tadhg refused to accept that
Eberians would not have been able to stand Eremonians without aid from
the druid, the descendant of *Ír*.

The versions of the Siege from the *Forbhuis Droma Damhghaire* or
Crichad an Chaoilli from The Book of Lismore include a detailed
description of druidic magic, which must have been too fabulous for
seventeenth-century scholars. Reacting to Tadhg's account of Mog Ruith's
wizardry Lughaidh criticizes the story itself:

---

[67] Ibid., §179.

[68] M.-L. Sjoestedt, "Forbhuis Droma Damghaire", 8.

[69] Comyn D., and Dinneen P., *Foras feasa ar Éirinn,* 320–321.

Creididh thu do na leabhraibh madh ni thaithneas léd mheanmain más faibhle is milis a mblas madhre síÉibhir beanas.

You believe the books if there be something in them that pleasures your feelings. Even if they be fables, sweet is their taste if they refer to Eibhear's race.[70]

Speaking about the Siege he makes a reference to one passage which is included in The Book of Lismore, but is absent in other versions:

Bréag ar Mogh Ruith do fheadar do chur sa sgéal so as Pheadar go ndubhairt ris ní radh ceart méaraidh choidhche do dhruidheacht.

I know that a lie about Mogruith is attributed in the tale to Peter, how Peter said to him–a wrong thing to say–"Your wizardry shall abide forever.[71]

Here Lughaidh may refer to the passage from the Lismore text, where Mog Ruith speaking about his magic speaks of Apostle Peter as his teacher. Only in this text, Peter is mentioned together with Simon as a teacher of the druid.

. . . uair ita briathar mh' oidi-se, .i. Shimoin meic Guill meic Iarguill, & Petair ris na soeidfider orum mo dana cein bear beo.'

. . . I have the assurance of my teacher Síomón mac Goill mhic Iarghoill and Peter, also, that my art will never fail me while I am alive.[72]

It could be that Lughaidh was familiar with the text from The Book of Lismore, or from the book of Monasterboice, from which the former manuscript had been copied.[73] However, while he does not doubt the existence of Mog Ruith as a historical figure, calling him the descendant

---

[70] McKenna, *Iomarbhágh na bhfileadh*, Vol. 1, 56–57, § 16.

[71] Ibid., 70–71, § 123.

[72] M.-L. Sjoestedt, "Forbhuis Droma Damghaire", 58.

[73] Donnchadh Ó Corráin, "The Book of Lismore: MS description, edition and history", *CELT: Corpus of Electronic Texts*, accessed December 2018, https://celt.ucc.ie//book_lismore.html.

of Fergus Mac Róich, and does not question his participation in the siege on behalf of Munster, he refuses to believe in the druid's wizardry:

> *Sgéal fuarara bhfionntar bréag ní cóir a chreideamh go n-eag 's gan cóngnam éin leabhair lair is mar sin atá th'fhorbhais.*

> An unlikely tale, of which the falsehood can be seen, should never be believed, especially when there is no book to support it. Such is your tale of the Siege.[74]

His opinion was supported by another bard of The Contention, Aodh Domhnal. In his poem *Measa do thagrais a Thaidhg* "Worse have you argued, O Tadhg" he calls the story of the wizardry of the old druid Mog Ruith a superstition,[75] and provides a list of "trustworthy" books of Ireland: *Lebor Gabála Érenn, Dindschenchas,* the Psalter of Cashel, "the history books of Art's Isle", "the Courts". "the Destructions", "the Wooings", "The Book of Armagh", etc.[76] The similar list of "recommended reading" appears later in Keating's "History of Ireland".[77] However, even though Aodh mentions these books, he does not say that he consulted them himself. Moreover, some of these books, for example, The Psalter of Cashel[78] had been already lost by the time of the poem's creation. Tadhg in his answer to Aodh—the poem *Ní breit orm do bhreith a Aodh* "No condemnation of me is your judgment O Aodh" notes that "there might easily be found things in that book [the Psalter of Cashel] without his [Aodh's] knowledge".[79] With this Tadhg points that neither he nor his opponent Aodh could be sure about the content of the Psalter, presumably because the manuscript had been lost by the time of the poems.

---

[74] McKenna, *Iomarbhágh na bhfileadh*, Vol. 1, 70–71, § 124.

[75] Ibid., 142–143, § 55.

[76] Ibid., 136–137, § 9–13.

[77] Comyn D., and Dinneen P., *Foras feasa ar Éirinn*, Vol. 1, 78–81.

[78] Aisling Byrne argues that the last known location of the manuscript was the library of the Earls of Kildare, from which it disappeared in the 1630s or 1640s, and the library itself was destroyed in 1642. Aisling Byrne, "The earls of Kildare and their books at the end of the Middle Ages", *The Library: Transactions of the Bibliographical Society* 14 (2013), 129–153, at 133–134.

[79] McKenna, *Iomarbhágh na bhfileadh*, Vol. 2, 192–193, § 117.

MOG RUITH

Measa do thagrais a Thaidhg by Aodh (the XV poem of The Contention) is the last poem in which Mog Ruith is mentioned. In his answer to Aodh, Tadhg no longer gives the name of the druid, saying one more time that it was Cormac, the unjust prince who was the first to employ wizardry, and Fiacha overcame Cormac's attack and wizardry too.[80]

To summarize the evidence on the druid in the literary controversy, the legend of Mog Ruith follows the central paradigm of The Contention–the conflict between *Leth Cuinn* and *Leth Moga*. The poet under southern patronage Tadhg who was representing the interests of Uí Briain, tries to omit Mogh Ruith's participation in the *Forbhuis Droma Damghaire* and attributes the victory to the king Fiacha Muillethan from the race of Eber. He does not mention the fosterage relationship between the king of Munster and the druid, just as he does not consider Mog Ruith to be from Munster, because according to the Book of Invasion the race of *Ír* belongs to the North of Ireland, as Tadhg's main opponent Lughaidh claimed. Another reason why Tadhg tries to distance his king from Mog Ruith could be the condemnation of wizardry in The Contention and generally in the seventeenth-century Ireland.[81] As the poets say several times, making use of wizardry is not honourable for a king.[82] However, the druid received good report in Lughaidh poems as one of the noble men of *Leth Cuinn.* The poet, disbelieving the narrative about Mog Ruith's wizardry, treats him as one of the outstanding heroes of *Leth Cuinn.*

It is difficult to say if the poets were familiar with Mog Ruith's adventures in the East, or with his murder of John the Baptist. These parts of the druid's biography are omitted in The Contention and only his participation in the conflict at *Druim Damghaire* is mentioned. They should be familiar at least with Mog Ruith's pupilage under Simon Magus, because it is mentioned in different versions of the Siege, which were known to them. There is also a reference to Peter as Mog Ruith's teacher, as well as, Simon Magus in The Book of Lismore. However, Lughaidh mentions only Peter's name in his poem. The execution of John

---

[80] Ibid., 192–193, § 116–121.

[81] For additional discussion see Andrew Sneddon, *Witchcraft and Magic in Ireland*, (London: Palgrave Macmillan, 2015).

[82] McKenna, *Iomarbhágh na bhfileadh*, Vol. 1, 50–51, § 176.

the Baptist appears in The Book of Lecan, The Yellow Book of Lecan, The Book of Uí Maine, which were in Ireland over the time of the Contention[83] and might have been available for the poets. Therefore, it is difficult to say whether the poets were not familiar with the story, or they omitted it on purpose. As we will see later, the Contention is not the only work of the seventeenth century, which mentions Mog Ruith and keeps silence about John the Baptist.

Foras Feasa ar Éirinn "The History of Ireland" (1629–1634)

Another cautious assessment of Mog Ruith could be found in the work of Geoffrey Keating, who was working under the patronage of Munster earls, the Butlers.[84] In his *Foras Feasa ar Éirinn* (composed between 1629–1634)[85] he mentions *Forbhuis Droma Damhghaire* only briefly, telling that because of the wizardry of Cormac's druids, whom he brought from Scotland, the men of Munster were left without water, so people were starving.[86] Therefore, Fiacha was obliged "gur bh'eigean do rígh Mumhan"[87] to send for druid Mog Ruith, and obliged to give him two cantreds of *Feara Muighe* "fá heigean don rígh dá thriúcha céad

---

[83] The Book of Lecan was kept in Ireland till 1640, when the manuscript was taken out of the country with other collection of James Ussher. In 1657 the manuscript was returned to Ireland, to Dublin castle, and in 1660 was given to Trinity College. Ó Muraíle, *The Celebrated Antiquary*, 194.

The Yellow Book of Lecan was in possession of clann Fhir Bhisigh over the seventeenth century till the death of the Dubhaltach Mac Fhir Bhisigh in January 1671, when it came into hands of his lord, O'Dowd, and then at around 1700 into possession of Irish historian Roderick O'Flaherty. Ó Muraíle, *The Celebrated Antiquary*, 303.

The Book of Uí Maine was compiled for Muircheartach Ó Ceallaigh, Bishop of Clonfert, later Bishop of Tuam (1378–1394), and stayed within the family until 1757. See N. Ó Muráile, "Leabhar Ua Maine alias Leabhar Uí Dhubhagáin", *Éigse* 23 (1989), 167–95.

[84] Bernadette Cunningham, *The world of Geoffrey Keating* (Cornwall: Four Courts Press, 2000), 60.

[85] Mícheál Mac Craith, "Literature in Irish, c.1550–1690", 213.

[86] Comyn D., and Dinneen P., *Foras feasa ar Éirinn*, 320–321.

[87] Ibid., 320.

Fearmuighe".[88] Thereupon the druid removed the barrier that had been put to the water withholding it, and at the same time threw up into the air a magic spear and in the place where the spear fell there bursts forth a well of spring water which relieved the men of Munster. Hereupon the king of Munster with his host made a sudden onset on Cormac and his followers and expelled them.[89] This brief description seems to be neutral, however, the adjective *éigean*[90] which means "necessity, compulsion" catches the eye. Still, Keating did not underestimate the druid's contribution to the victory of Munster, sharing victorious palms between Fiacha and the druid.

Another detail of Mog Ruith's biography, mentioned by Keating is the long life of the druid, who, as he narrates, lived in the time of nineteen kings.[91] This detail appears in the text *Mog Ruith rigfile gan gai* from The Book of Lecan,[92] mentioned above. The text mentions Mog Ruith learning wizardry from Simon Magus, and the druid's participation in the conflict between Simon and the Apostles, however, it omits the execution of John the Baptist. Other texts dedicated to Mog Ruith in the Book of Lecan also neglect the story of the execution. The text *Mog Ruith rigfile gan gai* mentions the druid's participation in the Siege and may be one of Keating's sources for writing the passage about it. Mícheál Ó Cléirigh used the manuscript for his transcription of the poem *Naemhshenchus* name *Insi Fail* in April 1636.[93] Bernadette Cunningham in her work suggested that Mícheál Ó Cléirigh and Keating belonged at that time to the same cultural circle, using some of the same manuscripts in their researches, though there is no evidence that these two scholars ever met in person.[94] Therefore, it could be that Keating also had access to the Great Book of Lecan and to the text *Mog Ruith rigfile gan gai* together with

---

[88] Ibid.

[89] Ibid.

[90] *Electronic Dictionary of the Irish Language,* s.v. "éigean", accessed December 7, 2018, http://dil.ie/19711.

[91] Comyn D., and Dinneen P., *Foras feasa ar Éirinn*, 320.

[92] Carey, "An Old Irish poem about Mug Ruith", 113–134.

[93] Ibid., 194.

[94] Cunningham, *The world of Geoffrey Keating*, 60.

other texts about the druid, preserved in this manuscript. Though there is no direct evidence to prove it.

Keating also might have access to The Book of Lismore with the expanded version of the *Forbhuis Droma Damhghaire*. He spent much of his life in Lismore and had strong connections with the southern families of *seanchaithe*,[95] through whom he could get hold of the Book of Lismore, whilst working on his *Foras Feasa*. It is known that in June 1629 Mícheál Ó Cléirigh copied certain items from the Book of Mac Cartaigh Riabhach.[96] The book was still probably within Mac Carthaig family by June 1642 (after the approximate date of the compilation of *Foras Feasa*), when Lord Kinalmeaky captured the Mac Carthaigh Riabhach castle at Kilbrittain. In a letter to his father, Lord Kinalmeaky reported that he acquired a manuscript, which is thought to be the Book of Lismore.[97] This means that by 1642 the Book was in the possession of a Gaelic family and was available to scholars. Therefore, Keating, as well as Ó Cléirigh, could have had access to it.

Keating's account of the Siege of Knocklong repeats the version from The Book of Lismore, though the texts are not identical. Two stanzas he quotes–one about Mog Ruith (where it is said that he lived during the reign of nineteen kings), the second about king Fiacha–are not found in the Lismore manuscript. Also, as contrasted with Lismore's version and the version from *Mog Ruith rigfile gan gai*, the main hero of the battle in *Foras Feasa* is king Fiacha, not the druid, who is given *Fer Maige* (Fermoy) land for his help. The fosterage relation between the druid and the king is also omitted.

Following the poets of the Contention, Keating mentions neither Mog Ruith's pupillage under Simon nor the execution of John the Baptist. However, for an Irish Catholic scholar who strived to write a praising history of the Catholic Irish nation (which united Gaels and Anglo-Normans who were born in Ireland and had been Catholic)[98] it would have been logical to omit the execution of John the Baptist by the Irishman. Especially during the time of European wars of religion and the

---

[95] Cunningham, *The world of Geoffrey Keating*, 17–31, 60.

[96] Brian Ó Cuív, "Observations on the Book of Lismore", 271.

[97] Ibid.

[98] Cunningham, *The world of Geoffrey Keating*, 106.

Reformation in Ireland, which caught Irish Catholics in a difficult state. The hard-line against Catholics in Ireland in the sixteenth-seventeenth centuries could also explain why Mog Ruith's relation to Simon Magus and John the Baptist is suppressed in the Contention.

Iomdha scéimh ar chur na cluana "Many petty settings" (1662–1667)

A small allusion to Mog Ruith's participation at *Druim Damhghaire* is presented in a wedding poem by Dáibhí Ó Bruadair (1625–1698). The poem *Iomdha sceimh ar chur na cluana* (Many petty settings)[99] was written between 1662–1667, after Cromwell's confiscations and was devoted to the marriage of Dominic Roche to the daughter of John Bourke and Anna Hurley.[100] Mog Ruith appears in prose rhetoric in the middle of the poem. Dáibhí Ó Bruadair one of whose primary sources was Keating's "History"[101] mentions the stream *Greadhnach*[102] (Ballingarry) which as he explained was given to Munster by Mogh Ruith during the Siege, when he opened the magic lock put on Munster water by Cormac's druids. As the poet says the stream was a clear, joyful and streamlet, and everyone benefitted from it till the time of Captain Odell, an English colonist frequently identified with John Odell, one of Cromwellian soldiers who seems to have been granted these lands approximately in 1667.[103] Once Odell got the lands and the town as his property, he modified its banks to use it for ministering grass, and made reservoirs to " . . . *ag beathughadh n-anmann n-anaithnidh*" (feed weird form of life),[104] and as a result the stream ceased to be free and profitable to all people in general.

In the poem, Mog Ruith appears in a positive way as a hero of Munster, who opposed English colonist Odell. The druid's stream *Greadhnach* which means "the Joyful" brings profit to nature and local people while the "art" of the colonist brings perversion on nature: "to feed

---

[99] MacErlean, John C*., Duanaire Dháibhidh Uí Bhruadair*, Vol. 1, 88–119.

[100] Griffin-Wilson, Margo "Mythical and Local Landscapes: Dáibhí Ó Bruadair's Iomdha sgéimh ar chur na cluana", *Celtica* 25 (2007) 40–60, at 40.

[101] Ibid., 50.

[102] MacErlean, John C., *Duanaire Dháibhidh Uí Bhruadair*, Vol. 1, 112–113.

[103] Griffin-Wilson "Mythical and Local Landscapes", 55–56.

[104] Ibid., 112–113.

weird forms of life". In the images of Mog Ruith and Odell, the poet probably notes a discontinuity between an idyllic past and the grimness of the present.[105] It is interesting that despite adopting the concept of the providentalism in 1650s and seeing the misfortunes of Irish as God's punishment for their sins,[106] the poet does not refer to the sins of Mog Ruith in his poetry. It could mean that the story of the execution was either unknown to Ó Bruadair or was generally considered fictional.

Mog Ruith is mentioned briefly in the poem. However, as Margo Griffin-Wilson, who analysed the description of a landscape in the poem, argues, this brief reference should have been enough for people gathered at a wedding to recall the exact legend and the exact place.[107] Speaking about the stream released by Mog Ruith Dáibhi Ó Bruadair describes the area of Ballingarry. Sources mention John Odell a Cromwellian soldier, who was granted the territories in co. Limerick, including the Castle, mill, and fair of Ballingarry in 1667.[108] The wedding and the poem should be dated to approximately the same year.[109] Therefore, this comparison of Mog Ruith and English colonist Odell in Ó Bruadair's poem could either refers to the particular events which took place already, as granting the lands to Odell, or shows expectations of the upcoming changes.

The reference to Mog Ruith and *Forbhuis Droma Damhghaire* had another meaning for a just married couple. The *Druim Damhghaire* or Knocklong [*Cnoc Luinge*] was the hereditary seat of Hurley, the family of the bride's mother.[110] The territory of *Fer Maige* which according to *Forbhuis Droma Damhghaire,* Mog Ruith chose for his descendants is identified in Keating's narrative with the land of the Roches, the family of the groom.[111] Therefore, we should assume that both families of the newlyweds were familiar with the legend.

---

[105] Mícheál Mac Craith, "Literature in Irish, c.1550–1690", 223.

[106] Ibid., p. 223

[107] Griffin-Wilson "Mythical and Local Landscapes", 51.

[108] Ibid., 56.

[109] Ibid., 40.

[110] Ibid., 58.

[111] Comyn D., and Dinneen P., *Foras feasa ar Éirinn*, 320–321.

MOG RUITH

Leabhar na nGenealach "The Book of Genealogies" (1649–1650)

The last seventeenth-century work in our list which mentions Mog Ruith is the Great Book of Irish Genealogies by Dubhaltach (Óg) Mac Fhirbhisigh, compiled in Galway in St. Nicholas's College house in 1649–1650.[112] Dubhaltach belonged to the hereditary learned family–clann Fhir Bhisigh–whose history could be traced back to the eleventh century.[113] The family produced many manuscripts, which we have, or about which we are aware, nowadays; those crucial for the current article are the Yellow Book of Lecan (Ó Muraíle names this part *Leabhar Giolla Íosa*)[114] and the Great Book of Lecan. The chief compiler of both manuscripts was Giolla Íosa Mór.[115] The various texts about Mog Ruith in these manuscripts demonstrate that clann Fhir Bhisigh was familiar with different aspects of the druids' biography: not only with his participation in the Siege and receiving Fir Maige, but also with his pupilage with Simon Magus, his participation in the conflict between Simon and the Apostles, and the execution of John the Baptist. Some rare genealogical traditions related to the druid, absent in other manuscripts, also could be found there. For example, Genealogical tract C from the Great Book of Lecan, mentions Meadbh Leithderg and Cormac mac Art as Mog Ruith's parents.[116]

As a member of the Mac Fhirbhisigh family, Dubhaltach would have access to manuscripts in its possession, as well as to scholarly networks, which would provide additional material for his *Leabhar na nGenealach* (LGen). Recent research by Ó Muraíle discovered which works Dubhaltach used or may have used, whilst working on his collection of genealogies.[117] This research gives an idea, from where the parts on Mog Ruith from LGen are derived.

---

[112] Ó Muraíle, *The Celebrated Antiquary*, 166.

[113] Ibid., 1.

[114] Ibid., 16.

[115] Nollaig Ó Muraíle, *The Celebrated Antiquary*, 16–7.

[116] Ed. Ó Toirdhealbhach Raithbheartaigh, *Genealogical tracts.* Vol. 1, (Dublin: Irish Manuscript Commission, 1932), 147.

[117] Ó Muraíle, *The Celebrated Antiquary*, 166–201.

TATIANA SHINGUROVA

There are few sections dedicated to the druid and his descendants in LGen. They are all included in the part *Síl Ír* (486–560).[118] This is considered as one of the earliest parts of LGen, because it is known that the Dubhaltach made a copy of *Senchas Síl Ír* in 1645.[119] It is believed, though there is no proof of it,[120] that Dubhaltach derived it from The Book of Uí Maine and later integrated it into his LGen. Dobbs argued that Dubhaltach version combined all extant versions:[121]

> 1) A short account of the oldest pedigrees and traditions (from Laud, LL, Rawl.)
>
> 2) A more extended version with detailed and later pedigrees of Dal Fiatach and Dal Araide (Lec. B., D.2.1.)
>
> 3) An extended version including people of Ulster descent in Louth, Meath, Queens Co. Fermanagh. (Represented by Lec. A. and BB).

The section on Mog Ruith and his descendants (535.1–537.1) begins with *Mogh Ruith mac Feargusa a quo Fir Muighe Féne.*[122] The text was most likely taken from The Book of Uí Maine,[123] because both texts are identical, though Dubhaltach corrected orthography[124]and expanded abbreviations. In the beginning of the section (535.1–535.2) there is an introduction about Mog Ruith, which mentions his origins to Fergus, his pupilage under Simon Magus, creation of the *roth ramach* with a prophecy that this tool will bring vengeance over Europe because there was a pupil of every people along with Simon when he was contending against Paul and Peter. This is followed by an account of Mog Ruith's mother–Cacht, and his foster father Roth mac Riogholl (535.2). Passages

---

[118]Ó Muraíle, Nollaig, *Leabhar mór na ngenealach*, 309–508.

[119] Ó Muraíle, *The Celebrated Antiquary*, 108.

[120] Ibid., 109.

[121] Dobbs, Margaret E., "The history of the descendants of Ir [part 1]", *Zeitschrift für celtische Philologie* 13 (1921): 308–359, at 309.

[122] Ó Muraíle, Leabhar mór na ngenealach, 414.

[123] RIA MS D ii 1, The Book of Uí Maine, f.72 verso col. a-b.

[124] Ó Muraíle, *The Celebrated Antiquary*, 103.

535.3–535.6 mention Mog Ruith's seven sons. The passage 537.7 is a short account of Tlachtga and her pregnancy with the sons of Simon. She is also mentioned as the one who broke *roth ramach*. Sections 535.8–536.13 are genealogical records on the kins, descendants of Mog Ruith, who are linked to him through his sons. Section 536.1, entitled *D'fhoisgeluibh Mogha Ruith* (Of the minor tales of Mog Ruith)[125]repeats the earliest surviving text on Mog Ruith from the Great Book of Lecan–*De fabulis Moga Ruith*–which describes Mog Ruith's studentship under Simon Magus and his adventures in the East before he came back home to the Isle of Daibre. He mentions Mog Ruith's participation in the conflict with the Apostles, and the loss of his two eyes: the first one he lost when he stopped the sun at An Bhuan, the second in the Alps during a siege.

Another section on Mog Ruith in LGen is *Genealach Síl Mogha Ruith mc Feargusa*. The same text is preserved in the Book of Uí Maine and is almost identical to its oldest versions from MSS. Laud 610 (De genealogia Dál Moga Ruith)[126]and Rawl. B.502. (Genelach Síl Moga Ruith).[127]

John the Baptist's execution is not mentioned, although it is also omitted in the original texts from The Book of Uí Maine, which Dubhaltach used while working on LGen. However, the latter manuscript contains two poems on the execution. The first poem, which was mentioned above, begins with *Absdolon adba na righ* and describes the beheading of John the Baptist by Mog Ruith for the saint's raiment.[128] The great mortality of the Irish as the punishment for the evil sin is also mentioned–*"nár fhagbat Gaídil na nglec biad is étach i n-aenfhecht"* ("may the contentious Irish never receive food and clothes together").[129] The second poem begins *"Clanna Israel uili scailseat fon mbith mbharrbuidi . . . ".*[130] The author's name is given in the last stanza "Flann

---

[125] Ó Muraíle, *Leabhar mór na ngenealach*, 418–419.

[126] Ed. Kuno Meyer, "The Laud genealogies and tribal histories", *Zeitschrift für celtische Philologie* 8 (1912): 291–338, at 334–6.

[127] Ed. Michael Ó Briain, *Corpus Genealogiarum Hiberniae*, (Dublin: Dublin Institute for Advanced Studies, 1962), 285.

[128] RIA MS D ii 1, The Book of Uí Maine, f. 211 verso col. a.

[129] Ó Cuív, "Two items from Irish Apocryphal Tradition", 109.

[130] RIA MS D ii 1, The Book ofUí Maine, f. 123 recto col. b –123 verso col. b.

mac Gossa aird meic Oraith on Gréigh glégaird" (who is identified with Altfrith mac Oss, the king of Northumbria 685–705).[131] The poem also mentioned the execution of John the Baptist by Mog Ruith the Irishman; however, the choice of maidens is mentioned as a payment. As a punishment for this deed, the "feast of John (will come) upon Gaels, so that there shall not be of the race of noble Gaels save one-third unslain".[132] This sinister part of Mog Ruith's biography is skipped by Dubhaltach. Although it could be explained by the absence of this story from the genealogical tract on *Síl Ír*, which was used for the section on Mog Ruith.

Another manuscript, including the rare texts about Mog Ruith's adventures on the East and his killing of John the Baptist, which had been in possession of the Dubhaltach, is the Yellow Book of Lecan, created and preserved by his family.[133] It contains the the *Imthechta Mogha Ruith* (Adventures of Mog Ruith) and an account on the beheading of John the Baptist by the druid;[134] with a request to pray for the scribe MacFhirbhis (Giolla Íosa Mór Mac Fhirbhisigh).[135] However, these texts have not been used as a source for the section on Mog Ruith's descendants in LGen.

Dubhaltach also could have been familiar with the context of The Book of Lecan. However, as it was noted, the book was out of the country with the rest of Ussher's collection by approximately 1657, whilst the principal portion of LGen was written in 1649–1650. Therefore, it is doubtful that Dubhaltach was able to consult it. However, LGen has references to the manuscript. For example, dealing with the genealogies of certain Viking leaders, the scholar states that they could be found in Lebhar Mór Leacáin Mec Fhirbhisigh.[136] Other parts of the book also related to the genealogical material from The Book of Lecan.[137] This suggests that he must have had another manuscript with a similar material

---

[131] Scarre, "The Beheading of John the Baptist", 173.

[132] Ibid., 181.

[133] Ó Muraíle, *The Celebrated Antiquary*, 16.

[134] Gwynn, *Catalogue of the Irish manuscripts in the Trinity college*, (Dublin: Dublin Institute for Advanced Studies, 1921), 106.

[135] Tomás Ó Concheanainn, "A personal reference by Giolla Íosa Mór Mac Fhirbhisigh", *Celtica* 18 (1986): 34.

[136] Ó Muraíle, *The Celebrated Antiquary*, 179.

[137] For example, sections on the Uí Bhriúin and Uí Fhiachrach. See Ó Muraíle, *The Celebrated Antiquary*, 194.

whilst working on his Book of Genealogies, possibly from the clann Fhir Bhisigh collection at Lackan.[138] However, the exact manuscript he was working with is unidentified, so it is difficult to judge with which texts about Mog Ruith from The Book of Lecan he was acknowledged.

The evidence above demonstrates that the Dubhaltach Mac Fhirbhisigh was familiar with the legend of Mog Ruith's beheading John the Baptist, or at least he had copies of the legend in his possession. This legend, however, stays beyond his genealogical tract, probably because it was not a part of the texts from The Book of Uí Maine, which he had been used for his section on *Síl Ír*. However, in his LGen he mentions all of Mog Ruith's other adventures in the East which are preserved in the Book of Uí Maine, among them the druid's participation in the conflict with Apostles and the creation of the tool of Apocalypse–*roth ramach*–together with Simon Magus. Therefore, it seems that the story of the execution was beyond the concept of LGen, and its sources, and consequently omitted. Probably because of the same reason, there is no reference to Mog Ruith's participation at Druim Damhghaire in Dubhaltach's work.

Conclusion

The evidence given above shows that the biography of Mog Ruith was well known in seventeenth-century Ireland. Scholars and bards have been familiar with different aspects of the druid's biography–with his participation in the Siege of Knocklong, his adventures in the East with Simon Magus, and his execution of John the Baptist. However, if Mog Ruith's studying under Simon and his participation in the conflict between his teacher and the Apostles are rarely mentioned, the story of the execution is completely omitted, and the scholars concentrate mainly on the local deeds of Mog Ruith–his participation in the Siege of Knocklong and receiving the territory of Fir Maige Féne. There is no direct evidence explaining why the "eastern" period of Mog Ruith's biography had been suppressed. One possible reason may lie in the confrontation between Catholics and Protestants in the seventeenth-century Ireland. During this period Catholic scholars had to be especially careful about their words, especially when they, as Keating, were writing the history of the Catholic

---

[138] Ibid.

nation. The description of Mog Ruith's wizardry, probably due to the same reason, was also generally condemned in the seventeenth century. Only Dáibhí Ó Bruadair mentions Mog Ruith's magic in a positive way. Geoffrey Keating and Tadhg Mac Daire, working in the south of Ireland try to distance Mog Ruith from the Eberian king Fiacha Muillethan, while the northern poet Lughaidh Ó Cléirigh denies the fact of Mog Ruith's wizardry and refers to the druid as a nobleman from the North of Ireland.

Another reason for omitting the story of the execution could be that it simply lost its significance by the seventeenth century and was not anymore considered trustworthy, just like the description of Mog Ruith's wizardry, which is called a falsehood by Lughaidh Ó Cléirigh. During the panic of the eleventh century, one can see references to the story of the execution.[139] However, in the seventeenth century, while many poets saw the misfortunes of Irish as the *Fearg Dé* (God's anger), there were no references to Mog Ruith's sins, to Simon Magus or the execution of John the Baptist. Instead of this, Irish pride was viewed as the main reason for the upheavals of the time.[140]

In the context of the Reformation and anglicization of Ireland, poets and scholars paid much attention to genealogies and origin stories, that have been used to create the "New History of Ireland", which united Catholic Gaels and Gaelicised Anglo-Normans under the new identity of *Éireannaigh*. The stories of Mog Ruith were recalled for the same purpose. The genealogies of the druid and his descendants, as well as the story of his participation in the conflict between the king of Leth Cuinn–Cormac mac Art, and the king of Leth Moga–Fiacha Muillethan, were considered as essential part of the local history, and therefore were taken into account by scholars and poets of the seventeenth century, and not only for the benefit of Gaelic aristocracy. Thus, Dáibhi Ó Bruadair places Mog Ruith in the poem, celebrating the marriage between the offspring of Irish family Hurley, and Anglo-Norman Roche. Ó Bruadair opposed both these families to Cromwellians.

---

[139] Although it should be borne in mind that the Annals of Four Masters, which provide these references, were compiled in the seventeenth century by Mícheál Ó Cléirigh (et al), and therefore these references should be treated with caution.

[140] Mícheál Mac Craith, "Literature in Irish", 220.

In these historical circumstances, the story of the beheading John the Baptist by Mog Ruith, which according to the *fabula* led to great mortality among the Irish seems to lose its value for the learned class, whose main creed was to match Catholic Éireannaigh against Protestant English. They had to meet real enemies and witness fateful political and economic changes that affected their country. Mathghamain Ó hIfearnáin, who was one of the bards of the Contention, uses the fable of a cat and a fox to describe the dispute between Eremonians and Eberians: "bickering over a fat piece of meat (Ireland) until a wolf comes and snatches it all".[141] This demonstrates that the poets of the seventeenth century saw the reason for their misfortunes in the disunion of Irish, rather than in the deeds of the mythical druid from the past. Therefore, the legend about the beheading of John the Baptist, even though it could have been available to these scholars through the manuscripts mentioned above, was probably outside of their interest.

Bibliography:

The Book of Ballymote, ed. Robert Atkinson. Facsimiles of Irish Manuscripts 4. Dublin: Royal Irish Academy, 1887.

The Book of Lecan, with descriptive introduction and indexes by Kathleen Mulchrone. Facsimiles in collotype of Irish Manuscripts II. Dublin, Irish Manuscripts Commission, 1937.

The Book of Lismore (Mac Carthaigh Riabhach), with introduction and indexes by R.A.S. Macalister. Facsimiles in collotype of Irish Manuscripts V. Dublin: Stationery Office, 1950.

The Book of Uí Maine, with introduction and indexes by R.A.S. Macalister. Facsimiles in collotype of Irish Manuscripts IV, Dublin: Stationery Office of Éire for the Irish Manuscripts Commission, 1942.

The Yellow Book of Lecan, ed. Robert Atkinson. Facsimiles of Irish Manuscripts 5. Dublin: Royal Irish Academy, 1896.

---

[141] McKenna, *Iomarbhágh na bhfileadh*, Vol. 1, 114–5.

Lands that time forgot: the early Cistercian settlement of Monasternenagh, Co. Limerick

Catherine Swift

Approaching Clairvaux, the great European Cistercian house of the earlier twelfth century, modern pilgrims can easily find themselves lost and wandering in a vast tract of commercial forestry. Within the extensive area of the original medieval *vallum* wall, there lies today a high security prison, founded in the days of Napoleon in the requisitioned buildings of the eighteenth-century monastery. Immediately outside its gates is a small hostel, run by sisters of the *Fraternité St. Bernard* who offer accommodation to relatives of the prisoners and to people following the ancient *Via Francigena*, a trans-European route from Canterbury to Rome. Irish visitors are greeted with particular delight and the sisters make a point of bringing them to a small well, located in a nearby water meadow, which is marked by a wooden post bearing an inscription: "*Source St Malachie.*"

For those who approach twelfth-century Cistercian history as an international phenomenon, Malachy (otherwise Mael-Madhóg Ua Morgair) is the subject of the only biography produced by the indefatigable St. Bernard–a man whose career provided Bernard with a paradigmatic model for those who, inspired by a "longing for the silence and austerity of the desert,"[1] yet found themselves becoming Cistercian bishops and important public leaders in twelfth-century society. For Irish historians, Malachy has traditionally been seen as the quintessential reformer, a man who struggled against the laicising tendencies of the Clann Sínaig dynasty of Armagh to establish international best practice, both monastic and diocesan, throughout Ireland. Much of the evidence for his efforts is drawn from Bernard's text with the result that the establishment of the Cistercian order within Ireland has often been described in heroic terms. Dedication and devotion in the face of barbarity

---

[1] Jeremiah F. O'Sullivan, trans., *Cistercians and Cluniacs: the case for Cîteaux.* Cistercian Fathers Series 33. (Kalamazoo: Cistercian Publications, 1977), 3; Hugh Jackson Lawlor, ed., *Saint Bernard of Clairvaux's life of Saint Malachy of Armagh* (London: Society for Promoting Christian Knowledge, 1920).

have been seen as the hallmarks of the processes involved and its rapid spread within the country has been a source of some pride. To quote Daphne Pochin-Mould:

> Ireland was in the most awful of spiritual morasses, according to Bernard, sunk in a rich variety of sins, both against God and against Church legislation. [2]

Once Malachy had introduced Continental teaching, however, as John Watt put it: "Mellifont prospered and Cistercianism took solid root in Ireland."[3]

Despite subsequent, more specialised, work on the history of the order within Ireland,[4] it is only with the recent publication of Marie-Therese Flanagan's *Transformation of the Irish church in the twelfth century*, that professional historians have begun to examine the wider context for the Cistercian establishments in more detail. Constance Hoffman Berman has pointed out that the single foundation date in the order's filiation tables often required a sequence of multiple events to be condensed and has referred to what she terms the "myth of apostolic gestation"—the image of the abbot and community of twelve who establish a new monastery in an uncultivated wilderness. Hoffman Berman has drawn attention instead to a significant number of instances where incorporation of pre-existing communities and their properties into

---

[2] Daphne Pochin-Mould, *The monasteries of Ireland* (London: B.T. Batsford Ltd., 1976), 50–51.

[3] John Watt, *The church in medieval Ireland* (Dublin: Gill & Macmillan, 1972), 21.

[4] John Watt, *The church and the two nations in medieval Ireland* (Cambridge: University Press, 1970); Barry W. O'Dwyer, trans., *Stephen of Lexington: letters from Ireland 1228–1229* Cistercian Fathers 28. (Kalamazoo: Cistercian Publications, 1982); Roger Stalley, *The Cistercian monasteries of Ireland* (New Haven: Yale University Press, 1987); Colmcille Ó Conbhuidhe, *The story of Mellifont* (Dublin: M.H. Gill and Son Ltd, 1958); Ó Conbhuidhe, *The Cistercian abbeys of Tipperary* ed. Finbarr Donovan (Dublin: Four Courts Press, 1999); Geraldine Carville, *The impact of the Cistercians on the landscape of Ireland* (Ashford: KB Publications 2002); Ann Lynch, *Tintern abbey, Co. Wexford: Cistercians and Colcloughs, Excavations 1982–2007* (Dublin: Wordwell Ltd., 2010); Breda Lynch, *A monastic landscape: the Cistercians in medieval Ireland* (Xlibris Corporation, 2010); Matthew and Geraldine Stout, *The Bective Abbey Project Co. Meath: archaeological excavations 2009–2012* (Dublin: Wordwell Ltd., 2016).

the Cistercian family occurred. In her book, Flanagan outlines Hoffman Berman's perspective and, applying it to the Irish evidence, points out the discrepancies between the foundation dates for Cistercian houses such as Killenny and Monasterevin in contemporary Irish charters and the official dates as conveyed in the filiation tables. She has also highlighted the fact that the place-names in such Irish charters often include settlement words such as *dún, ráith* and *baile*, indicating a strong probability that these lands were already occupied by pre-existing tenants.[5]

With these observations in mind, this paper examines evidence for the early Cistercian foundation of Monasternenagh, Co. Limerick, the possible motivations of those who endowed it, the nature of the lands which were given to it and the type of agricultural exploitation which may have taken place there in the later twelfth and early thirteenth century. The historiography of the Cistercian order in Ireland has focussed on the novelties introduced to Ireland from its Continental homeland and on sources written in Latin; in this paper, in contrast, stress is laid on pre-existing Irish systems of monastic organisation and settlement which shaped the reception and evolution of the new foundations within the local environment. Irish language sources are examined in some detail to elucidate this native perspective and the economic as well as the religious advantages for the patrons of the new order are considered.

Ireland in the twelfth century was ruled by *ard-ríg co fresabra*, (high-kings with opposition). These kings had emerged from the coastal fringes of the traditional polities of the pre-Viking age. Instead of a country divided into the two, relatively cohesive, halves of *Leth Cuinn* and *Leth Moga*, each ruled by multiple competing dynasties genealogically linked into the collectives known as the Uí Néill and the Eoganacht and with strong symbolic assembly points at Tara and Cashel respectively, there were now five strong kingdoms whose rulers vied for dominance of the entire island. In each case, the kingdom contained an important settlement which enjoyed royal patronage and which appears to have functioned as

---

[5] Marie-Therese Flanagan, *The transformation of the Irish church in the twelfth century.* Studies in Celtic History 29 (Woodbridge: Boydell, 2010), 123–134, quoting Constance Hoffman Berman, *The Cistercian Evolution: the invention of a religious order in twelfth-century Europe* (Philadelphia: University of Pennsylvannia Press, 1999), 95, 103–4; Colmán Etchingham, "The 'reform' of the Irish church in the eleventh and twelfth centuries," *Studia Hibernica* 37 (2011), 215–37, 233.

the regional *caput*: Derry in the case of the Meic Lochlainn of Ailech, Tuam in the case of Uí Chonchobair of Connacht, Ferns for the Mac Murchadha of Leinster, Cork under the Meic Carthaig of Desmond and Limerick in the case of the Uí Briain and Thomond. Of these urban or quasi-urban conclaves, Cork and Limerick had both been founded by Scandinavians and still retained important Ostmen communities despite the royal Irish presence. Largely independent of these five polities were the Hiberno-Norse city-states of Dublin and Waterford, each of which retained the potential to be ruled, at least sporadically, by Scandinavian leadership from abroad. Somewhat lower in political importance were the northern midland kingdoms of Breifne (stretching from Leitrim to Kells) and Airgialla (from Armagh to the river Boyne) as well as the southern kingdom of Osraige, uncomfortably sandwiched between the bigger power-blocks of Munster and Leinster. These three latter kingdoms, while not numbered among the leading powers, were still sufficiently important for their rulers to act as kingmakers on occasion.

At the beginning of the twelfth century, the Uí Briain kings of Thomond, who were then enjoying the position of greatest political power, presided over the creation of an all-island diocesan system at the synod of Rathbreasail in AD 1111. At this synod, Limerick was explicitly incorporated into the national structure with Bishop Gille's cathedral of St. Mary being linked to a diocese on the south bank of the Shannon, a unit which was also the most carefully defined of all the Irish dioceses. This is according to our only record of the Rathbreasail decisions, which was subsequently incorporated by the seventeenth-century Geoffrey Keating into his history of Ireland, *Foras Feasa ar Érinn*, which he completed *c.* AD 1634. Earlier sources, including contemporary annals, indicate the contemporary existence of other Ostman bishoprics with Dublin's first bishop dying in 1074 and with a request by Muirchertach Ua Briain and his brother Diarmait to the Archbishop of Canterbury to consecrate their chosen candidate as bishop for Waterford by *c.* AD 1096. [6] Keating's seventeenth-century account links Port Láirge or Waterford to a large

---

[6] Aubrey Gwynn, ed., *The writings of Bishop Patrick 1074–1084*. Scriptores Latini Hiberniae 1 (Dublin: Dublin Institute for Advanced Studies, 1955), 1–2; Walter Fröhlich, ed., *The letters of Saint Anselm of Canterbury Volume 2* (Kalamazoo: Cistercian Publications 97, 1993), 137–8. Ostman bishoprics refer to those affiliated with Canterbury.

south coast diocese which was also given an alternative centre at Lismore but oddly, the Ostman bishopric of Dublin is not mentioned by Keating at all. John Watt has pointed out that Dublin was incorporated into the region ascribed to the diocese of Glendalough, suggesting an early amalgamation along the lines of the later Norman creation but even if this existed, it was not a long term reality given that both Dublin and Waterford were given their own dioceses, strictly limited in area to their immediate hinterlands, in the synod of Kells in 1152.[7] The difficulties of interpretation posed by combining sources of very different periods is unfortunately typical of much twelfth-century Irish church history and makes the task of constructing a coherent narrative of events invariably a matter involving some degree of speculation.

The foundation records for the Cistercian foundation of Monasternenagh provide a classic illustration of such problems. Our most detailed accounts of early Irish Cistercian foundations are found in Sir James Ware's notices entitled *Coenobia Cisterciensia Hiberniae*, originally compiled in 1626 and rewritten in 1658. In his later account, *Nenay al. De Magio* or modern Monasternenagh is identified as *Monasterium Beatae Mariae* and is said to have been founded "*ab O'Briano ut putatur.*" Harris' eighteenth-century expansion of Ware's works add further details from an unknown source and was summarised by Thomas Westropp in 1889 as follows:

> King O'Brien vowed it to the Virgin in a desperate battle with the Danes, near Rathmore, where a massive tower and rath still stand east of the Abbey. The monastery was built beside a fair-green (Aenagh beg) between 1148 and 1151, by Turlough O'Brien, King of Limerick, on a plain near the river Cammogue, and dedicated by the name De Magio, probably meaning "the plain" (Magh), and not the river Maigue, a couple of miles distant.[8]

---

[7] John Mac Erlean, "Synod of Raith Breasail: Boundaries of the Dioceses of Ireland [AD 1110 or 1118]," *Archivium Hibernicum* 3 (1914), 1–33; Watt, *The church and the two nations*, 16–18, 28–31.

[8] Sir James Ware, *Coenobia Cisterciensia Hiberniae*, ed. John T. Gilbert, *Chartularies of St. Mary's Abbey*, Dublin vol. 2 (London: Rolls Series 1884), 218–237, 235; Walter Harris*, The whole works of Sir James Ware concerning Ireland,*

MONASTERNENAGH

This account has never been interrogated and is, in essence, what is provided in more modern surveys by Aubrey Gwynn and R.A. Hadcock, Lord Killanin and Michael Duignan, Roger Stalley and Richard Gem.[9] The identification of the founder as Toirdelbach Ua Briain seems inherently likely; he was the highest ranking member of the dynasty between 1142 and his death in 1167 and his successors were the foundation's most important patrons up to the mid thirteenth century.[10] It appears to have generally escaped remark, however, that there were no Viking armies operating as late as the twelfth century in Limerick and that the Irish annals provide no obvious contender for such a force.

The commonly accepted foundation date of 1148 for Monasternenagh derives ultimately from Bernard's life of Malachy which is thought to have been completed by the early months of 1149. By that time, Mellifont had produced five daughter houses. Bernard does not name these although he does mention elsewhere in his text the house of Suir (or Inislounaght). Precise dates for the Irish foundations are given in the official filiation tables of the Cistercian order tabulated by Father Leopold Janauschek in *Originum Cisterciensium* and published in Vienna in 1877. There, five Irish foundations are all given the date of 1148—the date of Malachy's death and a few months before Bernard completed his biography. These are: Bective, Boyle, Baltinglass, Monasternenagh, otherwise known as Magium, and Suir.

---

revised and improved in three volumes, vol. 2 (Dublin: S. Powell 1745), 275; Thomas Johnson Westropp, "History of the Abbey and Battles of Monasteranenagh, Croom, County Limerick 1148–1603," *Journal of the Royal Historical and Archaeological Association of Ireland* 9 (1889), 232–8, 232.

[9] Aubrey Gwynn and R. Neville Hadcock, *Medieval religious houses: Ireland with an appendix to early sites* (Harlow: Longmans 1988), 141; Lord Killanin and Michael V. Duignan, *Shell Guide to Ireland* (London: Ebury Press, 1962), 183; Stalley, *Cistercian monasteries*, 248–9; Richard Gem, "The Irish cathedral in the twelfth century: the dioceses of Limerick and Killaloe," in *Limerick and south-west Ireland: medieval art and architecture* ed. Sarah Brown, British Archaeological Association Conference Transactions 34. (Leeds: 2011), 63–88, 71

[10] Marie Therese Flanagan, *Irish royal charters: texts and contexts* (Oxford: University Press 2005), 232–3; 246–7, 341, 359; Catherine Swift, "The Uí Briain, the de Burgos and the Hiberno-Norman settlement of Limerick," *North Munster Antiquarian Society* 57 (2017), 1–18, 12–15.

In 1959, Gearóid Mac Niocaill produced a table of the foundation dates for these houses as listed in eleven manuscripts. Under the name Magium, Mac Niocaill's list gives foundation dates for Monasternenagh from eight manuscripts, ranging in date from the thirteenth to the seventeenth centuries, under the year 1148. A fifteenth-century Munich manuscript gives an earlier date of 1147 while the local records of the Cistercian abbey of St. Mary's in Dublin, ascribed by Aubrey Gwynn to the period 1230–40, has a rather later date of 1151.[11] The information provided by Bernard is thus the only contemporary evidence for the early foundation of Monasternenagh while the Cistercian records from Dublin, which opt for 1151, represent one of the earliest alternative sources available to us. A difference of three years is not, of course, a major one but the discrepancy does alert one to the idea that the decision-making processes surrounding foundations may have been rather more drawn out than in Bernard's idealised depiction.

If Viking armies are conspicuously absent from twelfth-century Irish annals, Scandinavian communities resident in Ireland can be readily identified in such records at Waterford (*Gall Puirt Láirge*), at Dublin (*Gall Átha Cliath*), at Cork (*Gaill Corcaighi*), at Wexford (*Gaill Locha Garman*) and at Limerick (*Gall Luimnigh*).[12] Fleets belonging to these communities are also attested—a Limerick fleet was on the Shannon in

---

[11] Gearóid Mac Niocaill, *Na Manaigh Liatha in Éirinn 1142– c. 1600* (Dublin: Cló Morainn, 1959), 4–5, (Table 1); Aubrey Gwynn, "Some unpublished texts from the Black Book of Christchurch, Dublin," *Analecta Hibernica* 16 (1946), 283–337, 318–9.

[12] W.M. Hennessey, ed. and trans., *The Annals of Loch Cé*. 2 vols Rolls series 54. (London: 1871). 1134: Séamus Ó hInnse ed. and trans., *Miscellaneous Irish Annals (AD 1114–1437)* (Dublin: Dublin Institute for Advanced Studies, 1947), 1134, 1136, 1139; W.M. Hennessey, ed. and trans., *Chronicon Scottorum*. Rolls Series 46. (London: 1866), 1130, 1134, 1148; Sean Mac Airt ed. and trans., *The Annals of Inisfallen M.S. Rawlinson B 503* (Dublin: Dublin Institute for Advanced Studies 1944), 1117, 1118, Whitley Stokes, ed. and trans., *The Annals of Tigernach*. 2 vols (Felinfach: Llanerch Press, 1993) 1130, 1145.

1130 and again in 1145 while Dublin fleets were hired by forces outside Ireland in 1051, 1055, 1088 and 1166.[13] In a Munster context, a literary account of a tenth-century king of Cashel, *Caithréim Chellacháin Chaisil* (thought to have been written in the 1130s–1140s),[14] which appears only loosely based on historical realities, refers to the *Danair 7 Duibhgeinnti in bhaili Corcaigh*[15], to a battle at Cashel against *Danair* where the Irish victors proceeded to consume the *flegha 7 fureca* (drinking feasts and provisions) *na n-Danar 7 na n-Dubloclannach* and to *Danair* and *Lochlannaigh* at Waterford—the latter apparently recent arrivals by ship.[16] In this tale, Limerick is solely associated with *Lochlannaigh* but a battle waged within the walled town is seen as the first step in a campaign against *Danair*.[17] The tenth or indeed twelfth-century validity of such references have to be evaluated within the context of an introduction to the text stressing the ubiquity of Scandinavians throughout Munster:

> *Ba hiatso cisa 7 cana na n-Gall ngrandha o mhiledaibh Muman .i. ri ar gach tricha 7 taisech ar gach tuaith, ab ar gach cill, maer ar gach mbaili, suaitreach gacha tighe. Gan coibeis ein-chirce ag duine da biadh fein na da digh gan brat gan blaithedach um righ na um romnai acht athbrait 7 aitheduigthi na nDanar 7 na ndaerLochlannach.*

These were the tributes and taxes of the abominable Foreigners [owed] from the soldiers of Munster, namely a king over every cantred and a chieftain over every people, an abbot over every church, a bailiff over every village and a billeted soldier in every house. Without so much as a clutch of eggs of one hen for a person's own food or

---

[13] Tig.,1130, 1145, Marie Therese Flanagan, *Irish society, Anglo-Norman settlers, Angevin kingship – interactions in Ireland in the late twelfth century* (Oxford: Clarendon Press, 1989), 57, 61, 66–7, 76, 144.

[14] Donnchadh Ó Corráin, "Caithréim Chellacháin Chaisil: history or propaganda," *Ériu* 25 (1974), 1–69, 9.

[15] Alexander Bugge, ed. and trans., *Caithréim Cellacháin Caisil: the victorious career of Cellachan of Cashel* (Christiania: J. Chr. Gundersens Bogtrykkeri, 1905), 10 (§20)

[16] *Caithr.CC* 13 (§22)

[17] *Caithr.CC*, 4–10 (§8–§19); (§9)

drink. Without a cloak or a good dress on king or noble
lady, but only the cast-off cloaks and clothes of the Danes
and the ignoble Lochlannachs.[18]

Danair and *Lochlannaigh* are also terms which are found in the
eleventh-century compilation known as the *Fragmentary Annals of
Ireland* where they are used of military forces in the later ninth and the
earlier tenth centuries.[19] The exact meaning of these terms is difficult to
establish.[20] It may be that rather than referring to Danes and Norwegians,
as in modern Irish, they should be understood as distinguishing between
Scandinavians who may have originally settled in England (ruled by the
Danish king Knútr until his death in 1035) before moving further west and
others who sailed directly to Ireland from Norway and the North Atlantic
colonies. The Icelandic chronicle *Morkinskinna*, for example, refers to the
defeat and occupation of Dublin by the Norwegian king Magnús Berfœttr
and its subsequent rule by his *gœzlumenn*, for close to a year in 1103/4
while he himself was resident in the west of Ireland.[21] No reference is

---

[18] *Caithr.CC,* 1–2, 58, §3. The relationship between this and a similar passage in §XL
in *Cogadh Gaedhel re Gallaibh* is clear as Ó Corráin has noted; Ó Corráin,
"*Caithréim*", 6.

[19] Joan Newlon Radner, ed. and trans., *Fragmentary annals of Ireland* (Dublin:
Dublin Institute for Advanced Studies, 1978): sub annis 851, 849/50, 852, 853, 858,
856, 859, 860, 862, 863, 864, 866, 867, 869, 870, 871, 873, 907, 913, 914.

[20] Alfred P. Smyth, "The Black Foreigners of York and the White Foreigners of
Dublin," *Saga-Book* 19 (1974–7), 101–117; Máire Ní Mhaonaigh, "The Vikings in
Medieval Irish Literature" in *The Vikings in Ireland* ed. Anne-Christine Larsen,
(Roskilde: Viking Ship Museum, 2001), 96–103 at 103–105; David N. Dumville,
"Old Dubliners and New Dubliners in Ireland and Britain: A Viking-Age story,"
Medieval Dublin 6 (2004), 78–93; Clare Downham, "Hiberno-Norwegians and
Anglo-Danes: anachronistic ethnicities and Viking-Age England," *Medieval
Scandinavia* 19 (2009), 139–69; Colmán Etchingham, "*Laithlinn,* 'Fair Foreigners'
and 'Dark Foreigners' : the identity and provenance of Vikings in ninth-century
Ireland" in *The Viking Age: Ireland and the West: Proceedings of the Fifteenth Viking
Congress* eds John Sheehan and Donnchadh Ó Corráin (Dublin: Four Courts Press,
2010), 80–88 at 81.

[21] Finnur Jónsson, *Morkinsinna* (Copenhagen: J.Jøregensen & Co., 1932), 333;
Theodore M. Andersson and Kari Ellen Gade, trans., *Morkinskinna: the earliest
Icelandic chronicle of the Norwegian kings (1090–1157)* (Ithaca: Cornell University
Press, 2000), 310 where *gœzlumenn* is translated as 'officers and administrators.'

made to this episode in the Irish annals, a fact which highlights the partial and subjective nature of these, our most important historical sources for medieval Ireland.

When trying to identify potential contenders for Harris's battle leading to the foundation of Monasternenagh, it is worth noting that, in *Caithréim Chellacháin Chaisil*, a battle was fought in the vicinity of Croom, immediately to the west of Monasternenagh. This encounter, however, is described as being between local Limerick groups (the Uí Chonaill and the Uí Cairbre) who were pitted against the Cashel king Cellachán, assisted by five hundred men of the Uí Chaím, kings of Eoganacht Glendamnach in north Cork. No reference is made to the participation of Scandinavians.[22] Of course, the *Caithréim* is a literary work, classified by Donnchadh Ó Corráin in 1974 as a "historical romance" and the Viking tyranny over Munster which it describes has been dismissed by Ó Corráin as "sheer fantasy and invention." He identifies the author as a secular man of learning, working in the Meic Carthaig interest in the earlier twelfth century and as a man who had access to many local genealogies, king-lists and perhaps some saga material. These genealogies had, however, been syncopated so that while they provide us with considerable detail on local kings such as the Uí Chaim or the Uí Cairbre, Ó Corráin describes them as quite untrustworthy. We know from the manuscript evidence that *Caithréim* was popular with later medieval and early modern Munster scribes and was often associated with heavily interpolated annals continuing in date to AD 1138.[23] It may be, therefore, that the traditions about a battle between the Uí Briain and the Danes reported by Harris are ultimately based on some, perhaps much later, interpolation of the *Cáithréim* or its associated annals. Meidbhín Ní Úrdail's work on *Cath Cluana Tarbh*, which often occurs in association with the *Caithréim* in surviving manuscripts, provides important evidence for the substantial reworking of earlier material in this way. In the absence of detailed perusal of the manuscript evidence for the *Caithréim,* however, this can only be speculation.

---

[22] *Caithr.CC*, 15, §25; Ó Corráin, "*Caithréim*," 16–18.

[23] Meidhbhín Ní Úrdail, *The scribe in eighteenth and nineteenth-century Ireland: motivations and milieu*, Studien und Texte zur Keltologie III (Münster: Nodus Publikationen, 2000), 190; *Cath Cluana Tarbh: the Battle of Clontarf* Irish Texts Society 64 (Dublin: 2011), 37, 226–230.

Historically, the *Annals of Tigernach* tell of a battle won by Toirdelbach Ua Chonchobair of Connacht in 1132 in which *"cor' airg ocus cor' mill Cromadh"* (he plundered and consumed Croom) immediately to the west of Monasternenagh. There is no reference to his enemies on that occasion and thus it is unknown whether either the Uí Briain leadership or Scandinavians were involved.

Another possibility is that the reference to Toirdelbach's battle with Danes is, in fact, to a battle between the Uí Briain king of Thomond and the cities of Cork or Waterford. The likelihood of this suggestion is enhanced by the fact that such a battle is described in considerable detail in *Mac Carthaigh's Book*[24] under the year 1151:

> *Do fassaigheadh o Luimneac co Corcaigh & o Port Lairge co Cnoc Brenaind don cogadh-sin. Do leanattur Sil m-Briain Diarmaid Mac Carrthaigh tri Musgraidhe bu dheas go Ceann Eith do argain. Do cuir Diarmaid mac Cormaic & maithi na n-Eoghanacht teachta uatha do iarraidh Toirrdhealbhaigh mic Ruaidhri, ri Condacht, & Diarmada Mic Murchadha, ri Laighean, a n-aighidh t-Sil m-Briain.*

> *An oidhche tangattur Connachtaigh & Laignigh co h-Abhainn Moir as i sin oighthe rangattur Sil m-Briain co Corcaigh. Do imighittur arnamaireac tri Moin Moir budh tuaigh ar n-denamh morain uilcc ar muintir Barra, & mac Cormaic & Í Mathgamhna & I Donnchadha & I Caim & I Muirceartaigh go maithibh Eoghanachta ina n-diaigh ac toraigheacht orra lá ciach, et nír airgittur Sil m-Briain Connachtaigh & Laighnigh noco tarla ina measg iad guro muidh ar Sil m-Briain roim na tri sluaighid-sin, dar marbhadh Concubur h-Briain &*

---

[24] *Mac Carthaigh's Book* is a small quarto volume of the late fifteenth century of Munster provenance. It was separated into two by 1846 and is now catalogued as MSS G 5 and 6 in the National Library of Ireland. It forms the first fragment edited and translated by Ó hInnse in his volume *Miscellaneous Irish Annals*; see *Misc. Ir. Ann.* vii; *Irish script on screen* s.v. National Library of Ireland MS G 5, accessed 12th April, 2019, https://www.isos.dias.ie/master.html?https://www.isos.dias.ie/libraries/NLI/english/index.html?ref=https://www.google.com/.

MONASTERNENAGH

Flaithbheartac h-Deaghaidh & Eineislis h-Grada & tri mili don t-sluagh o h-oin amach. Do fag Torrdhealbhach {folio 9a} h-Briain & Diarmaid Sugac h-Concubuir beacan marcac an cath tri an ceo gan airiughadh tar Abhaind Moir budh tuaigh.

From Limerick to Cork and from Waterford to Cnoc Bréanainn was laid waste in this war. Síol Briain pursued Diarmait Mac Carthaigh through Múscraighe southwards to Cenn Eich to plunder it. Diarmait son of Cormac and the nobles of the Eoghanachta sent messengers to ask the support of Toirdhealbhach son of Ruaidhrí, king of Connacht and Diarmaid Mac Murchadha, king of Leinster against Síol Briain.

It was the night the Connachtmen and the Leinstermen came to Ab Mór that Síol Briain came to Cork. They set out the following day through Móin Mhór northwards, having committed many outrages on the community of Barra and Cormac's son, the Uí Mhathghamhna, the Uí Dhonnchadha, the Uí Chaoimh and the Uí Mhuircheartaigh as well as the nobles of the Eóghanacht were in pursuit of them. The day being misty, Síol Briain did not perceive the Connachtmen and the Leinstermen until they found themselves in their midst. Síol Briain were defeated by these three hostings and Conchobar Ó Briain, Flaithbeheartach Ó Deadhaidh, Áineislis Ó Gráda and three thousand of the host were slain. Toirdhealbhach Ó Briain and Diarmaid Súdgach Ó Conchobhair with a few horsemen went from the battle unperceived through the mist, past Abhainn Mór northwards.[25]

The political significance of this battle has been elucidated by John V. Kelleher whose article concentrates on its national implications for the leading kings of mid twelfth-century Ireland.[26] To recount his arguments

---

[25] Misc. Ir. Ann. 1151.

[26] John V. Kelleher, "The battle of Móin Mhór, 1151" *Celtica* 20 (1988), 11–27; Whitley Stoke and Ernst Windisch, eds. *Irische Texte mit Wörterbuch* 4 vols, 3.1

in detail would be to stray too far from the purpose of this paper but two points seem particularly important. Upon escaping the battle, Toirdelbach Ua Briain fled to Limerick where he was compelled to hand over the enormous sum of two thousand ounces of gold and sixty treasures, including the drinking horn of Brian Bóroma, to the Connacht king. This was sufficient to buy him his freedom (although suffering the indignity of eviction from Thomond) but the sheer size of the sum provides a dramatic illustration of the scale of his defeat. That the battle left an impact on Irish literary imagination is indicated by the *Annals of Tigernach* entry describing it which states that, until sands of sea and stars of heaven are numbered, no one will count the numbers of Munster dead and by a verse describing the storm and the rain that poured down on the battlefield.

As Kelleher makes clear, Móin Mór was the culmination of a lengthy series of campaigns taking place across the midlands and southern half of Ireland. The battle began, however, with the sacking of Cork (identified by contemporaries with settlements of *Danair* and/or *Gaill*) and its major church of St. Finbarr by the Uí Briain leadership.[27] Furthermore, while clearly a major defeat for the Uí Briain king, he himself had an almost miraculous escape and *Mac Carthaigh's Book* goes on to state that despite a period of exile to the far northern kingdom of Ailech, Toirdelbach subsequently returned to Móin Mór to defeat the Meic Carthaigh in 1154.[28] We know that others were moved to found Cistercian monasteries out of gratitude; Latin annals explain that the abbey known as *De Voto* in Wexford derived its name from a vow made by William Marshal as a result of a miraculous escape from drowning.[29] Furthermore, the fact that Toirdelbach Ua Briain was indebted to Muirchertach Mac Lochlainn, in the very years leading up to the dedication ceremony of Mellifont by the latter, gives us a political context for Toirdelbach's enthusiasm for Cistercians which is otherwise entirely lacking. It can be nothing more than a suggestion, given the partial records involved but it may be that

---

(Leipzig: S. Hirzel, 1891), 67 Kenneth Hurlstone Jackson, trans., *Studies in Early Celtic Nature Poetry* (Cambridge: Cambridge University Press 1935), 33.

[27] Henry A Jeffries, "The history and topography of Viking Cork", *Journal of the Cork Historical and Archaelogical Society* 90 (1985), 14–25.

[28] Misc. Ir. Ann. 1154.

[29] J.H. Bernard, "The foundation of Tintern Abbey, Co. Wexford." *Proceedings of the Royal Irish Academy* 33C (1916/1917), 527–9.

MONASTERNENAGH

Móin Mór is the best available contender for Harris' eighteenth-century story of Toirdelbach's battle with Danes and its importance in triggering his endowment of Monasternenagh.

The place names *Ab Mór* and *Móin Mór*: 'big river' and 'big bog' are both generic descriptions in Ireland and it is therefore difficult to pin down the exact location of the battle. Donnchadh Ó Corráin has suggested that *Ab Mór* in a Munster context is the river Blackwater and *Móin Mór*, following a suggestion by John O'Donovan, may be Mourneabbey, just south of Mallow or possibly, following an alternative suggestion by O'Donovan, subsequently endorsed by Edmond Hogan, Moanmore in the parish of Emly, Co. Tipperary. The *Cenn Eich* of this entry he locates in the parish of Kinneigh, west of Bandon.[30] Kelleher, in contrast, located Móin Mór on the range of hills known as the Nagle Mountains and their westward extension, the Boggerach Mountains.[31] For what it is worth, however, there is also a Móin Mór within the later lands of Monasternenagh, in the parish of Fedamore, in County Limerick and it remains possible that this was the original battle site and the *ab mór* over which the Thomond king escaped was, in fact, the Shannon.

Even if we discount Harris's battle in its entirety as a much latter fabrication, a military rationale for the foundation of Monasternenagh can be put forward, albeit a defensive one. It is clear from the annals that a good deal of Toirdelbach Ua Briain's career was spent fighting the Meic Carthaigh and Kelleher has explained how this arose from a deliberate policy of the Uí Chonchobair kings of Connacht to weaken Munster by dividing it in two. The original homeland of the Uí Briain, in the days of Brian Bóroma, was around Killaloe in east Clare and by the mid twelfth century, the region under their over-lordship stretched across north Munster from Kerry to Offaly.[32] Monasternenagh, located north of the Galtee mountains, was close to their southern border which was symbolically marked by their claim in *Acallamh na Senórach* that their

---

[30] *Electronic Onomasticon Goedelicum* Entries 69, 21631, 8749 accessed 20th November, 2018, https://www.dias.ie/celt/celt-publications-2/onomasticon-goedelicum/; Edmund Hogan, *Onomasticon Goedelicum locorum et tribuum Hiberniae et Scotiae* (Dublin: Hodges Figgis & Co. Ltd., 1910), s.v. *ab mór*.

[31] Kelleher, "Móin Mhór", 11.

[32] Swift, "De Burgos," 3–4.

ultimate progenitor, Cormac Cass, was buried at Duntryleague, some thirty miles east of the Cistercian site.[33] Central Limerick was, moreover, the home of local kings, the Uí Chairbre, who claimed ancestral connections with Meic Carthaigh progenitors. *Caithréim Chellacháin* situates this group in the area around Croom, immediately to the west of Monasternenagh and it seems plausible that this reflected twelfth-century realities.[34] A twelfth-century Uí Briain king might well wish to weaken the Uí Chairbre by emulating the famous donation of Cashel to the church by Muirchertach Ua Briain of 1101, which had had the effect of removing that site from political importance and domination by hereditary Uí Briain enemies.[35]

The strategic value of such donations lies in the fact that churches were not deemed suitable locations from which to raise soldiers for royal armies. A poem in the twelfth-century *Book of Leinster*, attributed to the ninth-century figure Fothad na Canóne, outlines this ideology explicitly.[36] It begins "*Eclais Dé bí leic di a n-as n-ai. Bid a cert for leth feib as dech ro boí*" (The Church of the living God, leave to her that which is her own. Let her right be set aside as has been best). Even more relevantly, the next two verses read:

> *Cech fírmanach fail*
> *fora cubus glan*

---

[33] Catherine Swift, "Brian Boru's origins and the kingdom of North Munster," *History Ireland* 22.2 (2014), 18–22.

[34] *Caith.CC.* 15, 73 §25; Ó Corráin, "*Caithréim*," 23.

[35] Flanagan, *Irish royal charters*, 241.

[36] Fothad na Canóne is linked to the court of Áed Oirdnide in an entry in the *Annals of the Four Masters* listed under the year 799 in a tale of how the leader of Armagh and Fothad persuaded the king to listen to the demands of clerics to be exempted from military service. The tale finishes with the poem cited above. Its listing here is one of those instances in which ecclesiastical history was actively enhanced by the Four Masters; see Bernadette Cunningham, *The annals of the Four Masters: Irish history, kingship and society in the early seventeenth century* (Dublin: Four Courts, 2010), 242. Of this poem and *Cert cech ríg co réil* below, Gearóid Mac Eoin has remarked that they are "either much revised [from Fothad's original compositions] or were composed at a later date." Gearóid Mac Eoin "Irish literature [2]" in John T. Koch, ed., *Celtic Culture: an historical encyclopedia Vol III* (Santa Barbara: ABC-CLIO, 2006), 997–1003, 1000.

dind eclais dan dír
gnid amal cech mod.

Cech dílmain íar sin
fil cen recht cen réir
cet cia dig ri báig,
Aida nair meic Néil

Every true monk of enclosure,
on his clear conscience,
concerning the church to which it is due,
let him work like any man.

Every unattached man after that,
who is without authority (rule), without obedience,
he is allowed to go to the battle of
noble Aéd son of Níall.[37]

The precise status of a *firmanach fail* (a true monk of enclosure) is not entirely clear for the status of manual labour in the Irish monastic tradition is far from consistent.[38] According to this poem, however (and there are other records with similar implications),[39] an ecclesiastical labour force was not supposed to be available to royalty wishing to drum conscripts into their armed forces. One can see obvious advantages to this, particularly if the churches concerned were located in contested border areas for an encroaching enemy would then have to occupy and control a substantial proportion of his opponent's territory before he could hope to raise local reinforcements. To remove land from those who claimed kinship with their overlord's enemies in order to create such a defensive

---

[37] Richard Irvine Best and M.A. O'Brien, eds., *The Book of Leinster formerly Lebar na Núachongbála* vol. 3 (Dublin: Dublin Institute for Advanced Studies, 1957), 621. Translation based on Whitley Stokes, *Félire Óengusso Celi Dé–The Martyrology of Oengus the Culdee* ed. Whitley Stokes. Henry Bradshaw Society 29. London:1905, 5 with modifications to reflect the Book of Leinster wording.

[38] Catherine Swift, "Religion" in *More maps and texts: sources and the Irish Historic Towns Atlas* eds. Howard Clarke and Sarah Geary (Dublin: Royal Irish Academy 2018), 69–77.

[39] *Chron. Scottorum* 1089; Whitley Stokes, "Cath Cairn Conaill," *Zeitschrift für celtische Philologie* 3 (1901), 203–19, 206–7.

zone would surely have been attractive to a strategically-minded Uí Briain king. In this regard, it is interesting that, working from the standpoint of landscape analysis rather than that of texts, Harold Mytum has suggested that there is clear evidence for the foundation of Clare churches along the northern frontiers of the Uí Briain kingdom.[40]

Another poem, immediately preceding *Eclais Dé bí* in the Book of Leinster, is *Cert cech ríg co réil* (The clear right of every king). This refers, among other issues, to a king's responsibilities to churches and was apparently written within a context of ecclesiastical reformation for one particular verse refers to *athnúgud na cell* or the renewal of churches:

Na cella cen cáin
rit reimes raith réil
co rabais ós chách
7 cách dot réir.

Cádus don aes gráid
a nnárus dod réir.
A comét ar mnáib
a degmeic náir Néil.

Almsa menic maith
don relic dan toich
do Phatraic do Dia
bale I mbia fa cholich.

Aes gráid in cech cill
co saidbir is co soimm
cen díth bruit na bíd,
* eter mír is loimm.*
Athnúgud na cell
tria rathmúnud mind.
Crábud ecna óg
libuir lór rit lind.

---

[40] Harold Clive Mytum, "The location of early churches in northern Co. Clare" in *The early church in Western Britain and Ireland,* ed. Susan M. Pearce, *The early church in Western Britain and Ireland* British Archaeological Reports British series 102. (Oxford:1982), 351–61.

Leave the churches untaxed
during the course of clear success,
so that you be beyond all,
and that all may obey you.

Esteem for the clergy;
control over their dwelling;
their protection against women,
good noble son of Níall.

Give frequent and generous alms
to the church for which it is right,
for Patrick and for God,
the place in which you will be under a stone.

Have men of clerical grade in every church,
with wealth and with riches,
wanting neither clothing nor food,
whether bite or sup.

Let there be a renewal of the churches
by the gracious doctrine of relics,
piety, perfect wisdom,
with abundance of books, during your time.[41]

Katharine Simms has suggested that *Cert cech ríg co réil* shows knowledge of a Continental theory of "theocratic kingship" and links it to the presence of Irish kings at the reforming synods of the twelfth century.[42] The belief that churches should be left untaxed by secular authorities was certainly not limited to Irish poets in this period and a

[41] Best and O'Brien, *Book of Leinster* 3, 614 (ll.18864–7), 615 (ll.18888–91, ll.18896–9), 617 (ll.18963–6), 618 (ll. 18968–18971). Translation is based on T. O'Donoghue, "Cert cech ríg co réil" in *Miscellany presented to Kuno Meyer by some of his friends and pupils on the occasion of his appointment to the chair of Celtic philology in the University of Berlin* eds. Osborn Bergin & Carl Marstrander (Halle: M. Niemeyer, 1912), 258–77, verses 14, 20, 22, 62, 63, modified to represent the Book of Leinster manuscript.

[42] Katharine Simms, *From kings to warlords: the changing political structure of Gaelic Ireland* (Woodbridge: The Boydell Press, 1987), 25–26.

similar belief is also recorded in the charter confirming the lands of Monasternenagh by King John *c.* 1200. This refers to:

> *[O]mnas terras et tenementa quae de dono antecessorum nostrorum vel illorum qui post adventum nostrum in Hybernia illis benefecerunt, tam de dono regum vel principum Hyberniensium quam Francorum illis juste et rationabiliter data fuerunt unde munimentum vel warantum habeant secundum notitia in hoc volumine subscripta sicut in puram et perpetuam elemosinam absque omni seculari servicio secundum libertatem ordinis Cisterciensis.*[43]

> [A]ll the lands and holdings that by grant of our predecessors or of those who made grants to them after our arrival in Ireland; those that have been given to them legally and by due process by grants of Irish kings and princes as well as those of the Franks. For these they should hold confirmations or guarantees, as found on the record inscribed in this roll, as an unconditional and perpetual gift, free from all secular obligation, according to the liberty of the Cistercian order.[44]

This also makes it clear that, by this date, the Monasternenagh estate had been supplemented by further gifts. The holdings are identified by name but as a general description they are summed up as lands:

> . . . *in bosco et plano, in pratis et pascuis, in viis et semitis, in aquis et molendinis, in rivariis et piscariis, in stagnis et joncariis in mariscis et vivariiis, et turbariis et in omnibus aliis lociis et libertatibus et liberis consuetudinis ad predicas possessiones et terras pertinentibus absque omni seculari servicio . . .*

> . . . in wood and field, in meadows and pastures, in roads and footpaths, in waters and in mills, in rivers and in

---

[43] *Rotuli chartarum in turri Londinensi asservati ab anno 1199–1216* ed. T. D. Duffy (Record Commission London, 1837), 78.

[44] My thanks to Dr. Joseph Flahive of the Royal Irish Academy for his assistance with this translation.

fisheries, in ponds and reed-beds, in marshes and preserves and turf-cuttings as well as all the aforesaid possessions and lands belonging to them in all other places and liberties to be held in free custom, exempt from all secular service . . .

John wrote confirmation charters for other Irish Cistercian houses, including Baltinglass,[45] two charters for St. Mary's, Dublin, in 1185[46] as well as others of later date and two charters for Mellifont, one written in 1185/6 and the other in 1203.[47] It is clear from examination of these that the above quotation represents a charter formula which was in widespread use. At the same time, however, there are distinctive elements in each example such as the *joncarii* or reed-beds at Monasternenagh which do not exist in the other charters. (The most well-known use of reeds is for thatching and reed-cutting is still practiced for such purposes in the Shannon region.) In the Baltinglass charter, there is reference to *pasturae* 'grazing' and to *vintaria* 'wine-depots'[48] while in St. Mary's, the phrase immediately after *in bosco et plano* is *in ecclesiis et capellis et decimis* ([holdings] in churches and chapels and tithes) and their assets included both *piscariae et piscaturae* (fisheries and fish-traps).[49] In other words, far from being "a place of horror, a vast wilderness" as Cîteaux had originally been, according to the mid-twelfth-century *Exordium Cistercii*,[50] these Irish Cistercian foundations, by the time of King John,

---

[45] K.W. Nicholls, "The charter of John, Lord of Ireland, in favour of the Cistercian abbey of Baltinglass," *Peritia* 4 (1985), 187–206.

[46] John T Gilbert, *Chartularies of St. Mary's Abbey, Dublin*. 2 vols (Cambridge: Cambridge University Press), 2012, 1: 86–9.

[47] Colmcille Ó Conbhuí, "Seven documents from the Old Abbey of Mellifont," *Journal of the County Louth Archaeological Society*, 13 (1953), 35–67, 36–9, 41.

[48] Nicholls, "Baltinglass," 191. *Vinitarius* is translated as a vintner or the custodian of the wine in a convent while *vintarius* is a vintner or a commander of twenty soldiers: Charles Trice Martin, *The Record Interpreter* (Chichester: Phillimore & Co. Ltd, 1982), 340. The translation of *vintaria* as 'wine-depot' is my own suggestion.

[49] Gilbert, *Chartularies*, 1: 87, 89; *Medieval Latin word-list from British and Irish sources* ed. J.H. Baxter and Charles Johnson (Oxford: Oxford University Press, 1934), 311–2.

[50] Bede K. Lackner, trans., "*Exordium Cistercii*".in Louis J. Lekai, *The Cistercians: ideals and reality* (Kent: Kent State University Press, 1977), 443.

were estates marked by human habitation and agrarian assets. This was in line with the order's established requirements for feeding their communities as found in their *Summa Cartae Caritatis* of 1119:

> Food for the monks of our Order ought to come from manual labour, agriculture and the raising of animals. Hence we may possess, for our own use, streams, woodlands, vineyards, meadows, lands far removed from the dwellings of seculars, and animals.. To raise, feed and take care of animals, we may keep *grangiae*, either in the neighbourhood or at a greater distance. These are to be supervised and managed by the *conversi*.[51]

Grangia as a term is found in the Irish Pipe Roll of John in 1211-1212 where it is used of secular estates in Meath producing grain for Norman garrisons and for export; of fortified settlements in Co. Waterford; of a settlement with kiln and fulling mills in the central midlands and of others with byres and pig-sties in Ulster.[52] It seems probable that the novel word was being used to describe holdings organised under different principles from those of earlier Irish settlements but to what extent they mirrored the Cistercian estates, described by the same word, is unclear. The precise nature of the organisation of early Cistercian holdings has been under debate in recent times,[53] but it has classically been understood as a system in which forced peasant labour was replaced by voluntary labour performed by monks, *conversi* (lay brothers) and hired men. It was thus rather different from the high medieval manor and it seems to have often been considerably larger. Statistical surveys of south German houses have shown that the size of the average manor of a lay lord reached only one quarter or one fifth of a Cistercian grange in the same region.[54] It has also been suggested that the

---

[51] Bede K. Lackner, trans., "*Summa Cartae Caritatis*" in Lekai, *Ideals and reality*, 26, 449 §XV.

[52] Oliver Davies and David B Quinn, "The Irish Pipe Roll of 14 John 1211–1212," *Ulster Journal of Archaeology* 4 (1946, supplement), 35, 49, 53, 55, 57, 59, 65, 67, 71.

[53] Isabel Alfonso, "Cistercians and Feudalism," *Past and Present* 133 (1991), 3–30.

[54] Geraldine Stout, "The Cistercian grange: a medieval farming system" in *Agriculture and settlement in Ireland* eds. Margaret Murphy & Mathew Stout

Cistercian grange was managerially more efficient, especially in the early years, as the order was only feeding and sheltering productive labour as opposed to provisioning entire families. Furthermore, their workforce of celibate adult males could be moved more easily to wherever they were needed.[55]

At Mellifont, the charter of 1203 mentions a *grangia salinarum* (or 'grange of salt-works')[56] identified as a possession before the French arrival in Ireland and a *grangia vero de Bali meic Edugain scilicet quatuor carrucatas terre cum pertininentiis suis in pasturis et wastinis* (a grange belonging to the *baile* of the Meic Edugain, namely four ploughlands of land, grazing and waste). In the earlier Mellifont charter, eight granges were mentioned: Kulibudi, Melle, Drochetatha, Teachlenni, Rosnarrigh, Cnogva, Kelcalma, Finna.[57] The Irish words show that these estates included such man-made features as a bridge, a house and a church but perhaps the most telling are two which we know were linked closely to local royalty before ever the Cistercians came to Ireland. The site of Cnogbha or Knowth, for example, was used as a sobriquet for local kings from the early ninth century to the mid tenth, including references to kings who were killed *i taig Cnogba* 'in a house of Knowth.'[58]

The nearby site of Ros na ríg 'peninsula/wood of kings' was described in *Senchas na Relec*, an account of the pre-Christian cemeteries of Ireland incorporating poetry by the later tenth-century author, Cináed Ua hArtacáin and copied by the eleventh-century scholar Flann

---

(Dublin: Four Courts, 2015), 28–68, 28–32, 65–68; Emilia Jamroziak, *The Cistercian order in medieval Europe 1090–1500* (London: Routledge, 2013), 185–6.

[55] Constance Hoffman Berman, "Medieval agriculture, the southern French countryside and the early Cistercians; a study of 43 monasteries". *Transactions of the American Philosophical Society* (1986), 79–86.

[56] At Baltinglass, there was also a salt-working described as *salina apud Arclo* (Arklow, Co. Wicklow); Nicholls, "Baltinglass," 191.

[57] Ó Conbhuí, "Seven documents," 41.

[58] Francis John Byrne, "Historical note on Cnogba (Knowth)" in "Excavations at Knowth, Co. Meath, 1962–65" by George Eogan, *Proceedings of the Royal Irish Academy* 66C (1967–8), 299–400, 383–400; Catherine Swift, "The early history of Knowth" in *Historical Knowth and its hinterland* by Francis John Byrne, William Jenkins, Gillian Kenny and Catherine Swift. Excavations at Knowth 4 (Dublin: Royal Irish Academy, 2008), 10–36.

Manistrech before being transcribed into Lebor na hUidre.[59] In this text, Ros na Ríg is identified as the burial place of the prehistoric king Cormac mac Airt who was believed to have to have been blessed with a foreknowledge of Christianity when he died at the time of the Crucifixion. As a result, he told his household not to bury him at Brug (na Bóinne) *acht a adnocol i rRos na Ríg 7 a aiged sair* (but his burial in Ros na Ríg and his face eastwards).[60] According to the Middle Irish saga, *Cath Ruis na Ríg*, the vicinity of the cemetery was also the location of an important battle.[61]

Monasternenagh has a somewhat similar history. The site which may have given the site its name, *mainister an aenaigh* 'the monastery of the *oenach*' is listed in John's charter as ENACHCHULI IN CORBALI.[62] *Oenach Culi* was a possession of the Fir Muman in *Senchas na Relec* while more specifically it is identified with *Rigrad Muman I nÓenuch Cúli* (the Munstermen of royal status at Oenach Culi) and was marked by fifty burial mounds in the associated text *Aided Nath Í ocus á adnacol insó* (copied by Flann Mainistrech from manuscripts kept in Armagh along with *Senchas na Relec*). Here again, therefore, the *oenach* is given an important prehistoric royal ancestry.[63]

Patrick Gleeson has argued that Oenach Culi was located within a conglomeration of archaeological monuments around Knocklong in Co. Limerick, fifteen odd miles to the east of Monasternenagh.[64] This distance may imply that *Oenach Culi* was not, in fact, the site which gave rise to the name of the Cistercian monastery even if *Oenach Culi* formed part of their lands. Edmund Hogan identified *Oenach Culi* with another name,

---

[59] Máire Ní Mhaonaigh, 'Cináed ua hArtacáin' in *Medieval Ireland: An Encyclopedia* ed. Seán Duffy (London: Routledge, 2005), 87; 'Flann Mainistrech,' 181.

[60] Richard Irvine Best and Osborn Bergin, eds., *Lebor na hUidre: Book of the Dun Cow* (Dublin: Royal Irish Academy, 1929), 127.

[61] Edmund Hogan, ed., *Cath Ruis na* Ríg. Todd Lecture series 4 (Dublin, 1892); Patrick Wadden, "*Cath Ruis na Ríg for Bóinn*–history and literature in twelfth-century Ireland," *Aiste* 4 (2014), 11–44.

[62] The place-name forms in the Monasternenagh charter are listed here in capitals to distinguish them from others.

[63] *LU.*, 94, 128.

[64] Patrick Gleeson, "Assembly and elite culture in late antique Europe: a case study of Óenach Clochair and the Balline hoard," *Journal of Irish Archaeology* 23 (2014), 171–87.

Oenach Clochair, but this may have been an error and perhaps there were, in fact, two separate *oenach* sites within east Limerick. (This would also fit with Westropp's nineteenth-century identification of the Cistercian buildings as being at Aenagh Beg for a small *oenach* implies a contrast with another, larger *oenach*.) *Oenach Clochair* is described in the Book of Leinster as a place where races were held under the aegis of the prehistoric king Fiachu Muillethan.[65] This is significant for Fiachu, in the early twelfth century, was seen as the ancestor of the Meic Carthaig, the Uí Briain rivals for the kingship of Munster.[66] If this was the *oenach* which gave rise to the name Monasternenagh, it would therefore reinforce the idea that Toirdelbach's gift to the Cistercians was fuelled, in part, by the advantage of removing a key part of the social infrastructure of his enemies. *Óenaig* were places of assembly and communal celebration which took place under royal aegis in designated areas of open ground (often prehistoric cemeteries), normally but not invariably at key points within the agricultural year. They were characterised by political gatherings and markets as well as by marriages and race meetings.[67] A Cistercian monastery located by an *oenach* may have been "far removed from the dwellings of seculars" as in the requirements of *Summa Cartae Caritatis* but it was hardly an isolated desert.

There also appears to have been at least one pre-existing royal settlement amongst the Monasternenagh land-holdings. The grange of Loch Gur, GRANGIA LOCGEIR, in King John's charter of 1200 is followed by a list of place-names including DUNGEIR and an island which belongs to the VILLA LOCGEIR. *Dun nGair* is also identified as one of the *poirt ríg Caisil* 'places of the kings of Cashel' in *Lebor na Cert*,

---

[65] *The Book of Leinster formerly Lebar na Núachongbála IV* ed. R.I. Best and M.A. O'Brien (Dublin: Dublin Institute for Advanced Studies, 1965), 994.

[66] Hog, *Onom.*, s.v. óinach; Ó Corráin, "*Cáithréim*," 8.

[67] Catherine Swift, "*Óenach Tailten*, the Blackwater valley and the Uí Néill kings of Tara" in *Seanchas; Studies in Early and Medieval Irish Archaeology, History and Literature in honour of Francis J. Byrne* ed. Alfred P. Smyth (Dublin: Four Courts Press 2000), 109–120; Joe Wolf, "Arguing for an 'emergency óenach': reassessing the evidence for the seasonality of the Early Irish óenach", *Proceedings of the Harvard Celtic Colloquium* 35 (2015), 204–15; Catherine Swift, "Meeting with the taxing master: an investigation of the word *oireachtas* in modern and medieval Ireland," *Studia Hibernica* 43 (2017), 1–24.

a text which favours the Uí Briain as kings of Cashel and was compiled around the year 1100.[68] It is reasonable to suggest that it was somewhere around the *dún*, the lake, the *inis* and the *villa* of Loch Gur that Donnchad Mac Carthaigh was being kept by Toirdelbach Ua Briain when he died as the latter's hostage at Loch Gur (*do é gar Loch Gair*).[69] Irish royalty, therefore, was not only responsible for sponsoring the new Cistercian foundations; they were also prepared to contribute to such churchmen lands which had been royal centres, royal sites of assembly, royal prisons and royal burial places. It does appear, however, that in many if not most cases, these generous gifts represented lands which had been taken from their earlier royal owners by force of conquest.

The presence of pre-existing settlements among donated lands is particularly interesting given that the term *grangia* is not used of all Irish Cistercian holdings. It is not used at all in King John's Baltinglass charter for example where the text is said to be derived from the *carta memorati regis Dermatii* (the charter of the aforementioned king Diarmuid (mac Murchada)).[70] Nor does it occur in the early charters for St. Mary's of Dublin. These are first documented in a list put together by William Fitz Audelin in 1172 by which stage, the Cistercians controlled a major estate around Clonliffe (including holdings such as Culmine, a church location as early as the mid seventh century)[71] and another, separated holding, south of the river Liffey which ran from Monkstown to Bullock Harbour.[72] It appears that where *grangia* is used in Irish charters, it should perhaps be understood as representing estates as they had been re-shaped and re-formed into new and rather different units by the Cistercians themselves.

---

[68] Myles Dillon, ed. and trans., *Lebor na Cert: The Book of Rights* Irish Texts Society 46. (Dublin: 1962), 42; Kevin Murray, *"Lebor na Cert: language and date"* in *Lebor na Cert: Reassessments* ed. Kevin Murray. Irish Texts Society Subsidiary Series 25 (2013), 77–102.

[69] *Misc. Ir. Ann.* 1143.

[70] Nicholls, "Baltinglass," 189

[71] Catherine Swift, "St Patrick, Skerries and the earliest evidence for local church organisation in Ireland" in *The Island of Saint Patrick: Church and ruling dynasties in Fingal and Meath AD 400–1148* ed. Ailbhe MacShamhráin (Dublin: Four Courts, 2004), 61–78, 68.

[72] Columcille Ó Conbhuí, "The lands of St Mary's, Dublin," *Proceedings of the Royal Irish Academy* 62 (1961–3), 21–84, 22–23.

This, in turn, raises the question: did kings like Toirdelbach Ua Briain know, in advance of endowing their foundations, that the Cistercians would revolutionise the patterns of land-holding and agrarian activity in the lands they were given? For kings enjoined to have "men of clerical grade in every church, with wealth and with riches, wanting neither clothing nor food," it would obviously be a great advantage if such churchmen were proficient and self-sufficient farmers in their own right.

It has been noted by others that the charter for Monasternenagh lists eight granges in total.[73] Unfortunately, the mainstay of those seeking to identify Irish Cistercian lands, the Tudor dissolution extents of 1540–41, do not cover the lands of Monasternenagh in any detail.[74] In the Elizabethan *Fiants*,[75] there are summary notes to the effect that Elizabeth granted the Monasternenagh lands to Sir Warham Saint Leger, to Sir William Drury, to Sir Henry Wallop and to Robert Collam but in each case the grant is, at its most explicit, "the site of the abbey of Nenagh, Co. Limerick with appurtenances."[76] This minimal information, allied to such a confused chain of ownership, makes it difficult to trace all of the ninety-one place-names in John's charter although they appear to be concentrated within the area of the greater rivers in central Limerick, the Maigue, the Comoge (or Cammogue) and the Morning Star.[77]

The words used to qualify *grangia* in the Monasternenagh charter clearly indicate that its granges were topographically varied: e.g.

---

[73] Lynch, *Monastic Landscape*, 11; Stout, "The Cistercian grange," 32.

[74] N.B. White ed. *Extents of Irish Monastic Possessions 1540–1541* (Dublin: Irish Manuscripts Commission, 1943), 212: "Monastery of Nenanghe–issues, nil."

[75] A "fiant" was a warrant by the deputy or council to the Irish Chancery to convey a right, an office, title to property or a pardon to named individuals. They thus provide important information about land-holdings and their owners; Fiona Fitzsimmons, "Tudor Fiants," *History Ireland* 23.4 (2015)–digital edition (accessed 16th April, 2019): https://www.historyireland.com/featured-archive-post/tudor-fiants/.

[76] *The Irish Fiants of the Tudor sovereigns during the reigns of Henry VIII, Edward VI, Philip and Mary and Elizabeth I*, (Dublin: Eamonn de Búrca, 1994), §1143, §3174, §4124, §4757, §5116, §5964.

[77] John Begley, *The diocese of Limerick–ancient and medieval*, 3 vols (Dublin: Browne and Nolan), 1906, I 339–341. Begley lists the charter as 1201 but it is listed under 1st November 1200 in H. S. Sweetman, ed., *Calendar of documents relating to Ireland 1171–1251* (London: 1875), §136.

BRIDDAIN (*brí* 'hill'), NAHAVA (*ab* 'river'), CORACOIMGILLAIN (*cora* 'stone fence/weir'), NAGLOCHMIB (genitive plural of *cloch* 'stones'); CATHIRCORNII (*cathair* 'settlement'); LOCGEIR (*loch* 'lake'); CAMUIS (*cam* 'a winding or bend'); INTLEVI (*lem* 'elm'). The nature of agricultural exploitation taking place on these granges is not described although the names may hint at fishing, quarrying and timber extraction. The charter does, however, include place-names such as IN TABALLGORT otherwise, *int-aballgort*, 'the apple-orchard', SALCUARAIN incorporating the word *sál* or 'salt-working' and CLUAMCOLLAM or *cluain collán* 'the river meadow of hazel-nuts.' It should be noted in passing that there is no reference here to sheep, the classic animal associated with late twelfth and thirteenth-century Cistercians in England and Wales and one which was clearly a feature of many Irish Cistercian houses by 1242 when Henry III sought a year's worth of wool from each house.[78]

The monastery itself was located amongst the KENELMEGAN or *Cenél Megan*, an otherwise unknown dynasty whose name may derive from the Maigue river. Of the other place-names in the charter, which may, or may not include sub-units within the granges, the more common onomastic terms are *mag* 'cleared land' (two examples), *les* 'fort' (three), *cluain* 'river meadow' (four), *cathair* 'settlement' (five), *áth* 'ford' (six), *ceall* 'church' (eleven) a further four "CEAL/KEAL" which may be either a spelling variant of *ceall* or possibly *coill* 'wood' and, the most common, twenty-three examples of *baile*.

Some of the churches may have been very ancient foundations; one such is CEALLCRUMTIRLAPAN CUILLEAN which incorporates the very early borrowing of the word *presbyter* or priest which shows the replacement of "p" by a "c/k" as well as syncope (to produce *cruimthir*), thought to belong to the earliest phase of Latin loanwords into Irish.[79] The Cistercian estate of Monasternenagh, therefore, included a large variety of pre-existing churches, perhaps as many as fifteen, and some of these appear to have been dedicated to ecclesiastical use for a very considerable

---

[78] David H. Williams, *The Cistercians in the Early Middle Ages* (Leominster: Gracewing, 1998), 346; Breda Lynch, *Monastic Landscape*, 102–3, Sweetman, *Calendar* §2586.

[79] Damian McManus, "A chronology of Latin loan-words in Early Irish," *Ériu* 34 (1983), 21–71, 46.

time. It may be, in fact, that Toirdelbach's patronage should be seen as essentially representing a transformation of the extant religious presence in the locality rather than as the introduction of substantial numbers of new churchmen to the region.

The most common term in the Monasternenagh charter, *baile*, has been linked by Fergus Kelly to the word *fintiu* or 'kin-land,' divided between kin-members who farm as individuals but who have reciprocal rights and duties as a group.[80] As an onomastic term, it has been examined in some detail by both Liam Price and Gregory Toner.[81] Price made the point that though it is common in townland names today (the anglicised form "Bally-" accounting for approximately one sixth of the entire total), this does not mean that the modern townland units were necessarily extant in the middle ages.[82] The first occurrence of *baile* is recorded in the *Annals of Ulster* in 1011 and by the twelfth century, it already had a wide semantic range, from the fortified settlement of Limerick, marked by urban gates, towers and streets full of houses, down to individual farmsteads. In his summation, Toner highlights labour as the common denominator: "each place is important by virtue of the presence of people who imbue it with an economic and social function in relation to the provision of food and raising of revenue." He suggests that the most common twelfth-century *baile* units might be made up of small farms of between 25-30 acres, worked by a farmer and his immediate family and linked to others belonging to the same kin-group.[83] Such an interpretation fits with the *Bali meic Edugain* with its four ploughlands of grazing and waste in the Mellifont charter (above) and also agrees with the evidence for *baile* in the Monasternenagh charter for on three separate occasions, the *baile* therein is also described as an extended area as in:

> *BALI ISATCHILL a marisco ab oriente grangiae circa*
> *amnem ex utique usque ad vadeum Denndirg*

---

[80] Fergus Kelly, *Early Irish farming* (Dublin: Dublin Institute for Advanced Studies 1997), 402.

[81] Liam Price, "A note on the use of the word *baile* in place-names," *Celtica* 6 (1963), 119–26; Gregory Toner, "Baile: settlement and land-holding in medieval Ireland," *Éigse* 34 (2004), 25–43.

[82] Liam Price "A note," 123.

[83] Toner "Baile," 38–43.

BALI ISATCHILL from the marsh from east of the 'Grange around the River,' on both sides, to the ford of Denndirg.

In the Monasternenagh charter, *baile* is invariably found in the initial position apart from the single example of CORBALI, (a common townland name, apparently meaning a conspicuous *baile* or one characterised by rough ground).[84] The normal spelling in the Monasternenagh charter is BALI + I with the single exception of BALITARSNU, 'the crooked *baile.*' Another placename is BALI ICARRAIG or *baile i carraig* 'a *baile* at the stone.' A third, BALI INACALLIGI is *baile inna caillige*, 'the *baile* of the veiled woman' which may be a reference to the presence of female religious at Monasternenagh, as described by Stephen of Lexington, whose house was joined to that of the Cistercian brothers.[85]

The most common formula in the Monasternenagh charter is *baile* combined with personal names as eponyms, implying many were (or at any rate had once been) settlements occupied by extended families. Examples are BALI IBRENAIN or *baile Uí Bhrennáin,* BALI IDUB or *Bailie Uí Dubh,* BALLIRIAGAIN *or Baile Uí Riagáin.* Some are family names which can be traced in the surrounding region. Thus BALI IMELINNAN (perhaps originally *Baile Uí Mael Fhinnan*)[86] seems closely related to M. Omelinum, cantor of the Limerick cathedral chapter in the latter's foundation charter of 1204–6.[87] Others, such as BALI IDUBAN, BALI IDUIBGINI and BALI IGERRIDIR also appear in the charter for the Cistercian abbey of Holy Cross in Tipperary, another foundation by an Uí Briain king, Domnall Mór. This may imply land exchange between two Cistercian houses, as Marie Therese Flanagan has suggested,[88] or perhaps it represents multiple settlements occupied by related families or even

---

[84] https://www.logainm.ie/en/ s.v. Corbally (accessed 26th November, 2018).

[85] O'Dwyer, *Letters*, 185 (§88).

[86] Two grave slabs seeking prayers for a Mael Finnia, are known from Clonmacnois; R.A.S. Macalister, *Corpus Inscriptionum Insularum Celticarum* vol. 2 (Dublin: Stationary Office, 1949), 55, 58.

[87] James McCaffrey, *The Black Book of Limerick* (Dublin: Gill & Son, 1907), 116, 179.

[88] Flanagan, *Irish royal charters*, 309.

settlements referring to unrelated ancestors who shared a common personal name. So little is known about the adoption and use of Irish surnames in this period that it is impossible to be entirely sure. It is noteworthy, however, that a number of surnames appear to have been shared by fellow churchmen working in the same region in roughly the same time period.

In the mid-twelfth-century Kells charters, one finds *Baile Í Uidhrín* and *Baile Uí Comgáin* both being further characterised as *cona muiliund ocus cona fherund uili* (with its mill and all its farmland).[89] This indicates clearly that a *baile* identified with a family name had agricultural assets. An account in the Middle Irish text, *Betha Colmáin maic Lúacháin*, provides a statement that such *baile*-families could be in service to a church:

> *Dá aicme immurgu robátar hi Fidh Dorcha ar cind Colmáin maic Lúacháin, id est Hí Dubáin Caille ⁊ Húi Dubáin Maige. Táncatar malle dochum Colmáin ⁊ dorónsat a manchine dó eter bás ⁊ bethaid ⁊ a ferann ar bíthdílsi co bráth, conid síatt is fine Griein ac Laind ósin alle ⁊ dobert an rí do-som a saere dóib co bráth úaith féin ⁊ ó cach ríg 'na diáid co bráth ar cís ríg ⁊ flatha. Is síatt-so bailed Hú nDubán .i. Less na Fingaile cona dib lessaib beca ⁊ Less Dubán ar cúl Less Grúccáin . . . a ndílsi uile do Cholmán mac Lúacháin ⁊ don Choimded co bráth ó ríg ⁊ ó chíss na flatha ⁊ na túaithe archeanae.*

There were two groups in the Dark Wood before Colmán son of Luachan came there, viz. the Uí Dubáin of the Wood and the Uí Dubáin of the cleared land. They both came together and granted him service both in death and life and their land to be his own till Judgement so that from that time onward, they have been the kindred of Grian in Lann. And the king granted him [Colmán] their freedom till Judgement from himself and from every king after him till Judgement as regards tax of king or lord. These are the various *baile* of the Uí Dubáin .i.e Less na

---

[89] Toner, "Baile," 38; Gearóid Mac Niocaill, *Notitiae as Leabhar Cheanannais, 1033–1161* (Dublin: Cló Morainn, 1961), 28.

Fingaile with its two small *les* and Less Dubán behind Less Grucáin . . . and all these to be the property of Colman son of Luachan and of the Lord until Judgement [free] from king and from tax of lords and of laymen."[90]

In what may be merely an intriguing coincidence, Monasternenagh and Holy Cross both also have a *baile Uí Dubáin*. More generally, the existence of twenty-three *baile* farming units on the Monasternenagh lands not only confirms the settled nature of the landscape prior to the Cistercian foundation, it also makes one wonder about the origins and role of the *conversi* who formed part of the Cistercian community by the time of Stephen of Lexington's visit to the locality in 1228/9.[91]

Bernard tells us that the first lay *conversus* of the monastery of Suir met Malachy in his youth.[92] An obituary notice for Donnchad Úa Cerbhaill, early patron of Mellifont, in a later medieval antiphonary, states that 300 *conversi* (and 100 monks) were attached to Mellifont by the time of Donnchad's death in 1168.[93] In a writ from King John on behalf of St. Mary's Abbey, there is reference to *nativi et fugitivi sui, cum omnibus catallis suis et cum tota sequela sua . . . qui fugerunt de terra sua post captionem Dublin* (their local men and fugitives with all their cattle and their whole following . . . who fled from the abbey lands after the capture of Dublin). Another refers to the same abbey's *terrae et homines et omnes possessiones* 'lands and men and all possessions.'[94]

The *conversi* were the main labour force of the Cistercian monasteries throughout Europe although choir monks helped with harvesting. The *conversi* were vowed to obedience, lived a common life and might not marry. Upon joining the order, they had a year of religious training. They were illiterate but were expected to learn key prayers such as the *Pater Noster,* the *Credo Deum,* the *Miserere Mei* and the *Ave Maria*

---

[90] Kuno Meyer, ed. and trans*., Betha Colmáin maic Lúacháin* (Felinfach: Llanerch 1997), 36–39 (§39). I have slightly modified Meyer's translation to update his use of words such as tribe.

[91] O'Dwyer, *Letters*, 195–6 (§ 93), 188 (§ 89), 193 (§ 91).

[92] Lawlor, *Saint Bernard's life,* 114 (§64).

[93] George Petrie, *The ecclesiastical architecture of Ireland: an essay on the origin and uses of the Round Towers of Ireland* (Shannon: Irish University Press, 1970), 394.

[94] Gilbert, *Chartularies*, I, 87, 90.

off by heart. They were not tonsured and did not wear a cowl, being dressed instead in a tunic, hose, scapula and smock. The European norm was that they were of peasant origins although exceptions were known, especially in the earlier history of the order. The *conversi* ate in their own refectory, worshipped within their own choir, were expected to abstain from alcohol and much of the craftsmanship and the external trade of the monastery was in their hands.[95]

This description seems close, though not identical, to that proffered by Colmán Etchingham for the *manaig béothlusaig* or "monks possessed of livestock", a phrase used in the ninth-century legal text, *Bretha Nemed Tóisech*. These were entitled to receive baptism, communion and memorial services after death and attend Mass in exchange for submission of tithes and they could include entire families, alongside their womenfolk.[96] They appear to have represented people from a wide range of social backgrounds but whereas a *manach ríagaltae* 'a monk bound by a rule' is glossed as *saormanach* or 'enfranchised monk,' he could be contrasted with a *daormanach* or unfree monk who had no legal capacity. The model which bound these *manaig* together was one of kinship and, apparently, location. Depending on their status, they could receive land only (at the lower social levels) or land and livestock from their churches in return for which they appear to have provided labour.[97] Etchingham has argued for the continued existence of this married church workforce into the twelfth century, citing the tract by Bishop Gilli of Limerick who speaks of a category of married 'individuals who engaged in prayer' who were neither clerics or monks.[98]

If twelfth-century Irish society was already accustomed to an agrarian tenantry who provided the labour force to keep religious communities

---

[95] Williams, *The Cistercians*, 79–88.

[96] Colmnán Etchingham, "The early Irish church: some observations on pastoral care and dues," *Ériu* 42 (1991), 99–118, 105–6.

[97] Thomas Charles-Edwards, "The church and settlement" in *Irland und Europa: die Kirche im Frühmittelalter* ed. Próinséas Ní Chatháin and Michael Richter (Stuttgart: Klett-Cotta, 1984), 167–75; Neil McLeod, *Early Irish contract law*. Sydney Series in Celtic Studies 1 (Sydney: University of Sydney, 1992), 199–200; Colmán Etchingham, *Church organisation in Ireland AD 650 to 1000* (Maynooth: Laigin Publications 1999), 391–425.

[98] Etchingham, "*Reform*," 225.

sheltered and fed, this provides yet another explanation for Irish interest in a religious order organised on economic principles quite akin to their own. Rather than viewing the Cistercian grange as a radically different model of agrarian organisation from the feudal manor,[99] one might visualise it rather as slotting reasonably neatly into an extant Irish church system, perhaps with some preliminary amalgamation of individual land units. Such original units may have been those identified with the word *ceall* in the Monasternenagh charter or they may have been composite *ceall* and *baile* entities. (It may be significant that in the verses from *Cert cech ríg co réil* cited above, a *baile* is associated with Christian burial).

A characteristic of some new Cistercian foundations elsewhere in Europe was their determination to move peasant families belonging to pre-existing settlements off their newly acquired lands while converting at least a proportion of the men-folk to the status of *conversi*.[100] Just as the modern townland does not necessarily represent the original *baile* which provides its name, so, too, the Monasternenagh charter of 1200 may merely represent the existence of various kin-groups who had already been evicted from the land, leaving behind only their name embedded in local place names.

As against this possibility, however, it is noteworthy that, in his recommendations to Irish Cistercians, drawn up in August 1228, Stephen of Lexington insisted that:

> *Item omnes consanguinei tam monachorum quam conuersorum ab abbatial et grangiis penitus amoueantur. Alioquin prior et cellerarius et magister conuersorum insimul conuersi magistri grangiarum, quamdiu id omissum fuerit, omni VI feria sint in pane et aqua et in capitulo uapulent.*

> All blood-relatives of monks and *conversi* shall be completely removed from the monastery and the granges. Otherwise, the prior, the cellarer, the master of *conversi*, and the *conversi* masters of the granges shall be on bread

---

[99] Stout, "The Cistercian grange," 28–30.

[100] R.A. Donkin, "The Cistercian order and the settlement of Northern England," *Geographical Review* 59 (1969), 403–416, 407–412; C.N.L. Brooke, *Churches and churchmen in medieval Europe* (London: Hambledon Press, 1999), 198–209.

and water every Friday and shall be flogged in chapter as often as they transgress in this.[101]

Stephen goes on to state that monks and *conversi* should not ride to visit their relatives unless for the business of the house. *Conversi* should not have a certain portion of the goods of granges allotted to them by custom. Monastic officials should guard the celibacy of monks and *conversi* were forbidden to sell anything without the permission of the abbot or cellarer.[102] These prescriptions clearly relate to *conversi* who were closely related to the surrounding population groups and Stephen's criticisms would seem to refer to people continuing to live in the manner of the earlier *manaig béothlusaig*.

In Stephen's description of events which took place at Monasternenagh in October 1228, he refers to a group identified as allies of the rebellious *conversi* and *monachi* but who were distinguishable from both:

> [. . .] *gillae domus et ribaldos prouintie circiter CC sibi adiunxerunt cum armis, partim pro mercede, partim modis aliis.*[103]

> [. . .] about two hundred house servants and lay-abouts of the districts, joined with themselves, partly by money, partly by other means.[104]

O'Dwyer's translation of *gillae* as house servants minimizes the obvious Latinisation of Irish *gilla*, who, at least by implication, are said here to belong to families of the immediate locality. Another of Stephen's letters, describing the situation in Ireland generally, refers to Irish monks living outside the cloister, in groups of three and four, each *equum cum puero proprio habente* (having a horse along with his own boy-servant).[105] Finally, a letter addressed to the abbot of Furness states explicitly that Stephen had chosen not to evict the Irish residents on the lands of their

---

[101] P. Bruno Greisser, ed., *Registrum epistolarum Stephani de Lexinton. Analecta sacri ordinis Cisterciensis* 2 (1946), 99 §CIV:5; O'Dwyer, *Letters* 157 (§8:5). (The letters are ordered differently by Greisser and O'Dwyer).

[102] O'Dwyer, *Letters* 157, 162, 163 (§80).

[103] Greisser, *Registrum*, 16 (§4).

[104] O'Dwyer, *Letters*, 189, (§89).

[105] Greisser, *Registrum* 4, (§2); O'Dwyer, *Letters* 183, (§87).

new daughter house at Suir in order to avoid repercussions from those living nearby who might react badly.[106] It appears then that Irish Cistercian houses did not evict the pre-existing peasant tenantry represented by families living in the *baile* farms. These appear to have functioned, at least on occasion, as a separate serving class as well as, perhaps, being absorbed as *conversi* of somewhat higher status. While the Monasternenagh estates might have been organized into new granges with new systems of agricultural exploitation by the Cistercian authorities, the population of the locality appears to have remained largely unchanged although the status of the women and children belonging to these local families after the Cistercian takeover remains unclear.

One *baile* unit in the Monasternenagh charter seems to have been occupied by craftsmen rather than farmers, namely BALIISODER or *Baile Uí Sútaire*. This name derived ultimately from Latin *sutor* meaning 'shoemaker' or 'cobbler'. Such men were seen elsewhere as important members of the Cistercian *conversi*. In the *Breve et Memoriale Scriptum de Conversatione Laicorum Fratrum*, written in the latter half of the twelfth century, chapter 13 is headed *De sutoribus et pellipariis et textoribus* (on cobblers and tanners and weavers) and it is said that these are to speak to none other than the abbot and the prior except through their grange master.[107]

Sútaire may not have been a direct borrowing from Latin for *sutor* was also borrowed into Norse where *sútari* means a tanner.[108] This possibility is enhanced by the use of Irish *sútaire* as a family eponym for individuals named *Sútari* are known from eastern England and the word exists as a by-name in Western Scandinavian languages.[109] There are examples of such occupational names in Irish: modern examples include the Ó Troighthigh or Troy (from *traigthech* a footsoldier) or Ó Treabhair,

---

[106] O'Dwyer, *Letters*, 35 (§15); *Registrum* (§25).

[107] Chrysogonus Waddell, *Cistercian lay-brothers: twelfth-century usages with related texts*. Commentarii cistercienses, studia et documenta 10 (Cîteaux: 2000), 152–4, 159, 207.

[108] Richard Cleasby and Gudbrand Vigfusson, eds., *An Icelandic-English Dictionary* (Oxford: Clarendon Press, 1957), 605.

[109] Gillian Fellows Jensen, *Scandinavian personal names in Lincolnshire and Yorkshire*. Navnestudier udgivet af Institut for Navneforskning 7, (Copenhagen: I Kommision hos Akademisk Forlag, 1968), 272–3.

Travers (from *trebaire*, 'a farmer') but they are far more common in English and Norse naming traditions.[110] It seems likely, in what was the ethnically mixed context of early medieval Limerick, that *Baile Uí Sútaire* may have been a family group who made some or all of their income through leather-working. Parallels for Cistercian craft groups living in distinct communities can be found in Tuelachnacornary or *Tulach na Cornaire* 'the hill of the horn-players' in the 1185/6 Mellifont charter and possibly Balivkerde or *Baile Uí Cerd* 'the *baile* of metal-craft workers', granted to St. Mary's by Adam de Feipo around the year 1185.[111]

While *Uí Sútaire* would clearly be an example of an occupational kin-name, the case is not quite so clear when examining individuals with similar professions from the vicinity of Monasternenagh. In the *Dublin Guild Merchant Roll*, under the years 1224–5, a *Willelmus de Athdare le Tannur* is recorded and some fifteen years later, in 1239–40, a *Walterus Tannator de Addare*. (As an aside, the *Merchant Roll* also has a Hugo Sutor of Baligaueran in Co. Down, confirming the contemporary existence of this word in Ireland as a surname.)[112] These men may have been travelers who registered with the guild in order to carry out trade within Dublin and it is not known whether they were long-term residents in that city. On the other hand, their place of origin, Adare, is less than ten miles to the west of Monasternenagh. It may also be significant that among the *praepositi* or reeves of Limerick, we find a Walter de Adare who is witness to a charter of the abbot of Monasternenagh dating roughly to this same period of 1230–1240. Were William and Walter also members of a putative kin-group, the Uí Sútaire, a group of whom lived on the lands of

---

[110] David Hey, *Family History and Local History in England* (Harlow: Longman & Co., 1987), 26–34.

[111] Ó Conbhuí, "Seven documents," 49; Gilbert, *Chartularies*, I 86,88. Middle Irish legal commentaries on the eighth-century law tract *Córus Bésgnai* refer to land obtained by practicing one's *dán* and this could include craftsmenship in wood, stone and metalwork; Liam Breatnach *Córus Bésgnai: An Old Irish law tract on the church and society* Early Irish Law Series VII (Dublin: Dublin Institute for Advanced Studies 2017),172–5, 230–1; Fergus Kelly, *Early Irish farming* Early Irish law series IV (Dublin: Dublin Institute for Advanced Studies 1997), 419.

[112] Philomena Connolly and Geoffrey Martin, eds., *The Dublin Guild Merchant Roll* c. *1190–1265* (Dublin: Dublin Corporation, 1992), 51, 76, 84.

the Cistercian monastery? They clearly held a craft, an approximate location and an interest in the affairs of Monasternenagh in common.

Interestingly, the Limerick charter that Walter witnessed may bespeak an interest in tanning as well as referring to Monasternenagh holdings within the walled city. Such holdings were already attested in King John's confirmation charter where the list of Monasternenagh lands ends: *curia praedictorum monachorum in Limerich cum pertinenciis suis scilicet Bearninnlith* (the court of the aforesaid monks in Limerick, with its assets, that is BEARNINNLITH). *Curia*, as used by Cistercians, was a synonym for grange (there are numerous examples of granges known by their Welsh form *cwrt*) but it could also be a reference to a specific building complex.[113] If the holding in Limerick had assets or *pertinentiae*, it was presumably of a certain size. Its name can be understood as *Bearn Imlech* or land bordering a lake or marsh and incorporating a gap or breach.[114] The name no longer exists and in the marshy, low-lying environment of King's Island, it would be difficult to identify today. The key feature of the city, in the eyes of contemporaries, was *Linn Luimnig* or the pool of Limerick[115] which is a widening of the Shannon just at the point where the Abbey river, the branch of water which cuts off the island city from the mainland, re-enters the mainstream. As a guess, this may have been the breach, known as *Bearn Imlech*, because this area marked the southern edge of the walled city and there is reference to land owned by the abbey and community of Monasternenagh, *circa albam crucem lapideam ex parte australi civitatis Lymeric* (around the white stone cross in the southern part of the city of Limerick). The pool in this southern area was the harbour for shipping arriving into Limerick from the Atlantic so that these Cistercian landholdings were in a very prominent location.[116]

---

[113] David H. Williams, *The Welsh Cistercians*. 2 vols (Norwich: Cyhoeddiadau Sistersiaidd, 1983), II 227, 228, index.

[114] *DIL (Dictionary of the Irish Language)* B s.v. *bern*; I s.v. *imlech* 1.

[115] J. Carmichael Watson, ed., *Mesca Ulad.* Medieval and Modern Irish series 13 (Dublin: Dublin Institute for Advanced Studies, 1941), 13, l.301.

[116] McCaffrey, *Black Book*, 40. Interestingly, the Cistercians of Owney (in the modern parish of Abington in north-east Limerick), a foundation endowed by Theobald Walter during the reign of Richard Lionheart, also owned a burgage in Limerick city. St John Seymour, "Abbey Owney, County Limerick," *Journal of the Royal Society of Antiquaries of Ireland* 37 (1907), 170.

MONASTERNENAGH

However, the southern edge of the city is clearly not the Monasternenagh land involved in the charter signed by Walter de Adare since one of the boundary references in that charter is to the Dominican house of St. Saviours, founded by Domnall Cairpreach Ua Briain in the northern half of the city in 1227.[117] The key features read as follow:

> *Abbas et conventus monasterii de May . . . Hac presenti carta nostra confirmasse David Longo civi Lymeric totam terram nostram infra muros civitatis Lymeric, illam scilicet que extendit a vico de Polmanath usque ad murum civitatis in longitudine et iacet inter terram monialium ex una parte et terram quondam Willelmi le Parmeter ex altera in latitudine et illam terram nostram que se extendit a nona porta juxta aream Fratrum Minorum versus terram monialium in longitudine, et iacet inter predictum murum ex una parte et tenementa quondam dicti Willelmi le Parmeter et Radulphi Carpentari et tenementum quondam Rogeri Mey ex altera in latitudine . . .*

> *Hiis testibus Symonne Herewardo, tunc maiori Lymeric, Mauricio Blundo, Waltero de Adaro, tunc prepositiis eiusdem civitatis, Reginaldo de Sanco Jacobo, Jordano Dykellystoun, Adam Russell, Willelmo Brun, Waltero Croppe, Willelmo filio Willelmi Longi et aliis.*[118]

The abbot and community of the monastery of Maigue (otherwise Monasternenagh) . . . in this, our present charter, all our land between the walls of the city of Limerick are confirmed to David Longus, citizen of Limerick, that is, the land which, in length, extends from the street of Polmanath to the wall of the city and in width, lies between the land of the nuns on one side and the land of a certain William le Parmeter on the other.

---

[117] Brian Hodkinson, *Aspects of Medieval North Munster* (Limerick: Thomond Archaeological and Historical Society, 2012), 28; Significant text underlined for emphasis.

[118] McCaffrey, *Black Book*, 35–6, (§36).

Also our land which, in length, extends itself from the ninth gate next to the open ground of the Brothers Minor to the land of the sisters and in width lies between the aforesaid wall on one hand and the holdings of the aforesaid William le Parmeter and Radulphus the Carpenter and the holding of a certain Roger Mey on the other . . .

By these witnessed: Symon Herewardus, now mayor of Limerick, Maurice Blundus and Walterus de Adare, now reeves of the same city, Reginaldus de Sancto Jacobo, Jordanus Dykellystoun, Adam Russell, Willelmus Brun, Walterus Croppe, Willelmus son of Willelmus Longus and others.

According to this charter, the Cistercians seem to have occupied a substantial portion of urban land before they transferred it to David Long. The boundary marker of Polmanath is not otherwise attested.[119] The first element, *poll* means 'hole,' 'cavity' or 'pit'; the second may be *mónaid*, used of bog or moor although it is hard to believe that one particular bog-hole would have been distinctive enough on King's Island to have given rise to the name of an urban *vicus*. The *Dictionary of Irish language* also identifies *menad* as an 'awl' or 'borer' and *fer menath* as a 'man of awls' or 'shoemaker.'[120] Shoemakers, of course, use leather as well as awls and cavities and pits are an integral part of leather-working so *Polmanath* may refer to tanning-pits used by leather-workers as well as cobblers. A tanning complex of late twelfth- and thirteenth-century date has been found south of the Poddle river in Dublin, immediately outside the city walls.[121] In the case of Limerick, Polmanath appears to have been outside

---

[119] A *poll mónad* may lie behind Polmuntath, listed in the boundaries of a fishing area in the river Barrow given to the Cistercians of Duiske by Henry Fitz Henry Roche; Geraldine Carville, "The economic activities of the Cistercian order in medieval Ireland 1142–1541," *Cîteaux* 3–4, (1971), 278–299, 288; https://www.logainm.ie/en/ *s.v. Poulmounty* (accessed 17th November, 2018).

[120] *DIL* M s.v. *menad, manath.*

[121] Linzi Simpson, "Excavations on the southern side of the medieval town at Ship Street Little, Dublin" in *Medieval Dublin V* ed. Sean Duffy (Dublin: Friends of Medieval Dublin, 2004), 9–51,15–16, 32–34.

the original core walled city (represented by the medieval parish of the Cathedral church, St. Mary's). The northern part of the city described in the above extract appears to have represented a recent expansion into what had previously been extra-mural settlement for a murage grant by Henry III exists for the year 1237, indicating a rebuilding of the city wall at that time. [122] Certainly the phrase *area Fratrum Minorum* indicates that some of what had been thus enclosed was open ground.

The witnesses to the *Polmanath* charter includes Simon Hereward, the mayor, as well as Reginald de Sancto Jacobo, identified elsewhere as *seneschallus* or steward of the city and Walter Crop, owner of five urban burgages as well as a knight's fee in the surrounding hinterland.[123] Given the high status of these individuals, it seems a reasonable guess to identify the Walter de Adare who also signs this charter with the contemporary man of the same name belonging to the Merchant Guild of Dublin. The affairs of Monasternenagh were evidently considered matters of some importance within the city and indeed the 1237 murage grant makes it clear that hides were of considerable economic value for city authorities:

> For every crannock of wheat coming to the city on sale ½ d; every crannock of oats ½ d; every horse, ox or cow 1d; every 4 hogs 1d; every 6 sheep 1d; every last of hides 20d; every sack of wool 4d; every hogshead of wine 2d; every wey of iron 2d; every cartload of lead 2d; every truss of cloth or other merchandise 4d; every crannock of salt 1/2d; every crannock of woad 2d; every wey of onions or cheese 1d; every hogshead of honey or butter 4d; every mease of herrings ½ d; every horse-burden of salmon 1d; every hundred of wares 2d.[124]

The evidence is hardly conclusive but adding it all together, one can put forward the following. By AD 1200, the Cistercians of Monasternenagh held land to the south of the city, known as Bearn Imlech, later marked by a white stone cross. By the 1230s and 40s, they also held land within the newly expanded city walls to the north. Since we know that these northern lands were held by Uí Briain kings (who granted

---

[122] Hodkinson, *Aspects North Munster*, 6, 32.

[123] McCaffrey, *Black Book*, 53, 101; Hodkinson, *Aspects North Munster*, 39.

[124] Sweetman, *Calendar*, (§2405), underlining added.

territory to the Brothers Minor and to Augustinian nuns in this same area), it seems reasonable to see the Cistercian holdings as deriving from the same patrons, the Uí Briain dynasty which had originally endowed Monasternenagh. These lands were bounded by a place-name which may refer to leather-workers; Monasternenagh also had a settlement of leather-workers and one of the witnesses to transactions involving this land appears to have been a merchant specialising in leather-working. The most lucrative urban trade in Limerick at the time appears to have been one involving hides given that these were taxed at a rate at least five times higher than any of the other goods coming into the city.

Since cattle were the major economic asset of early Ireland, it is impossible to identify where the hides entering Limerick were originally produced and, indeed, more than one source seems inherently likely. On the other hand, the very large estate of Monasternenagh, with its centralised control and eight granges, would appear to be very well situated to exploit such a trade. We know from Stephen of Lexington that the Irish Cistercian *conversi* were involved in commercial leather-working:

> *Item conversus sutrini habeat aliquen monachum conscium omnium eorum que facit uendendo, emendo, dando, acomodando. Qui ea scripto commendet et sciat inde manifestas reddere conputationes.*[125]

> The *conversus* cobbler shall have a monk with him who is informed of all the things which he does in selling, buying, giving and lending. He will put these down in writing and will know how to make clear assessments of them.[126]

Other references in Stephen's letters state that the *sutrinus* shall not provide sandals for any member of the community or any other person without the permission of the abbot, the cellarer or another monk deputised by the abbot.[127] These recommendations indicate that leather-

---

[125] Greisser, *Registrum*, 104 (§66).
[126] O'Dwyer, *Letters*, 165
[127] *Registrum* 101, 105, 106 (§104); O'Dwyer, *Letters*, 161, 165, 167, 170 (§80).

working was important to the Irish Cistercian communities, not just for their own use but also for external trade and that, as elsewhere in Europe, it was carried out by members of the *conversi*.

One last piece can be added to the story. In the tempestuous period of Stephen's visitation of 1228/29, a major leader at Monasternenagh was Thomas, a nephew of the Uí Briain king of Thomond, who had been castrated and blinded by his relatives before he took the Cistercian habit. Stephen, who was a close ally of the De Burgos (the Norman rivals of the Uí Briain for control of Limerick in his day),[128] described the Cistercian foundation as "stony of heart and unyielding of neck", engaged in wickedness, and with its pride growing from day to day. He writes how, on hearing that Stephen was planning on leaving Ireland, the monks under their Uí Briain leadership, expelled the abbot and their Norman *confrères*. They then stored thirty salted head of cattle under the dormitory, they brought in large amounts of grain, hay and flour which they stored in the church and they led thirty head of cattle on the hoof into the cloister "grazing them on the grass there and on hay stored in the church."[129] Stephen then goes on to say that the rebels went on to eat "flesh-meat publicly," which, allied to everything else, left the visitor "utterly astounded and also perplexed about what ought to be done."[130]

It is evident that the monks of Monasternenagh were engaged in cattle-rearing even if they were not normally meat-eaters. In this, they resembled other early Cistercian houses of northern and western England where cattle in specialised *vaccariae* are also known to have been farmed.[131] In the light of this paper, however, what is perhaps most

---

[128] Swift, "Uí Briain and De Burgos," 12–15; Greisser, *Registrum*, 111, (§110): "quidam monachus de Magio, Thomas nomine, nepos regum Teomon(ie) a parentibus suis ante susceptionem habitus exoculatus et membris genitalibus privatus; ipse uero principalis machinator Th auctor erat conspirationis inaudite olim facte in domo de Magio, cuius conspirationis seriem euidenter habetis inter scripta que anno preterito delata errant ad curiam."

[129] Registrum,16 (§4): "tam bladum quam fenum, farina et alia necessaria" . . . "ad ultimum XXX bouses uiuos intra claustrum introderunt in pratello et de feno in eccelsia recondito ipsos pascentes."

[130] O'Dwyer, Letters, 149 (§77); 188 (§89).

[131] R.A. Donkin, "Cattle on the estates of medieval Cistercian monasteries in England and Wales," *The Economic History Review* 15 (1962), 31–53.

interesting is that the monks of Monasternenagh were also farming hay. Hay was not produced in any quantity in pre-Norman Ireland[132] but a *haggardum*, possibly translating Norse *heygarðr,* was noted at Trim in the Irish Pipe Roll of King John under the heading *Exitus grangiarum Midie.*[133] Perhaps then, hay-making was a feature of the agricultural practices on early Irish granges in general. Certainly hay-making seems to have been conducted on a substantial scale elsewhere in the Cistercian world if the 150 wagon-loads of hay stored in the barn of a grange belonging to the Italian house of Morimondo Milano in 1237 is any sort of guide.[134] Hoffman Berman has argued, in fact, that systematic flooding of meadows in southern France, with the specific intention of increasing hay production, enabled Cistercian communities there to overwinter more stock and, in turn, to improve land fertility with added manure.[135] The river basins of central Limerick are unlikely to have required human intervention to achieve the same effect while the grass-growing season in Ireland was notoriously long in comparison to other parts of Europe. Nevertheless, a more systematic use of hay for overwintering might well have had important economic advantages in lessening the traditional Irish necessity to reduce herds (especially male yearlings) through slaughter at the period of Samain.[136]

Case studies of individual monasteries in their regional and temporal context have much to add to our understanding of the spread of Cistercian practice within Ireland. Marie-Therese Flanagan has pointed out that the word 'reform' was not widely used by contemporaries to describe the twelfth-century changes in church organisation but rather *renovatio* or renewal.[137] The Irish equivalent was *áthnugud*, the term used by the Irish poet who composed the poem *Cert cech ríg co réil*. To think in such terms is to lessen the dramatic novelty and heroic nature ascribed to the

---

[132] Kelly, *Farming*, 46–7.

[133] Davies and Quinn, "The Irish Pipe Roll," 34; Margaret Murphy, "Manor centres, settlement and agricultural systems in medieval Ireland, 1250–1350" in *Agriculture and settlement in Ireland* eds. Margaret Murphy & Mathew Stout (Dublin: Four Courts, 2015), 69–100, 87.

[134] Williams, *Cistercians*, 382.

[135] Berman, *Medieval agriculture*, 88–92.

[136] Kelly, *Farming*, 51–2, 59–60, 320. Samain is the harvest period in fall.

[137] Flanagan, *The transformation*, 247.

Cistercians by writers such as Daphne Pochin-Mould but it does help to make popular enthusiasm for the new order in Ireland rather easier to comprehend.

Previous studies of Irish Cistercians have tended to treat the evidence for the order in isolation from the society in which they operated and considerable weight has been attached to the evidence for their land-holdings at the time of Dissolution as indicative of their original endowments. This paper, in contrast, has sought to confine itself to one particular site, Monasternenagh, in the first hundred years of its existence. These fragmentary records have deliberately been interpreted through the lens of local regional history and by highlighting the relevance of sources in the Irish language. This has allowed the possible motivations of the man who made the original foundation grant, King Toirdelbach Ua Briain, to emerge more clearly from the now shadowy world of the mid-twelfth century.

Toirdelbach may have chosen to endow a Cistercian house at Monasternenagh in thanksgiving for his miraculous escape from the major battle between himself and a powerful coalition of his enemies, including the kings of Leinster, Connacht, the Meic Carthaig of Desmond and the men of Cork. His choice of Cistercians rather than any other form of religious community may have been politically opportune, given his dependence for patronage on a northern Mac Lochlainn king who was himself to endow Mellifont at its consecration. His location of his new community in the southern reaches of his kingdom would have removed border-lands threatened by other power-blocks, especially the Meic Carthaig, from military exploitation by potential invaders and his decision to make over local assembly sites or *óinaig* to the church would have fundamentally transformed a key part of the social infrastructure which such enemies had once enjoyed.

Toirdelbach's new foundation had amassed a very large estate, supplemented by grants from both other Irish as well as Norman patrons, and including eight of the new agricultural units known as *grangiae*, by the time King John issued a charter confirming its possessions in 1200. This estate included an apple orchard, a salt-works, hazels, elm trees and reed-beds as well as mills, fisheries, woods, pastures, meadows and turf-cuttings. It seems to have included a house for female religious as well as at least eleven churches but its most common settlements were termed *baile*, a word understood to represent areas of farmland occupied and exploited by kin-groups who shared a common surname. It appears that some of these families continued to provide a serving class for the new foundation, as well as others who became *conversi*, the men who would have provided the bulk of the agrarian work-force for the Cistercian house. One such kin-group (who apparently had become *conversi*) were named after the Norse word for a tanner and may well have been related to similarly named individuals who were prominent in the urban life of Limerick, a city situated "not more than seven leagues away" from Monasternenagh as Stephen of Lexington pointed out.[138]

In fact, Monasternenagh also owned important land holdings in the immediate vicinity of urban Limerick and had done so from 1200 if not earlier. By the 1240s, these included lands both to the south of the city, by the area of the harbor, and lands to the north, in the vicinity of other Uí Briain foundations of Dominicans and Augustinian nuns. The boundary of the Cistercian lands was marked by the place-name Pollmanath which has been understood as referring to tanning pits. It is clear that a trade in hides was highly valued by the city authorities at the time and it is suggested that one of the key interests of the Cistercian house at Monasternenagh was in cattle farming and the newly developed techniques of hay-making to produce feed. The results from such a trade contributed in a major way to exports in hides through the port of Limerick and may also have included fabrication of leather goods.

The evidence does not allow us to know whether Toirdelbach was conscious that, in endowing a Cistercian house, he was introducing a system of agricultural exploitation that was proving remarkably successful in other parts of Europe at the time.[139] If he did, he may well have been pleased to think that these churchmen would be self-sufficient in raising the wealth needed to run a major monastic house, operating under the aegis of his family. To consider that Irish kings may have been provident with their resources and far-seeing in their endowments is not to undermine a belief in their piety or in their religious beliefs; the Cistercian

---

[138] O'Dwyer, *Letters*, 137 (§69).

[139] Sister James Eugene Madden, "Business monks, banker monks, bankrupt monks: the English Cistercians in the thirteenth century," *The Catholic Historical Review* 49 (1963), 341–364.

order spread rapidly throughout Europe in the twelfth century precisely because medieval society admired both their spirituality and their practical skills. In Idung of Prüfening's *Dialogue between a Cluniac and a Cistercian*, written in the third quarter of the twelfth century, the Cistercian paraphrases St. Augustine: "I would like to know what monks do who do not want to work physically" and sums up his order's perspective:

> You, who think you are contemplatives, are wrong because you do not do manual labour . . . manual labour is a furtherance rather than a hindrance to contemplatives . . . we put great effort into farming which God created and instituted. We all work in common, we choir monks, our *conversi* and our hired hands, each according to his own capability and we all make our living in common by our labour.[140]

Such dedication to farming produced agricultural surpluses which in turn led to trade and a Cistercian involvement in towns and ports. The early history of Monasternenagh provides a microcosm of the processes by which such developments worked themselves out in Ireland.

---

[140] O'Sullivan, *Cistercians and Cluniacs*, 63, 92–94.

Is Iceland Hell? Realism and Reality in
the *Navigatio sancti Brendani*

Nicholas Thyr

The *Navigatio sancti Brendani*,[1] likely written by an Irish monk before or during the middle part of the eighth century,[2] follows the voyage

---

[1] Rossana Guglielmetti and Giovanni Orlandi, eds., *Navigatio sancti Brendanii: Alla scoperta dei segreti meravigliosi del mondo* (Firenze: Edizioni del Galluzzo, 2014), henceforth *NSB*. This edition retains the chapter numbering found in Carl Selmer, ed., *Navigatio Sancti Brendani Abbatis: From Early Latin Manuscripts* (Dublin: Four Courts Press, 1959), henceforth *NSBa*.

[2] It is generally assumed to be the work is of a singular author, e.g. "The author of the Navigatio shows a particular interet in the Divine Office." (Martin McNamara, "Navigatio sancti Brendani. Some Possible Connections with Liturgical, Apocryphal, and Irish Tradition," *The Brendan Legend: Texts and Versions*, ed. Glyn Burgess and Clara Strijbosch [Leiden: Brill, 2006], p. 159). Guglielmetti, in the introduction to *NSB*, notes several discrepancies of plot and time in the received text. Though reserving final judgment, she notes that, regardless of the number of authors, "Resta, fortunamente, un'unitá di concezione strutturale ben visible" ("There remains, fortunately, a quite visible unity of structural conception"). Rossana Guglielmetti, introduction to NSB, pp. cxvi–cxix, quote at cxix. For the Irish origins of the author, see Giovanni Orlandi, *Navigatio Sancti Brendani* (Milan: Instituto Editoriale Cisalpino, 1968), pp. 131–40. The text's date is as yet unsettled. Prior to the recent edition, Jonathan Wooding argued for a date in the first half of the ninth century (Jonathan Wooding, "The Date of Navigatio S. Brendani abbatis," *Studia Hibernica* 37 [2011]: 9–26). Guglielmetti argues for a date considerably earlier, on the following grounds: one, she accepts the argument David Dumville put forth in 1988 for a date prior to 786, due to attribution of Brendan's origins to the Eoganach Locha Léin (David Dumville, "Two Approaches to the Dating of Nauigatio Sancti Brendani," *Studi Medievali* 29 [1988], 87–102, reprinted in Jonathan Wooding, ed., *The Otherworld Voyage in Early Irish Literature: An Anthology of Criticism* [Dublin: Four Courts Press, 2000], 120–132; for Guglielmetti's discussion, introduction to *NSB*, pp. cii–cxix). She further bolsters this claim with linguistic evidence (ciii–cx), noting that the Latinity of the author points to a pre-Carolingian date. Michael Herren, in his review, agrees with her assessment (Michael Herren, review of *NSB*, *Journal of Medieval Latin* 26 [2016]: 383–7).

of the quasi-historical[3] St. Brendan and a number of his monks as they explore the wonders of God's creation. Because the text so obviously draws from a wide variety of sources, a lively enterprise of Brendanian source-sifting has sprung up, attempting to tease out the *Navigatio*'s connections to St. Brendan's various Lives in Latin and Irish;[4] to other voyage tales, such as *Immram Curaig Maíle Dúin*;[5] to texts of foreign extraction, both ecclesiastical[6] and secular[7] in origin; and even to the Grail legend.[8] Such a density of textual reference is no accident; the *Navigatio* is clearly part and parcel of the *ars grammatica*, the dominant literary paradigm of Western Christendom in the early Middle Ages.[9] The effect of this style was reliant on a deep knowledge of "authorities"—most

---

[3] Guglielmetti, introduction to *NSB*, pp. xvii–xxviii; Pádraig Ó Riain, *A Dictionary of Irish Saints* (Dublin: Four Courts Press, 2011), pp. 115–7.

[4] E.g. Guglielmetti, introduction to *NSB*, pp. lxxviii–ci; Séamus MacMathúna, "The *Irish Life of Saint Brendan*: Textual History, Structure, and Date," *The Brendan Legend: Texts and Versions*, eds. Glyn Burgess and Clara Strijbosch (Leiden: Brill, 2006), pp. 117–59.

[5] For a brief discussion of the Immrama and their dates, see Guglielmetti, introduction to *NSB*, pp. xlv–xlvii; much broader in scope is Clara Strijbosch, *The Seafaring Saint: Sources and Analogues of the Twelfth-Century Voyage of Saint Brendan* (Dublin: Four Courts, 2000), which also, besides the Immrama, covers several Continental vernacular versions of the Brendan-legend; for narrower analyses of their interrelationships, James Carney, review of *Navigatio sancti Brendani Abbatis* [Selmer, n. 2 above], *Medium Aevum* 32 (1963), 37–44; reprinted in Wooding, ed., *The Otherworld Voyage*, 42–51, especially pp. 45–51; MacMathúna, "Motif and Episode Clustering in Early Irish Voyage Literarture," *(Re)Oralisierung*, ed. H. L. C. Tristram (Tübingen: G. Narr, 1996), 247–62; Walter Haug, "Von Imram zur Aventiure-Fahrt," *Wolfram-Studien* 1 (1970), 264–98.

[6] To give two examples from the same volume (*The Brendan Legend*, eds. Strijbosch and Burgess, cited above, n. 6): Anna Marie Fagnoni, "Oriental Eremitical Motifs in the *Navigatio sancti Brendani*," 53–80; Peter Christian Jacobsen, "The Island of the Birds in the *Navigatio sancti Brendani*," 99–116.

[7] For example, Dora Faraci, "*Navigatio Sancti Brendani* and its Relationship with *Physiologus*," *Romanobarbarica* 11 (1991), 149–73, p. 155–6.

[8] John Carey, *Ireland and the Grail* (Aberystwyth: Celtic Studies Publications, 2007), pp. 262–4.

[9] Martin Irvine, *The Making of Textual Culture: 'Grammatica' and Literary Theory, 350–1100* (Cambridge: Cambridge University Press, 1994), p. 8. The rest of this description is based on Irvine's account.

commonly, the Bible and its glosses. The label, however, could be extended to any other *auctor* of sufficient *auctoritas*: Virgil, for instance, or the encyclopedist Isidore of Seville. Within this "grammatical culture,"[10] any literary composition worth the name would draw from a common stock of images derived from these authorities, helping to infuse the events under discussion with allegorical resonance. Therefore, understanding the textual background of the *Navigatio* helps to unlock many of the symbols present in the text, often providing insight into some of the finer points of medieval theology.[11] Nonetheless, the story disguises its erudition well, presenting a simple, charming façade, with a strong tendency toward naturalistic detail.[12]

"Naturalistic," however, does not entail actual observation of the natural world, a distinction not always observed in scholarship on the *Navigatio*. Even though few today would claim that the *Navigatio* is true, in the straightforward way that Tom Severin believed as he sailed across the Atlantic in his leather boat,[13] time and again, various aspects of St. Brendan's journey are referred to landmasses and natural phenomena of the North Atlantic, such as icebergs[14] or the Faroe Islands.[15] One scene in particular has been the subject of many such attempts: §§23–4, when Brendan and his monks enter the confines of Hell. In the course of their voyage through this marine Inferno, the travellers encounter fiery mountains, a terrible stench, and ominous rumblings underground. These features are clearly volcanic; and, given that "Ireland is not known for its

---

[10] Irvine, *Textual Culture*, p. 8.

[11] Jacobsen, "Island of the Birds," pp. 108–16.

[12] "Ma certo nessun testo come il nostro ha il potere di rappresentare le soglie dell'aldilà come uno spettacolo della natura." Orlandi and Guglielmetti, notes to *NSB*, p. 171, n. 14.

[13] The subtitle says it all, really: Tim Severin, *The Brendan Voyage: Sailing to America in a Leather Boat to Prove the Legend of the Irish Sailor Saints* (New York: Modern Library, 2000 [1978]).

[14] Selmer, notes to *NSBa*, p. 90, n.85. Cf. Orlandi, "Temi e correnti," p. 562: "Che si tratti di un iceberg, com'è stato suggerito, è una barzelletta."

[15] Wooding, "Monastic Voyaging," pp. 237–41.

high level [of] volcanic activity,"[16] there has been quite a bit of speculation about the source(s) of such a description.[17] Despite the absence of any firm evidence, scholars have, by and large, accepted the tantalizing possibility that the *Navigatio* preserves a record of an early visit to Iceland.[18] I do not mean to deny this possibility here; in fact, I regard it as entirely possible, though not certain.[19] Nevertheless, the focus on a possible eyewitness account has led to a meaningless game of pinpointing *which* volcano, precisely, the travellers saw;[20] this has often obscured other plausible means by which knowledge of volcanoes might have reached the author. For instance, Carl Selmer, in his 1959 edition, noted a general similarity to Book III, ll. 639 ff. of the *Aeneid*—and then

---

[16] "Volcanoes," *Geological Survey Ireland*, Department of Communications, Climate Action, and Environment, 2018. https://www.gsi.ie/en-ie/geoscience-topics/natural-hazards/Pages/Volcanoes.aspx.

[17] This is a long-running tradition in the scholarship: see Selmer, notes to *NSBa*, p. 90, n. 88, where he refers back to suppositions made in 1892 (Mt. Hekla) and 1845 ("the Isle of Teneriffe").

[18] Many accounts state the matter with a great deal of confidence: E.g. Selmer, notes to *NSBa*, p. 90, n.86 ("This episode probably represents the eruption of a volcano which the travelers witnessed on their voyage"); Donnchadh Ó Corráin, "Irish and Nordic Exchange: What They Gave and What They Took," in J. M. Fladmark, ed., *Heritage and Identity: Shaping the Nations of the North* (New York: Routledge, 2015 [2002]), 61–72, at pp. 64–6 ("That knowledge [of the North Atlantic] extended to a volcano, which is well described, and a dramatic account of a volcanic eruption in Iceland," p. 65). Wooding, for his part, is considerably more circumspect: "The vision of barren land with adjacent fiery mountain might come from a classical, perhaps Aegean, source." Jonathan Wooding, "Monastic Voyaging and the *Navigatio*," in Wooding, ed., *Otherworld Voyage*, 226–45, at p. 243.

19 It is strange that what is likely the first written record we have with confirmed knowledge of Iceland—*De mensura orbis terrae*, written by an Irish monk, Dicuil—doesn't mention any volcanic activity on the island. See Wooding, "Monastic Voyaging," pp. 241–4; for the text itself, see Dicuil, *Liber de Mensura Orbis Terrae*, ed. J. J. Tierney, *Scriptores Latini Hiberniae* 6 (Dublin: Dublin Institute for Advanced Studies, 1967), Book VII, §§11–13. For another skeptical take on Irish voyagers, see Arni Hjartarson, "Hekla og Heilagur Brendan," *Saga* 46, no. 1 (2007), 161–71.

20 This tendency does seem to have dropped off in the new millennium, but there has been at least one attempt: Margaret Burrell, ("Hell as a Geological Construct," *Florilegium* 24 [2007]): 37–54) suggests Reykjaneshryggur and Santorini (at pp. 41–2).

dismissed it out of hand, preferring German mythology (explaining the smiths) and vision of Hekla (explaining the rest)[21] Though recent work (especially in the new edition of Guglielmetti and Orlandi) has started to build evidence for possible connections from this segment to other texts,[22] the possible connections of many particular details in the passage to other texts remain unexplored.

What follows is a preliminary attempt at such an exploration. I have consulted texts on a somewhat ad-hoc basis, limiting my focus, by and large, to post-Classical works from before the second half of the eighth century, though I have pointed out Classical parallels where it seemed proper; furthermore, I have searched only within the two broad categories of visions and voyages, as this provides a shared context between a given text and the *Navigatio*. Since proving direct relationships between medieval texts is a thorny process—time-consuming, exhausting, and often inconclusive[23]—I will, in general, avoid claiming that *x* was a source for the *Navigatio*; instead, I will merely note that *x* and the *Navigatio* share common motifs or ideas.[24] Where I do suggest that a text is a source, I have done so for two reasons: one, someone else has proven it to my satisfaction; two, there are one or more direct verbal parallels that, given the context, seem more than coincidental. Lastly, I have attempted to

---

[21] Selmer, notes to *NSBa*, p. 90, n.86.

[22] See the notes to *NSB*, pp. 169–73, also Guglielmetti's introduction, p. lxxv. Several of my ideas regarding which works to pursue (in particular, the *Cosmography*) were provided in these pages; I have cited these notes whenever I reproduce a particular quote or passage mentioned in them below.

[23] See, for instance, Leopold Peeters' attempt to show reliance of the *Navigatio* and its Dutch relative on the thought of Eriugena, and the reaction it provokes in the appended discussion to the article. Peeters, "Neue Perspektiven in den Forschungsstand der *Navigatio Sancti Brendani abbatis* und der Reise-Texte," *De Studie van de Middelnederlandse Letterkunde: Stand en Toekomst: Symposium, Antwerpen, 22–24 September 1988* (*Middeleeuwse studies en bronnen* 14 [1989]), 169–86; pp. 174–82, 185–6.

[24] An article with similar methodology, but with a much wider scope, is Giovanni Orlandi's "Temi e correnti nelle leggende di viaggio dell'Occidente altomedievali," in *Popoli e paesi nella cultura altomedievale: 23–29 aprile 1981*, Settimane di studio del Centro italiano di studi sull'alto Medioevo 29 (Spoleto: Presso la sede del Centro, 1983), 523–71.

confine myself to the physical description of the first two islands in Hell. This is done for convenience: volcanic imagery is, compared to, say, monstrous smiths or foul-looking demons, considerably easier to track in the textual record. Given these limitations, the parallels adduced below will be, of necessity, somewhat impressionistic. Yet, in the end, I am not after plausibility, but rather evidence of shared ideas, and such evidence emerges best by aggregating several different instances of a particular motif. I have selected six such motifs below. They are arranged in no particular order; the way various descriptions repeat themselves throughout the passage at hand would frustrate any strictly logical system of organization.

1. Fire and brimstone

[V]iderunt montem discoopertum a fumo et a se spumantem flammas usque ad aethera et iterum ad se easdem flammas respirantem (§24.10)

They saw the mountain, no longer covered by smoke, and it was spewing flames from itself up to the ether and breathing them in again back to itself

. . . atque ad nares ingens fetor. (§23.14)

. . . and a great stench [came] to [their] noses

Although it is hard to imagine a Hell without lapping flames and pits of sulfur, it had to be invented at some point, and from there somehow conveyed into lands where volcanic activity—the basis for such imagery—was unknown.[25] While the creation of a volcanic Hell was long prior to the composition of the *Navigatio*, two important early medieval reference works of the early seventh century provide a connection between particular Mediterranean volcanoes and Hell: Gregory's *Dialogues*, wherein a monk reports having see the former King Theodoric trapped inside the pit of Vulcano;[26] and in the work *De Natura Rerum* by Isidore of Seville, who states that Etna is a prefiguration of Gehenna,

---

[25] See Thomas O'Loughlin, "The Gates of Hell: From Metaphor to Fact," *Milltown Studies* 38 (1996): 98–114.

[26] Gregory, *Dialogues*, ed. Adalbert de Vogüé (Paris: Les éditions du Cerf, 1978–80): IV.31 (vol. 3); see O'Loughlin, "The Gates of Hell," pp. 99–102.

"whose perpetual fires" will torment sinners "into the ages of ages."[27] The *Cosmography of Aethicus Ister*, a deeply strange, perhaps parodic work of the early eighth century,[28] also makes the direct connection:

> . . . *a parte inferorum prope gehennam fontem manantem, ob uaporem terribilem illius ardoris ipsum fontem feruescentem, et fauillas inferorum illuc decendetes crepitare, nam ut Ethna et Vulgaus aut Cimera, quae ex sulphoria terra . . .*[29]

> . . . at the part of the underworld near Gehenna {there is} a dripping fountain, {and} the same fountain seethes on account of the terrible vapour from that heat, and ashes of the underworld falling from it crackle, for it emits fire and brimstone just like Aetna or Vulcan or Chimaera, which {pour these out} from the sulphurous earth . . .

Above all, however, it is *Visio Pauli* that matches this milieu the best.[30] Sulfur, molten fire, demons snatching away a woebegone sinner

---

[27] "*Constat* [Aetna] *autem ad exemplum Gehennae, cuius ignis perpetua incendia spirabunt ad puniendos peccatores qui cruciabuntur in saecula saeculorum.*" Isidore of Seville, *Isidore de Séville: Traité de la nature; suivi de l'Épître en vers du roi Sisibut à Isidore*, ed. Jacques Fontaine, Bibliothèque de l'École des Hautes Études Hispaniques 28 (Bordeaux: Féret, 1960): §48.4, p. 422–3; qtd. in O'Loughlin, "The Gates of Hell," p. 104.

[28] Michael Herren, ed. and trans., *The Cosmography of Aethicus Ister* (Turnhout: Brepols, 2011); henceforth *CAI*. While Orlandi suggests the *Cosmography* had an Irish background, though written on the continent ("Temi e correnti," pp. 550–1), Herren prefers to see the author as from the hinterland of the Eastern Mediterranean (Sklavinia?), and who composed the text at, perhaps, Malmesbury and Bobbio, completing it shortly after 727 (Herren, introduction to *CAI*, pp. lv–lccviii). For its genre, see idem, pp. xvi–xx. I am not the first to note its similarity to the *Navigatio*; see note in Guglielmetti and Orlandi, *NSB*, p. 171, n. 14.

[29] *CAI* §59a.12–15. All translations are Herren's; words in curly brackets are his as well.

[30] The textual history of the *Visio Pauli* (henceforth *VP*) and its various relations and descendants is extremely complicated, as the Lenka Jiroušková's recent edition demonstrates. Some forms of the text were clearly in existence by the time the *Navigatio* was written, and Irish monks certainly had access to it, as two of the many redactions demonstrate. When I do quote from the *Visio Pauli*, I have made sure to

into the bowels of Hell[31] there are any number of images in the *Visio* and the *Navigatio* that seem to draw on some common stock of imagery[32]

Regarding the smell: Scripture often uses sulfur as a symbol of divine wrath;[33] moreover, visions of Hell often mention a wretched odor, as in Bede:

> *Sed et fetor incomparabilis cum eisdem uaporibus ebulliens omnia illa tenebrarum loca replebat[.]*

> Also, an incomparable stench, welling up with these vapors, filled all these places of darkness.[34]

So, too, the *Cosmography*:

> *Infernum in [ima parte] infimo uoraginem asperum [in] baratrum fore teterrimum ab alto sulphure.*

> {He says that} hell is a pungent whirlpool in the deepest part {of the world}, an abyss most foul from the deep sulphur.[35]

As for the odd image of the volcano "respiring," Guglielmetti cites the vision of Wenlock in a letter of St. Boniface's.[36] This appears to be a

---

cite a reading present in multiple textual traditions, unless noted otherwise. Charles Wright, "Some Evidence for an Irish Origin of Redaction XI of the *Visio Pauli*," *Manuscripta* 34/5 (1990/1), 34–44; Lenka Jiroušková, ed., *Die Visio Pauli: Wege und Wandlungen einer oreientalischen Apokryphe im lateinischen Mittelalter* (Leiden: Brill, 2006).

[31] At the very least, *Visio Pauli* should put paid to the suggestion by Selmer, notes to *NSBa*, n.87, that the similar scene in the *Navigatio* may represent some poor soul falling into Icelandic lava.

[32] Here is a single example, which likewise features leaping flames: "*Et erat ibi flumen ut ignis fervens et fluctibus eius exaltans usque ad celum*" ("And there was a river like boiling fire and reaching with its waves up to the sky"). *VP* A.7b.

[33] O'Loughlin, "The Gates of Hell," p. 113, n.30, lists Genesis 19.24, Deuteronomy 29.23, Job 18.15, Isaiah 30.33, 34.9, and Ezekiel 38.22.

[34] *EH* V.12, 490.

[35] *CAI* §5.1–2.

[36] "*Et in circuitu totius mundi ignem ardentem videbam et flammam inmensae magnitudinis anhelantes et terribiliter ad superiora ascendentem, non aliter pene quam ut sub uno globo totius mundi machinam complectentem . . .*" Epist. 10, *Epistolae Merowingici et Karolini aevi*, ed. Societas Aperiendis Fontibus Rerum Germanicarum

somewhat common trope; Bede's *Ecclesiastical History* features a similar passage in the vision of Dryhthelm.[37]

2. Hell in the North.

Sic ferebatur per octo dies navicula contra aquilonem. (§22.21)

Thus the little boat was carried for eight days into the north.

The combination of Hell, fire, and brimstone has lingered on well past the Middle Ages; the notion that Hell is located to the north, however, has not. Yet this, too, had a widespread following in early medieval texts.[38] Whatever its origins, such deep distrust of the higher latitudes receives a certain amount of Scriptural support in the book of Jeremiah:

> *et dixit Dominus ad me / ab aquilone pandetur malum super omnes habitatores terrae[.]*

> and the Lord said to me / evil shall be extended from the north over all the inhabitants of the earth.[39]

The *Cosmography* takes this passage as a starting-point for a long diatribe against the various regions of the barbarian North, "mother of dragons," and "pit of demons."[40] In the vision of Dryhthelm, the imagined locations of Hell and Paradise are directly opposed to each other: Hell is to the northeast, "against the rising of the solstice sun," while Paradise is

---

Medii Aevi, Monumenta Germaniae Historica, vol. 3, second ed. (Berlin: Weidmann, 1957), pp. 252–3; qtd. in Guglielmetti and Orlandi, notes to NSB, p. 173, n. 10.

[37] Bede, *Bede's Ecclesiastical History of the English People*, eds. and trans. Bertram Colgrave and R. A. Mynors (Oxford: Clarendon, 1969) [*EH* henceforth]: "*At cum idem globi ignium sine intermissione modo alta peterent, modo ima baratri repeterent, cerno omnia quae ascendebant fastigia flammarum plena esse spiritibus hominum, qui instar fauillarum cum fumo ascendentium nunc ad sublimiora proicerentur, nunc retractis ignium vaporibus relaberentur in profunda[.]*" V.12, 490.

[38] Claude Carozzi, *Le voyage de l'âme dans l'au-delà d'après la littérature Latine (V^e–XIIIe siècle)* (Rome: École Française de Rome, 1994), p. 290.

[39] Jeremiah 1.14: Robert Weber and Roger Gryson, eds., Biblia Sacra: Iuxta Vulgatam versionem, fifth ed. (Stuttgart: Deutsche Bibelgesellschaft, 2007).

[40] "O et tu aquilon! / mater draconum / et nutrix scorpionum / fouea serpentium / lacusque demonum" (CAI §33.19–23).

associated with the southeast, and the summer solstice.[41] A similar orientation is also present in the *Visio Pauli*:

> *Et tulit illum a[d] septentrionem, hoc est in orientem partem super puteum signatum sigillis septem*

> And he brought him to the north, that is in the eastern part above the pit of the seven seals.[42]

3. A barren, rocky, uncultivated land

> *Transactis autem diebus octo viderunt insulam non longe, valde rusticam, saxosam atque scoriosam, sine arboribus et herba. (§23.1)*

> After eight days had gone by, they saw an island not far away, quite uncultivated, rocky and slag-filled, without trees or grass.

We should not take this as a straightforward description of the Icelandic countryside. Virgil refers to the "smoking rocks" (*fumantibus . . . saxis*) of Vulcano;[43] the *Cosmography* describes Hell in similar terms:

> *"In ipsos enim montes," inquid, "nullius arboris uirgultum aut saltus uirentia folia aut sucrulis emitti possunt."*

> "In these same mountains," he says, "there is no shoot of a tree, nor can the greening leaves of the woodland be emitted from branches."[44]

Some have seen this passage as describing a new-born volcanic island, like Surtsey;[45] I would rather put it down to rocky barrenness just being part of how volcanoes, and northern climes in general, were described.[46]

---

[41] EH V.12, p. 488. That is, northeast, as opposed to Paradise, which lies to the southeast (EH V.12, p. 492).

[42] VP A.28.

[43] *Aeneid* VIII.417. Virgil. *Aeneid*: Books 7–12. Appendix Virgiliana. Translated by H. Rushton Fairclough. Revised by G. P. Goold. Loeb Classical Library 64. (Cambridge, MA: Harvard University Press, 1918).

[44] CAI §59b.4–6.

[45] Guglielmetti and Orlandi, notes to NSB, p. 171, n. 14.

The allegorical thrust of this description hinges on two words: *rusticam* and *scoriosam*. The first may seem simple enough: literally, it means "of the countryside," and is often used neutrally in opposition to *urbanus*, though moral judgments often work their way into the connotations. As is the case today, what is 'rustic' could either connote some form of moral purity, untainted by city ways, or of retrograde unsophistication. Given the context, we may safely suspect 'rusticus,' here, is not intended in a particularly positive manner.

But what does the word mean, precisely, in this context? Typically, *rusticus* is an adjective used for people, not land; it is frequently substantive, a synonym for 'peasant' or 'villein,' or some such provincial laborer. Virgil, for instance, uses it three times, all in reference to humans.[47] There is no sign this ever changed; *rusticus*, in the *Dictionary of Medieval Latin from British Sources*, covers much the same ground.[48] What, then, is meant by "*insula rustica*"? In all likelihood, the word is only intended to stress the lack of communal spirit: the opposite of the busy *civitas* of the monastery. Both the ugly smiths and the virtuous monks have their own cells, but only one group lives *unanimiter*:

> *Erat enim habitatio eorum sparse; tamen, unanimiter illorum conversatio in spe et fide et caritate, una refectio, ad opus Dei una ecclesia perficiendum.*

> For they dwelled apart: nonetheless, their way of life was as one in hope and faith and charity: a single place for eating; for doing the work of God, a single church.[49]

---

[46] CAI §19.2–3: " ... nullo umquam tempore in eas nihil uiride aut floridum, quandoquidem nullatenus[que] prae rigore ualeant." CAI §20.8–9: "Quae reuera sicut illa nimio frigore inculta, ma<r>ceda, sterelis adeo in diuersa torreda ac pruinose a septentione."

47 *Georgics* II.405–6, ("*acer curas uenientem extendit in annum / rusticus*"); *Eclogues* II.56 ("*Rusticus es, Corydon*"); *Eclogues* III.84 ("Pollio amat nostram, quamvis est rustica, Musam"). Virgil. *Eclogues. Georgics. Aeneid: Books 1–6.* Translated by H. Rushton Fairclough. Revised by G. P. Goold. Loeb Classical Library 63. Cambridge, MA: Harvard University Press, 1916.

[48] *Dictionary of Medieval Latin from British Sources* (Brepols, 2015) s.v. *rusticus*.

[49] *NSB* §1.11.

For its part, *scoriosus* refers to *scoria*, the broken lumps of rock and ore left over from the smelting process.[50] This word is unattested outside the *Navigatio*,[51] but there is no reason to consider it a possible scribal error—if the island is one enormous smithy, the neologism makes a good deal of sense. Furthermore, there is a certain Scriptural justice to Hell being '*scorious*':

> *fili hominis versa est mihi domus Israhel in scoriam /*
> *omnes isti aes et stannum et ferrum et plumbum / in medio*
> *fornacis scoria argenti facti sunt / propterea haec dicit*
> *Dominus Deus / eo quod versi estis omnes in scoriam /*
> *propterea ecce ego congregabo vos in medio Hierusalem*
> */ congregatione argenti et aeris et stanni et ferri et plumbi*
> *in medio fornacis / ut succendam in ea ignem ad*
> *conflandum / sic congregabo in furore meo et in ira mea*
> *et requiescam et conflabo vos[.]*[52]

> Son of man, the house of Israel has become dross to me: all of them bronze and tin and iron and lead in the middle of the furnace: they have become the dross of silver. Therefore the Lord God says: Since you have all become dross, lo, I will therefore gather you in the middle of Jerusalem, with the gathering of silver and bronze and tin and iron and lead, in the middle of the furnace, so I may kindle a fire in it to refine [the gathering]. Thus I will gather [you] in my fury, and in my rage and I will rest and I will melt and refine you.

Given that one unfortunate monk is snatched to away to burn in Hell, the metaphor follows: the monks' passage by the island is like ore's passage through a medieval bloomery, where the metal escapes, and the dross is left.

In combination, these two adjectives create a familiar contrast between the evils of human industry (all the monsters are smiths, living by

---

[50] Nancy Edwards, *The Archaeology of Early Medieval Ireland* (Philadelphia: University of Pennsylvania Press, 1990), pp. 86–92.

[51] Guglielmetti and Orlandi, notes to *NSB*, p. 169, n. 1.

[52] Ezekiel 22:18–20.

themselves in their own little caves) and the richness of nature's gifts (by which, for instance, the hermit Paul is supported in §26 of the *Navigatio*, until he ceases to need food at all). This opposition is ancient; it is found, for instance, in the Book of Genesis.[53]

4. Smithing, Volcanic Action

Ergo illis praetereuntibus parumper quasi iactus lapidis, audierunt sonitus follium sufflantium quasi tonitruum, atque malleorum collisiones contra ferrum et cudes. (§23.3)

Thus swiftly passing by [the island] about a stone's throw [away], they heard the sound of breathing bellows, like thunder, and the striking of hammers against iron and anvils.

This description parallels Virgil's account of Vulcano quite straightforwardly: smiths, volcano, thunder, hammers.[54] The *Aeneid* is, in all likelihood, not the only origin of this description (the comparison between this scene and one in *ICMD*, which has smiths but no volcanic rumbling, is instructive),[55] but there is a clear relationship here between the Roman text and the Irish.

5. Burning Sea

Nam ubi cecidit in mare coepit fervere, quasi ruina montis ignei fuisset ibi, et ascendebat fumus de mare sicut de clibano ignis. (§23.10)

---

[53] According to Genesis, Cain founded the first city, and his great-great-great-great grandson invented smithing: Genesis 4:17–22.

[54] Virgil, *Aeneid*, VIII.416–23: *Insula Sicanium iuxta latus Aeoliamque/ erigitur Liparen fumantibus ardua saxis,/ quam subter specus et Cyclopum exesa caminis/ antra Aetnaea tonant, validique incudibus ictus/ auditi referunt gemitus, striduntque cavernis/ stricturae Chalybum et fornacibus ignis anhelat,/ Volcani domus et Volcania nomine tellus./ huc tunc ignipotens caelo descendit ab alto.* This reference from Guglielmetti, introduction to *NSB*, p. lxxv. See the notes to *NSB*, p. 170, n. 8, for several more parallels (suggested by Neil Wright)

[55] *The Voyage of Máel Dúin: A Study in Early Irish Voyage Literature*, ed. H. P. A. Oskamp (Groningen: Wolters-Noordhof, 1970), §21.

IS ICELAND HELL?

[. . .]

et simul apparuit quasi tota arsa illa insula sicut unus globus, et mare aestuabat sicut cacabus plenus carnibus aestuans quando bene ministratur ab igne (§23.13)

And [the place] where it fell in the sea began to boil, as if the ruin of a fire-mount were there, and smoke rose from the sea as if from a fire-pot.[56]

[. . .]

and at once the island appeared as though utterly burnt, just like a single round mass (?), and the sea simmered like a simmering cauldron filled with meat, when it is well tended-to by the fire

This passage in particular has been linked to a "subterranean eruption" on Iceland.[57] Yet the words used to construct this image echo other accounts. The word 'fire-pot' (above, *clibano ignis*) perhaps derives from Biblical commentary, on either Genesis 15:17 or Psalms 20:10.[58] Bede, in his glosses to the Genesis text, claims,

*Haec caligo et **clibanus ignis** post occasum solis factus significat iam in fine seculi per ignem iudicandos esse carnales.*

This darkness and **the fire-pot** created after the setting of the sun already signifies that, at the end of time, flesh shall be judged by fire.[59]

---

[56] "Fire pot" is the translation of the phrase in the *The New Oxford Annotated Bible* (New Revised Standard Version [NRSV]), third ed. (Oxford: Oxford UP, 2007), Gen. 15:17.

[57] Orlandi and Guglielmetti, notes to *NSB*, p. 171, n. 14.

[58] Ps. 21:9, in the NRSV.

[59] Bede, *Libri quattuor in principium Genesis usque ad natiuitatem Isaac et eiectionem Ismahelis adnotationum*, ed. C. W. Jones (Turnout: Brepols, 1967), CCSL 118A: IV.15. Interestingly, a branch of the *Visio Pauli* manuscript tradition seems to make the same connection: "*Et erat ibi draco ingens... et erant oculi eius ardentes tamquam clibanus ignis*" (*VP* A1.13, StO², p. 514); both other A1 manuscripts presented use "*clibanus ignis.*" All three manuscripts are from the twelfth to thirteenth centuries (*VP* pp. 30, 45–6, 123–4). According to Jiroušková, however, "It is . . . the sub-group A1 which represents the closest textual form (*Textgestalt*) of the HF [Hell-

His description, in turn, may derive from liturgical practice, as can be seen in this excerpt from the Stowe Missal (written at Tallaght around 800):[60]

> *Nec té lateat Satanas inminere tibi poenas inmine[re] tibi Gehinam diem iudici diem suplicii sempiterni diem qui uenturus est uelud **clibanus ignis** ardens in quo tibi adque angelis tuis sempiternus preparatus est interitus et ideo pro tua nequitia dampnate atque damnande.*

> Nor let it be hidden to you, Satan, your threatening with punishments, with Gehenna, the day of judgment, the day of eternal suffering, the day which draws nigh like a burning **fire-pot** in which ruin was ever-prepared for you and your angels and thus by your iniquity condemned and condemning.[61]

This text is a variant of the baptismal exorcism (i.e., "the prayer of exorcism over the baptismal candidates, which originally took place on the morning of Easter Saturday") present in other early-medieval liturgies.[62] These other rites, though, typically refer only to a *clibanus*, not the *clibanus ignis* of Bede and the *Navigatio*; given, however, that the Bible itself vacillates between just *clibanus* (Gen. 15:17) and *clibanum ignis* (Ps. 20:10), the conclusion that one of these texts influenced the other does not follow. Furthermore, as befits the rather Apocalyptic milieu, this passage features syntax similar to the Book of Revelations' description of an

---

versions, *Hölle-Fassungen*] to the HHF [Heaven-Hell-versions, *Himmel-Hölle-Fassungen*, i.e. the Latin descendant of the original Greek]" (*VP* p. 276). Given the difference in context there is likely no relation.

[60] Introduction to *The Stowe Missal: MS. D. II. 3 in the Library of the Royal Irish Academy, Dublin*, ed. George F. Warner (London: Harrison and Sons, 1915), Henry Bradshaw Society, vol. 32.

[61] *Stowe Missal*, p. 26. That Bede may have had this rite in mind is indicated by the end of the next paragraph: "*in nomine domini nostri Iesu Christi qui iudicaturus est iudicare uiuos et mortuos et saeculum per ignem*", "in the name of our lord Jesus Christ who shall soon [come to] judge the quick and the dead and the world through fire" (with *iudicaturus* a likely mistake for *venturus*).

[62] G. M. Lukken, *Original Sin in the Roman Liturgy: Research into the Theology of Original Sin in the Roman Sacramentaria and the Early Baptismal Liturgy* (Leiden: Brill, 1973), at pp. 32–33.

infernal pit, where the "smoke arises" "just as" smoke from a furnace, beclouding the sky.[63]

Regarding the second passage, in the *Cosmography*, a passage describes a river that runs through Hell in much the same manner:

> . . . *mare in tam magno feruore turbolento fore, ita ut nullus accessus fieri possit, quia quemadmodum sartago fervens in calore et uapore ignis, ita mare in modum sartaginis ingressu ipsius amnis feruescit.*

> . . . the sea is in such great and turbulent ferment that no access is possible, for just as a frying-pan seethes with the heat and steam of the fire, so the sea, like a frying-pan, seethes at the entrance of the same River.[64]

In the *Cosmography*, this description occurs near the entrance to Hell. Thus, in a very similar context, we are faced with very similar imagery, even if the texts differ with regards to the terminology of the cooking vessel.[65] Was this a common way to describe infernal waters in the Middle Ages? If not, what explains its presence in both texts?

Lastly, some comment should be made on the phrase "*quasi ruina monti* . . ." which is rather hard to parse ("as if the remnants/debris/ruin of a [fire-]mount were there"?).[66] Based on the texts contained in Brepols' databases,[67] the phrase "*ruina[que] montis*," prior to the tenth century, is limited to both Plinies, the *Navigatio*, and a handful of other texts. At first glance, then, this passage seems to contain a striking parallel with the

---

[63] "*et aperuit puteum abyssi / et ascendit fumus putei sicut fumus fornacis magnae / et obscuratus est sol et aer de fumo putei*" Revelations 9:2

[64] *CAI* §59c.10–12.

[65] There is a similar metaphor on the previous page: " '*tunc enim,* ' inquid, '*strepidum undarum feruentium quasi in olla uel cacabum cernentes contemplantur[.]* '" *CAI* §59a.8–9.

[66] Selmer, p. 97, conjectures "*pruna,*" on no evidence.

[67] Brepolis (Brepols Publishers Online), Cross-Database Searchtool, Brepols, 2018. Searching for 'ruina* + monti*' in the Cross-Database Searchtool gives 70 results, drawn from every Latin text Brepols has made available online. All but a few of the results were either written well past 800, or were false positives (i.e., 'ruin*' and 'monti*' belonged to separate clauses).

letter on Vesuvius by Pliny the Younger.[68] In this letter, Pliny describes how ash and rock fell down on his uncle's boat from above:

> *Iam nauibus cinis incidebat, quo propius accederent, calidior et densior; iam pumices etiam nigrique et ambusti et fracti igne lapides; iam uadum subitum* **ruinaque montis** *litora obstantia.*

> Already the ash fell upon the boats, [growing] hotter and thicker as they neared; already the pumice-stones were blackened and scorched and shattered by fire; already a sudden shallowness and the **mountain's ruin** were blocking the shore.[69]

While the context is of note—burning rocks falling down from the sky—this is probably no more than coincidence: why should the author of the *Navigatio*, of all texts, have access to a letter unattested for centuries in either direction? [70]

---

[68] Pliny the Elder, in his *Natural History*, twice uses a version of the same while discussing various mining techniques: "*ruina montium*," "the debris of the mountains" (33.xxi, §66, §74). In between these two instances, there is a detour to metallurgy, where slag is mentioned (§69). *Natural History, Volume IX: Books 33–5*, ed. E. F. Warmington, Loeb Classical Library vol. 394.

[69] Pliny, Pliny the Younger, *C. Caecilii Plinii Secundi Epistolarum libri decem*, ed. R. A. B. Mynors (Oxford: Clarendon Press, 1963), VI.xvi.11.

[70] The greatest obstacle to this parallel is the matter of the author's access to the text. There is little scholarly discussion of Pliny's transmission after Antiquity; what is known, though, is unpromising: Betty Radice bluntly states, "In the writings of the Middle Ages he leaves no trace." (Betty Radice, introduction to Pliny the Younger, *Letters, Books 1–7; Panegyricus*, trans. Betty Radice, Loeb Classical Library 55 [Cambridge, MA: Harvard UP, 1969]). The fullest account of the transmission can be found in Mynors' introduction to the Oxford edition, pp. v–xxii. ***Ruinaque montis***, *cf. ruitura montium* in the same passage of the *Cosmography* discussed above (§59b.12) is also suggestive. As Michael Herren suggests (review of *NSB*, p. 386), it is worth considering whether these two texts may be related. If they are, it would place the *Navigatio*'s composition within a much narrower timeframe than currently obtains.

6. Wind

*"Filioli, **tendite** in altum plus **vela** . . . atque fugiamus istam insulam." (§23.7)*

. . .

Et statim rapidissimo cursu ventus traxit illos ad litus eiusdem insulae[.] (§24.2)

. . .

Iterum arripuit illos prosper ventus ad australem plagam. (§24.9)

"Little sons, stretch out the sails to greater height . . . and let us flee this island."

. . .

And at once the wind brought them, very rapidly, to the shore of the same island[.]

. . .

Again a favorable wind snatched them to the south.

In both §23 and §24, the same pattern presents itself: the wind blows the ship to the island; in §24, the wind—blowing from the north—delivers them. This is in clear imitation of *Aeneid* III, where the wind causes the Trojans to drift towards Etna (albeit by deserting them, not by blowing— *ventus cum sole reliquit*); the next day, a north wind saves them from the Cyclopes, Scylla, and Charybdis.[71] This scene provides several close verbal parallels to the *Navigatio*. The first quote above reflects ll. 682–3 of the *Aeneid*: *"praecipitis metus acer agit quocumque rudentis / excutere et ventis **intendere vela** secundis"* (a parallel supported by Brendan's uncharacteristic exhortation to "flee").[72] Further evidenece of the adaptation is the change from "Boreas" (the personified North Wind) to "ad australem plagam," "towards the south."[73] The author thereby rids his text of the obvious Classical reference and holds onto the substance.

Most, if not all, of the details in *Navigatio*'s description of Hell cited above are congruent with other early medieval visions of the afterlife or

---

[71] Virgil, *Aeneid*, III.568; 687–8.

[72] "Sharp fear of danger drives [us] to cast out the rigging wherever and stretch out the sails for favorable winds."

73 *"ecce autem Boreas... / missus adest."* Virgil, *Aeneid*, III.687–8.

Classical accounts of volcanic eruptions. This does not rule out a voyage from Europe to Iceland and back in the early Middle Ages, from which certain details made their way into the text. In the end, however, §§23–4 of the *Navigatio* describe neither Hekla, Vulcano, nor Etna; there is not now, nor was there then, any volcano on Earth that precisely fulfills the different attributes contained in the passage. Viewing this island through the lens of Iceland, tempting though it may be, brushes aside those nuances, and waves away the many unnatural oddities present within the text, many of which are clearly taken from exegetical or visionary material. For instance, when the volcano breathes its smoke back in (possible in Hollywood, perhaps, but not in reality),[74] it's not that the author of the *Navigatio* is retailing some garbled vision of Icelandic volcanism; rather, he is hewing to the visionary, exegetical tradition of Bede and Boniface. Therefore, to determine just which islands Irish monks had visited, we must first reckon with what texts they had read, what purpose a given detail in the desciption serves—and, most fundamentally, what sort of truth the story is trying to tell.

In a well-known article, Gregory Toner stresses the necessity of "tak[ing] seriously the claims of medieval authors to be telling, or at least seeking, the truth";[75] at heart, the need to find Iceland in the *Navigatio* stems from a misguided application of this dictum, conflating our own version of the truth with the author's. Certainly, there is no reason to doubt the sincerity of the *Navigatio*'s tale; the text takes a great deal of care to portray a vision of Hell congruent with scholarly commentary and tradition: its position in a volcano, its location in the north, and so on. In short, its depiction of Hell is one that strives to place itself within the bounds of believability. In a way, therefore, the *Navigatio* simply engages in the sort of persuasion I am doing right now: it presents a varation on familiar ideas, and adds, as support, useful details and references to suitable authorities. Yet just because the text tells a particular version of

---

74 Unfortunately, this problem does not seem to have been considered in great detail by vulcanologists. See, however, "Can a volcano suck stuff back in?" *Yahoo! Answers*. Yahoo.com. Accessed April 4 2019.
https://answers.yahoo.com/question/index?qid=20120323141147AAF5hJB
[75] Gregory Toner, "The Ulster Cycle: Historiography or Fiction?" *Cambrian Medieval Celtic Studies* 40 (2000), 1–20, at p. 19.

"the truth" does not mean we should go looking for demonstrable facts. Geologic reality should not be the final comparandum of the *Navigatio*; many of the details in the passage, whatever their ultimate source, were carefully chosen to fit the wider exegetical and allegorical thrust of the story. Rather than crisp cartographic accuracy, the *Navigatio* presents us a landscape shaped to a different sort of truth, where the landmarks are not shoals or headlands, but texts. In other words, St. Brendan may have gone to Iceland—but Aeneas went to Etna first.

Abstracts of Other Papers Read at the
Thirty-Eighth Harvard Celtic Colloquium

What, if anything, is Gruffudd Gryg's
Yr Ywen uwchben Bedd Dafydd?
John K. Bollard

Modern tradition continues to assert that Dafydd ap Gwilym lies buried under the ancient yew that grows beside St. Mary's parish church at Strata Florida. The earliest evidence for such a belief is found in Gruffudd Gryg's poem Yr Ywen uwchben Bedd Dafydd. However, this poem is classified by many as a *marwnad ffug*, a false elegy composed while Dafydd was still alive. If that were the case, then the poem itself may have been an important contributor to, if not indeed the progenitor of, the tradition of the Strata Florida burial, in contradistinction to the sixteenth-century evidence that Dafydd was buried at Talyllychau Abbey. This paper will re-examine Gruffudd Gryg's poem in the light of the other likely *marwnadau ffug* by the fourteenth-century *cywyddwyr*, as well as that of their true elegies, *marwnadau gwir*, if you will, in order to assess the poem's place among Gruffudd's oeuvre and in his relationship with Dafydd, and in the context of the development of the *cywydd* as a medium suitable for lament alongside the ancient and more prestigious *awdl*.

On the Historical Dimension in the Inter-Comprehension Between
Dialects in Modern Breton
Myrzinn Boucher-Durand

On the historical dimension in the inter-comprehension between dialects in Modern Breton: this presentation is a case study of the more recent and more frequent use of the post-positioned preposition 'a' as a means of replacing the pronoun in preverbial positions in the KLT dialects. It also considers the difficulties raised by the conservatism of the pronoun form in the Vannetais dialect.

ABSTRACTS

ML 4080 "The Seal Woman" in Its Irish
and International Context
Gregory R. Darwin

The migratory legend known as "The Seal Woman" or "The Mermaid Legend" (ML 4080) recounts how a human man captures an aquatic supernatural female being (mermaid, selkie, etc.) by stealing her magical cloak or skin, without which she cannot return to the water. She remains on land, often marrying her captor and having children with him, until one day she recovers her stolen skin or cloak and returns home to the sea. This legend has been collected throughout Ireland, Scotland, Iceland, the Faroe Islands, and continental Scandinavia, from as early as the end of the eighteenth century, and continues to be told up until the present day.

As part of the preparation of my doctoral dissertation, I spend the 2017–2018 academic year visiting archives in Ireland, Scotland, Norway, and Sweden, and have assembled a catalogue of nearly 500 individual versions of this legend from published and archival sources. In this presentation, I discuss the size of this corpus, the geographic distribution of the legend, and its demographics: especially the gender and age of informants and collectors, and the patterns of transmission which can be traced. I also examine the distribution of a number of specific details, such as the depiction of the supernatural woman as a mermaid or seal-woman, the location where the man hides her stolen skin or cloak, or the means by which the woman recovers this object, and argue on the basis of these details that the legend disseminated from the Gaelic-speaking world to eastern Scotland, and to the Nordic countries via the Shetland and Orkney islands.

'A most venerable ruin': word, image
and ideology in Guest's Geraint
Sioned Davies

This paper will explore the relationship between text and image in Charlotte Guest's English translation of Geraint, first published in 1840. In her revised second edition (1877), she firmly re-iterates the tale's links with Cardiff Castle in an attempt, I would argue, to anchor events firmly in the South Wales landscape. By doing so she is reminding her readers of the Welsh context of Geraint in the wake of Tennyson's appropriation of the tale in his Idylls of the King.

Laryngeal Realism, Articulatory Phonetics, and Early Insular Celtic Orthography
Joe Eska

It has been the communis opinio since at least Kenneth Jackson's Language and history in early Britain that early Insular Celtic orthography is based upon Latin orthography after a time at which the pronunciation of Latin in Britain had assimilated to the neo-Brittonic phonological system. Of this there can be no doubt. It has been assumed, however, that the neo-Brittonic contrast between the plosive series was via the laryngeal feature [voice] and that the frication of 'voiced' plosives occurred shortly before the earliest non-ogam attestations of the Insular Celtic languages. We now know that both of these assumptions are incorrect. This paper describes the chronology, phonology, and articulatory phonetics of lenition in Celtic and outlines how we should understand the rationale for the features of early Insular Celtic orthography and its subsequent development.

Stops and Sonority: the Historical-Phonological Development of S+Consonant Clusters in Irish
Mary Gilbert

In Modern Irish, there are some sequences of consonants that appear to pose some interesting irregularities. The consonant clusters sp, sm, st, sk, and sc do not undergo mutation, and are present in initial 3-consonant clusters, the longest allowable in Irish base forms (i.e. not induced by mutation). Cross-dialectically, they also do not always palatalize with slender vowels, as would be expected. In Old Irish, they are already displaying more unusual behavior in unexpected patterns of deletion, reduction, and assimilation. In Old Irish poetry, which was heavily alliterative, the consonant clusters sb/sp, sd/st, sg/sc, and sm only alliterate with the identical consonant cluster, i.e. not with other clusters and not with just initial s and a vowel, in contrast to sequences like sl, sn, sr, which can alliterate with each other or with initial s and a vowel. The question is, then, why and how do these clusters display such unexpected behavior?

In this paper, I will seek to explain these irregularities with a historical-phonological analysis. This analysis will also consider modern phonetic data, articulatory phonology, phonological theories of single vs. complex segments, and cross-linguistic research about sC clusters, which behave atypically across languages, to comprehensively describe the development of these historical patterns in Irish. While the focus of this paper is on phonology and historical linguistics, I will strive to make the argument as accessible as possible to people who have had minimal exposure to these fields.

Reading Objects, Exchanging Meaning: Material Culture in the 'Four Branches of the Mabinogi'
Jerry Hunter

This paper will examine aspects of the "Four Branches of the Mabinogi," focussing on the role of material culture. In addition to considering objects in terms of immediate narrative function, their place in broader patterns of unfolding meaning will be discussed. While the analysis will touch upon all four tales, the focus will be on the Second and Third Branches—more specifically, the character Llassar Llaes Gyfnewit (or Gygnwyt) and the *calch llasar* used by Manawydan and Pryderi to colour items which they fashion. It will be suggested that the tales are driven in part by a thematic emphasis on creation, transaction and circulation, both in terms of exchanging goods and exchanging meaning. This reading will be set against the backdrop of cultural and economic connections between Wales, Ireland and England.

Piracy in the Celtic and Breton areas
in the Lower Middle Ages
Kentigwern Jaouen

Giving an account of piracy as a phenomenon in the late Middle Age equates to giving a picture of the maritime and economical activities in the Celtic areas. It is a recurring phenomenon undergoing profound changes during the last three centuries of the medieval period, as well as being the centre of diplomatic, economical and social exchanges between the different Celtic populations of Ireland, Wales, Scotland, Brittany, and, to a certain extent, the Iberian Peninsula. Sea-going piracy, through its central aspect to all exchanges, links the different 'Celtic' countries in a tangible way. The contacts, violent or not, are reflected in this piracy, where the sea is used as a chessboard.

Brittany is at the heart of this Celto-Atlantic space, where it plays a key role. As the centre of this maritime network, Brittany witnessed all the struggles. The Breton powers were the main participants of the different interactions, be it diplomatic or martial. Through the prism of piracy, it is the everyday life of the maritime populations of the Celtic areas that we can uncover.

Filial Duty in the Welsh Gentry: The Saleburys of Rhug as Fatherless Sons, 1581–1660
Sadie Jarrett

The relationship between a father and his son was an important aspect of the early modern gentleman's education. In particular, the plethora of contemporary advice books demonstrates the value attributed to that relationship. However, there is considerable scope to understand how the early death of a father affected his sons, including their relationship with each other and the wider family. This paper explores how a son gained an understanding of the roles and responsibilities of the Welsh gentry, including filial duty, despite the early death of his father. When John Salesbury of Rhug died in 1581, he left three sons still in their minority. Using family correspondence, estate papers and legal records, this study assesses how the three sons were integrated into their kinship networks. It also examines the relationship between the youngest son, William Salesbury, and his own children. The paper finds that the fatherless sons of John Salesbury were supported by their kinship networks. These networks could produce strong bonds that remained with the Salesburys even once they reached their majority. Despite John's early death, there is clear evidence that at least one of his sons had a strong sense of filial duty, expressed in his relationship with his own sons. This paper therefore highlights the importance of the Welsh gentry's kinship network for the support and education of their sons.

ABSTRACTS

The Immersive Nurseries in Breton, an Essential Tool of the Transmission of the Language
Stephanie Le Pelleter

Since the late 1990s, Breton has gradually entered the nurseries, first by localized actions in Finistere, and then, spread over the years, throughout the territory of historic Brittany. This entry has taken many forms, from punctual initiation to the immersion nurseries. Since 2011 and the opening of a first nursery in Vannes, by the association Babigoù Breizh, four other immersive nursery projects have emerged in the east of Brittany, most successfully conducted.

This link with professionals in early childhood will be important in a child's language learning. The immersive nurseries in Breton therefore have a primordial place in the transmission of the language. The purpose of this study is to analyze and understand the place of immersive nurseries in Breton in the transmission of language through the more particular study of the nursery Kerbihan and the association that administates it, Babigoù Breizh.

The problematic of this project will lead to a deeper understanding of the notion of linguistic transmission, in the light of the authors who studied it, notably Joseph Fishman, on the Reversing Language Shift; also, to an understanding of the context, both political and cultural, which allowed the establishment of this nursery. The first data is being collected, I will focus, after redefining the notion of linguistic transmission, on highlighting the cultural and political context that led to the establishment of this nursery and its linguistic functioning.

Heroic poetry in the manuscripts of Tomáisín Bacach Ó Dubhgáin (c.1800–1874)
William Mahon

In spite of the fact that only two manuscripts from his hand are extant in catalogued collections, Tomáisín Bacach Ó Dubhgáin was well-known in the Parish of Claregalway (Co. Galway) as a schoolmaster and scribe. The older of the these manuscripts (Irish Folklore Collection MS 196) was produced in the period 1840–58. The younger manuscript (Hardiman Library MS B218), made in 1860, is a transcription of the same material, for which reason one might refer to the underlying compilation as

"Leabhar Thomáisín". For the most part, its contents include late medieval religious poetry (dánta), local song-poetry (amhráin), and heroic verse (including laoithe fiannaíochta and laments belonging to Oidheadh Chloinne Uisnigh and Oidheadh Chonlaoich mic Con gCulainn). This paper, dealing primarily with the last group of texts, will give consideration to: the categorization and phusical arrangement of the texts; orthographic and textual difference between between copies of the same material; and evidence for dictation used in manuscript production. Some observations will also be made in regard to the scribe's purpose in producing his manuscripts and to manuscript copies of similar material produced by other East Galway scribes.

The Irish Language, TV and translation
Clíona Ní Ríordáin

Scúp is a Northern Irish drama television series broadcast on TG4 and BBC Northern Ireland in 2013–14. The series was nominated to the Special Irish Language Award at the 11th Irish Film & Television Awards in 2014. The premise concerns a journalist named Rob Cullan who is sacked from his job at The Guardian following a phone hacking scandal. He returns home to Belfast where Diarmuid Black puts him in charge of a failing Irish language newspaper titled 'An Nuacht.' This talk will present an analysis of the bilingual TV series Scúp and will discuss the various techniques and approaches in use in writing and producing the program placing particular stress and emphasis on the use and promotion of the Irish language and the depiction of Irish-language locales in the series.

Walter Macken and Theatre in Irish
Philip O'Leary

Walter Macken was one of twentieth-century Ireland's most versatile and prolific men of letters. He is perhaps best known for the best-selling novels of Irish life he published in the 1950s and 60s, novels that reached a wide audience not only at home but also in Britain and North America, as well as, through translation, in many other countries. (Many of these titles are still on print.) It was, however, in the theatre that he began his artistic career. During the 1930s and 1940s, he was the dominant figure in Taibhdhearc na Gaillimhe, not only writing and acting in plays, but also directing nearly every production for many years. After he left An Taibhdhearc, he repeated his success at the Abbey Theatre in Dublin, acting many major roles and writing several successful plays in English. Indeed, at one time his "Home Is the Hero" (1953) was the longest-running play in the Abbey's history and was later made into a feature film in the UK. This paper will focus on his five plays in Irish performed at An Taibhdhearc during his years there, plays that were at one time staples of the Gaelic amateur theatre movement.

From dialectology to history, a new window open on the diachrony of Breton. The dialectometrical contribution.
Tanguy Solliec

Dialectometry is a quantitative method for the evaluation of dialectal distance (Wieling & Nerbonne 2015). When applied to Breton, it produced interesting results whose distribution correlates with socio-historical structures (German 1984, 1993 ; Costaouec 2012). The diachrony of Breton (Jackson 1967 ; Schrijver 2011a, 2011b) is based mainly on written sources and is seen as a quite unitarian development (Fleuriot 1987). The status of these sources is a debated issue whether it reflects spontaneous speech or is a literary Koine (Guyonvarc'h 1984, Le Duc et al. 2006). Falc'hun studied the linguistic geography of Breton and showed the dialectal structure of the language has been composed of three long-established and distinct areas (north-western, central and south-eastern). The scarcity of the sources does not allow drawing firm conclusions regarding the history of these dialects.

I carried on a dialectometrical analysis of the Nouvel Atlas Linguistique de la Basse-Bretagne (Le Dû 2001) based on an aggregate analysis of phonetic features. In this talk, we would like to present an alternative view on the diachrony of Breton based on these conclusions and on discrete linguistic facts. My results (see following map) actually suggest a situation founded on the convergence between distinct ancient dialects (Dixon 1997, Mufwene 1997) and possibly, ancient languages. Interestingly, our findings match with the distribution of the cystic fibrosis gene whose prevalence is high in Lower Brittany (Pellen 2015). Such a quantitative approach as dialectometry offers a possibility to understand the history of a language whose written sources are nonexistent or limited.

The Otherworld and the Hunt:
Dogs and the Tristan Legend
Rue Taylor

The Tristan legend underwent many iterations throughout the Middle Ages, propelled by its popularity beyond its Celtic origins while still retaining increasingly obscure pieces of its early variants. One such feature is Tristan's consistent association with dogs. In the Celtic tradition, polychromatic hunting hounds from the Otherworld feature prominently across the legendary cycles and folklore. However, upon Tristan's movement into the French corpus, the hunting and otherworldly qualities diverge into two separate animals. Despite their shared origin in Thomas of Britain's French Tristan, Gottfried von Strassburg's German translation retains this separation, while the Norse Tristrams saga ok Ísöndar merges the two dogs back into a single otherworldly hunting hound. This paper will look at how the dog's Celtic characteristics have reunited in Tristrams saga despite the lineage of translations, and the implications of the dog within its newfound Scandinavian context. The retention of the dog's unmistakable Celtic qualities makes him a control case against which to measure cultural contingencies that alter his function between the French, German, and Norse variants. Due to the dog's specific association with Tristan, these various functions ultimately reflect each translator's treatment of and perspective on the character of Tristan and, by association, his romance with Isold. Thus the dog offers a unique window into the ideological evolution inherent in the cross-cultural transmission of the Tristan legend.

Adomnán, Bede and the Religious Underpinning
of Northumbrian Power
Patrick Wadden

Adomnán, ninth abbot of Iona, hagiographer of St. Columba, scholar and jurist, was a figure of international standing in his own lifetime. A member of the ruling dynasty of Cenél Conaill, he was also an acquaintance of Aldfrith, king of Northumbria, whom he visited twice. On one of these visits, Adomnán left a copy of his work "On the holy places in Northumbria" and it was later used by Bede. This paper will suggest that another of Adomnán's works, his Life of St. Columba, might have had a different, more subtle influence on Bede. Adomnán, writing at least in part for an English audience, claims in the Life that Northumbrian political power was founded in part on the relationship between its kings and Columba. During the reign of Aldfrith, who had spent time on Iona prior to his accession to the kingship, and just two decades after the synod of Whitby, this might be interpreted as an effort to promote the reestablishment of a formal relationship between the Northumbrian kingdom and Adomnán's monastery. For Bede, Northumbria's "Golden Age"—and that of all the English—while it might have been initiated by kings with links to Iona, reached its apogee at a later date, after the formal link between Iona and Lindisfarne had been broken and the English Church united under Canterbury. This paper will ask whether Bede's assertion might reflect an awareness and rejection of Adomnán's proposition.

Ríastrad Revisited
Thomas R. Walsh

There is always occasion to examine the signature iconography of the Ulster Cycle, in particular, the *ríastrad* of Cúchulainn. In a short chapter of an obscure book (Walsh 2005), I suggest that the congeners of this display of anger involving a facial distortion include comparative epic from both Indo-European culture families and from non-IE ones, from the Gorgon to Humbaba. Since then, explanations of this image of the hero's wrath have tried to focus the discussion on monastic appropriations of classical sources. (See Miles 2011: 208–22 et passim, with literature, including Dooley 2006.)

In this paper, I explore the value of Cúchulainn's display within Irish saga narrative. What is the function for the narrative of this remarkable example of shape-shifting within a textual martial context? After reviewing the contexts of *ríastrad* in our texts, I suggest that recent interventions regarding "wonder" in cultural imaginaries (e.g., Daston and Park 1999) as well as more seasoned discussions of the "grotesque" or the "fantastic" may convincingly deepen our understanding of early Irish narrative artistry.

Returning to Bodily "Wholeness" in
Medieval Irish Literature
Sharon Wofford

In this paper, I examine literary examples of men using prostheses, both mechanical and magical, to circumvent the physical standards required of Irish kings. Irish kingship belonged to a system of sacral kingship, in which the king becomes an avatar for the land itself, often through his coupling with a sovereignty goddess figure. Because of this, physical wholeness is seen as a mark of divine favor and points towards one's status as a "true" king. In the "Tochmarc Étaíne" and the "Lebor Gabála Érenn", the kings Midir and Nuadu are badly injured and their physical wholeness is compromised by a "blemish," which disqualifies them from further rule. They both successfully use prostheses, which I define in this paper as a body part that has either been magically restored or crafted as a replacement, to correct the "blemish" and continue in the role of king. In the case of Nuadu in the Lebor Gabála, this is done by means of a spectacular, and fully functional, prosthetic silver arm.

I argue that the acceptance of these prosthetics as a return to bodily wholeness is likely based on the medieval Irish emphasis placed on cleverness that appears in much of the literature. The use of prostheses by Midir and Nuadu in these texts are a result of resourcefulness, well-connectedness, and material wealth, which have inherent social value and could aid in proving one's "truth." If a physical blemish marks a loss of divine favor under sacral kingship, then perhaps the return to wholeness by means of a clever prosthesis indicates a reversal of fate.